HERVÉ RYSSEN

PSYCHOANALYSIS OF JUDAISM

Hervé Ryssen

Hervé Ryssen (France) is a historian and an exhaustive researcher of the Jewish intellectual world. He is the author of twelve books and several video documentaries on the Jewish question. In 2005, he published *Planetary Hopes*, a book in which he demonstrates the religious origins of the globalist project. *Psychoanalysis of Judaism*, published in 2006, shows how intellectual Judaism displays all the symptoms of hysterical pathology. There is no "divine choice", but the manifestation of a disorder that has its origins in the practice of incest. Freud had patiently studied this question on the basis of what he observed in his own community.
France is home to one of the largest Jewish communities in the Diaspora, with a very intense cultural and intellectual life. Hervé Ryssen has been able to develop his extensive work on the basis of numerous historical and contemporary sources, both international and French.

Psychoanalysis of Judaism

Psychanalyse du Judaïsme, Levallois-Perret, Baskerville, 2006.

Translated and Published by
Omnia Veritas Limited

www.omnia-veritas.com

PART ONE **11**

JEWISH MESSIANISM 11

1. Planetary propaganda *13*

A unified world at last 13

The disregard for deep-rooted cultures 16

Jewish intellectuals and immigration 21

The blame game 27

Islam and Cosmopolitanism 31

Europe and the US model 36

Planetary cinema 41

2. The mission of the Jewish people *64*

Jewish activism 64

Messianic Hope 70

The true face of Israel 83

PART TWO **99**

THE COSMOPOLITAN MINDSET 99

1. The Jewish Personality *99*

The darkest hours 101

Jewish sensibility 111

Entrepreneurship 118

An insolent success 123

Jewish solidarity 127

Ethnocentrism 134

A fertile imagination 139

A surprising plasticity 145

Jewish humour 164

The scandal 165

Contempt for the goy 173

The spirit of revenge 178

Rage and the passion to destroy 182

Evil 185

Hatred of the "others 190

2. Anti-Semitism *195*

Inexplicable anti-Semitism 195

Jews and Communism 201

Going off the rails 208

The mirror of the anti-Semite 213

Anti-Semitic paranoia 216

Anti-Semitic madness 218

Psychoanalysis of the anti-Semite 222

PART THREE **226**

PSYCHOPATHOLOGY OF JUDAISM 226

1. Jewish neurosis *226*

Role reversal 226

The Mirror of Judaism 235

The Jewish obsession 246
The symptoms of madness 250
The inferiority complex 260
Self-hatred 267
Suicides 278
2. Psychoanalysis of Judaism 282
Clinical picture of histrionics 282
The diagnosis 287
The idealisation of the father 306
The birth of psychoanalysis 309
Incest in the Jewish tradition 311
Incest: a burning issue in Judaism 316
Incest and paedophilia 324
Paedophilia among rabbis 328
The prescriptions of the Talmud 333
The Oedipus Complex finally explained 336
Kabbalah, Hasidism and psychoanalysis 341
The issue of patricide 343
How to erase the trace 345
Feminism and matriarchy 347
Sexual disorders 354
Freudian bisexuality 359
Caves and Cellars of Civilisation 362
Judaism in psychiatry 365

ANNEX I 377

THE TALMUD 377

ANNEX II 380

EL ZOHAR 380

ANNEX III 383

THE LURIA CABALA 383

ANNEX IV 386

CHASSIDISM AND THE TEACHERS JABAB LUBAVITCH 386

ANNEX V 394

JACOB AND ESAU IN KABBALISTIC EXEGESIS 394

ANNEX VI 397

SHABTAI TZVI AND SABBATISM 397

ANNEX VII 401

JUDAISM ACCORDING TO WERNER SOMBART AND KARL MARX 401

ANNEX VIII 403

SHEHINAH AND THE COMMUNITY OF ISRAEL.. 403
OTHER TITLES 407

PART ONE

JEWISH MESSIANISM

Judaism[1] is not only a religion. It is also a political project based

[1] The term "Judaism", which designates the religion of the Hebrews, although it also encompasses ethnic and cultural aspects, deserves a preliminary clarification. According to Rabbi Adolph Moses, "of all the misfortunes that have occurred, the one whose consequences were most regrettable was the invention of the word "Judaism". (…) Worse still, the Jews themselves came to designate their own religion by the name of "Judaism", (…) whereas neither in the Bible, nor in later writings, nor in the Talmud, is there a single mention of this term (…) It was Flavius Josephus who coined the term "Judaism" in order to instruct the Greeks and Romans on this question, and to distinguish this religion from Hellenism (…)…) Thus the term "Judaism", coined by Flavius Josephus, remained completely unknown to the Jews, (…) and was not used by them until a relatively recent period, after the Jews began to read Christian works. Therefore, they also began to call their religion Judaism." (in Adolph Moses, *Yahvism and Other Discourses*, 1903). In fact, in the *Encyclopaedia Universalis* we read in its article on the Pharisees the following: "Pharisaism is a great movement which, for many centuries and until recently, ensured the permanence of a Judaism without a Temple and a religion without a State. The Pharisees were left alone on the Jewish scene and, no longer having any reason to call themselves Pharisees, since the label reflected a distinction that was no longer relevant (the representatives of the other three sects [Sadducees, Essenes and Zealots] having disappeared), they became and remained simply: "the Jews" (…) Thus, under the name of Pharisee, they became and remained the Jews (…)…) Thus, under the name of Judaism, Pharisaism became a true religion: parallel to Christianity, it became rabbinical and then Talmudic."
The doctrine of the Pharisees was the most orthodox and accepted all the books of the Torah as inspired by God. The Pharisees promoted the religion of the synagogue and placed great importance on oral tradition (the vast majority of the scribes were Pharisees). Only the Pharisees believed in the oral law. This is a very important thing to keep in mind.
The eminent American rabbi Louis Finkelstein would write: "Pharisaism became Talmudism, Talmudism became medieval rabbinism, and medieval rabbinism became modern rabbinism. But through all these changes of name (…), the spirit of the ancient Pharisees remained the same (…) From Palestine to Babylon, from Babylon to North Africa, then to Italy, Spain, France and Germany, and thence to Poland, Russia and all Eastern Europe, ancient Pharisaism continued its journey, (…) proving its importance as one of the great religions of the world." (in Louis Finkelstein, *The Pharisees: The Sociological Background of Their Faith*, 1962). It should also be emphasised that the rabbis are not priests, but the leaders who gather the Jewish community in the

on one main idea: the disappearance of borders, the unification of the earth and the establishment of a world of "peace". For religious Jews, this aspiration for a pacified, unified and globalised world is confused with the feverish hope for the coming of a Messiah that they have been awaiting for three thousand years. He will come to restore the "kingdom of David". For non-believing Jews, this messianism has taken the form of secularised political activism in favour of all the utopias of globalism.

That is why so many Jews engaged in the communist adventure throughout the 20th century with such special enthusiasm and abandon. But even before the fall of the Soviet system, many had realised that liberal democracy was far more effective in erasing borders and dissolving national identities. It is a question of working tirelessly for the establishment of the global Empire, which must also be the Empire of Peace. This is the "mission" of the Jewish people.

For centuries, this hope has nourished and shaped the spirit of Jews all over the world, isolated among other peoples and strongly encouraging this isolation as if there were a future revenge to take on the rest of humanity. This spirit of revenge manifests itself in numerous texts of cosmopolitan literature. It is one of the characteristic features of Judaism. The study of religious, philosophical, literary and cinematographic production does indeed make it possible to reveal and expose the predominant ideas of Judaism in general, particularly the Jewish intellectual personality. We then observe a striking homogeneity of thought among Jews in the four corners of the world, whether they are believers or atheists. They all seem to have been trained in the same school, speaking and expressing themselves in different languages only to spread the same ideas, the same emotions, the same paradoxes, the same messianic hope, the same faith in the final victory.

---

synagogues. The priests of the Hebrew religion disappeared with the destruction of the Temple in Jerusalem in the year 70.

1. Planetary propaganda

The Jewish people are the militant people par excellence. They are a people of propagandists, a people of "priests" who have a message to convey to the rest of humanity and a "mission" to accomplish. But unlike Christianity or Islam, the Jews do not seek to convert others to Judaism, but to make them renounce their religion, their race, their identity, their family and all their traditions in the name of "Humanity" and "human rights". The global empire, in fact, can only rise on the remains of the great civilisations, with the human dust produced by democratic societies and the capitalist mercantile system.

A unified world at last

The idea of a world without borders is a prospect that has long been a source of enthusiasm for Western youth. But whereas in the twentieth century this ideal was mainly espoused by militant Marxism, today it seems to have found its true realisation through the triumphant liberal ideology and plural democracy. The collapse of the Soviet bloc was the opportunity to redouble efforts in this direction. It was hoped that the end of the bipolar world and the triumph of democracy would bring about a world of peace and the "end of history", as some philosophers somewhat naively thought. The main representatives of this cosmopolitan current of thought are, by the way, often former Marxists. Edgar Morin, for example, is a French sociologist from the second half of the 20th century who perfectly personifies the "planetary" spirit. He is the author of numerous works and press articles which have invariably advocated, for many years, a "planetary confederation" and world unification. In a book entitled *A New Beginning*, published in 1991, he reminded the reader that the process of unifying humanity was quite recent, having begun to materialise in the 16th century with the discovery of the Americas: "Christopher Columbus had brought humanity into the planetary era." In that sense, Morin stated the following: "We are still in the iron age of the planetary era", in "the prehistory of the human spirit... We have not separated from the primates, we have become super-primates[2]."

It is an idea that Edgar Morin takes up systematically in all his books. Thus, in *Terre-Patrie*, in 1993, he reiterated his cosmopolitan convictions. Our task, he said, is to "reform Western civilisation", to "federate the Earth" in order to "bring about the era of planetary citizenship[3]". We must "consider planetary citizenship, which would give and guarantee earthly rights to all." It is, according to him, the only way "out of this planetary iron age".

Planetary consciousness" must first be anthropological: all human beings are brothers and sisters. But it must also be ecological, and even cosmic, because, after all, we are only Humans lost in the universe: "Our Earth is already only a tiny planet lost in a gigantic cosmos where billions of stars and galaxies proliferate. It is a tiny, warm planet in an endless space where an icy cold reigns[4]."

Presented in this way, we will understand that human solidarity imposes itself, beyond all divergences. Let us also note that this intergalactic vision of life on earth is also the plot of many catastrophic and futuristic film scripts produced by Hollywood. In this quest for the universal, the struggle for respect for the environment is nowadays an essential reason for mobilisation, all the more so as pollution of all kinds threatens our planet: "The ecological threat ignores national borders," wrote Morin. A threat on a planetary scale hangs over humanity." We must therefore "think of everything in a planetary perspective."

In order to force people to merge into a common nation, the cosmopolitan intellectual seems to take the Earth hostage under the threat of an apocalyptic catastrophism: "Civilising the Earth, transforming the human species into humanity, becomes the fundamental and global objective of any policy that aspires not only to progress but also to the survival of humanity[5]." You have understood: our life is at stake, our survival is at stake.

Nations must therefore be destroyed as soon as possible, borders abolished, old civilisations transformed into human dust from which a unified world can at last be moulded and the "world confederation", the condition of our salvation, realised: "Nation-states are in themselves uncontrollable paranoid monsters… The ideal to be announced to the world is no longer the independence of nations, but the confederation

[2]Edgar Morin, *Un nouveau commencement*, Seuil, 1991, p. 192, 23, 186.

[3]Edgar Morin and Anne Brigitte Kern, *Tierra-Patria*, Editorial Kairós, 2005, Barcelona, p. 136, 143.

[4]Edgar Morin, *Un nouveau commencement*, Seuil, 1991, p. 19, 21.

[5]*Le Monde*, 21 April 1993

of nations." And there is no reason to limit these grandiose projects to little Europe: "the confederative idea is an idea not only valid for Europe, but is universal in scope."

"This is the new future, uncertain and fragile, which we must nurture. We do not have the Promised Land, but we have an aspiration, a desire, a myth, a dream: to realise the homeland[6]." It is towards a world of peace that the philosopher wants to lead us, for this unified and pacified world will finally be the Promised Land.

Jacques Attali's thinking is also totally imbued with cosmopolitan ideas. In his 2003 book *The Nomadic Man*, he also prophesied the world of tomorrow with a very personal vision: "After many disorders, even dreadful disasters, the planet will become a single entity, without borders; people will be both sedentary and nomadic, enjoying rights and assuming new types of duties: a universal democracy in the service of a "common good" of humanity." In this New World Order, "*hypernomads* (artists, holders of a nomadic asset, patent or know-how)" will form a *hyperclass* of tens of millions of people." They will constitute "the network that governs the world in search of new conquests and colonies to populate in real and virtual space[7]."

In order to make us accept the idea of the future domination of nomads, Jacques Attali rewrote the history of humanity from a cosmopolitan point of view: "Sedentarism is only a brief parenthesis in human history. For most of his adventure, man has been shaped by nomadism and is now returning to being a traveller." In this new world, reviewed by Jacques Attali, traditional identities no longer serve. There are no Bretons, Flemish or French anymore:

"The transhuman will have the right to belong to several tribes at the same time, obeying, depending on where he is, different rules of affiliation, multiple rites of passage, various forms of courtesy and codes of hospitality. He will have to come to terms with his multiple affiliations honestly… Polyandry and polygamy will allow you to share with others, temporarily or permanently, a roof, goods, projects, a partner, without wishing to have or raise children, or to bear the same name, or to maintain sentimental or sexual relations, thus rediscovering the varied practices of some nomadic peoples such as the Nuer of Africa, where childless women marry each other and pool their goods, while others reconcile polygamy and polyandry with the same tolerance. He will be able to mix cultures, faiths, doctrines, religions, to take as he pleases elements from one or the other without being obliged

[6]Edgar Morin, *Un nouveau commencement*, Seuil, 1991, p, p. 190, 204-206, 9
[7]Jacques Attali, *L'Homme nomade*, Fayard, 2003, Livre de Poche, p. 451, 32

to join such a Church or party in charge of thinking for him[8].”

Indeed, in the future world described by the prophet Attali, the old European civilisation will have definitively disappeared, replaced by the nomadic African model considered clearly superior. Democratic globalisation “will not only involve technology, but also the reinvention of new ways of life, inspired by those of the original peoples. This will require rethinking cultures and the organisation of work in cities and in politics; inventing a government of the planet; a transhuman democracy… One will then glimpse, beyond immense disorders, a promising planetary miscegenation, an Earth hospitable to all travellers of life.”

In this new organisation, “the government of the planet will be a final utopia organised around a set of agents and networks dependent on a planetary Parliament” and will be “at the service of the Common Good”. It will be the blessed time “of a serene and united planet”. Jacques Attali concluded his book with these words: “The travellers of life will then emerge as a promise of an Earth that is at last welcoming to all humans.” At the beginning of his book, he wrote: “The nomad will end up having only one dream: to stop, to settle down, to take his time; to make the world a promised land[9].”

Beyond the poetry that underpins the discourse of their worldview, we can observe a certain similarity of vocabulary in the two philosophers. Between Edgar Morin’s “Fatherland” and Jacques Attali’s “Promised Land”, one might almost think that through these profane books aimed at the general public, a secular interpretation of ancient Hebrew prophecies is actually being put forward.

The disregard for deep-rooted cultures

The promise of a unified world does not go without virulent denunciation by cosmopolitan intellectuals of traditional societies. The contempt for “deep France” and local traditions had already been expressed in a hurtful way by the very media-friendly philosopher Bernard-Henri Levy in his 1981 book *La ideologie française*[10]. François Mitterrand and the Socialists were then coming to power in France, and one could dream of a better world. In the midst of these liberating hopes, another cosmopolitan author, Guy Konopnicki, in his turn, was

---

[8]Jacques Attali, *L’Homme nomade*, Fayard, 2003, Livre de Poche, p. 451, 32

[9]Jacques Attali, *L’Homme nomade*, Fayard, 2003, Livre de Poche, p. 35, 471, 472, 34

[10]Read in Hervé Ryssen, *Planetary Hopes*, 2022, p. 97.

shattering the old traditional values and the prejudices of those Frenchmen who were still too "timorous" in the face of modernity. In 1983, in a book entitled *The Place of the Nation, he* sought to rid the country of everything exasperating that it could still have: "The cult of the land, ecstasy before peasant virtues, spontaneous philosophy, popular common sense and all the reactionary antiquities."

And to further discredit this abhorred deep France, Konopnicki equated it with a political regime on which heaps of rubbish had already been poured since the end of the war and which had been clearly reproached by all: "That image is due to Vichy and remains its dominant feature[11]." Thus, Marcel Pagnol[12] symbolises for Konopnicki all that France's impoverished nature can produce most deeply rooted: "*La Fille du puisatier* cleansed the national soul of the stains inflicted by the cosmopolitanism of the Parisian intellectuals," he wrote. Certainly, a film by Pagnol such as *Regain,* for example, would make today's intellectuals shudder with its beauty and the artistic direction it took, against the grain of the values of rootlessness and nomadism. This overly French culture can only inspire disdain: "The country had lost a battle, but it still had Tino Rossi and Marcel Pagnol." And we must recognise, agreeing with Konopnicki, that "there has never been a more French cinema than that produced during the German occupation".

After the resounding defeat of 1940, France was indeed trying to lick its wounds and to recover by drawing on its history, its culture and its national values. Certainly, twenty years after the massacre of the First World War, the French had reluctantly launched a new war in the name of "democracy" and "human rights", and had not shown the warlike ardour that intellectuals had expected of them to fight the Hitler regime. For Guy Konopnicki, this attitude was hard to forgive. He did not understand the Gauls' lack of combativeness and criticised their lack of spirit of sacrifice: "How many officers resigned? How many officers committed suicide rather than be taken prisoner? All those professional Frenchmen remained at their posts[13]." We must understand Guy Konopnicki's disgust and indignation at the cowardice of those who refused to die for "human rights".

---

[11]Guy Konopnicki, *La Place de la nation,* Olivier Orban, 1983, p. 112, 60, 62. The Vichy regime was Marshal Petain's collaborationist regime set up after the defeat of France in June 1940.

[12]Marcel Pagnol, French novelist and filmmaker whose work was characterised by a popular and realistic vision of the world, and a concern for regional themes. He is considered a forerunner of Italian neo-realism.

[13]Guy Konopnicki, *La Place de la nation,* Olivier Orban, 1983, p. 55, 56.

This French baseness has never ceased to manifest itself in reality. In the 1950s, this "stunted" France continued to drag the country down with its inertia, incarnated in the father figure of Antoine Pinay. Pinay, Konopnicki wrote without disguising his contempt, was a man "very popular in that deep France which stocks potatoes at the slightest strike and which boasts of no longer investing in industry since they gambled with the Suez crisis and the Russian railway loans."

The small French saver is undoubtedly exasperating, with his mania for saving for his old age and his instinctive distrust of the hucksters of finance." The tradition of right-wing anti-capitalism, a very French tradition", which drew its references from anti-Semitic authors such as Edouard Drumont, could not satisfy our intellectual, who pointed out: "It is a fundamentally hypocritical tradition, because under the pretext of preferring the noble values of land and stone, it makes money take refuge in securities and real estate. In France, you don't invest, you hide your money. You don't gamble with money. It is buried, hidden in piles of sheets and mattresses. And when the cock is beaten, there remains the little squirrel of the savings banks[14]."

It is true that after the continuous financial scandals and countless swindles that had punctuated the history of the Third Republic, deceived small savers tended to view financial investments with suspicion. We can therefore understand Konopnicki's pain, who would obviously have preferred the loot to be handed over to international speculators.

This very French meanness naturally continued right up to the Fifth Republic, whose constitution and practices followed the same logic: "Institutional umbrella of a presidential constitution, economic umbrella of the gold reserves of the Bank of France, not forgetting, of course, our little nuclear "cucumber"[15]. "This way of reinforcing the protective state is constitutive of the French spirit." This way of reinforcing the protective state is constitutive of the French spirit: "The state invested in gold, the French in stone and land... Thus, France once again freed itself from the taste for industrial, cultural and political risk." This pusillanimity can only inspire the highest contempt of our intellectual: "Under the feathers of the cockerel, Gaullism saw a hen... The Hexagon[16] had become a French garden: no surprises in our

[14]Guy Konopnicki, *La Place de la nation*, Olivier Orban, 1983, p. 77, 173 [The squirrel is the effigy of a well-known French savings bank (La Caisse d'Epargne)].

[15]Alain Minc uses the same language when he speaks of a "France hiding behind its nuclear capability." (*La Grande illusion*, Grasset, 1989, p. 255).

[16]France's geography forms a hexagon. France is often referred to as a hexagon.

avenues, no disorder on our lawns." Certainly, the gardens of Louis XIV—beauty, restraint and harmony—are the exact opposite of what the cosmopolitan spirit of a Konopnicki can produce.

But the intellectual's contempt was not only for "reactionary" France, clinging to its old peasant and "petit-bourgeois" virtues. It was also against a part of the left-wing culture represented by the Communist Party, which still spread concepts too impregnated with the idea of terroir: The PCF, he said, "supported by corporatism", only wraps its reactionary positions in a plebeian discourse." To him we owe the paternity of the slogan "Let's make French."

Part of the French left thus coincided with the right in its veneration of national values. For Konopnicki, it was precisely this clinging to their identity that explained why the French were still somewhat impregnated with the dungy stench of their peasant ancestors: "How can we be surprised, then, that imagination and novelty have so little place in this country? For a long time now, two forces have united to marginalise all those who, from the old Mendesists[17] to the German Jews of May'68, have tried to look beyond a horizon enclosed on six sides. Gaullism and Stalinism are the two jaws that grip France, the two pillars of French conformism. The two converge to forbid audacity; they coincide in the fear provoked in them by all philosophies which do not exhale the terroir."

But if Konopnicki honours us all by living in France, despite everything that bothers him, it is because he nevertheless likes some things: "It would be very unfair to pass over the ideological landscape without mentioning the existence of breaths of fresh air like *Libé* or the *Canard* that make France still bearable[18]." We are happy to be able to give him at least that much satisfaction.

The intellectual was naturally pleased with the mass immigration that has profoundly transformed the French population in recent decades. This is how he celebrated this "irreversible mutation": "In the suburbs of the big cities, generations have grown up together, attended the same schools and vibrated to the sound of the same rhythms. Like it or not, miscegenation is there, irremediable, definitive... The old republic is dead."

In fact, according to him, the "French people" no longer

---

[17]Supporters of Pierre Mendès-France, former Prime Minister of the Fourth French Republic.

[18]Guy Konopnicki, *La Place de la nation*, Olivier Orban, 1983, p. 79, 87, 115. [*Libération*, a progressive left-wing newspaper and *Le Canard enchaîné, a* satirical and investigative newspaper].

corresponds to anything: "The expression is either laughable or repellent. Nobody speaks like that any more except in the courts to condemn in the name of …; the French people no longer have any internal coherence, if they ever had any, they are united only by geographical chance and administrative and political tutelage." So it is all over.

"Fortunately, the reactionaries are too late: the traditional France of which they speak is not threatened; it is dead and buried."

Cosmopolitan propaganda has in a few decades overcome the mistrust and anxieties of those despicable little targets: mission accomplished. Victory!

"Capitalism can never be thanked enough for having uprooted the peasants from their land to take them to the city. That is where the mixing of populations takes place, where the exchange of the most valuable things takes place, more essential than all those old rural huts: cinemas, theatres, entertainment venues forced to constantly renew themselves under the pressure of the most cultural laws possible such as those of the market and of competition[19]."

All French people can nowadays enjoy the spectacles offered by the cosmopolitan Hollywood cinema and modern art exhibitions. That is the real culture. However, Konopnicki did not hide the fact that there are superior cultures and others that are definitely inferior: "Even the lousiest of Broadway revues will always surpass the pitiful spectacle of folk dancing with souks."

One might object that African peoples, the tribes of the Maghreb, the Amazonian Indians or Asian peoples might be offended by such words. But it seems that Guy Konopnicki only despises European cultures, according to this passage he wrote after attending a "festival of the Soviet republics" during a trip to the USSR: "I have never seen anything as embarrassing as those folk dances that all look the same, with those village braids, scarves and souks[20]."

We can assume that Guy Konopnicki longed for the time of the Bolsheviks, before the war, when numerous Jews had taken complete control of the state apparatus, ridiculed Russian traditions, arrested hundreds of thousands of people, massacred millions of Christians and destroyed churches and everything that could remind us of the old Russia[21]. Konopnicki acknowledged: "Not much attention was paid during those crazy years to the folklore of the Soviet republics." But

[19]Guy Konopnicki, *La Place de la nation*, Olivier Orban, 1983, p. 114, 122, 123, 113

[20]Guy Konopnicki, *La Place de la nation*, Olivier Orban, 1983, p. 175, 176.

[21]See Aleksandr Solzhenitsyn, *Deux Siècles ensemble*, Fayard, 2003.

like his peers, he preferred to remain discreet about that tragic pre-war period. For him, as for all planetary intellectuals, the great one, the only one responsible for those abominations was none other than Stalin, on whom one prefers to throw the full weight of ignominy[22].

Ultimately, according to Konopnicki, everything that is not cosmopolitan must be discarded. Only "the great crossbreeding of cultures, which prefigures and accompanies the general crossbreeding of humanity", can triumph over resistance and open the way to that world of Peace announced by the prophets. "Something is appearing, something that surpasses us and escapes us[23]", he wrote enigmatically.

Jewish intellectuals and immigration

The apology of immigration is a constant in the planetary discourse. The highly publicised liberal essayist Alain Minc gave us a good example of this relentless desire to impose the idea of a plural society on people's minds. In a book entitled *The Revenge of the Nations*, published in 1990, he constantly lashed out at the retrograde attitude of the indigenous French who did not seem to understand the benefits of this evolution and who were alarmed by what they considered an invasion. Alain Minc thus restored the truth to the facts:

"Immigrants are hardly more numerous today than they were fifteen years ago; they represent a weaker part of the population than they did in the 1930s. However, the problem has reached an unprecedented dimension, as if the facts were blurring in the face of a stronger reality: a collective anguish under siege."

Under these conditions, the advance of the extreme right in France at the end of the 20th century is an alarming and incomprehensible phenomenon. This anomaly "makes us look like a crazy people" to the rest of the world. France, in fact, "has invented the problem of immigration… The more the French are maddened by immigration, the less they understand the reality of the phenomenon." The fears and "anxieties of the small, medium and even big bourgeoisie" are in reality completely ridiculous: "Fantasies and phobias are always fed by collective ignorance: but at this point, it's astonishing! One would almost have to turn the conspiracy theory so dear to Le Pen on its head and claim that ignorance is deliberately cultivated to make way for

---

[22]Hervé Ryssen, *The Planetary Hopes*, 2022, p. 268

[23]Guy Konopnicki, *La Place de la nation*, Olivier Orban, 1983, p. 185, 220, 114.

fear[24]."

Alain Minc's analyses can be disconcerting when one looks back at the evolution of the French population over the last twenty years. In reality, this is because it is an ideological discourse of "sensitisation" rather than a social analysis. Minc's words prove it: The immigrant population is in reality "smaller than is claimed"; "the numbers are still lower than political agitation might lead one to believe." The number of illegal immigrants, for example, "must not be higher than it was in 1981". For Alain Minc, immigration is fortunate for France, for in reality it represents "less a problem for the population than an excuse for the malaise of French society … for it is growing weakly and is contributing, as it has been doing for a century, to the regeneration of French demography." We can therefore conclude with Alain Minc that it is indeed "ignorance" that "feeds xenophobia" and that an "invasion" is not taking place, since it only exists in the stupid brains of extreme right-wing doctrinaires.

For the cosmopolitan intellectual, "the question of immigration does not arise" because there is only "the drama of ghettos as in the United States". Radical Islam may be a problem, but Alain Minc proposed a solution that could be perplexing: "The most intelligent response, he wrote, would be to accelerate normalisation and not, through an attitude of rejection, to drive Muslims to turn in on themselves. Hence a policy that runs counter to that desired by the enlightened xenophobes: more places of worship, special authorisations for Muslims similar to those for Jewish festivals, simplified organisation of ritual slaughter, provision of space for Muslims in cemeteries[25]."

With the same honesty and a keen sense of observation, Minc denounced the "myth of the tolerance threshold" and the typical French fantasies about insecurity. Indeed, according to his personal statistics, "incidents are numerous in the Var, with a low percentage of immigration, and rare in Seine-Saint-Denis where immigration is massive."

To think that "immigration is the major cause of insecurity" is indeed a mistaken belief. One would have to be in very bad faith to assert such things. Although immigrants do indeed represent "27% of inmates in French prisons, i.e. four times their demographic weight in France [26]… a closer look, taking into account the type of offences,

[24]Alain Minc, *La Vengeance des nations*, Grasset, 1990, p. 11, 21, 15, 154.
[25]Alain Minc, *La Vengeance des nations*, Grasset, 1990, p. 155-160, 166, 171-174.
[26]The 2005 figures were closer to 70%.

brings nuances to the question: since immigration stopped in 1974, illegal residence offences have multiplied... They account for 20% of immigrant imprisonment ... and do not correspond to any form of insecurity."

On the other hand, "social factors and age mitigate immigrant specificity with respect to insecurity... It would therefore be better to restore immigration in its proper measure, rather than feeding xenophobic campaigns with abusive rebuttals."

Immigrants, as you will understand, are in fact the first victims of French society: they are "long-term unemployed, marginalised, people in vulnerable situations, victims of a series of disadvantages that leave them by the wayside", as well as being the "scapegoats" of French malaise.

Faced with the incomprehensible racism of the pusillanimous little whites, the cosmopolitan intellectual asked himself a few questions: "How should the psychological illness of the French be treated? "What collective psychoanalysis will rid us of this paranoia? Well, let's say it again: "There is no problem with immigration, only the sum of some local difficulties around the ghettos and a collective paranoia... France is paranoid. France is paranoid. It has to heal itself and its elites must do their duty." It must therefore "fight against xenophobic delirium", "carry out tireless information work on the figures, the reality of immigration, and the nature of the phenomena of social exclusion of which immigrants are the unfortunate victims[27]."

The very liberal Alain Minc finally proposed a very concrete solution, which consisted of copying the American model of "positive discrimination", also known as "foreign preference": "Successful integration requires that we move away from the French egalitarian model, recognising the specific disadvantages of immigrants." It is therefore a question of "breaking with our mental rigidity", and "applying non-egalitarian methods", taking an example from the United States, where quotas are applied that "reserve a number of places for minorities in universities and the administration[28]."

Finally, Alain Minc tactfully warned us that immigration was going to increase anyway. It is "an inevitable prospect", he said with a certain ill-concealed satisfaction: "Immigration is going to increase: it is better to prepare for it than to let the French fantasise about a current situation that is much less critical than they think[29]." The best way to

[27]Alain Minc, *La Vengeance des nations*, Grasset, 1990, p. 176-179, 207, 208.

[28]Alain Minc, *La Vengeance des nations*, Grasset, 1990, p. 206, 194, 195.

[29]Alain Minc, *La Vengeance des nations*, Grasset, 1990, p. 11, 158.

prepare for it is undoubtedly to read Alain Minc's books.

Unlike Alain Minc, Guy Konopnicki is a left-wing journalist. However, there is a certain convergence of views between these two cosmopolitan intellectuals, for Konopnicki also defends the idea of a multiracial society and denounces the myth of immigration as the cause of insecurity:

"There is certainly an impressive increase in the number of crimes, he wrote, but the statistics include financial crime, including the two national sports of tax fraud and legal offences involving bank cheques. The increase in assaults is appreciable, but in much smaller proportions than might have been feared in a country that is breaking all historical records for unemployment. No one has yet demonstrated with figures to prove that the proportion of immigrants is a determining factor in the increase in crime. The immigrant criminal, easily identifiable, is more vulnerable to repression; he is more easily declared against and more harshly condemned."

In reality, wrote Konopnicki, "the main criminogenic social category is not the one we think it is: the most prolific nursery of criminals is recognisable by the camouflage clothing worn there. It is called the French army. The proportion of criminals peaks among the former Algerian and Indochinese volunteers. There are very few crooks and murderers who have not fought in the rice paddies and djebels. Since the end of the colonial wars, the aggression curve has been on the rise. One could also mention other highly criminogenic groups such as the police, the gendarmerie or private militias. How many former cops we have seen sitting in court! But little is said about that[30]."

To complete the picture, Konopnicki could well have spoken of the financial crime and swindles of all kinds in which his fellows have excelled for centuries[31].

As we can see, the discourse of the cosmopolitan intellectual corresponds less to reality than to a vision of the world centred on the obsessive idea of achieving, whatever the cost, a world without borders. He reasons only on the basis of his prophetic visions, and dismisses all "collateral damage", which can only be temporary. It is a propaganda discourse, in which the end seems to justify the means. Thus, as we have seen in the communist experience, everything is justified in the name of the ideal, even the worst atrocities.

This apology for immigration and the mixing of European peoples is not a new phenomenon. There are ancient precedents, such as Spain

[30]Guy Konopnicki, *La Place de la nation*, Olivier Orban, 1983, p. 102, 103.

[31]Hervé Ryssen, *The Planetary Hopes,* 2022 and *The Jewish Mafia,* 2022

in the early eighth century, which was to suffer the Muslim invasion. The Jews of the time exuded defeatist ideas and became the invader's "collaborators", as Jacques Attali himself wrote: "With their help, the Muslim troops defeated King Roderic in July 711 and quickly conquered the entire peninsula, with the exception of a few enclaves in the north which remained Christian. Relations between Jews and Muslims became more intense." Thus, the archbishop of Toledo accused the Jews of treason in favour of the Saracens, thus provoking an uprising; he also organised the sacking of synagogues. In Barcelona, in Tortosa, the "disputes "become trials against the Hebrew texts[32]."

Spain under Muslim rule, when Christians had to ride donkeys and pay a special tax, while Muslims rode horses, remains a golden age that Jews long for. The great Jewish historian Leon Poliakov wrote: "In 711, the Arab invasion catapulted them to the top of the social ladder, as advisors and allies of the conquerors[33]." Jacques Attali confirmed it: "The Jews have never known a more beautiful place to stay than this European Islam of the 8th century".

We may also have noticed that the cosmopolitan discourse always expresses itself with an unerring aplomb, allowing itself to make unbelievable false claims. The end always justifies the means.

The former Minister of Culture, Jack Lang, expressed himself with the same aplomb as his peers on the subject: on 3 September 2005, for example, on a prime-time talk show in front of millions of viewers, he responded to a sudden, unexpected question: "Don't you think there are too many immigrants in France? —No, he answered immediately, you know that France is the country in Europe with the fewest immigrants[34]."

This point-blank reflex is actually very revealing of a probably natural tendency to take "others" for retards. Such unrestrained brazenness is absolutely characteristic of the cosmopolitan mentality. Jews call it "*chutzpah*[35]".

---

[32]Jacques Attali, *Los judíos, el mundo y el dinero*, Fondo de cultura económica, 2005, Buenos Aires, p. 134, 204. ["It is known that the invasion of the Arabs was solely sponsored by the Jews living in Spain. They opened the gates of the main cities to them. For they were numerous and rich, and already in the time of Egica they had conspired, seriously endangering the security of the kingdom." Marcelino Menendez Pelayo, *Historia de los Heterodoxos españoles, Tomo I*, Ed. F. Maroto, Madrid, 1880. p. 216].

[33]Léon Poliakov, *Histoires des crises d'identité juives*, Austral, 1994, p. 22.

[34]Programme *Tout le monde en parle*, France 2, Saturday 3 September 2005.

[35]*Chutzpah*: Yiddish word. *Chutzpah* is the most insolent and shameless impudence. It would be the quality of the man who, having murdered his parents, invokes the leniency of the court because he is an orphan. (NdT).

It is this *chutzpah that* also allowed the Marxist philosopher Jacques Derrida to write the following: "I stressed that there was much more room than was claimed to receive more foreigners, and that immigration had not increased, contrary to what was being claimed[36]."

That same *chutzpah,* with which the former anarchist and student leader of May '68, Daniel Cohn-Bendit (who now admits quite coherently to being a "libertarian liberal") declared: ""We could deduce that in order to curb xenophobia it would be better to increase, and not want to decrease, the number of foreigners[37]."

The same *chutzpah* with which the liberal essayist Guy Sorman dared to write: "Consequently, it would not be the presence of foreigners that would provoke racism, but their absence: it would be the ghost of the immigrant, rather than the immigrant himself, that would provoke violence." And Guy Sorman added in the same vein: "On the other hand, France, which counted hundreds of dialects, *patois* and regional languages a century ago, was more multicultural then than it is today[38]."

Cosmopolitan thinking also aims to make us understand that the phenomenon of immigration is unavoidable, and that there is therefore no point in opposing it. Jacques Attali prophesied the following about the large migratory flows that we will have to accept: "France, the first country, will have to radically change its attitude in terms of effort and movement. It will have to give itself the means for a remarkable rejuvenation and accept the entry of a large number of foreigners[39]."

This is what the press director Jean Daniel (Bensaid) explained in the magazine *Le Nouvel Observateur* of 13 October 2005: "Nothing will stop the movements of miserable populations towards an old and rich West... This is why, from now on, wisdom and reason consist in preparing to receive and welcome more and more migrants... We must accept the idea that nations will no longer be what they are today."

Let us simply note that in Marxist discourse it was the "classless society" that was "ineluctable". But you have understood, we are not dealing here with social analyses, but with propagandistic discourses which try to eliminate from our minds the idea of defending ourselves. This tendency is the reflection of a prophetic discourse very characteristic of the cosmopolitan mentality: one projects oneself into

---

[36]Jacques Derrida, Élisabeth Roudinesco, *Y mañana, qué...* Fondo de Cultura Económica, Buenos Aires, 2002, p. 71.

[37]Daniel Cohn-Bendit, *Xénophobies,* Hamburg, 1992, Grasset, 1998, p. 43–45.

[38]Guy Sorman, *Waiting for the Barbarians,* Seix Barral, 1993, Barcelona, p. 47, 163.

[39]Jacques Attali, *L'Homme nomade,* Fayard, 2003, Livre de poche, p. 436.

the future, carried away by "prophecies", and declares that everything that is "written" must inevitably come to pass.

The process of blaming

In order to make the ideal of plural society and planetary unification better penetrate the "others", cosmopolitan thinking has to undermine all feelings of ethnic, national, racial, familial or religious belonging. Thus, the history of Europeans will be presented to us as a succession of ignominies and their ancestors as criminals. In a book published in 2005 with the explicit title *European Culture and Barbarism,* Edgar Morin wrote for example: "It can be affirmed that, through the memories of the victims of Nazism, but also of the enslavement of deported African populations and colonial oppression, what emerges in the consciousness is the barbarism of Western Europe… Nazism is only the last phase."

This blaming process never forgets to spit in the face of Catholicism and to open new perspectives to fight another competing religion:

"One of the weapons of Christian barbarism has been the use of Satan, wrote Morin… It is with this delirious argumentative [sic] machine that Christianity has exercised its barbarism. Evidently, it has not had the exclusive use of the Satanic weapon. We see Satan returning today through the virulent Islamist discourse[40]."

Viviane Forrester also worked in the same direction in her book entitled *Western Crime* (with a capital letter). In it, we see how the ignominy of Europeans is not limited to the episode of the Second World War. Their entire history demonstrates their cruelty and abjectness. Viviane Forrester insisted on this point: "Spoliation, massacres and genocide of peoples have been perpetrated on other continents for centuries by and for Europeans. All this in good conscience, with the public's approval and admiration of such feats and their gratitude once their taste for possessions has been satiated. All this thanks to the aptitude of Westerners to manage, erase and conceal what makes them uncomfortable, without altering the image of the world they have, or the role they pretend to play? In the name of their supremacy, with an innate sense of arrogance and the certainty of a natural superiority that justifies their universal arrogance, Westerners have given themselves the right to decree, without scruples, and as if it

---

[40]Edgar Morin, *Culture et barbarie européennes,* Bayard, 2005, p. 89, 90, 16

were a matter of course, the non-importance of numerous living beings judged to be annoying and the subhuman nullity of entire populations, even their presumed harmfulness. From then on, spoliating, oppressing, persecuting, murdering without limits these halogenous masses considered unwelcome and often disastrous, became admissible, even necessary, or better still: demandable[41]." The style is a little gritty, but the idea is there.

In *Récidives,* a compendium of articles published in 2004, Bernard-Henri Levy crushed the beast even further under his heel, declaring that it was not only the ignominy of European civilisation that should be incriminated, but the white man himself who is intrinsically perverse and rotten to the core: "Western man, structured and defined for hundreds or thousands of years," wrote Bernard-Henri Lévy, citing Jean-Claude Milner's 2003 book *The Criminal Tendencies of Democratic Europe,* is "potentially criminal[42]."

This tendency to besmirch the past of European man is not specific to cosmopolitan intellectuals living in France. It is also found in their colleagues on the other side of the Atlantic, such as Michael Moore, who published in 2002 a book kindly entitled *Stupid White Men,* which was widely covered by the media[43] in Europe. In the introduction, Michael Moore explained the origin of the evils that currently overwhelm the United States:

"Everything went down the drain. Everything started to fall apart. The faltering economy and energy stocks, the fading peace in the world, no more job security, no more social security… It was clear to Americans that nothing was working." And if it all went wrong, it could only be because of those racist white cretins in power: "That virus of white stupidity is so powerful that it even infected Blacks like Colin Powel, Interior Secretary Gale Norton, or National Security Advisor Condoleeza Rice… Those stupid white Men [President Bush's team] must be stopped." Of course, Michael Moore forgot to mention the countless Jews who held important positions in successive US administrations and who gravitated closely to the US presidency…

Chapter IV was simply entitled: *"Kill Whitney"*. Michael frankly declared his hatred of the white man: "I don't know why it is, but every time I see a white man walking towards me I get tense. My heart races and I immediately look for some place to escape or some way to defend

---

[41]Viviane Forrester, *Le Crime occidental*, Fayard, 2004, p. 57, 65.

[42]Bernard-Henri Lévy, *Récidives*, Grasset, 2004, p. 436, 448, 455.

[43]Michael Moore, *Mike contre-attaque!* 2001, La découverte, 2002. *Stupid white men*, Ediciones B, 2005, Barcelona (http://biblioteca.d2g.com)

myself... White people scare me to death. It may be difficult to understand since I am white, but that is exactly why I say it... You must take my word for it: if you suddenly find yourself surrounded by white people, be very careful. Anything could happen... All those who have harmed me in life were white... I don't think I am the only white person who can make such claims. Every venomous word, every act of cruelty, all the pain and suffering I have experienced in life had Caucasian features. Why on earth should I fear blacks?"

Of course, if Michael Moore were to walk around with a revolving headlamp on his head and a fluorescent jumpsuit, we would be much more suspicious. But let Michael speak:

"I take a look at the world we live in and, guys, I hate to be a gossip, but it's not African-Americans who have turned this planet into the pitiful, fetid place we inhabit today. Recently, a front-page headline in the science section of the New York Times asked, "Who Built H-Bomb? "The article delved into the debate about the device, which was being fought over by two men. Frankly, I didn't care, because I already knew the answer that interested me: It was a white man. No black man ever built or used a bomb designed to wipe out thousands of people, whether in Oklahoma City or Hiroshima. Yes, my friends. There's always a white man behind it.

Lucky Michael! It is true that Einstein, Hahn and Oppenheimer, the fathers of the atomic bomb, are pure Galicians, as are Cohen, the inventor of the neutron bomb, or Weizmann and Fritz Haber, the inventors of asphyxiating gases during the First World War. This mania for projecting one's own vileness onto others is undeniably a characteristic feature of the cosmopolitan mentality, and we shall see later that this tendency is deeply rooted in the minds of certain intellectuals. We also know, on the other hand, that the role and responsibility of Jewish slave traders in the slave trade, for example, is simply overwhelming and irrefutable. But let us move on and take a closer look at what our friend Michael was saying:

"Who spread the Black Death? Who invented PCBs, PVC, BPB and all the other chemicals that kill us every day? It was white people. Who started all the wars that the United States has been involved in? White men. Who are the people responsible for Fox programming? Whites. Who invented the butterfly ballot? A white woman. Whose idea was it to pollute the world with the combustion engine? A white man. The Holocaust? That guy gave us a real bad name. That's why we prefer to call him a Nazi and his helpers Germans. The genocide of the Native Americans? It was the whites. Slavery? The same. In the year 2001,

American companies have laid off more than 700,000 people. White executives. Who keeps blowing up my internet connection? Some white cunt. If one day I find out who it is, it will be a white stiff[44]."

In his fierce hatred of the white man, Michael Moore could only end with a call for miscegenation to put an end to those arrogant goyim: "Why don't we run like hell when we see a white man? Why don't we shit our pants when our daughters introduce us to their white boyfriends? ... There is a foolproof method to help create a world without chromatic distinctions: marry someone black and have children. Blacks and whites making love together ... will result in a country of one colour. And when we are all the same colour, we won't have to hate each other and we won't have to argue." It will then be a perfect world; or almost: only the Jews will be left to interbreed.

At the end of 2004, the *Nouvel Observateur* carried a large photo of Mr. Moore on its front page with the headline: "The America we love, not Bush's America". *The Nouvel Observateur* thus offered us limited choices, as democracy traditionally does: if you don't like the "right", you can always take the "left". The important thing is, as you well know, to stay within the circle, otherwise you are "lost".

This systematic blaming is in full swing in all democratic media systems. In this respect, the Second World War is a very fertile ground to grow all the poisonous plants that will feed the new transgenic historiography for future generations. Elie Wiesel, for example, sought to denounce the collective responsibility of Whites for the Holocaust; of all Whites, not just Germans: "Since Moscow and Washington were aware of what the murderers were doing in the death camps, why was nothing done to at least reduce "production"? The fact that no military aircraft attempted to destroy the railways around Auschwitz remains a shocking mystery to me. At the time, Birkenau "treated" ten thousand Jews a day[45]... But whether the Jews lived or died, whether they disappeared today or tomorrow, that was all the same to the free world."

Elie Wiesel was therefore truly outraged by the hypocrisy of the Allies: "There was a time when everything made me angry and indignant. Against complicit humanity. Later, I felt above all sadness... Cowardly, men refused to listen[46]."

The writer Marek Halter approached the matter in the same way: "What was the world doing while Jews were being slaughtered? This obsessive question haunts my thoughts every time I express my

---

[44]This is probably an anti-Semitic individual.

[45]On the down low!

[46]Elie Wiesel, *Mémoires, tome I,* Seuil, 1994, p. 97, 133, 134.

solidarity with the persecuted victims... I want to understand: Why is the death of Rwandan children unbearable for us today, when yesterday the death of Jewish children left world public opinion indifferent[47]?"

For Elie Wiesel and Marek Halter, the tens of millions of European Goyim who died during the war were apparently not enough to atone for the crimes of their leaders. We will limit ourselves here to pointing out that neither Churchill's memoirs, nor those of General de Gaulle, nor those of Roosevelt, mention the gas chambers during the war. But this is probably because these people were cowards.

We will leave the last word on this terrible chapter of the holocaust to the philosopher Bernard-Henri Levy: "This crime without traces, this crime without archives ... this crime without traces, this crime without ruins, this crime without graves is a perfect crime, not in the sense that it would go unpunished, but in the sense that it would be as if it had never happened."

And to those who asked: "When will the time for mourning come? When will the wound be closed? "Bernard-Henri Levy replied: "It is a wound without suture, without scar, without possible mourning, it is one of those wounds that Emmanuel Levinas said in the 1960s "must bleed until the end of time"... This infinite memory, Levy wrote, this endless work, I believe very deeply that it is not only a matter for the victims and survivors, even less so for the Jews alone. I believe it is incumbent on all nations in general[48]."

You have understood: all peoples on all continents must atone until the end of time for this "crime without vestiges, without traces, without ruins and without archives." It is the new religion of modern times. This astonishing egocentrism is undoubtedly another characteristic feature of the planetary mentality.

Islam and cosmopolitanism

While most people in the West have now realised that Judaism is to be welcomed, Muslims seem to see things differently. Islam is now effectively the main force opposing Judaism. So much so that planetary intellectuals, while frantically promoting immigration in European countries for decades, keep warning us of the danger of radical Islam that threatens them directly. Since the second Intifada in Palestine in September 2000, many young French-born Muslims have begun to

---

[47]Marek Halter, *La force du Bien*, Robert Laffont, 1995, p. 154.

[48]Bernard-Henri Levy, *Récidives*, Grasset, 2004, p. 435.

oppose, sometimes violently, the Jewish community. And it is precisely this new threat that has provoked the media establishment to demonise radical Islam as a new avatar of fascism.

After having destroyed Europe's ethnic homogeneity and greatly weakened its traditional religion, it is now a question of dissolving the threatening internal force of Islam: "Christianity and Islam, wrote Pascal Bruckner in *Le Figaro* of 5 November 2003, have in common that they are two imperialist religions, convinced that they possess the truth and are always ready to bring salvation to mankind, whether by the sword, the auto de fe or the burning of books." The essayist recalled that in France, the integration of the Catholic Church into the Republic had not taken place without clashes: "The extraordinary virulence of the anticlerical combat in France and in Europe sometimes bordered on barbarism: churches, temples, convents burned and razed to the ground, objects of worship degraded, priests, bishops, nuns guillotined, hanged, massacred... A terrible price was paid in an unconscionable sectarian struggle, but which freed us from ecclesiastical tutelage."

With the 1905 law on the separation of church and state, the problem of Catholicism was solved, and the Church also developed favourably towards democratic ideals after the Second Vatican Council in 1965[49].

"This long process of mending is still to be done in Islam, for Islam is certain to be the last revealed religion, and therefore the authentic one... It will have to engage in a kind of reformation just as radical as the Catholics and Protestants have done throughout the last century." After which, we suppose, it will be up to the Jews to do their own reformation.

The question of Islam is now at the centre of the concerns of cosmopolitan intellectuals, not only because of the growing and worrying weight of Muslims in France, but also because of the rise of Islamic radicalism in the world. This was manifested once again with the election of President Ahmadinejad in Iran in June 2005 and the victory of Hamas in Palestine in January 2006.

In the weekly *Le Point* of 13 October 2005 (page 100), the great international Peruvian novelist Mario Vargas Llosa gave his opinion on the Palestinian question. After an excursion in an armoured Range Rover in the Gaza Strip, the writer recounted his impressions and

---

[49]On these religious and political developments, read Vicomte Léon de Poncins, *Judaism and Vatican, an attempt at spiritual subversion,* Christian Book Club of America, 1967, Léon de Poncins, *El Judaísmo y la Cristiandad,* Ediciones Acervo, Barcelona, 1966.

sympathised with the situation of those unfortunate people: "Atrocious… What I have seen is atrocious… Worse than the worst shantytowns in Latin America… And the future is not rosy for these poor people who live there." We are not used to hearing this kind of compassionate discourse towards the oppressed Palestinians, but you have to read Mario Vargas Llosa to the end: "Sharon was right to eliminate Gaza."

On the situation in France on the eve of the serious ethnic riots in November 2005, the progressive writer made no secret of his preferences. Sarkozy: "A small hope for France." Islamism: "The greatest danger of our times."

If Mario Vargas Llosa moved from the extreme left to support the "hard", pro-American liberal right, like many of his colleagues, it is not because he calls plural society into question, but rather because it is a question of restoring order in order to better establish it.

Let us now listen to a dialogue between two eminent figures of late 20th century French democracy: Daniel Cohn-Bendit, the former anarchist leader of the May '68 revolt and prominent MEP, and his compadre Bernard Kouchner, former socialist minister and co-founder of Médecins sans frontières.

Bernard Kouchner: "Every time I read the Koran, I am frightened by the spirit of superiority expressed by this proselytising and conquering religion. It so subordinates trade, the rule of men and the subjugation of women to dogmas and rites that it can only—unless it evolves—appear provocative… I remain convinced that one day Europe will have to face up to this obscurantism. It is useless to present ourselves with a white flag: the Islamic fascists are our enemies." To which Daniel Cohn-Bendit replied:"… Like Europe in the 19th and early 20th centuries, Islam has a great secular reform to carry out. This will be done through struggle and pain."

For cosmopolitan intellectuals, it is not a question of expelling Muslims, who have been introduced en masse in Europe, but of neutralising them, as was done with the Catholic religion and the European peoples. This was clearly expressed by Bernard Kouchner when he said he wanted to favour Islam and then tame it: "This communitarianism, let's be clear, would simply be the first stage necessary for integration, the time needed to harmonise family and religious cultures. It is up to us to build the mosques, and not in basements[50]! "

[50]B. Cohn-Bendit, B. Kouchner, *Quand tu seras président*, Robert Laffont, 2004, p. 320, 183, 190

The same reasoning led Bernard Kouchner to support positive discrimination projects that favour immigrants to the detriment of native French and Europeans: “I’m quite in favour”, he would simply say.

On the international scene, on the other hand, there is no reason not to fight Islam and the Arab world by all means. Daniel Cohn-Bendit had opposed the US intervention in Iraq in 2003 because he feared that the war would “destabilise the whole region and strengthen the most destructive forces by uniting the opposing sides.” But once the country was crushed under bombs, he expressed his true thoughts: “The US intervention has liberated the Iraqis,” he finally acknowledged. The former anarchist had been more forceful in his support for the first US intervention. In 1991, at the end of the first Gulf War, he declared that the coalition “had to go on to Baghdad and bring down Saddam Hussein. Koweit had been liberated, but not the Kurds or the Shiites… It is legitimate to say that for twenty years we had the right and the duty to overthrow Saddam Hussein.”

Enthused by his words, his friend Bernard Kouchner replied: “Thank you Dany, you are a true supporter of interference! [51]“He added: “It is Wolfowitz, the neo-conservative ideologue at the Pentagon, who is behind this decision. He even wanted to deal with Afghanistan and Iraq at the same time[52].” Indeed, many Jews play a decisive role in US policy.

With the Iraqi question barely resolved, Iran emerged in 2006 as the standard-bearer of Muslim resistance. Even before the election of President Ahmadinejad, the mullahs’ regime was worrying intellectuals and they were already dreaming of armed intervention. This is what Daniel Cohn-Bendit suggested in a somewhat veiled way: “When you talk to students in Iran, you can see perfectly well, even though they claim not to want an American intervention, that they actually dream about it at night[53].”

In 1983, after the Islamic revolution, Guy Konopnicki confused his personal desires with reality, insinuating that Iranians also wanted to be bombed so that they could adopt the Western democratic system and American culture: “In Tehran, it is not the Shah that is missed, but rather

---

[51]Bernard Kouchner distinguished himself by campaigning before international bodies in defence of the principle of humanitarian interference. In 2010, *The Jerusalem Post* ranked him 15th among the 50 most influential Jews in the world.

[52]Cohn-Bendit, Kouchner, *Quand tu seras président*, Robert Laffont, 2004, p. 228, 229, 219, 222.

[53]Cohn-Bendit, Kouchner, *Quand tu seras président*, Robert Laffont, 2004, p. 326.

American films and the debauchery imported from the West[54]."

Former Israeli Prime Minister Ehud Barak, visiting the US on the eve of the anti-US attacks of 11 September 2001, gave an analysis of what the anti-terrorist response should be. Writing in *Le Monde* on 14 September, he wrote: "The very scale of these acts and the challenge they pose are such that they should provoke a global fight against terrorism… The time has come to launch a global war against terrorism, in the same way that Europe once fought maritime piracy."

You have understood: if Israel is threatened, and if New York, the first Jewish city in the world and the heart of international finance, could have been the target of these attacks, then it is the Westerners who must fight back and go to war against the Muslim world and the "enemies of civilisation". Israel, in fact, seems to want to wage its wars with the blood of others. Islamists are demonised just as "fascists" and in general all enemies of international finance and cosmopolitanism were once demonised. Ehud Barak wrote: "The only cause of what has happened is the diabolical nature of terrorism… They want to destroy the Western way of life, even if they do not know it, out of various frustrations. They want to threaten the West, impose their decisions on it and humiliate it."

We recognise the same discourse in the philosopher Bernard-Henri Levy when he wrote in November 2003: "The same demon manipulates the militants of today's radical Islam as it did the Maurrasians in his time[55]. And that demon is anti-Semitism[56]."

The internationally renowned American novelist Norman Mailer was also able to detect and denounce the presence of the devil: "That is why I am inclined to think that the best explanation of 9/11 is that the devil won a great battle that day. Yes, Satan was the pilot who guided those planes to that atrocious outcome." [57]."

White men, who had been portrayed for decades as perverse, hypocritical and inherently evil, were now supposed to go out and defeat Muslims in the Middle East while being forced to integrate them en masse into their own countries. This is all a bit fat, but the media hammering allows these cognitive contradictions to be masked. In the weekly *Le Point* of 22 December 2005, Bernard-Henri Levy headlined his article: "Is it still possible to stop Tehran's fascislamists? "Compared

[54]Guy Konopnicki, *La Place de la nation*, Olivier Orban, 1983, p. 138.

[55]Supporters of Charles Maurras (1868–1952). Nationalist, monarchist, anti-parliamentary and anti-Semitic ideologue of the *Action Française*.

[56]Bernard-Henri Levy, *Récidives*, Grasset, 2004, p. 886.

[57]Norman Mailer, *Why are we at war?* Editorial Anagrama, 2003, Barcelona, p. 121.

to the current Iranian regime that is threatening to get its hands on the atomic bomb, Saddam Hussein's "warlike veleities" were in reality "a good joke", wrote Levy. It was therefore a matter of overcoming the "pusillanimity of the free world": "We must hurry, wrote the philosopher, because we have very little time left."

After leading us to war against Iraq in 1990, against Serbia in 1999, against Afghanistan in 2002, and again against Iraq in 2003, the cosmopolitan intellectuals are now leading us to war against Iran with an exaggerated propaganda that pretends to make us believe that it is our duty to go and "liberate" these "frightened" peoples who only "aspire to human rights". A little more and we might think that these are the same people who would have led us into war against the German-Nippon axis in 1940. But, after all, isn't it all about building the Empire of "Peace"?

Europe and the US model

Cosmopolitan intellectuals have the same enthusiasm for the American model as they once had for the Bolshevik revolution and communism. It was not until after the Second World War that this fervour towards the Soviet system waned, due to the new anti-Zionist orientation of the regime. These intellectuals became massively committed to the various currents of Trotskyism, and played a decisive role during the events of May '68. Since then, many of them have realised that democracy was ultimately much more effective than Marxism in building the foundations of the desired world society. The famous novelist Mario Vargas Llosa is an example of how many of these intellectuals now exalt the United States. In *Le Point* of 13 October 2005, he was presented thus: " In France, Vargas Llosa could pass for a right-wing man—but with a left-wing memory… Once upon a time, he thought he was a Marxist—but in the 1970s, everything slowly changed."

The truth is that today the political divergence is no longer between the right and the left, but between the supporters of the global Empire and the supporters of national resistances. Mario Vargas Llosa is clearly a supporter of the Empire and the Great Hodgepodge:

"I was horrified by the victory of the No vote in the referendum on the European constitution" in May 2005, Vargas Llosas declared, bitterly regretting this reactionary and almost unbearable vote of the French: "How long will France, this historically exemplary country, remain angry with globalisation, with liberalism, even with the laws of gravity? I wish you with all my heart … to revive the universalism that has always made, against nationalism, the greatness of your nation[58]." A globalist when he was a communist, Mario Vargas Llosa remains a globalist from his liberal capitalist positions.

This point of view sheds light on the ideological foundations of European construction, which in the end is nothing more than another version of the American model and a step towards the construction of world government. The sociologist Edgar Morin realised the universal scope of the American model: "Just as the dream of the French Revolution became the horizon of all the peoples of Europe, so the American dream of a society in which it is possible to invent concrete and diverse forms of utopia has become the inalienable heritage of the peoples of the world[59]."

In 1991, Edgar Morin was already calling for a "European confederation": "The confederal idea," he wrote, "enables Europe to tackle the problems of planetary civilisation." He thus envisaged the possibility of a system that would make it possible to "liberate" a people who had unfortunately allowed themselves to be led astray by voting the wrong way: "When the civil and democratic rights of the citizen are threatened in one of the countries of the confederation, we can consider a right of joint intervention by the confederation[60]." The unleashing of wars, as we have seen in recent years, is indeed a major speciality of cosmopolitan politics.

Bernard-Henri Levy was much more explicit. His words perfectly expressed this cosmopolitan will to destroy nations: "The European machine, he wrote, has come to stand against these mystical nationalisms and has already begun to expel them to the museum of historical horrors. With the death of these messianic nationalisms, the Jews get rid of the most fearsome of their adversaries."

This was very enlightening, and Bernard-Henri Levy hastened to specify the nature of this democratic Europe which should not, according to him, be "just another nation", but "a device whose function is to work, fracture, pulverise and finally cause the necrosis of national identities and fixations[61]."

It is for this very reason that he reveres American cosmopolitan society. For him, anti-Americanism is a "morbid passion": "Since the time of Maurras and Drieu, all regressions have been cited in it. It

---

[58]*Le Point*, 13 October 2005, p.100

[59]Edgar Morin, *Un nouveau commencement*, Seuil, 1991, p. 124.

[60]Edgar Morin, *Un nouveau commencement*, Seuil, 1991, p. 90, 94.

[61]Bernard-Henri Levy, *Récidives*, Grasset, 2004, p. 458.

attracts like a magnet the worst and most nauseating of every political family[62]." Twenty years earlier, Levy had already written in *The French Ideology:* " I affirm that the brutal and total hatred of America as such is definitely the hatred of liberty[63]."

Planetary intellectuals, who can afford to insult their adversaries without fearing legal action against them, are generally quite virulent when criticising the sacrosanct American model. In the wake of Bernard-Henri Levy's powerful genius, Bernard Cohen, a lesser writer, also believed he had the right to insult those who did not think like him. In *The Return of the Puritans* (no wonder there are publishers to publish such a nullity), he let loose his little spittle and proclaimed his "will to turn away from European anti-Americanism which, rather than exhaling like good terroir, smells in the end of dung[64]." Intolerance of frustration is a characteristic feature of the cosmopolitan mentality.

The American model embodies the ideal of cosmopolitan uprootedness and multiracial society that these intellectuals are so enthusiastic about. Guy Konopnicki was not wrong when he wrote: "The anguish of Americanisation is linked to the fear of immigration. The "Americanised" France is that of the gangs of young North Africans, of the black musicians in the metro, of the night people in the centre of the big cities. This mix is our future. It has long been the nightmare of all the regimes of order on the planet." It would be logical then for people on the left to support the American model, instead of fighting it, and to make a political turn, just as all the cosmopolitan intellectuals did, from the old militant Marxism to democratic liberalism. For it is only this multiracial and multicultural society that allows the voices of the "racist" Whites to be silenced. The integration of immigrants is, after all, the possibility of dissolving the resistance of European peoples still too reluctant to the global domination of international finance. Certainly, these new hybrid and uprooted identities will be the most permeable and manageable for the messages of cosmopolitan propaganda: "The population of France and Western Europe increasingly resembles that of the United States", Konopnicki rejoiced. This "movement of cultural universalisation" is "globally liberating[65]." Konopnicki wrote these lines in 1983. Twenty years later, after numerous anti-white aggressions during the March 2005 demonstrations and the November riots in almost all French cities, one

---

[62]Bernard-Henri Levy, *Récidives,* Grasset, 2004, p. 830.

[63]Bernard-Henri Levy, *Récidives,* Grasset, 2004, p. 280.

[64]Bernard Cohen, *Le Retour des puritains,* Albin Michel, 1992, p. 16.

[65]Guy Konopnicki, *La Place de la nation,* Olivier Orban, 1983, p. 123, 124, 175, 148.

can legitimately point to these intellectuals as the main culprits of this situation[66]. But we all know that it would be illusory to call them to account in a public debate. The philosopher André Glucksman, a former Maoist leader during the events of May '68, also made his ideological mutation in order to better maintain the course towards globalisation[67]. In his book, *The 11th Commandment*, he went a step further in explaining the defence of the American model, drawing a parallel between anti-Americanism and anti-Semitism: "Tied in the hate score … the two pillars of fundamentalist catechism—Jew-hatred and anti-Yankee rage—are complementary and feed back on each other. When one becomes momentarily unusable through overuse, the other takes over[68]." Indeed, the two concepts are related, for we know that the Jewish community exerts great influence over the various American governments and that its financial and media power make the United States the heart of world Jewry.

In fact, this is exactly what the press director Jean Daniel, who saw the United States, rather than the state of Israel, as the "homeland of world Jewry", stated: "It is superficial, though not useless, to emphasise the power of American Jews in the press and thus in the making of news throughout the West. This explanation must be mentioned, but then quickly superseded. It is true that the United States is the home of journalism, whatever its flaws or the bias of its press. It is true that, within this news factory, this laboratory of information, Jews play a fundamental role, and they are also a very influential financial and cultural minority. In that sense, I can say that the vitality, the vigour, the splendour of Judaism have impressed me much more in New York than in Tel-Aviv… I have been so impressed by the Jewish cultural effervescence, the genius of its writers, its artists, its academics, the incredible fecundity of its humour, and also, of course, its unassuming financial might, that it has seemed to me that the homeland of world Jewry was not in the beleaguered fortress of the pioneers of the Hebrew State, but in the bastions built by the founders of the New World for the

---

[66]Note the very serious deterioration of the current situation in Western Europe and the United States.

[67]André Glucksmann is also known for having supported NATO's intervention in Serbia, along with other intellectuals. He also spoke out in favour of the Chechen cause, where he stayed for a month, denouncing the complacent attitude of Western countries towards Vladimir Putin's policies. His son Rafael Glucksmann supported the Euromaiden coup and the Ukrainian "revolution" in 2013 and is currently a vehement defender of the cause of the Uighur Muslim minority in China. (NdT).

[68]André Glucksmann, *Le XIe commandement*, Flammarion, 1991, p. 142.

greater glory of free enterprise[69]."

So, after such considerations, we can allow Guy Konopnicki to speak freely and declare his love for America: "The United States of America has been the place in the world where the greatest miscegenation of all times has taken place". It is today "the prefiguration of world culture."

And this world culture has no better vehicle than images, which require little effort on the part of the spectator to absorb them. It is through the cinema that the planetary masses will become aware of the advantages of liberal and cosmopolitan civilisation: "I sincerely believe," wrote Konopnicki, "that Metro Goldwyn Mayer, Warner Brothers, Fox and Columbia are in our time what cathedrals were in the Middle Ages[70]." Indeed, Konopnicki devoted a separate chapter to this religious worship of Hollywood; a chapter eloquently entitled: "*Yerushalayim - Hollywood, Hallelujah*!"

Hollywood symbolises the power of propaganda and the domination of the mind. As the prophecies of Israel foretold, all peoples finally submit to the cosmopolitan model, abandoning their own traditions to kneel at the feet of the Jewish people: "In the city of the cinema, all curses are over, including that of the tower of Babel, annihilated by dubbing and subtitles. All the tribes of Israel, all the nations of creation have been reunited with their flocks and their horses… It was said that history would begin again, that there would be a great *remake* and that *Hallelujah* would be sung with a soundtrack by Leonard Bernstein[71]." Ultimately, for Konopnicki, redemption will come through cinema: "Some prophets even said that the Messiah would be Light", he wrote. The cosmopolitan intellectual's discourse is strangely impregnated with prophetic terms:

"Something is growing that is nothing like the revolutions foreseen by the bearded men of the last century, nor the triumphant progress announced at the time of the Enlightenment. Something impalpable that is born through the confrontations and crises of our time… Something will emerge from this crisis. As in all previous crises, something that will be neither French, nor American, nor Russian[72]."

---

[69]Jean Daniel, *L'Ère des ruptures*, Grasset, 1979, p. 106, 107.

[70]Guy Konopnicki, *La Place de la nation*, Olivier Orban, 1983, p. 145, 155.

[71]Jacques Attali tells us in *The Jews, the World and Money* that Hollywood is a Jewish fiefdom: "Today's essential firms are: Universal, Fox, Paramount, Warner Bros, MGM, RCA and CBS are all creations of Jewish immigrants from Eastern Europe…" *(Los judíos, el mundo y el dinero,* Fondo de cultura económica, 2005, Buenos Aires, p. 413).

[72]Guy Konopnicki, *La Place de la nation*, Olivier Orban, 1983, p. 215, 225-229.

Doesn't this resemble the words of Edgar Morin: "The eruption of racial hatreds, religion, ideology, always entails wars, massacres, tortures, hatred and contempt. The world is going through agonising pains of something that we do not know whether it is birth or death. Humanity has not yet succeeded in giving birth to Humanity[73]." This singular vocabulary secretly conceals religious convictions that we are impatient to present to you.

Planetary cinema

In *The Planetary Hopes*, we had already identified and succinctly commented on some eighty cosmopolitan propaganda films produced by the progressive "Matrix". This chapter completes that study, without, of course, claiming to be exhaustive.

Planetary cinema has always extolled the virtues of multicultural democracy and miscegenation. As early as the 1950s, a cosmopolitan filmmaker sought to raise public awareness of racism in American society. *No way out (*USA, 1950) tells the story of a black hospital intern, Dr. Brooks. One day he treats two criminals, Ray and John Biddle, injured during a robbery. John dies and Ray accuses Dr. Brooks of killing him..." An anti-racist allegation that caused something of a stir at the time" reported historian Jean Tulard's *Guide to the Movies* (2002). The film is by Joseph Mankiewicz.

*La Frontera (*USA, 1982) tells the story of a US immigration police officer policing illegal immigrants in El Paso. One day he finds himself in a moral dilemma when the baby of a young Mexican woman is kidnapped to be sold to a sterile couple. We can deduce that Tony Richardson's film aims to teach us about universal brotherhood.

In Above *All* (USA, 1992), Michelle Pfeiffer plays the role of a beautiful blonde who loves black people. It is 1963 in the United States, and President Kennedy has just been assassinated. Shocked, Lurene decides to go to the funeral in Washington despite the opposition of her husband, an asshole of the moment. On the bus she meets a black man and his young daughter. But he is cold and distant. She finds the behaviour of this "coloured man" strange, and the girl seems to have been kidnapped. At one stop, Lurene decides to call the police before she realises her mistake: the little girl is indeed her daughter, whom she has freed from a horrible orphanage after the death of her mother. Fond of the little girl, the beautiful blonde decides not to abandon them and

[73]Edgar Morin, *Un nouveau commencement*, Seuil, 1991, p. 206.

runs away with them. The police are now on their trail, convinced that this “nigger” has kidnapped the girl and the young blonde who was going to report him. The scene of racist violence takes a while to arrive, but it finally happens as planned: while the stolen car is broken down, the good Negro is beaten to a pulp by three White bastards in the middle of a lost road. The beautiful blonde tries to cure him in a farmhouse and offers him her body. From then on, the die is cast. At a motel where her jealous and enraged husband is waiting for her, a fight breaks out between the two men. The Black, good and kind, will obviously win over the White, repressed, mean and “pusillanimous”, as Alain Minc would say. The flight forward will not last forever, of course, and everything will return to normal after the arrests. The beautiful blonde will divorce to live as a couple with the Negro. This beautiful film is by Jonathan Kaplan. This director, who had hesitated between a career as a filmmaker and that of a rabbi, thus achieved an anti-racist masterpiece.

Men in Black (USA, 1997) is a film that teaches us to welcome the foreigner, all foreigners, even aliens. We don’t know it yet, but there are already many of them living among us in human form. Members of an ultra-secret special agency are in charge of monitoring and regulating this new type of migration flows and keeping the existence of these aliens secret so as not to alarm the population. The two super special agents—a Black and a White—are tasked with hunting down a hostile Alien, which will not be able to resist the efficiency of the ruthless duo. But, although both are very competent, the White one is a little tired. Black will be the one to continue the fight and enjoy the favours of his new teammate—a white one. The film directed by Barry Sonnenfeld, based on a screenplay by Ed Solomon and music by Danny Elfmann, is produced by Steven Spielberg. They are all aliens disguised as humans and agents of the “Matrix”.

In *Tears of the Sun* (USA, 2003), black director Antoine Fugua depicted a civil war between black tribes in Africa. A US army unit is tasked with rescuing a young American woman who runs a hospital. She, as we can imagine, is an idealist full of humanitarian principles; so much so that she refuses to follow Bruce Willis and his shock commando if the wounded Africans are not evacuated as well. Bruce Willis disobeys orders and goes so far as to massacre half the men in the unit under his command in order to save the Africans. A dialogue in the film allows the viewer to understand that if the Americans act in this way, it is to “redeem” themselves for all the crimes committed by the white man throughout history. But this is to quickly overlook the fact that many of the Blacks sold to the Whites during slavery were sold by their racial brothers. Moreover, if director Antoine Fugua had remembered the role and the irrefutable responsibility of the Jewish traders in the slave trade of the Blacks, not to mention the Muslim slavers in the Indian Ocean for fourteen centuries, he would certainly not have been able to produce his film.

The Day After Tomorrow (USA, 2004) is a catastrophic film. After volcanoes, tornadoes and meteors, global warming causes a tidal wave followed by a glacial cold snap. The film is tedious, but the ending is revealing of the director's mentality. Indeed, the people of the North are forced to migrate south. The American president declares: "The Americans, and many other peoples as well, are now the guests of what we once called the Third World. We were in need and they let us into their countries, they took us in; I want to express my gratitude for their hospitality." The director's message is clear: we must let immigrants into our countries because it is possible that, in a future, let's say hypothetical and uncertain, we too will need their help. Let's remember that Roland Emmerich is also the director of the film *Independence Day*, which tells how the Earth is saved from catastrophe by a Black and a Hasidic Jew. A great guy, this Roland.

France has no shortage of anti-racist and moralising films. In *Sacred Union* (*L'Union sacrée*, France, 1989), two policemen are forced to investigate together a network of Islamists who are financed by all kinds of trafficking. The Jew Simon Atlan (Patrick Bruel) and the Arab Karim Hamida (Richard Berry) hate each other. However, in the face of the intolerance and fanaticism of the evil Islamists, they gradually become friends. In this film, the Jew is a little crazy and sympathetic, while the Arab is serious and efficient. The commissioner, played by Bruno Kremer, speaks to his men in very direct language: "You have to behave like crusaders, defenders of the Western world! With these bastards, everything is allowed! "With these words we must understand that the indigenous French must go to war against the evil Islamists who threaten our beautiful multicultural democracy. The Islamists are obviously described as ferocious beasts. Let's look at the words of one of these dangerous morons that the film's director has probably heard on the terrace of a bar: "We are going to turn the life of this country into a nightmare. Today we strike here, tomorrow we strike there. There are no innocents worth a damn."

Simon is separated from his wife Lisa. She is a goy, a very cute French woman who loves Jews but who has not been able to stand living with Simon, who is too childish. Lisa can't stand him any more; besides, as she tells Karim, her mother-in-law has circumcised her son when she has never had him baptised in church. Lisa is in charge of openings and exhibitions in an art gallery. When an embassy official, a certain Rafjani, turns up at the tapestry exhibition she is organising, she does not hesitate to reprimand him for the status of women in his country. That's how French women are: preachy, know-it-all, and, above all, very open to the winds of the East. That's how we like them. And indeed, Lisa, who has left the Jew, will fall under Karim's charms.

But it so happens that Rafkhani is also the head of the Islamist network. The two supercops have located the headquarters of this mafia network. It is a pseudo-cultural centre which, according to the two protagonists, is "a real arsenal; it looks like Beyrouth." There, the Islamists, who are really very bad guys, torture a poor Kabyle by pouring two bottles of whisky through a funnel into his mouth. When he comes face to face with Rafjani, good cop Karim tells him: "I'm ashamed to be the same race as you! That's how we like Muslims: divided, full of rancour and shame, and ready to kill each other. But before being expelled from the territory, Rafjani exclaims in hatred: "I will take revenge, even if I have to put Paris in blood and fire. *Allah Akbar*! "

Another embarrassing scene occurs when Lisa, the pretty French girl, has dinner in the restaurant with Karim. Simon, who is still in love with her, suddenly appears: "You're fucking my wife on the sly! "Always impulsive, Simon decides to play Russian roulette: "If you win, you get my wife". Bravely, he puts the gun to his temple and fires: click. Karim refuses to take part in this stupid game and stands up. Then the Jew pulls the trigger, and this time the gun goes off: "You're dead, get out! "Karim, however, will not go away with his head down and, very dignifiedly, slaps Simon before leaving. We see how in this tremendous duel to conquer the white woman, the two Semites know how to compete gallantly.

But the evil Islamists are determined to liquidate these two overly meddlesome cops. Here is an anthological scene in French cinema. Simon's mother's *kosher* restaurant*74* is machine-gunned in broad daylight, just like in Chicago! Lisa, seriously wounded, dies in hospital. During the funeral ceremony in the church, Simon, filled with hatred and revenge, can't take it any longer and rushes out, interrupting the Catholic ceremony (a recurring theme in planetary cinema, of course). The next scene shows Simon praying in the synagogue with a kippah

[74] A type of ritually prepared food authorised by Jewish law to be eaten.

and a prayer shawl over his head. We also hear his father praying for him in the restaurant: "Lord, give him strength, give him fury"!

The Islamist diplomat is finally expelled without Simon having been able to quench his thirst for revenge. In front of the TV cameras, Rafjani still tries to play the victim, complaining about the harsh treatment he received from "the homeland of Voltaire and Anatole France, protector of the oppressed" (the perfidy of these Islamists knows no bounds). Fortunately, this Islamist bastard doesn't get away with it, and we see his car explode at night, with the Eiffel Tower illuminated in the background. The film ends with a few lines that appear on the screen: "Simon and Karim have probably dreamt of this revenge. The law of Talion will never be an answer to violence. This story is a fiction. The reality is just as cruel." Beautiful, isn't it? Finally, the faces of the Jew and the Arab appear, looking at the distant horizon, like statues of Soviet proletarians. This is cinema in capital letters. The director is Arcady, who has never taken us for a ride…

Trop de bonheur (France, 1994) shows the life of four teenagers in the south of France during the summer: Valerie, Mathilde, Kamel and their friend Didier. They meet one night with some friends at Mathilde's mansion while their parents are away. Kamel loves Valerie. Music, dancing, alcohol, emotions and feelings, betrayal and violence. When they meet again years later, they hardly recognise each other. Kamel now lives with Mathilde. This film with the cosmopolitan stamp is by Cedric Kahn.

In *The City is Quiet* (France, 2000) we see how the destinies of several characters intersect: Michelle, a worker in the Marseilles port fish market, is married to an unemployed alcoholic. At the end of her hard day's work, she still has to look after the baby of her drug addict daughter, a teenager who prostitutes herself to pay for her heroin. Viviane, a mature bourgeois and singing teacher, is fed up with her husband's cynicism. She falls in love with one of her former pupils, the young Abderaman… The director is the same as the director of the film *Marius et Jeanette*, another work with the same obsession for the miscegenation of the white race: Robert Guediguian.

Fatou the Malian (France, 2001) is 18 years old. She was born in France of Malian parents and has just passed her baccalaureate. She works in an African hairdresser's in Paris. She is beautiful, cheerful, full of life and ambition. The Malian family is perfectly integrated. The father works in a grocery shop. The flat is very clean and well decorated. The African costumes are magnificent and colourful, just like in the theatre. Unfortunately, Fatu's parents decide to marry her off to her cousin whom she does not love, and she is literally kidnapped with no chance of escape on the sixth floor, right next to her parents' flat. But Fatou is saved by her friend Gaelle, a young French girl who has a great time with her Maghrebi friends, an example of a girl! Gaelle is going to free her friend Fatou and take her to Brittany to open a hairdressing salon. Brittany will thus be enriched with new little Bretons. The film by Daniel Vigne, presented by Fabienne Servan-Schreiber, was obviously awarded a prize in 2001." A success" according to *L'Express*; "outstanding" for *France Soir*; "moving" according to *Télé 7 Jours*.

On Friday 19 August 2005, the TV series *P.J.* (Police Judiciaire)—a "very French" series—presented an episode on anti-Semitism: a Molotov cocktail was thrown at a synagogue. Agathe is in charge of the investigation, which allows her to return to her religion. The suspects are paraded at the police station. An insolent young Moor implied—unbelievably!—that "the gas chambers did not exist". Enraged and out of her depth, the police rushed at him before being pushed away by her colleagues. The second suspect entered the room for questioning. He is a black colossus who does not paint a good picture of immigrant youth either. The third man is an extreme right-wing white man who seems more humane and sympathetic compared to the other two. The indigenous French are not usually treated very well in these series, but it seems that, at the beginning of the 21st century, the Jewish community has realised that the extreme right, which has always been demonised by the media establishment, represents less of a risk than the gangs of fanatical immigrants that are allowed to enter the territory. However, it is not one of these suspects who is the culprit, but a young Jew in rebellion against his teachers in the Chabad-Lubavitch community. One of the rabbis is interrogated at the police station. In effect, we see a religious man who seems to be living on "another planet", who rejects any idea of happiness provided by Western liberal society. Imprisoned by such a reactionary specimen, the young Jew, who longed for "fun" and freedom, has lost his mind. This script actually corresponded to some events of the same kind that had recently been in the news.

Indeed, in August 2004, a fire was set in a Parisian Jewish social centre. The case was highly publicised, as usual when a representative of the holy community is trampled underfoot. But it turned out that the culprit had been an outcast Jew, whom the media hastened to describe as "mentally ill".

Finally, all is not lost in this chapter, as everything ends quite well. The other policewoman is pregnant: "—Is it Karim? —No, no, answer.

I won't tell you. But she has something in common with Karim." This ideologically charged episode is by Gilles-Yves Caro, with a script by Brigitte Coscas.

Another series: *Josephine, guardian angel, The Colour of Love* (France, 2005)." Hired as a farm worker on the Revel farm, Josephine meets the owner Tomas, who is about to marry Aminata, a young Senegalese woman known on the Internet. Despite her best efforts, Aminata cannot get Claudine, her mother-in-law, to accept her." We can easily imagine that she is a bit of a racist, stubborn and a meathead. This TV series is by Laurent Levy. For *TV Grandes Chaînes, it* is undoubtedly "an episode full of good humour and generosity" which deserves to be "the darling" of the critics.

White Marriage (France, 2005) is an episode of another "very French" series: Tutor in Marseille, François Etchegaray helps those on the margins of society. René is one of his protégés. He's a big, burly man in his forties with a handsome Nordic face, but he's a bit of a simpleton and a bit of a tantrum. In fact, nothing goes right for him. He fails at every little job his tutor gets him, and at forty he still lives at home with his mother who seems to tell him what to do. This unmanly Frenchman suddenly falls in love with an African woman. He shows up at François' house, proud to show him the photo of his fiancée, Lela, whom he naturally wants to marry, even though he has never seen her in person. The *Amistad Africa* association helped him find the love of his life in exchange for a considerable amount of money. Because an African woman is the ultimate for a French idiot—the poor man's Rolls Royce! However, the amount of money asked by the association makes François Etchegaray doubt the honesty of these intermediaries. He quickly realises that René is being fooled like a fool, and that the African woman really only wants a marriage of convenience. It's a nice story, isn't it?

At the beginning of the episode, the viewer was able to see that the generous François also took tender care of a couple of old homosexuals who were a little bitter and worried about their inheritance rights. Apology for miscegenation and homosexuality: this is the trademark of Edouard Molinaro's planetary cinema. Unfortunately, the end of this magnificent series will never be known.

Homosexuality advocacy is indeed a central theme of cosmopolitan cinema. *In and out* (USA, 1997) is a "hilarious" comedy: Professor Howard Brackett teaches literature at the university in a small town in Indiana, USA. He is loved by all his students and the local community, until one day his reputation is turned upside down when, during a TV show, a former student turned movie star publicly thanks his "gay" former professor. Obviously, the teacher is shocked by this statement. Parents, students and friends now look at him with suspicion. He therefore decides to quickly marry his girlfriend to nip the rumours in the bud. But this is without the journalist who follows him everywhere with his camera, encouraging him to "*come out* of the wardrobe". On the day of the wedding, in the middle of the ceremony at the altar, when he is about to say "yes" to his bride, he finally gives up and declares half-heartedly and resignedly: "I'm gay". The attendants are stunned and the bride suffers a nervous breakdown. The religious ceremony is interrupted (a cosmopolitan obsession) and the couple end up arguing in public. However, the director makes us understand that it is better this way. Howard's entourage, family and friends are finally sympathetic. The problem lies in the fact that he lost his job at the university, a victim of the intolerance of those prudish Christians. The final scene is another great moment of cosmopolitan cinema: at the university, during the graduation ceremony, students and parents learn that the professor has been fired. Then they all stand up one by one to declare that they too are "gay". The film is by Frank Oz.

In the same vein, *A Taste of Honey* (UK, 1961) tells the story of the relationship of two outcasts: a teenage girl pregnant from a one-night stand with a black man, and a homosexual. The director is Tony Richardson. *First Summer* (*Presque rien*, France, 1999) is another film that makes an apology for white male homosexuality. It is "a film about love that tries to trivialise male homosexuality by showing very crude scenes", according to Jean Tulard's *Guide des films*. The film is by director Sebastian Lifshitz.

The cosmopolitan propaganda coming out of the "Matrix" is not only "anti-racist". Numerous "racist" films are regularly produced by Hollywood film studios. *In Heat of the Night* (USA, 1967), a Philadelphia criminal police officer is sent to a small Southern town to help the local police solve an industrialist's murder case. Problem: he's Black, and those White assholes can't stand him. But Virgile Tibbs, a specialist criminalist, quickly discovers that the white cops are wrong. He is a calm, rigorous and intelligent man, and he always keeps his cool in the face of the disgusting racism of those arrogant Whites who can't keep up with him. But as stupid as they are, they finally realise they can't do without him. Several times they have to go to the station and beg him to stay. Their investigation quickly leads them to the biggest farmer in the region. He is suspected of having ordered the murder of the industrialist because he was planning to set up a factory and hire hundreds of coloured people. The young people of this "backward" town do not take kindly to this, and will savagely persecute and round up Vigile Tibbs. The matter will be settled with blows in an abandoned factory, with chains and iron bars. Four against one, because that's what Whites are like: vile, cowardly and despicable. Fortunately, the chief of police arrives at the perfect moment and saves Virgile from certain death. This sheriff, initially prejudiced, seals the reconciliation between the two communities. The film naturally received five Oscars. Perhaps it would have won a sixth, if Virgile had returned to Philadelphia with the widow of the murdered industrialist. For she was a very pretty white woman. But in 1967, director Norman Jewison probably didn't want to go too far, lest those unpredictable White assholes react.

Barton Fink (USA, 1991): In 1941, Barton Fink is a young actor who rises to stardom thanks to a play. The first scene of the film puts us right into the atmosphere. He is backstage, gawking at the phenomenal success of his play: it's a triumph! The audience gives him a thunderous ovation and rises to its feet, enthusiastic about the sublime genius of this little unknown Jewish playwright. But Barton Fink is a shy and self-absorbed person. His newfound notoriety enables him to get a contract in Hollywood, although he initially turns it down: "It would take me away from the village", he says. Indeed, Barton has quickly become the new Broadway idol. However, unable to resist the temptation of greater glory, he travels to Los Angeles, where he meets a scheming producer. He is expeditious and very flashy. He is a Jew from Minsk, who claims to be "smarter than the other Jews in the area".

Here is Barton Fink in the hotel in front of his typewriter. But his neighbour in the next room is too noisy and prevents him from concentrating. He suddenly bursts into his life. He is fat, red, crude and an alcoholic: he is a goy! However, the shy and delicate intellectual Barton Fink will appreciate this simple and authentic individual. But he must finish the script very quickly for the film to be shot. The problem is that Barton is having great difficulty writing the script he is asked to write. He remains blocked for several weeks. When his producer receives him at his home by the pool, Barton, saddened, has no choice but to confess that inspiration has not yet struck him. He then receives the sarcasm of the assistant, who does not expect the violent reaction of the producer, who throws him out without a second thought before reiterating his confidence in the little genius he has taken under his wing. His admiration for Barton is such that he even goes so far as to lick the sole of his shoe, out of respect for the noble function of a writer!

Barton is able to return to the hotel in peace. Fortunately, inspiration finally strikes, and Barton manages to write his script in one night in one go. The result is simply brilliant: Yes, Barton Fink is a genius! He is overflowing with joy in the morning. Never before has he achieved such a degree of subtlety and perfection: "I am a creator! "In the evening, he celebrates in style by dancing in a jazz club. In the following days, he meets a great writer, but who turns out to be a very disappointing, alcoholic, brutal and rude individual, who also treats his girlfriend badly. In a misunderstanding, so to speak, Barton spends the night with her at her hotel. But the next morning, he discovers with shock and horror the woman's bloody body in his bed. What happened? He had nothing to do with it, of course, and immediately alerts his neighbour. The latter believes him, and takes it upon himself to make the body disappear.

Suddenly everything is falling apart around him. On top of that his producer is very disappointed with his script. When Barton appears before him, he is this time treated like the last of the scum and heavily insulted. Everything goes wrong for Barton. The police soon investigate the young woman's disappearance: but it turns out that his chubby, blushing, alcoholic neighbour is a dangerous psychopath who has a habit of scalping his victims. He is also a Nazi: "Heil Hitler!" he shouts before shooting two policemen dead with his shotgun in the burning hotel. The film ends like this. In the end, all Whites are ultimately rubbish in this film by the brothers Ethan and Joel Coen. The film was evidently awarded the Palme d'Or at the Cannes Film Festival in 1991. John Turturo is truly magnificent in the role of the Jewish intellectual "close to the people".

Desperately Seeking Susan (USA, 1985): a slightly repressed young woman is transformed into a shameless punk by amnesia. The indigent script is of no importance whatsoever. We simply observe how in an "open", "liberated" and very multicultural society, the black saxophonist in his flat occupies the place of the democratic icon, and that the role of the bad bastard unfailingly falls to a blond man. Is this a coincidence? The film is by Susan Seidelman.

Music box (USA, 1989) is a film that recalls the atrocities of the Second World War: Michael Laszlo is a Hungarian refugee who has been living in the United States for 37 years. From one day to the next he is accused of war crimes. Witness statements were blocked for forty years in the UN archives. He is a widower, but his lawyer daughter is there to defend him. Of course, she doesn't believe these sordid stories and decides to defend her poor father." The communists are behind all this," he says to reassure her. However, he is forced to confess that, before leaving his native Hungary after the war, he had been a policeman under the fascist regime, if only as a "clerk in an office", nothing more. His daughter, however, begins to doubt her father's role during the war: "They have a photo of your membership card of the special sections with your signature on it. The Hungarian government sent it." Moreover, witnesses identified him and accuse him of horrible things: "When I stop to think about all this, I'm ashamed to be Hungarian, Dad," the daughter says (that's how sorry we Hungarians want to be).

A group of survivors then came to demonstrate in front of his house with banners to make life miserable for the well-known anti-communist militant. The window panes were smashed with stones. A new hint alarms the woman when her son naively repeats to her the words of his grandfather: "He said that the holocaust has been fabricated, that it is exaggerated!"

The trial finally begins, and the prosecution witnesses appear one after the other to recount the atrocities committed by the Hungarian fascists, each one more horrible than the last, and of which we retain that "the beautiful blue Danube was red with blood": "Michka was the worst of them all. He loved to kill Jews. He was after gold and money … the beautiful blue Danube was red. It was him, I admit it." The daughter manages to get him off the hook, however, by demonstrating the suspicious links of these witnesses to communist governments and the KGB. Fortunately, her father was exonerated.

But later in Budapest, during a trip to interrogate a witness, he discovers in a music box the atrocious photos that betray his own father. This time the proof of his guilt is irrefutable: "I never want to see you again, Dad. I don't want you to see my son ever again," he tells her, his heart full of hatred and contempt. And when the daughter threatens to tell her son everything, the evil grandfather replies, self-assured and arrogant: "They won't believe you, they won't believe you. They won't believe you. They'll say you're crazy!" This is how we like to see Hungarian families: torn apart and ready to kill each other. The lawyer finally sends the photos to the press, and the film ends with her looking at the photo of her father in militia uniform on the front page of a newspaper. Note that Costa Gavras has taken care to integrate images and music from Hungarian folklore throughout the film. Probably to make it even more repugnant to the viewer.

False Seduction (USA, 1992) begins with a surprising scene: in a villa in a nice suburban town, a young couple discovers a burglar trying to break into their house at night. The man manages to escape by threatening the young woman with a kitchen knife. The aggressor is Black and the victims are White, which is not common in planetary cinema. We suspect that the director would not stop there, and indeed, in the next scene, we realise that there are also sympathetic Blacks, for one of the two policemen who appear to reassure the pretty couple is a black man. His colleague—a White—is also a very nice and professional guy … but only in appearance. For in reality he is a dangerous psychopath who has fallen in love with the young woman and is going to make her husband's life miserable. He even goes so far as to kill his black colleague along with a young drug dealer, making the crime look like a shootout between the two men, which won't stop him from mourning his friend's death in front of the TV cameras. Finally, the black man's knife-wielding assault is forgotten by the end of the film and the blue-eyed psychopath takes centre stage. We have M. Jonathan Kaplan (him again!) to thank for this film.

Cop Land (USA, 1997) reveals the unorthodox policing methods of some New York cops. Most of them have left the big cosmopolitan city they loathe to settle in Garrisson, a quiet little town on the other side of the great Hudson River where they can live in peace—among Whites. We soon realise that these white cops, who bury their dead to the sound of Irish music, are highly organised, and that they do not hesitate to falsify investigations and liquidate cops who get in their way. It's a real mafia gang. But the little sheriff of the area, who until then had turned a blind eye to the situation, finally gets up the courage to take action. All these bastards are white cops, while the multiracial police in New York are really super nice. This "brand" film is by the very astute James "Mangold".

In *Conspiracy* (1997), there are the bad guys and there are the good guys. But not everything is so simple, because among the bad guys, some are not so bad, and even turn out to be good guys. There is only one certainty: all the bad guys are White. Once again, in this respect, the obligatory quotas are not respected. The film is by Richard Donner.

The racism of planetary cinema can also be directed at other communities. *Lethal Weapon 4* (USA, 1998) sets the scene for two Los Angeles police officers, a Black and a White, who have uncovered a Chinese immigration smuggling ring. The two colleagues discover four hundred destitute people crammed into the hold of a ship, but the Black, in pity, and perhaps remembering his slave ancestors, decides to break the law and take in a forgotten family on a salvage boat. The two policemen soon discover the boss of this mafia that brings thousands of Chinese into the United States. They have to work for years to reimburse the cost of their journey and the false documents. It is a fearsome criminal organisation that also manufactures counterfeit currency. Richard Donner's film is undeniably funny and spectacular. But it is also one of the most racist films ever made. As far as we know, no community, apart from the white community, has ever been depicted by Jewish filmmakers in such an offensive and outrageous way. This treatment is perhaps due to the fact that the Chinese community is the only one to push back the Jewish community in the realm of business and community organisation.

In the same vein, one can see the French film *XXL* (France, 1997), which presents the Chinese in Paris in a very bad light, as their commercial activity competes advantageously with the businesses of the Jewish community in the Sentier district[75]. Here we have an Auvergne bar owner and a Jewish textile merchant who are going to join forces against the unbearable Asian invasion. The Auvergne (Gerard Depardieu) is a self-confident, self-assured, conquering showman, while the Jew (Michel Boujenah) is an anxious, shy and restless fellow. But the viewer must realise that their differences are superficial and that they have common interests to defend against these corrupt Chinese, so they can be insulted unceremoniously and without fear of being taken to court. The director of this film is Ariel Zeitoun.

In *The Panic Room (*USA, 2001), a wealthy young woman (Jodie Foster) and her daughter move into a huge mansion in the heart of Manhattan. The house is equipped with a vault designed to resist outside aggression. One night, three burglars break into the house. A terrifying adventure begins that will end very badly, as the loot they are looking for is precisely in the vault where the two women, who are completely unaware of the assailants' intentions, have taken refuge. Of the three thieves, the black colossus is the only one who is a little clever: in fact, it was he who conceived the vault. He is also technical and the most scrupulous of the three criminals, rejecting the use of violence from the outset. The team leader, on the other hand, is Blanco, a tall, nervous and unpredictable guy who will end up with a bullet in his head when he tries to escape. The third, another, very calm Blanco, turns out to be a dangerous psychopath and a crazed killer. At the end of the film, this moron is about to smash the woman in the face. Fortunately, Black intervenes in extremis. The Negro also manages to save the girl from certain death by giving her an injection under very difficult conditions. Whites are bad, Blacks are good; the film is by David Fincher.

---

[75]Traditional Parisian Jewish quarter with a textile trade.

In *O Brother!* (USA, 2000), three likeable rogues manage to escape from a penitentiary in the American South. The beginning of the film seems to be a homage to the culture of the Deep South, with the escape of the three fugitives set to *country* music. But, as usual, the anti-racist message comes through after a while: white male politicians are aggressive, racist, unscrupulous racketeers. The Ku Klux Klan is naturally given a good dressing down, and we realise that there is nothing better than a good multiracial society. The political message is skilfully embodied by a crew of three cronies and a "Negro" guitarist. Admittedly, their music is really stimulating. Not to be left unmentioned, the electoral system—*one man, one vote*—is described for what it is: a scam, where the winning candidate is the one with the best advertising campaign. A plus point, then, for the Joel and Ethan Coen brothers.

Planetary cinema is often characterised as anti-Christian. On television and in films, Christians, mainly Catholics, are indeed often portrayed as priggish, stubborn and intolerant people, and even as rapists and disturbed murderers. As for the Catholic clergy, they are more often than not depicted as a den of sadists and perverse polymorphs.

We have already analysed in *Planetary Hopes* the cases of films such as Richard Brooks' *Elmer Gantry* (USA, 1960), Ingmar Bergman's *Fanny and Alexander,* Jean-Jacques Annaud's *The Name of the Rose,* Robert Mandel's *The Difference,* Frank Darabont's *Life Sentence,* Sofia Coppola's *The Virgin Suicides,* David Fincher's *Seven* and Constantin Costa-Gavras' *Amen.* We will complete the list here.

The Night of the Hunter (USA, 1955), Robert Mitchum plays a Protestant pastor with a good and generous soul. But all this is only a false appearance, for in reality he turns out to be a dangerously unbalanced man in search of a large sum of money given by a father to his children before his imprisonment. Pursued mercilessly by this psychopathic pastor, the two children desperately flee. This Charles Laughton film perfectly embodies the cosmopolitan will to sully the Christian religion.

The Cardinal (USA, 1963) is a film remarkable for the beauty of its images and the nobility of spirit of the future cardinal. Although the Vatican and the Church are relatively well treated, the burden of ignominy falls on the ordinary, practising people. So it is, for Catholics who still refuse to marry their daughters to a Jew show that they are hateful bigots. The same goes for abortion. And given that the film is a series of clichés, we understand very well why the Vatican looks the other way modestly when it comes to taking a stand on the racial issue roiling America in the 1960s. The hero, an American bishop, officially intervenes in this Southern city where a Catholic church has been burned down because the priest was black. The racists of the area do not accept him, and we then witness an anthological scene when the young and intrepid bishop is kidnapped by the militants of the Ku Klux Klan. He will be flogged until he bleeds, amidst a gaggle of hooded men singing and pounding Dixieland rhythms to the sound of the harmonica, while a giant crucifix burns in the night in the background. Geniuses of staging, these Klansmen!—or rather Otto Preminger, if you prefer.

Guy Konopnicki wrote about the film *Ben-Hur* (USA, 1959): "William Wyler is the prototype of the unbearable cosmopolitan: born in Mulhouse in 1901, he arrived in Hollywood when France had just regained Alsace. German? French? Swiss? American? An international filmmaker, Wyler played with all the legends of the world. The model of Christianity that emerges from Wyler's masterpiece prefigures the Second Vatican Council, and Judas Ben-Hur issues a warning to Pontius Pilate addressed to both Washington and Rome[76]." We have been warned.

In *A Girl as Decent as Me (*France, 1972), Charles Denner plays the role of a Catholic who is dedicated to rooting out farms… The film is by François "Truffaut" and the screenplay by Jean-Loup Dabadie. *The Black Widow,* by Arturo Ripstein (Mexico, 1977) is a blasphemous film that denounces the Church and the "bien pensantes". *The Runner Stumbles* by Stanley Kramer (USA, 1979) is the story of a priest who falls in love with a young woman and ends up in court.

Monsignore (USA, 1982) is the story of a depraved cardinal who manages to seduce a man and also ends up in court. But the cardinal is powerful: he manages the bank accounts and liaises with the mafia. The Pope, who is aware of the case, remains discreetly silent about it. The film is by Frank Perry.

In *Crimes of Passion* (USA, 1984), Anthony Perkins plays a docile and very pious evangelical pastor who reads the Bible with fervour, but who frequents X-rated cinemas and falls in love with a kleptomaniac. He ends up killing her in a scene of unbridled depravity to "save his soul"!

Agnes of God (USA, 1985) is set in a Canadian convent. During a winter night, a nun gives birth to a baby found strangled to death in a rubbish bin. Sister Agnes is accused of the murder, but tells the judge

[76]Guy Konopnicki, *La Place de la nation*, Olivier Orban, 1983, p. 209.

she has no memory of it. Dr Livingstone, a young court-appointed psychiatrist, arrives at the convent to try to elucidate the case. The nun who opens the door to her is evidently of a detestable appearance. The psychiatrist questioned the mother superior, who confirmed that no one knew anything. For her, the baby is a miracle; but the psychiatrist is much more pragmatic and realistic: "You refuse to see that Agnes has been raped or seduced." The interview with Sister Agnes is much more interesting: she is totally innocent, as well as ignorant of sexuality and procreation. On the other hand, she often goes into ecstasy and speaks of her love for the Virgin Mary. We finally learn that this poor girl, who was martyred by an alcoholic mother, was in fact raped in a secret passageway through which she sometimes passed, and whose existence the psychiatrist discovered while snooping through the archives of the place. This pitiful girl is the only somewhat sympathetic person in the convent, for all the other sisters are unpleasant as hell. And apparently this is the case with all Catholics, for even Dr. Livingstone's mother, alone in her hospice room, is a grumpy, self-righteous, xenophobic nag. This clunky, heavy-handed film is by Norman Jewison, who apparently doesn't seem to appreciate Catholics very much.

Silver Bullet (USA, 1985): A small American town lives under the terror of a beast that kills and mutilates its inhabitants at night. In reality, it is the shepherd who transforms into a werewolf. Fortunately he will be killed with a silver bullet. The film is by Daniel Attias and the screenplay by Stephen King, who is apparently a "great" writer. Do you know of any films about a rabbi who turns into a vampire on the night of the full moon?

In Cliff Osmond's *The Penitent (*USA, 1988), Paul Julia plays a New Mexico farmer who embarks on a primitive and brutal Catholic cult where followers gleefully enjoy human sacrifices in which the victims are crucified... It is said that in other films of the same kind we can witness scenes of Christian child sacrifices by bloodthirsty rabbis. But all this is, fortunately, nothing more than fiction.

In 1988 again, Martin Scorsese's *The Last Temptation of Christ* showed a homosexual Christ, fond of carnal pleasures and possessed by the devil.

The Handmaid's Tale (USA, 1990) is a dystopia that depicts a horrific United States ruled by Christian fundamentalists. The theocratic government bans books that do not spread the biblical message, rallies the masses to attend hangings and torture, and uses force and brutality to enforce the laws of the Bible, even the most obsolete ones. Moreover, it institutes genocidal policies against ethnic minorities. All this nonsense does not stop hypocritical Christians from frequenting brothels. The film is by Volker Schlöndorff.

The Favour, the Watch and the Very Big Fish (USA, 1991): Luis is a fine art photographer at the studio Norberto runs, specialising in religiously inspired compositions. They are looking for a new photographic model to embody Jesus when they find a slightly mad pianist with the face of Christ (Jeff Goldblum!). The deal is done. The new model embodies Christ beautifully, on the cross, at the supper with the apostles and in all the biblical pictures. But lo and behold, little by little, the false Christ begins to blend in with the real one. In a comical scene, Jeff returns home with a swordfish on his shoulder, which he places on the kitchen table and which his wife is going to prepare for dinner. She throws it into the grinder with the duck's feet! The dish she serves on the table, under her husband's nose, is a filthy, nauseating black stew. She then asks him: "Have you found our Lord Jesus Christ (close-up on the disgusting dish)? It is therefore very clear that this "Jesus" is vomitous for the director, and that Ben Lewin wishes to share his contempt with the whole audience.

Cape Fear (USA, 1991) is the story of an inmate wrongly convicted of rape. After fourteen years in prison, he is finally released with the firm intention of taking revenge on his corrupt lawyer. Robert de Niro plays a dangerous, psychopathic character, and Martin Scorsese has had the good idea of placing a huge crucifix tattoo on his back so that we can identify exactly where his dangerousness comes from. Occasionally, this Pentecostal Christian smokes opium and tries to seduce young girls, rapes a woman, and chases a family, before finally drowning in a torrent. Martin Scorsese is a rather strange Italian, isn't he?

Francis Ford Coppola's famous *Godfather* trilogy depicts the ways of the Sicilian Mafia in the United States in the early 20th century. The third part (1991) exposes the full might of the Catholic Church. In fact, the Vatican owns a huge real estate empire in the world. It is a colossal financial power that does business with the mafia. The Catholic mafia is therefore fearsome, and we can be sure that Western governments obey it to the letter. The Jewish mafia is far from being as powerful.

In *Alien 3* (USA, 1992), Lieutenant Ripley's ship crashes on a planet where the "company" has left only a penitentiary housing dangerous criminals: murderers, rapists, psychopaths. Not reassuring for a woman, even more so when she realises that an Alien was travelling with her on the ship. The commander of the penitentiary is a kind of stubborn fascist who wants nothing to do with the Alien's presence. Fortunately, he will be eaten at the beginning of the film. The prisoners are subjected to a very strict religious discipline, a mixture of "Christian fundamentalism tinged with apocalyptic millenarianism". They are dressed as monks and give a Roman salute by raising their arms after their leader's speech. But make no mistake, these are dangerous mental patients who are best kept away from, especially when they haven't seen a woman for years. The bastards who try to rape her are all evil Whites, while the one who comes to her rescue is a big Black man who has the upper hand over the others: he's the boss! He will sacrifice himself to save Ripley's life and catch the Alien. The film is by David Fincher—there's an Alien on my TV!

Priest (UK, 1994) features a homosexual priest who lives with his butler in plain sight, another alcoholic priest, a pitiful bishop and a young girl whose father regularly abuses her. All are adherents of the Catholic religion, though each conforms to it in his own way.

In *Star Trek V: The Final Frontier* (USA, 1989), God is depicted as a malevolent being and all religions were created by men and will soon have no meaning. God is depicted as a malevolent being and all religions were created by men and will soon no longer have any meaning. All of them? No, because it is a message mainly intended for export.

Johnny Mnemonics (USA, 1995) shows the evil nature of a preacher who has a habit of killing people with a crucifix.

The Two Faces of Truth (*Primal Fear*, USA, 1996): In Chicago, an archbishop is savagely murdered. A suspect is quickly apprehended. He is a mentally limited teenager found dazed and disoriented and with blood on his clothes. He was one of the boys protected by the archbishopric who sang in the choir. We will find out at the end that he was indeed guilty and that he pretended to have amnesia. He wanted to take revenge for all the disgusting vileness that the churchman forced him to do during orgies with his girlfriend and the rest of the choristers in the archbishopric. Nothing less! With such imagination, we can bet that Gregory Hoblit's next film will take place in the crypt of a synagogue. Here's the script: Pious Jews dance to a devilish sarabande, howling like possessed people. In the middle of a circle, an unconscious Christian child is being abused before being sacrificed. Fortunately, Mrs. Moreira, the Portuguese cleaning woman who has pretended to be Jewish in order to get the job, manages by trickery to free the child and take refuge in the police station where she tells everything she saw. Thus begins a new Dreyfus case. Incredible, isn't it?

Flight of the Black Angel (USA, 1991) sets the scene for a US Air

Force pilot who is also a fundamentalist Christian. As if by chance, he suddenly becomes a murderous madman and massacres his family and some colleagues in the squadron. After that, he imagines to clean up Las Vegas with a tactical nuclear bomb, justifying it with that he must fulfil God's will: "Everything on earth must be destroyed... I bring the light of heaven to the sick, to the impure, to the corrupt, to the liars." No doubt about it, he is a Marrano!

In *Rivers of Purple 2: Angels of the Apocalypse* (France, 2003), the director remains faithful to the first part in the sense that the corpses recovered by the two protagonists are just as horrible. Evidently, we are once again confronted with a dangerous network of highly organised neo-Nazis, whose headquarters is a monastery in Lorraine connected by underground galleries to the Maginot line. The monks, who fight "for a white and believing Europe", have contacts with high European personalities who act in the shadows in an underground way: they are everywhere, they control everything, but you don't see them! The scene in which the car is machine-gunned for a very long minute, pierced by at least two or three thousand bullets, is probably the great moment of Olivier Dahan's film, whose script is in any case amply sufficient for the target audience.

In the same vein, we have recently seen a Broadway play, *Corpus Christi*, which stages a homosexual Jesus with close ties to Juda and other disciples...

To relax a little after watching so many films, we can read Gore Vidal's book, *Live from Golgotha*, which apparently depicts St. Paul and Timothy as a homosexual couple. The author does not fail to stress that Christianity was "the greatest disaster to hit the West".

Planetary cinema also sometimes deals with the life of the Jewish community. More often than not, the image that stands out is that of an unjustly persecuted community. This trend in film propaganda is not new, judging by what Jonathan Weiss says: "In 1929, the cinema was producing films like Jean Kemm's *The Polish Jew*, in which a Jew was unjustly accused of a crime[77]." It is indeed the classic posture of the persecuted Jew reflecting the mirror of Judaism.

Norman Jewison's musical comedy, *Fiddler on the Roof* (USA, 1971), recounts the life of a small traditional Jewish community in a Ukrainian village on the eve of the Bolshevik revolution. The atmosphere is folksy; the traditional music and songs stir the hearts: "Thanks to our traditions, everyone knows who he is, and what God

---

[77]Jonathan Weiss, *Irène Némirovsky*, Éditions du Félin, 2005, p. 58.

expects of him," cries the milkman. We recognise in this village the picturesque characters of the time, such as the rabbi surrounded by his faithful, the matchmaker, or the book peddler. Tradition" is at the heart of the universe of this shtetl (Eastern European Jewish people). However, we see it crumble little by little over the course of the film, as the milkman's daughters do as they please and decide to marry the young men they have fallen in love with. For the milkman it is a new and incomprehensible situation. The "tradition" is simply being lost and we understand his suffering. His daughter is not in love with the butcher, but with the young carver: that's the way things are, that's a fact. After painful reflections, she finally consents and agrees to the union. Unfortunately, however, her second daughter chooses for her husband a young Jewish revolutionary who has little respect for "tradition". We see him haranguing the crowd in a Kiev square before he is arrested by the Tsar's police. As for his third daughter, she falls in love with none other than ... a goy! This time it is too much. Jewish law does not joke about such things, and the parents disown her. For them, from now on, she no longer exists.

Against the backdrop of this story, the political upheavals of the time are added, and soon the Russian policemen warn the Jews that they will have to leave the shtetl by order of the Tsar. The Jews, after the three-day deadline they were given, decide to leave after a brief outburst of indignation: after all, what does it matter to the Jews whether they live here or there? The violinist, who played on the roof at the beginning of the film, continues with the same melody behind the convoy of Jews as they set off on a long journey. This beautiful chronicle of the life of a shtetl is perhaps idealised, but it reflects quite well the mutations that Jews have had to accept in order to enter the modern world, as well as their surprising ability to adapt to the situations and needs of the times.

Barbara Streisand's *Yentl* (USA, 1983) is an entertaining film based on the novel by Isaac Bashevis Singer. In a Jewish village in Poland at the beginning of the 20th century, Tentl is a young girl who lives with her father, an educated man. In the market square, the peddler appears, shouting: "Picture books for women, holy books for men". This sums up a lot of things, for indeed, Jewish tradition pays little heed to women, who are forbidden to teach holy things. But Yentl loves books and has only one desire: to study the Talmud[78] like men. When his father dies, he decides to cut his hair short and pretend to be a boy. He goes to the city where he meets Avigdor, who takes his new "friend"

[78]See translator's note in Annex I.

to Bechev, where the *yeshiva*[79], the centre of study, is located.

At night, the two friends sleep at Avigdor's parents' house, and Yentl realises with horror that there is only one room and that he must sleep in the same bed as him. The scene is hilarious, for how will Yentl keep Avigdor from realising that his companion is actually a woman? The tension is at its peak when Avigdor, lying down and tired, loses his patience when he sees that Yentl does not turn off the light and continues to study. Yentl then makes up a ruse as he goes along, revealing that ability to get away with twisting sacred texts if necessary with unnerving aplomb. Thus we learn that, in Judaism, "two unmarried men in the same bed must lie on their backs". Avigdor is a little taken aback, but probably too tired to discuss it.

In the *yeshiva*, Avigdor is Yentl's study partner. One day he introduces him to his girlfriend. To Yentl's question about her: "What does she think," he replies simply: "I don't need her to think." And this brief dialogue confirms the situation of women in Judaism. Under her false identity, Yentl avenges this injustice done to women by becoming the best student in the *yeshiva*. Disheartened at not being reciprocated by her friend to whom she declared her love, who takes tradition very seriously, Yentl will eventually leave for America. On the ship that takes her there, she sings once again of her love for God and her father, whom she confuses in her melodic lament." I'm looking at you, I'm looking at you in the sky... Look daddy, look at me fly! "

In *I Ivan, Your Abraham (*France, 1993), Yolande Zauberman showed us the life of Polish Jews in 1933. In this village where Catholics also live, all Jews are easily blamed for all evils. Christian traditions are certainly steeped in intolerance and madness. Don't Christians see in the eyes of little Abraham the eyes of the devil?

One Shabbat night, an angry and suspicious Christian breaks into an old Jewish man's house to find out at last what is going on behind those closed shutters. He wants to be sure and see with his own eyes all the atrocities of which the Jews are accused. He rushes into the house, and is stunned! The camera slowly records the house: a table, some chairs, the candles burning in the dark; in short, nothing that could validate the plot thesis. All suspicions against the Jews are obviously ridiculous, for the Jews have nothing to hide: nothing. These prejudices must one day disappear. This is the only interesting thing about the film, which is why the fast-forward button on the remote control is indispensable. But the critics were ecstatic about such a work, giving it

[79]A yeshiva is a centre of Torah and Talmudic studies generally reserved for men in Orthodox Judaism. They are also often referred to as Talmudic schools.

the thumbs up: "Yolande Zaubermann has made an indispensable film" (Danièle Heymann, *Le Monde*); "The staging is of extraordinary sensitivity and emotion" (Jooshka Schidlow, *Télérama*); "Yolande Zaubermann achieves the universal" (Claude Lanzmann, *Le Journal du Dimanche*).

Jewish characters are also present in films for "the general public". Their prominent role in communist ideology is quite well reflected in *The Way We Were* (USA, 1973), which tells the story of a communist militant at an American university in the late 1930s. Barbara Streisand plays the role of a young Jewish girl who goes out of her way for the cause. She perfectly embodies that tireless activism so characteristic of Jewish intellectuals. With great courage, she will take the floor on the university campus to denounce "fascism and big business", defend the Spanish "Republicans", and "Peace". Evidently, she manages to move all the students. However, his frenetic activism is annoying for his entourage. Despite this, he manages to seduce Robert Redford, the typical quiet goy who always finds it a little difficult to understand what is happening to him. The film is by Sidney Pollack.

*The Pianist (*Europa, 2001) tells the story of a virtuoso pianist from Warsaw who is a big hit with his Polish fans." M. Szpilman, you are really wonderful," says a beautiful blonde. But the international situation is very tense, and the war is going to destroy our hero's life. However, things couldn't get off to a better start in September 1939, when the Szpilman family, gathered around the radio, learns that England and France have declared war on Germany. Everyone bursts with joy and congratulates each other: "That's wonderful! Unfortunately, however, everything quickly takes a turn for the worse with the victory of the German armies. We then see some repulsive scenes, such as the poor old man slapped in the street by a soldier who orders him to get off the pavement (it's really outrageous!).

In order to survive, our Jewish family is forced to sell the piano to a Polish bastard who takes advantage of the situation. During the frugal dinner, the old father gives his opinion: "The Jewish bankers should convince the United States to declare war on Germany" (Nothing new under the sun). Then an atrocious scene occurs: rampaging German soldiers break into the building across the street, interrupting a family's dinner and forcing them to get up. Since the old man in the wheelchair does not obey immediately, the Germans ... atrociously ... throw him and his chair out of the window. Everyone is finally taken to a labour camp. The streets are covered with corpses. A woman cries because she has been forced to suffocate her baby so that the Germans would not discover them both. Summary executions multiply in the streets ... it is atrocious... Roman Polanski ... film ... atrocious...

We will not recapitulate here all the films about this period that systematically revolve around the theme of persecution. The aim is always the same: to brainwash people about this "dark" period of history. Historians do not look very closely at these materials either, as we already know that these films are not aimed at them.

Cosmopolitan propaganda has been extraordinarily rampant in recent years. For a long time it could not show itself in the light of day, because of the weight of the "prejudices" of the goyim with which one always had to be careful. This propaganda was expressed above all through the apology of "licentiousness", with the aim of progressively undermining the ideal of the family cell, the pillar and nucleus of European civilisation since time immemorial. Cosmopolitan filmmakers sought their inspiration in this direction, unable to give free rein to their feverish imagination. Works that present adultery in a favourable light are innumerable. Later on, homosexuality was more openly advocated. It took several decades to work on the psyche of "the beast" until he could be shown images in which his own kind played the role of homosexuals, while his most beautiful women went off with "coloured men".

But we have probably not yet reached the bottom of this plunge into the cesspool. The times are coming when we will see on the screens a motley, cosmopolitan crowd, fawning over the High Priests and prostrating themselves before the king of the house of David. That would certainly be ideal, but will the LORD let us have a taste of that ecstasy?

2. The mission of the Jewish people

Cosmopolitan intellectuals and artists seem to write or produce their works with the sole purpose of conveying a message and teaching the public the virtues of cosmopolitanism. This militancy tends towards a very specific terrestrial objective: the disappearance of borders and religions, the universal application of the principles of democracy and human rights, and, finally, the establishment of the Global Empire. This permanent tension seems invariably to determine the orientation of his intellectual production, to the extent that we can wonder whether any novel written by a Jew can be totally ideologically neutral. Albert Memmi openly acknowledged this: "Jewishness is in general much more present than one might think in the behaviour and thinking, even in the confessions, of most Jews[80]." This propaganda never stops, for it is motivated by religious zeal and purpose. The Jewish people, indeed, have a "mission" to fulfil.

Jewish activism

There is always a message, however faint, in the literary and artistic productions of the representatives of cosmopolitanism. This tireless propaganda, which aims to convince people of the legitimacy of its doctrine, is undoubtedly one of the first characteristics of the Jewish people. It is a people of propagandists, or a "people of priests [81]", as the philosopher Jacob Leib Talmon put it, who expressed the very idea that the Jewish people must carry out a mission. This unbridled militancy also manifests itself in a more prosaic form through political combat. Indeed, we find Jewish militants in all extreme-left currents, where faith and revolutionary hope animate souls thirsting for messianism and a world finally liberated from all oppressions.

This "people of priests" is also heavily involved in the advertising

[80]Albert Memmi, in endnote to David Bakan's book, *Freud et la tradition mystique juive*, 1963, Payot, 2001, p. 342.

[81]J.-L. Talmon, *Destin d'Israël*, 1965, Calmann-Lévy, 1967, p. 25. [The same diagnosis that made by Friedrich Nietzsche in his *Genealogy of Morals*].

industry[82], which is, of course, another form of propaganda and public awareness-raising. Flamboyant publicity and laudatory press articles are indeed very useful in launching the "great" and "incomparable" works produced by the chosen people. This is why the "people of the book", as they define themselves, seem to us above all to be "the people of the megaphone", i.e. of activism, propaganda and publicity.

The former editor of the weekly *L'Express*, Françoise Giroud, gave an account of this militant spirit that animates the cosmopolitan intellectual. A journalist and writer, Françoise Giroud was at the side of Jean-Jacques Servan-Schreiber when the weekly was founded in 1953. At the time, the aim was to support the politics of Pierre Mendès France. In her book *Leçons particulières*, published in 1990, she underlined this commitment:

"Jean-Jacques Servan-Schreiber was a warlord, he wrote… His life is nothing but combat: combat to raise Pierre Mendès France to power—*L'Express* was created for this sole purpose—combat against the Algerian war, combat to win over the radical party, combat to win an unassailable constituency, combat to strengthen the reform movement, combat to win the 1978 legislative elections for Valéry Giscard d'Estaing. He never rests. Acting is his way of expressing his ego. He feels as responsible for the affairs of the planet as any head of state, and is capable, here and there, of influencing events. Indeed, he has been on equal footing with great leaders. Many willingly consult him[83]."

In other of his books, we can see that this typical agitation also concerns other characters who constitute the media caste par excellence in democratic societies, and that it always manifests itself when it comes to "great international causes":

"We had come together to found *Action Internationale contre la Faim (Action Internationale contre la Faim)* with some friends like Jacques Attali, Guy Sorman, Patrick Siegler Lathrop, Marek Halter,

---

[82]Mention can be made here of Edwards Louis Bernays (1891–1995), publicist, journalist and inventor of the theory of propaganda and public relations. An Austrian Jew, he was the nephew of Sigmund Freud, and used ideas related to the unconscious in North America for the persuasion of the *self* in mass advertising. Also noteworthy is the role of Walter Lippmann (1889–1974), a prominent German-Jewish intellectual and journalist who theorised the concept of public opinion and coined the famous slogan "the manufacture of consent" in his works *Liberty and the News* (1920) and *Public Opinion* (1922). Regarding these issues, the reader can watch the interesting documentary by Adam Curtis, writer and BBC documentary filmmaker, entitled: The *Century of the Self*, 2002.

[83]Françoise Giroud, *Leçons particulières*, Fayard, 1990, p. 176, 178.

etc.... We wanted to draw public attention, take action, call on the Pope, set up committees all over France, what do you know... Alfred Kastler, Nobel Prize winner, was to be our first president. Bernard-Henri Levy had written some magnificent statutes. All that remained was to put our good intentions into practice[84]."

Let us recall here that the human rights association *Amnesty International* was founded in 1961 by Sean Mac Bride and Peter Beneson-Salomon[85]. The latter was the son of the founder of the department store Mark & Spencer, which did not prevent him from being a member of the Communist International, as was his partner, by the way. In fact, there is no contradiction in this, as soon as we understand that business and communism work hand in hand in the abolition of borders and the establishment of global empire.

This fierce militant spirit was also seen in the former socialist minister, Bernard Kouchner, who announced to us in 2004 his vocation as a "priest", his "will to change the course of things, to influence society", and to convert us to his planetary logic. In such a way that he already saw a "world social security" as possible:

"The problem of minimum income is a global one, he wrote. It is not tolerable that hundreds of millions of people should be left destitute in the face of hunger." He therefore proposed for France the "abolition of health co-payment for the poorest and the illegal", so that foreigners from all over the world could benefit free of charge from health care paid for by the French. But the "project that I wish for with all my heart is the next and necessary fight" which represents "world social security: everyone, whatever their country or situation, must be able to have a minimum of medical care... We will call it *Sick without borders*[86]." We will see a little later in this study this singular predisposition of cosmopolitan intellectuals to generalise their personal cases on a universal level.

Bernard Kouchner was in fact just as aggressive in his fight as Jean-Jacques Servan-Schreiber was: "In the fight for peace, it is the fight that interests us." His support for the US army, engaged in a great democratic project in Afghanistan, was another clear example: "In Afghanistan, we will triumph in the end", he proclaimed. To which Daniel Cohn-Bendit nodded in agreement, expressing his own strong

---

[84]Françoise Giroud, *Arthur ou le bonheur de vivre,* Poche, 1993, p. 162, 163.

[85]Nicolaï Davidoff, *L'Ours et la chandelle, ou Faut-il détruire Amnesty international?* Éditions Ulysse, 1997

[86]D.Cohm-Bendit, B. Kouchner, *Quand tu seras président, Robert Laffont,* 2004, p. 18, 375

commitment to "the fight against intolerance and the current Islamic fundamentalism in Europe".

In this line of planetary combat, Bernard Kouchner is, like Edgar Morin, a fervent supporter of interference: "If I invented the right to interfere, it is because I want the Jews to be able to fight against oppression and, like them, all minorities as well." And he concluded with these words: "I would like to die a violent death, in a great gesture against oppression. When I was little I wished I could die killing a bastard[87]." This might be a bit problematic given the rather broad notion of a bastard that some people have…

This frenetic agitation, this incessant scurrying around the planet is undeniably a characteristic of the cosmopolitan spirit. They travel the globe in all directions to convey a message; they are involved in all humanitarian causes in the four corners of the world. The cases of Marek Halter, Bernard-Henri Levy and Elie Wiesel are very symptomatic of these writers who never stop travelling the world, hopping from airport to airport, to spread the good word[88].

The weekly *Le Point* of 13 October 2005 published an interview with the writer Mario Vargas Llosa. Vargas Llosa was born in Peru and has published more than thirty books translated into all languages. In 1990, he ran in the presidential elections, but was defeated in the second round by Alberto Fujimori. On the occasion of the publication of his *Dictionnaire amoureux de l'Amérique latine (Dictionary of Latin America in Love)*, the journalist from *Le Point* wrote: "It is not easy these days to get hold of this traveller-writer." Would you like to meet in Salzburg?" A brief hesitation, and the appointment was cancelled, because "Mario" had gone to Gaza." Would it be better to meet in London? "But Mario is already in Madrid. I'm coming, wait for me! "All right, but at 5 p.m. sharp, because I have to fly to Barcelona, and then to Paris."

This testimony recalls what Franz Kafka wrote in 1923: "I cannot stay long in one place; there are people who feel at home only when they travel[89]."

The very wealthy socialist businessman Samuel Pisar also expressed this incessant agitation in his autobiography. During the events of 1968, he was, like many of his peers, in a state of feverish exaltation: "I was constantly in dialogue with those young rebels from

---

[87]D.Cohm-Bendit, B. Kouchner, *Quand tu seras président, Robert Laffont,* 2004, p. 256, 332, 348, 349

[88]Hervé Ryssen, *Planetary Hopes,* 2022.

[89]Laurent Cohen, *Variations autour de K.*, Intertextes, Paris, 1991, p. 119.

Copenhagen to the Sorbonne, from Chicago to Sao Paulo and Kyoto... What is the most important mission? Which mission is more important?" So much so that one of his friends told him one day: "You're still too busy[90]".

For his part, Elie Wiesel was well aware that cosmopolitan activism could be annoying for those who are continually subjected to the ideological offensives of the chosen people. But we must understand that such behaviour, which may seem inappropriate, in reality corresponds only to an altruistic and charitable commitment:

"For me, literature must have an ethical dimension and an ethical requirement. I want to go beyond literature. I want to help. I want to raise awareness. I have not lived or survived to "make novels". The aim of literature—which I will call testimony—is not to please or to reassure, but to discomfort; others have said it before, and I am only repeating it insistently. I disturb the believer because, within my faith, I dare to question God, who is the source of all faith. I disturb the atheist because, despite my doubts and questions, I refuse to break with the religious and mystical world that has built my own. I disturb above all those who are installed in a system—political, psychological, theological—in which they feel very comfortable[91]."

To "disturb", "disturb", "disturb" and "irritate" are therefore virtues of cosmopolitan thought. Guy Konopnicki was also aware of this when he wrote: "I know perfectly well that, for every irritating page of this book, and there are irritating pages for everyone, the reader will say: "I beg your pardon? Identity? You pretend to have none, but yours looks like the nose in the middle of your face"—indeed, on the day the noses were handed out I was copiously served. And yet I insist and persist[92]."

This kind of "paradox", which we see regularly in planetary literature, is actually very practical, for it allows one to avoid explaining away the contradictions of one's own reasoning and approach. Other cosmopolitan thinkers have expressed this morbid need to disturb others: "So the Jews, wrote Steiner, have thrice called for individual and social perfection, they have been the night watchmen who do not ensure repose, but, on the contrary, awaken man from the sleep of self-esteem and ordinary comfort. (Freud awakened us even from the innocence of

---

[90]Samuel Pisar, *La Sangre de la esperanza,* Editorial Planeta, 1990, Barcelona, p. 236, 241.

[91]Elie Wiesel, *Mémoires, tome I,* Seuil, 1994, p. 438.

[92]Guy Konopnicki, *La Place de la nation,* Olivier Orban, 1983, p. 214.

sleep[93].)"

This echoes the words of Daniel Cohn-Bendit when he declared: "The contract signed with the multicultural society must prevent us from becoming too homely and comfortable, traditionalist and complacent in our familiar sphere."

And we hear the same in the words of the great rationalist philosopher Emmanuel Levinas: "The Jews are necessary for the future of a humanity that, knowing it is saved, has nothing more to hope for. The presence of the Jews reminds conformists of all kinds that all is not well in the best of all worlds[94]."

It is quite amusing to read these eminent personages naively confirming their willingness to provoke unrest in the rest of humanity. But it must be understood that these planetary intellectuals are conscious of having a divine mission that compels them to do everything possible to unify the earth. This is exactly what Ralph Schor, an "anti-racist" writer and author of several books on immigration and anti-Semitism, told us in the 1990s: "It must be taught that theories of hatred lead to fratricidal strife and deny the essential principle of the unity of mankind[95]." As you will understand, hatred and war is the business of others, while Jews embody the ideals of peace and love. Another second-rate writer, although a member of the French Academy, Maurice Rheims, also expressed this idea: "We would need a great central office in charge of administering humanity[96]." The famous Elie Wiesel in turn confirmed this permanent tension of the Jewish intellectual and his aspiration to build the global empire: "To save our people, we must save all of humanity[97]." The former Chief Rabbi of France in the 1980s, René Samuel Sirat, said exactly the same thing: "The role of the Jewish people is to bring both blessing to all peoples and the notion of the infinite dignity of mankind[98]."

The entire Jewish people is in tension towards the planetary ideal. This is what makes them the proselytising people, the militant people par excellence. But unlike Christians and Muslims, the mission of the Jews is not to convert others to their religion. It is simply to incite them

---

[93]George Steiner, *Pasión intacta. A través de ese espejo, en en enigma*, Ediciones Siruela, Madrid, 1997, p. 447.

[94]Emmanuel Levinas, *Difficile liberté*, Albin Michel, 1963, 1995, p. 231, 261.

[95]Ralph Schor, *L'Antisemitisme en France pendant les années trente*, Éd. Complexe, Brussels, 1992, p. 325-326.

[96]Maurice Rheims, *Une Mémoire vagabonde*, Gallimard, 1997, p. 133.

[97]Elie Wiesel, *Mémoires, Tome I*, Seuil, 1994, p. 51.

[98]Serge Moati, *La Haine antisémite*, Flammarion, 1991, p. 59.

to renounce their religion, without giving anything in return. It is sometimes a little “irritating”.

Messianic Hope

This continual agitation actually reflects a religious dimension. It expresses the feverish expectation of something—“something”—that must inevitably come to pass, and for which the Jews seem to be working ceaselessly. That “something”, which will at last usher in “Peace” in the world, is in fact the Messiah himself, the central figure of Judaism. It is indeed the messianic expectation that is the intellectual ferment and source of inspiration for modern philosophers and planetary thinkers. And the world of “Peace” they promise us is the one announced by the most ancient prophecies of the Torah.

The philosopher Emmanuel Levinas has brought us some clarity in this respect: “It is indeed possible to group the promises of the prophets into two categories: political and social. The injustice and alienation introduced by the arbitrary dimension of political powers in all human endeavours will disappear; but social injustice, the domination exercised by the rich over the poor, will disappear at the same time as political violence… As for the future world, it seems to be situated on another plane. Our text defines it as “the privilege of the one who awaits you”. It is, in principle, a personal and intimate order, external to the realisations of history that await a humanity on the way to unite in a collective destiny… Samuel affirms: “Between this world and the messianic age, there is no other difference than the end of the ‘yoke of nations’-of violence and political oppression[99]—”.”

The Hebrew prophecies thus promise us the progress of humanity towards a borderless, unified world and, parallel to that, the elimination of social inequalities. This will be the perfect society. Peace will reign throughout the universe, there will be abundance and people will live free and happy, in a perfect world of equality. We recognise here, of course, the primitive sources of Marxism as well as those which inspire today’s cosmopolitan planetary ideology at the beginning of the third millennium, and which many of our fellow citizens are dreaming of through great publicity.

The liberation of man is only conceivable on the scale of humanity as a whole.” The very idea of a fraternal humanity, united in the same

---

[99]Emmanuel Levinas, *Difficult Freedom, Essays on Judaism*. Ediciones Lilmod, Buenos Aires, 2004, p. 283-284.

destiny, is a Mosaic revelation [100]", Levinas confirmed. It is through the destruction of the nations that the divine promises can be fulfilled and Israel can finally lead humanity to happiness and prosperity: "[Our] old texts teach universalism purified of all particularism of one's own land, of all memory of what has been planted. They teach the human solidarity of a nation united by ideas[101]."

In *The Eleventh Commandment*, published in 1991, the philosopher André Glucksmann referred to the thought of the great Gershom Scholem to recall the words of the prophets: "Hosea, Amos and Isaiah know only a world in which all events take place, including the great events of the end of time. Their eschatology is national in character; it speaks of the restoration of the house of David, then in ruins, and of the future glory of an Israel that has returned to God. It speaks of perpetual peace, of the return of all nations to the one God of Israel and of their rejection of pagan and idolatrous cults[102]."

It is this same religious substratum that seems to be glimpsed in a secularised form in this dialogue between Daniel Cohn-Bendit and Bernard Kouchner. Their activism in favour of a federal Europe was explained by the desire to destroy all national resistance and to dissolve the identity referents of the European peoples: "A federal Europe is within our reach", declared Daniel Cohn-Bendit, affirming moreover the "legitimacy of Turkey to join the European Union". Bernard Kouchner nodded in agreement and said: "You cannot let Europe be like a Christian club and stop it where the crosses end." Cohn-Bendit then revealed what he really thought and expressed an old resentment: "The Europe of tomorrow will reconcile Christians and atheists, Jews and Muslims. This will turn the page on the terrible chapter opened by the Catholic Church in Cordoba in the 16th century when it expelled the Jews and Muslims." Thus, according to his own wishes, federal Europe will constitute "a fundamental step towards the pacification of the world[103]." We can imagine that at that time everything will be ready for the coming of the Messiah.

Let us recall how, before the May 2005 referendum on the draft European constitution, Daniel Cohn-Bendit, who was anticipating the victory of his opponents, had violently rebuked and insulted a politician

---

[100]Emmanuel Levinas, *Difficile liberté*, Albin Michel, 1963, 1995, p. 310.

[101]Emmanuel Levinas, *Difficult Freedom, Essays on Judaism*. Ediciones Lilmod, Buenos Aires, 2004, p. 254.

[102]André Glucksmann, *Le XIe commandement*, Flammarion, 1991, p. 208.

[103]D.Cohm-Bendit, B. Kouchner, *Quand tu seras président, Robert Laffont*, 2004, p. 367, 174-177

in favour of the "no" vote in a television studio, losing his temper in an unfortunate way. The anger and hatred that could be seen on his face could easily be explained in religious terms. Put yourself in his place: he has been waiting for the Messiah for 3000 years. They tell him that he is there, just around the corner, that he is finally coming, that everything is ready to receive him ... and suddenly: cataplum, everything collapses because a bunch of reactionary cretins, who don't understand anything at all, have preferred their vulgar national freedom instead of the opening to the messianic times. You have to admit that it's maddening!

Peace" is, however, always a very seductive concept in cosmopolitan discourse. But this time, it seems, our compatriots preferred to politely refuse the insistent offer of the miracle cure salesmen. But the idea remains attractive, despite all the deceptions behind the scenes. It is what motivated for example some artists like Clara Halter, the wife of activist Marek Halter, when she created the *Wall for Peace* inaugurated by Jacques Chirac on the Champs de Mars to celebrate the year 2000. On a kind of mound of earth, little Clara wrote the word "Peace" in thirty-two languages and thirteen alphabets; probably to make fun of the students of the military school for officers located just in front of it.

Gershom Scholem is one of the four or five great Jewish thinkers of the 20th century along with Walter Benjamin, Franz Rosenzweig, Emmanuel Levinas and Martin Buber. It is to him that we owe the explanations of the idea of messianism that we are now going to discuss, and which he expressed in a seminal book published in 1971 entitled *Jewish Messianism*.

Messianism has been for the Jewish people a "source of comfort and hope" that has enabled them to overcome the difficult times they have had to go through throughout history. But while waiting for the Messiah is a source of hope, it also generates a permanent dissatisfaction, fuelling the idea that "something" is always missing that will ensure redemption and put an end to all evils." What is called "Jewish existence", Scholem wrote, involves a tension that never relaxes, that is never resolved."

The conditions of the coming of the Messiah are in any case subject to debate." We know nothing of the manner in which that day of the Lord will come about which closes history and during which the world will be shaken to its foundations." The light of the Messiah that is to illuminate the world "is not always conceived as arising absolutely unexpectedly. It may manifest itself in degrees and stages[104]." In "the Talmudic *Aggadah*[105]," Scholem wrote, "the appearance of the messianic light that is to light the world was not to come suddenly, as dreamers and visionaries think, but progressively."

This idea of the stages of redemption was during the Middle Ages the view of most eschatologists who were engaged in calculating the date of redemption. It is, moreover, what can be read in the Zohar, the major classical work of Kabbalah written in the last quarter of the 13th century: "For just as the healing of the sick does not come suddenly but slowly so that he may grow stronger little by little", so the foreign peoples (symbolised by Esau or Edom) will have a reverse fate: having received the light of this world all at once, they will lose it slowly in order to allow Israel to grow stronger and overcome them. And when the spirit of impurity is expelled from this world and the light of the Almighty shines upon Israel without barrier and hindrance, all things will return to their perfect state and become flawless again, as they were in paradise before Adam's sin[106]." You have read correctly: Israel must overcome all nations.

But there are still more interpretations of the coming of the Messiah, Scholem wrote: "The conviction that it was impossible to foresee the date of the Messiah's coming gave rise in the Messianic *Aggadah to the* idea of the 'hidden Messiah'. According to this *Aggadah*, the Messiah would always be present everywhere. A profound legend even assures us, not without reason, that he was born on the day of the destruction of the Temple[107]... To this sort of perpetual redemption offered corresponds the idea of a waiting and perpetually hidden Messiah. This idea has taken many forms throughout history. The most famous is that which, by extravagant anticipation, places the Messiah at the gates of Rome among the lepers and beggars of the eternal City (Talmud, *Sanhedrin, 98a*). This truly astonishing rabbinical story appears as early as the second century... This symbolic antithesis between the true Messiah sitting at the gates of Rome, the seat of the head of Christendom and where he has his throne, was throughout the centuries constantly present in the spirit of the Jews when they pondered about the Messiah. We will see on several occasions aspirants to

---

[104]Gershom Scholem, *Le Messianisme juif*, 1971, Calmann-Lévy, 1974, p. 66, 31, 32

[105]The *Aggadah*: the narrative or allegorical, non-legal interpretation of *Midrash* [see note 109]. The *Aggadah is a* mixture of narratives and anecdotes about rabbis, biblical figures, angels, demons, sorcery, miracles, etc...

[106]Gershom Scholem, *Le Messianisme juif*, 1971, Calmann-Lévy, 1974, p. 82, 83.

[107]Destruction of the Second Temple by the Roman legions of Titus in AD 70.

Messianic dignity make the pilgrimage to Rome and sit on the bridge in front of Castel Sant Angelo to perform a symbolic ritual[108]."

Two currents of messianism within Judaism can be distinguished: the current that announces the coming of great cataclysms and the utopian current. The first current is an apocalyptic messianism: "it stresses the cataclysms and destructions that must accompany the coming of redemption... The origin and nature of Jewish messianism is—it cannot be stressed enough, Scholem wrote—the expectation of historical cataclysms. It announces revolutions, catastrophes that must occur during the passage of time from present history to future messianic times. Isaiah's "day of the Lord" is a day of calamities described in visions announcing these final cataclysms." The coming of the Messiah is thus confused with times of great desolation: "That is why this period is seen by Judaism as the period of the 'birth pangs' of the Messiah." This is a key concept in Judaism.

Scholem explained that the authors of the Apocalypses always had a pessimistic view of the world." For them, history deserves only one thing: to perish. Their optimism, their hope was not directed towards what history can bring but towards what will emerge from its ruins, thus revealing itself after history, at the end of time."

Thus, according to this theologian, humanity must therefore reach the lowest point, the darkest darkness, in order to finally be reborn in the messianic times.

"In all these texts, in all these traditions, the announcement of cataclysms, without which the Apocalypse cannot be conceived, is described with dazzling images in all sorts of forms: world wars, revolutions, epidemics, famines, economic catastrophes, but also apostasies, profanations of the name of God, forgetfulness of the Torah and rejection of all moral order and the laws of nature. The pages of tractate Sanhedrin of the Talmud dealing with the messianic age are full of extravagant formulas announcing that the Messiah will come when man is either totally pure or totally sinful and corrupt."

It is a worldview that could indeed explain many events and behaviours at the beginning of this millennium, as we sometimes have the impression that many influential personalities seem to want to lead us into catastrophes and terrible wars.

But the messianic times, Scholem explained, have also been described in a utopian light, with the re-establishment of Israel and the kingdom of David, thus realising the kingdom of God on earth and the

[108]Gershom Scholem, *Le Messianisme juif*, 1971, Calmann-Lévy, 1974, p. 37.

return of the paradisiacal condition." This is what is suggested by several ancient *Midrashim*[109] and above all by Jewish mystics, for whom the analogy of the Beginning and the End was always a living reality[110]."

In this book published and marketed to the general public, Scholem nevertheless remained rather discreet about the true meaning of

---

[109]*Midrash* ("explanation or commentary", plural *midrashim*), is a Hebrew term for a method of exegesis and interpretation of the biblical text, aimed at study and research that facilitates understanding of the Torah. It consists of interpretations and elaborations (commentaries) on written biblical texts, including stories, parables and legal deductions. Midrash is a text that is spoken orally, but linked to a written text. A Midrash cannot be made without a written text to quote from.

"Rabbi Joshua ben Levi, a Palestinian teacher of the third century, has said: "Scripture, Mishnah, Talmud [Gemara, ndt], and Aggadah, even what a precocious disciple will one day propose before his teacher, everything was already told to Moses at Sinai" (*Midrash Tankuma, 60a, 58b*) (…)…) One of the classical authors of Hassidic literature, Ephraim of Sedylkov, says: "Until the Sages [the Doctors of the Law] investigate it, there is only half of the Torah, until through their investigations the Torah becomes a complete book. For in every generation the Torah is researched [interpreted] according to the needs of that generation, and God enlightens the eyes of the sages of the corresponding generation [so that they] in their Torah perceive what is suitable [for them] (*Degel Makneh Ephrayim*, 1808, 3a)." Gershom Scholem, *Basic Concepts of Judaism: God, Creation, Revelation, Tradition, Salvation*. Editorial Trotta, 1998–2018, Madrid, p. 83–84.

"The true form in which it is possible to recognise truth is not systematic thought but commentary. This observation is very important for understanding the kind of literary creation found in Judaism… Commentary is the characteristic form of the Jewish search for truth, and the mode of expression proper to rabbinic genius… Many different ways of interpreting the Torah can be proposed; tradition has precisely the function of collecting them all. It defends contradictory ideas with surprising assurance and fearlessness, so that we must always ask ourselves whether a position rejected at one time might not become at another time the cornerstone of an entirely new edifice". Gershom Scholem, *Le Messianisme juif*, 1971, Les Belles Lettres, 2020, p. 407, 408.

Earl Doherty, author of the controversial best-seller *The Jesus Puzzle*, explained *Midrash* thus: "It was an ancient Jewish method of presenting some kind of spiritual truth, an insight, communicating a moral or instructive point, by embodying it in a new commentary, even a narrative. The details of that story, the pointers pointing to the insight or truth, were to be found in the Scriptures [the Torah]… The procedure of *midrash* was to develop the meaning of a given passage, to combine perhaps two or more passages and create a composite picture. Sometimes a Bible story was retold, but placed in a new, modern context, to illustrate that the ideas behind the old version not only still applied, but that God had given them a new meaning. *El Puzzle de Jesús*, La Factoría de Ideas, 2006, Madrid, p. 386, 387.

Midrash is the freedom to comment on the Scriptures, to take the text and take it out of its literal sense, extrapolate it and update it to contemporary times, even if it is absurd. (NdT).

[110]Gershom Scholem, *Le Messianisme juif*, 1971, Calmann-Lévy, p. 31, 32, 35, 38. The "Jewish mystics": i.e. the Jewish kabbalists.

redemption, which in reality concerns only the people of Israel and has a strictly national character: 'The content of this messianic hope, based on a collapse of history, has always been the end of exile and liberation from the yoke of empires. The liberation of the subjugated nation was to result from a hoped-for divine intervention and the establishment of a new world unrelated to the world in which we live... The essential thing, Scholem wrote, is the liberation of the nation, even if this must take place at the same time as the liberation of the whole world. The hope of a world that would regain its perfection in the state of redemption always had a very pronounced national aspect."

Jewish literature dealing with messianism thus insists on two ideas, Scholem wrote: 'That of the final war, of the final collapse of history which must bring about the coming of redemption, and that of national liberation. Redemption appears here as the culmination of a national and popular myth, deeply rooted in the national consciousness[111]."

It is a veiled way of affirming that the people of Israel are at permanent war against the rest of the nations, and that "perpetual peace", as well as "the liberation of the whole world", are ultimately no more than concepts that include the idea of "liberation" of the chosen people from the "yoke of empires", and that other more explicit texts present as absolute and definitive domination.

Since the time of the Enlightenment and the French Revolution, messianic expectation has taken the form of a faith in the continued progress of humanity. This "faith in progress", which underpinned the

---

[111]Gershom Scholem, *Le Messianisme juif*, 1971, Calmann-Lévy, 1974, p. 78-80. [Judaism has always and everywhere seen redemption as a public event which must take place on the stage of history and in the heart of the Jewish community, in short, as an event which must take place visibly and which would be unthinkable without this external manifestation. Christianity, on the other hand, sees redemption as an event that takes place in the spiritual and invisible realm, as an event that takes place in the soul, ultimately in the personal universe of the individual, and which calls him to an inner transformation without necessarily changing the course of history." Gershom Scholem, *Le Messianisme juif*, 1971, Les Belles Lettres, 2020, p. 23. Thus, the Jewish Messiah (*Mashiah*, in Hebrew, comes from the verb *Masha* which means to anoint to consecrate a king; the *Mashiah* is the one anointed to be King) is a political and national figure who must reign, literally and actually, as a descendant of the house of David and re-establish the sovereignty of Israel. Prophetic redemption is linked to political kingship and national independence. Thus, we believe that Judaism is not a religion, but first and foremost a religious nationalism forged in the struggle against neighbouring empires (Egyptian, Babylonian, Assyrian, etc.), and especially against the Roman Empire. On the contrary, for Christians, the figure of Jesus, after his death and resurrection, is linked to the notion of *Christos* (Greek word), the Saviour, a reinterpretation of the Jewish notion of Messiah in a diametrically opposed sense, totally spiritual, depoliticised and universal].

ideology of the victorious bourgeoisie throughout the industrial revolution, took shape in the doctrine of Sansimonism[112]. The philosopher Jacob Leib Talmon recalled in his book *Destiny of Israel* that, in the 19th century, the Sansimonian ideological foundations were largely steeped in utopian messianism.

"Sansimonism, he said, is intimately and explicitly related to Jewish messianic hopes. Jews were the soul of the influential and extremely interesting school founded in the 19th century by the first apostle of the socialist transformation of Europe. The Sansimonians strongly expressed their conviction that they were the heirs of the eternal messianic mission of Judaism."

According to Saint-Simon's doctrine, "the future city of universal harmony was to be directed by technicians and bankers, who would be both artists and priests; it was to be based on a universal religion of humanity, the New Christianity, where the old division between Church and State, Matter and Spirit, theory and practice, would be definitively abolished." Jacob Talmon further stated, "It is very significant that Jewish Samsonians like Rodriguez, Pereire and d'Eichtal, later became the architects of the French industrial and financial revolution, and were the promoters of much of European banking and industry."

While it is true that Jewish financiers have always played an important role in history, it would surely be very risky to attribute to them the paternity of the industrial revolution. On the other hand, at the other end of the ideological spectrum of the time, revolutionary socialism was imbued with this "faith in progress", and could also be related to Jewish eschatology, as Talmon wrote:

"It is thanks to the Jewish messianic tradition that the social discontent of the victims of the industrial revolution ... has taken the form of a prelude to the Last Judgement which must usher in the reign of justice and peace: for when all conflicts and contradictions are resolved, history will truly begin[113]."

We will not return here to the predominant role of Jewish

---

[112]Sansimonism was the ideological movement with political aims founded by the followers of the aristocratic socialist Henri de Saint-Simon after his death in 1825. In France, it was the first practical experience of socialism, although it is disputed whether its proposals were truly socialist. Its influence spread outside France and reached practically the whole planet, presenting itself not so much as a "socialist or social movement as a technical-political grouping, with reformist objectives, financial and mystical-philosophical goals that were not too well defined". In Gian Mario Bravo, (1976). *Historia del socialismo 1789-1848. Socialist thought before Marx,* (NdT).

[113]J-L. Talmon, *Destin d'Israël,* 1965, Calmann-Lévy, 1967, p. 31. (See note 543 in *Planetary Hopes*).

doctrinaires and leaders in Marxism, nor to their overwhelming responsibility for the atrocities that were perpetrated in the USSR and Eastern Europe[114]. Let us note once again that Marxism is ultimately nothing more than a rationalised and secularised form of Jewish eschatology, and that the hopes nourished by that doctrine are perfectly akin to messianic expectation.

The feverish activity of the Jews in preparation for the coming of the Messiah has taken different forms in different periods and has been adapted to the different political situations of the time. However, this messianic activism, this tendency to believe that each Jew, personally, has the duty and mission to prepare the redemption, is hardly present in rabbinic Judaism. The teachers of the Talmud then wondered whether it was possible to "hasten the end", to use the common Jewish expression, i.e. whether it was possible to force the coming of the Messiah. Gershom Scholem recalled the following: "In the biblical texts that constitute the source, the messianic advent is never described as the result of man's action. Neither Amos' Day of the Lord nor Isaiah's visions of the end times are presented as the result of human initiative. Likewise, the authors of the ancient Apocalyptics who set out to unveil the secrets of the end never mention a human initiative[115]." This is a fundamental issue, for this idea seems to determine the current behaviour of Jewish intellectuals, who think and act together with the aim of establishing the universal republic. The secularised and utopian form of messianic hopes, first of the French Revolution and then of liberalism, Marxism, and finally of today's globalism, is to this day still predominant in Judaism:

"We live within the legacy of the 19th century, especially as far as messianism is concerned. We live within the legacy of 19th century Judaism,' Scholem wrote. For contemporary Jews, in fact, "messianism contains the idea of the progress of the human race, of the salvation of mankind through its ever-increasing achievements, which will continue by virtue of continuous progress". Apocalyptic messianism has thus been largely eclipsed by utopian messianism. At this point, Gershom Scholem informed us that "the roots of this idea must be sought in the Kabbalah. Indeed, we find no other trace of it in the ancient traditions[116]."

Kabbalah is nothing other than the mystical stream of Judaism

---

[114]Hervé Ryssen, *Planetary Hopes, (*2022) and *Jewish Fanaticism (*2019).

[115]Gershom Scholem, *Le Messianisme juif*, 1971, Calmann-Lévy, 1974, p. 39, 40.

[116]Gershom Scholem, *Le Messianisme juif*, 1971, Calmann-Lévy, 1974, p. 76, 77.

through the study of the Hebrew language of the Scriptures[117]. It is there that the Jew must seek salvation, in the depths of his conscience, in order to find individual redemption in a direct dialogue with God. Kabbalah is thus from the beginning a mysticism of the individual. It is sometimes referred to as Occult Wisdom, in the sense that the Kabbalists consider that the Scriptures contain truths that cannot be grasped by a simple literal reading, and are therefore only understood by initiates who know the mysteries. We know that, for pious Jews, every word, even every letter of the Scriptures has its significance. We also know that each Hebrew letter corresponds to a number, and it is precisely on the basis of the numbers derived from the letters and words of the Scriptures that the Kabalists base their secret doctrine. The Scriptures are for the Kabbalists a kind of code, so that the Kabbalah is also a kind of numerical or mathematical mysticism[118].

The origins of modern Kabbalah may date back to the year 1200, but its golden age is later. The most important Kabbalistic document, the Zohar (*The Book of Splendour*), is officially the work of Shimon Bar Yochai, who is said to have written it between the 1st and 2nd century. It consists, for the most part, of a long commentary on Torah passages, with various other writings. Moses of Leon published it at the end of the 13th century in Spain[119]. It remained in the shadows for two centuries before its influence began to grow, until it became one of the most common writings of Jewish thought. The Zohar then became a

---

[117]"Jewish mysticism is essentially theosophy: a deepening of the secrets of the divinity and its action with regard to creation and the enigma of existence. An important result of modern research on the Kabbalah is precisely that the earliest Jewish mysticism did not live on the fringes, but right in the centre of Pharisaic and Rabbinic Judaism, at the time when it was being formed". In Gershom Scholem"... *Everything is Kabbalah". Dialogue with Jorg Drews, followed by Ten ahistorical theses on Kabbalah,* Editorial Trotta, Madrid, 2001, p. 14.

[118]Asked about this, Gershom Scholem replied: "Numerical mysticism does indeed play a great role in the Kabbalah. This, however, was the factor that attracted me the least. In the writings that go by the name of Kabbalah I found philosophical matters that interested me, and also religious ones, which also interested me. The factor which is numerical mysticism, and which was for the Kabalists only an auxiliary resource in their speculations or in their researches, did not seem essential to me. It did not appeal to me then, nor does it appeal to me now. For many years I have been receiving letters from people who are occupied with mystical numerological speculations, to which I always have to reply coldly that this is a subject which does not fascinate me very much." In"... *Everything is Kabbalah". Dialogue with Jorg Drews, followed by Ten ahistorical theses on the Kabbalah.* Gershom Scholem, Editorial Trotta, Madrid, 2001, p. 58.

[119]G. Scholem believes that the *Zohar* was written in its entirety by Moses of Leon in Castile. See translator's note in Annex II.

canonical text. For several centuries it had the same status as the Torah and the Talmud.

How could the Kabbalah, a mystical movement, an aristocratic movement if ever there was one ... come to impose itself in this way," Scholem asked, "how could the Kabbalah "transform itself into a collective movement and become an extraordinarily powerful historical factor? "How was the Kabbalah able to "transform itself into a collective movement and become an extraordinarily powerful historical factor", Scholem asked. We must point to the situation of the Jews of Spain, whose powerful community was expelled in 1492 by the Catholic Monarchs, for this mass expulsion, "which caused astonishment among the Kabbalists", was the essential and determining factor that re-launched a great Jewish messianic movement.

"It seems that after the expulsion of the Jews from Spain, Scholem wrote, a radical metamorphosis took place within the Kabbalah... The Kabbalah after 1492 changed its physiognomy and a new Kabbalah was then formed, properly speaking... It is precisely in this context that the two hitherto distinct spiritual currents of Messianism and Kabbalah united and became one[120]."

The Kabbalists had to find justifications for the catastrophe that loomed over their community. For them, the expulsion from Spain was "the beginning of the birth pangs" of the Messiah, i.e. cataclysms and terrible trials that were to be the first fruits of redemption and mark the end of history. The only thing to look forward to now, full of hope, was the final redemption. The "forty years" that followed the expulsion from Spain were a time of ferment and messianic awakening. However, as we know, redemption did not come, and the hopes ended in frustration. So once all hopes were extinguished, the whole matter was re-examined and a movement was formed which saw the birth and gave shape to a new religious universe." The new Kabbalah took hold because it provided an answer to the dominant preoccupation of the Jew of that time: what is exile and what is redemption?"

It was Isaac Luria Ashkenazi who gave Kabbalah its messianic aspect. The Hebrew initials of the name of the "divine teacher Isaac" have given his nickname *Ari*, i.e. the "Lion", and so his work was given the name "Kabbalah of Ari[121]". Born in Jerusalem in the year 5294 of

[120]Gershom Scholem, *Le Messianisme juif*, 1971, Calmann-Lévy, 1974, p. 85.

[121]The Lurianic Kabbalah, or Kabbalah of Ari, gave a new and seminal account of Kabbalistic thought that its followers synthesised and read into the earlier Kabbalah of the Zohar that had been disseminated in medieval circles. Lurianism became the near-

the Hebrew calendar, he died in Safed, Palestine, in 5332 (1534–1572). His ideas, which responded to the hopes of the initiated mystics, but also of the popular masses, played a decisive role in Judaism.

In his system[122], redemption becomes a historical process." We see here for the first time, Scholem wrote, this reversal of notions which transforms the catastrophic vision of redemption into a process of history." From now on, it is up to the whole people of Israel to "prepare the world of Reparation".

It is the duty of every Jew to "gather the [divine] sparks scattered in the four corners of the world[123]", and to do so, he must remain in exile, in the diaspora." Exile is not a mere coincidence, it is a mission [124]", Scholem wrote.

Franz Rosenzweig, another leading thinker of Judaism, stated in *The Star of Redemption*: "The glory of God, scattered throughout the world in innumerable sparks, he [the Jew] is going to gather it from its dispersion and one day bring it back to the house of the one who stripped himself of his glory. Each of his deeds, each fulfilment of a law, realises a piece of this unification. The Jew calls the confession of God's unity to unite with God. For this unity is in its becoming: it is becoming unity[125]."

Thus, everywhere on earth, in their exile, "the children of Israel raise sparks" and contribute to the unification of God, but also to the unification of mankind. Redemption thus becomes the logical consequence of a historical process. It is no longer the Messiah who inaugurates redemption, but on the contrary, his coming symbolises the completion of the work of Reparation." So it should come as no surprise that the figure of the Messiah is ultimately of little importance in Luria's Kabbalah... The Messiah becomes here the people of Israel. It is the people of Israel, as a whole, who are prepared to repair the primordial deterioration[126]."

However, this progressive messianism has not totally eclipsed the

universal dominant Jewish theology in the early modern age, both in academic circles and in the popular imagination. The Lurianic schema became the basis for later developments in Jewish mysticism, for example in Hasidism.

[122]See translator's note in Annex III. 1.

[123]See translator's note in Annex III. 2.

[124]Gershom Scholem, *Le Messianisme juif*, 1971, Calmann-Lévy, 1974, p. 97.

[125]Franz Rosenzweig, *La Estrella de la Redención*, Hermenia 43, Ediciones Sígueme, Salamanca, 1997, p. 481.

[126]Gershom Scholem, *Le Messianisme juif*, 1971, Calmann-Lévy, 1974, p. 97, 99-101. See translator's note in Annex III. 3.

apocalyptic messianism that predicts cataclysms, epidemics, wars and revolutions. In fact, Jewish thought has never abandoned the catastrophic vision of history. We can even safely say that some of the influential men in this community push in this direction and regularly threaten world peace with unbridled warmongering propaganda against regimes they dislike, be it Germany, Iraq, Afghanistan, Serbia or Iran.

Listen for example to this dialogue with a rabbi, written in one of the novels of a very influential man, Jacques Attali, who was the main advisor to President Mitterrand (and also to his successors):

The Jews, with their madness, are capable of causing many massacres and cataclysms," Eliav mutters, turning in on himself.

—They are certainly not the only ones! They alone cannot unleash the Apocalypse!

—Let us say that Jewish follies can more easily than others have universal consequences.

—That is true! If the crazies of the Reconstruction Party were to start rebuilding the Temple, it would surely provoke a planetary war.

—I agree! However, it is our right, perhaps even our duty. We are the discoverers of God, the priestly people of humanity. It would be normal for us to have our Temple there where our religion has been founded long before the others. Nobody can do anything about it. Not even us[127]."

In his book on *Messianism*, David Banon presented the worldview of the Chabad-Lubavitch Chassidic Jews[128], who perceive every crisis "as the birth pangs of the Messiah". This is how their leader Rabbi Yosef Yitzchak Schneerson[129] analysed the situation since the end of World War II: 'The sufferings of Israel have now reached a terrifying level; the people of Israel are overwhelmed by the birth pangs. The time of imminent deliverance has come. It is the only true answer to the destruction of the world and to the sufferings that have befallen our people… Prepare yourselves for the redemption that is soon to come! … The deliverer of righteousness is behind our walls, and the time to prepare to receive Him is very short[130]!"

---

[127]Jacques Attali, *Il viendra*, Fayard, 1994, p. 309.

[128]Chabad-Lubavitch is an orthodox Jewish Hasidic dynasty founded by Shneur Zalman of Ladi in 1772. It is one of the largest Hasidic groups and Jewish religious organisations in the world, and probably the best known and most influential Hasidic movement, especially for its outreach activities. It is currently headquartered in Brooklyn, New York. The reader can enter the Hasidic mental universe by consulting its website www.Chabad.org. See translator's note in Annex IV. 1.

[129]See translator's note in Annex IV. 2

[130]David Banon, *Le Messianisme*, Presses Universitaires de France, 1998, p. 120.

You have understood, we are on the eve of terrible changes: "It is impossible," continued Rabbi Schneerson, "that consolation should not come, for the sufferings are unbearable."

As we can see, utopian messianism has not managed to completely elude the "birth pangs" of the Messiah. The Jewish eschatological universe is strongly ambivalent. In fact, ambivalence is a notion that we will encounter at every step of this study.

The true face of Israel

Gershom Scholem has been more discreet about the more earthly nature of messianism and the universal consequences of Jewish eschatology. For a better understanding of what will be the kingdom of "Peace" and "Justice" according to the children of Israel, we can read Jean-Christophe Attias' interesting book on the work of Isaac Abravanel, published in 1992 and entitled *Isaac Abravanel, Memory and Hope.*

Isaac Abravanel (1437–1508) is one of the great mythical figures of Judaism. Born in Lisbon into a family noted for its financial and political success, Abravanel was the son of a powerful Jewish courtier. In 1484, he put his experience as a financial adviser at the service of the kingdom of Spain. He became tax collector and was the great treasurer of King Ferdinand of Aragon and Queen Isabella of Castile. Thanks to the large profits and gains in his numerous ventures, Abravanel was able to grant considerable loans to the royal treasury.

In 1492, when the decision to expel the Jews from the kingdom was taken—for reasons about which Jewish historians are always discreet—Abravanel decided to remain faithful to his God, preferring exile to apostasy. He took refuge in Italy, where he served the king of Naples, and then the Republic of Venice. This figure who led the Jewish community in exile is still surrounded by an aura of mystery due to the messianic speculations and calculations he developed as a prolific exegete. His writings allow us to better understand the traumatic rupture resulting from the expulsion of the Jews from Spain and the consequent very strong resentment that still survives today in the words of Daniel Cohn-Bendit quoted above, five hundred years after the event.

The idea of vengeance is indeed very present in Jewish eschatology. Regarding the visions of the prophet Zechariah, who saw "four horns" that scattered Juda, Israel and Jerusalem [*Zechariah 1:18-19*], Abravanel explained that Zechariah was alluding to the four kingdoms of Babylon, Persia, Greece and Rome, "which dominated

Israel and did so much harm… Indeed, the Persians and the Medes were together the carpenter who destroyed Babylon. Greece was the carpenter who destroyed Persia and Media. Rome was the carpenter who destroyed Greece. And the kingdom of Israel will be the carpenter who will destroy Rome[131]." The prophets have spoken concerning "a great cloud and a turbulent fire" [*Ezekiel, 1:4*] which allude to calamities, and "Daniel said that the salvation of our nation would come with "heavenly clouds," accompanied by suffering and darkness." (page 120).

On Daniel's prophetic texts, Abravanel commented as follows: "He meant that at the time when the Eternal will take vengeance on the nations, then Israel will pass from darkness to light and come out of bondage" (page 140). This vengeance will fall concretely "on the day of judgment", which is actually "the day of punishment and vengeance that will fall upon the nations. This is what clearly emerges from the words of the Sages and the scriptural texts," explained Jean-Christophe Attias." This vengeance will be exercised especially against Edom and Ishmael", i.e. against Christianity and Islam that dominated the Holy Land (page 145).

The prophecies of Ezekiel (25:12-14) are equally avenging: "Therefore thus says the Lord, Yahweh: I will also stretch out my hand upon Edom, and will exterminate man and beast, and reduce it to ruins; from Teman even to Dedan they shall fall by the sword… And I will lay vengeance upon Edom in the hand of my people Israel, who shall deal with Edom according to the fierceness of my wrath, and they shall know that I am Yahweh, and that vengeance is mine. Thus says the Lord, Yahweh[132]." Abravanel noted here the following: "This prophecy, we must interpret it in reference to the future and applying to Rome and to all Christians" (page 252). Abravanel also echoed the Jews' spirit of continuity when he encouraged "all nations to go up to war against the land of Edom" (page 256). A little more and we would think we hear the same words of our cosmopolitan intellectuals when they assure us that immigration is an inevitable phenomenon.

The reading from the prophet Obadiah inspired Abravanel with other reflections: "The day is near when the eternal one will retaliate against all the nations that have destroyed the First Temple and subdued Israel in exile. And you too, Edom, as you did in the destruction of the Second Temple, will know the sword and vengeance, and retaliation

---

131 Jean-Christophe Attias, *Isaac Abravanel, la mémoire et l'espérance,* Les Editions du Cerf, Paris, 1992, p. 86.

132 *Ezekiel (XXV, 12–14),* Nacar-Colunga Bible.

will fall on your head." And it should be clear that this vengeance will be especially visited on Christendom, which will be "more affected than other nations" (page 268). And to make things even clearer, Abravanel specified, on the basis of the prophecies of Obadiah[133], that "nothing shall survive of the house of Esau[134]"." The divine throne will not be fully re-established until it has exterminated the descendants of Esau" [*Psalms 9, 7135*] (page 274)." Indeed, any deliverance promised by Israel is associated with the fall of Edom [*Lamentations 4, 22136*]" (page 276).

Regarding the prophecies of Daniel (2, 44[137]), Abravanel specified that the God of heaven will establish "a fifth kingdom … which will crush and annihilate the four kingdoms. And that fifth kingdom will arise and stand forever, and that is the kingdom of Israel in the hour of its deliverance" (page 111). Israel will then establish its power over all nations and unlike the four preceding kingdoms, its dominion will be "absolutely everlasting": " And there was given him dominion, glory and kingdom, that all peoples, nations and languages should serve him; his dominion is an everlasting dominion, which shall not pass away, and his kingdom one that shall not be destroyed" [*Daniel 7:14*[138]] (page 126, 127).

"In the Messianic age, Samuel thought that all nations would be subjected to Israel, according to what is written: "His dominion shall be from sea to sea, and from the river to the ends of the earth".

133Will I not in that day destroy the wise men of Edom, the wise men of the mountain of Esau," declares the Lord, "City of Teman, your warriors will fall down in fear, so that every man will be exterminated from the mountain of Esau by slaughter. For the violence done to your brother Jacob, shame shall cover you, and you shall be exterminated forever." (*Obadiah 1: 8–10,* New International Version) "But on Mount Zion there will be deliverance, and it will be holy. The people of Jacob will regain their possessions. Jacob's descendants will be fire, and Joseph's descendants will be flame; but the royal house of Esau will be stubble: they will set fire to it and consume it, so that there will be no survivor left among the descendants of Esau. The Lord has said." (*Obadiah 1: 17-18* NIV).

134 See translator's note in Annex V.

135"The enemies are destroyed; they are perpetual ruins; you have destroyed the cities; the memory of them has perished."

136"Daughter of Edom, He [Yahweh] will punish your iniquity and lay bare your sins."

137"In the time of those kings, the God of heaven will raise up a kingdom which shall never be destroyed and which shall not pass into the power of another people; he will destroy and break in pieces all those kingdoms, but he will remain forever."

138"He was given dominion, glory and empire, and all peoples, nations and languages served him, and his dominion is an everlasting dominion that will not end, and his empire, an empire that will never disappear."

[*Zechariah 9, 10*[139]] (page 181)." During the deliverance to come, a king of the house of David will reign and be called by name" (page 228)." The peoples will look to the Messiah-King and submit to His authority, as prophesied by the Ancient [in note: *Jacob*] (page 202).

In that "age of the Messiah-King", a "great peace" will then reign over the earth." It will be a time when justice, righteousness and peace will increase ... wars will disappear, and men will no longer harm one another. This is what is said in the passage: 'The wolf shall dwell with the lamb, and the tiger shall lie down with the kid'" [*Isaiah, XI, 6–9140*] (page 198). In "the Messianic age, all will form one people and one nation, and nothing will divide them." (page 205)." After the Redemption to come, the majority of the nations that will have survived will adopt the faith of the Holy Blessed One, all will recognise His divinity and submit to Him[141]." We have here a fairly clear picture of the world of "Peace" proposed to us by the prophets of Israel.

These prophetic visions, which are glimpsed here and there in many speeches of today's intellectuals, nourish a deep resentment against the other nations, guilty of having destroyed the Temple and humiliated Israel, and also an immense pride. For, although the Jewish people's mission is to lead the world to perpetual peace, redemption can only come after they have defeated the other nations. After the crushing of the enemies, indeed, one is always in favour of "Peace". These feelings of hatred and revenge rarely appear in broad daylight, for the people of Israel have suffered too many accusations from their enemies throughout history. They are almost always expressed in a veiled manner, or in restricted books of limited circulation.

Les Editions des Belles Lettres, for example, has recently republished some interesting texts in a collection entitled *L'Arbre de*

---

139 "He will remove the chariots of Ephraim and the horses in Jerusalem, and the bow of war shall be broken, and he will promulgate peace to the nations, and his dominion shall be from sea to sea, and from the river to the ends of the earth."

140 "The wolf shall dwell with the lamb, the leopard shall lie down with the kid; the calf, the beast of prey, and the fatling together, and a little child shall lead them. The cow and the bear shall graze, their young ones shall lie down together; and the lion shall eat straw like the ox. A sucking child shall play over the cobra's den, and a weanling shall stretch out his hand over the viper's den. Nothing evil or vile shall be done on all my holy mountain; for the earth shall be full of devotion to Yahweh, as the waters cover the sea." (Israelite Nazarene Bible, 2011).

141 Jean-Christophe Attias, *Isaac Abravanel, la mémoire et l'espérance*, Les Éditions du Cerf, Paris, 1992, p. 231.

"(...) For once the Messiah comes, all the nations will be subservient to the Jewish people, and they will help him to prepare whatever is necessary for Shabbat." (Talmud, *Eruvin, 43b*).

Judée (The Tree of Judea), including a novel by a certain Camille Marbo, the pen name of Madame Emile Borel, who was president of the *Société des Gens de Lettres* in 1937–1938 and a feminist when it was still a scandal to be one: "She has left several novels that tell with modesty the difficult beginnings of women's emancipation." In a book entitled *Flammes juives*, published in 1936 and republished in 1999, Camille Marbo told the story of young Moroccan Jews who left their *mellah*[142] in the 1920s to settle in the land of Jauja that was Republican France.

Some specific features of the Hebraic mentality of the time appear here and there. The contempt for the Arabs, for example, partly explained the strong tension that existed between the two communities: "Daniel knew from the moment he opened his eyes that he was a Jew, that is, superior to the Arabs who were stronger than he was and who persecuted him" (page 12). We also find this passage: "Benatar and Mardoche despised the Muslims who left the poor in their midst and let the Christians organise hospitals and dispensaries" (page 14). On the other hand, this Jewish family had an inordinate love for republican France: "The French immediately protect the Jews" against the Arabs. Old Benatar told his grandson: "I have seen the noble Jews who have come from France. A new dawn is breaking. You will go to Paris, Daniel. You will receive from the French the torch of an ideal of civilisation and justice. You will be one of those who will lead the Hebrew people to their destiny[143]."

Indeed, through this republican France, the Jewish people seem to glimpse the great visions of world conquest promised by the prophets. Their destiny seems to be inevitably fulfilled. The will to power and the feeling of pride perfectly characterise the "race". But look at these passages: "Sarah's father and Daniel's uncle had raised and sent much money for the cause… Nathan's hall seemed to them the command post of Israel's conquest of the world" (page 10). Grandfather Benatar envisioned a bright future for Daniel: "I will take this boy to Fez. He will go to the school of the French and become a glory of the people of Israel" (page 14). From an early age, the young boy understood very

---

[142]Mellah: The walled Jewish quarters existing in some localities in Morocco; an analogue of the European Jewry or ghetto.

[143]Camille Marbo, *Flammes juives*, 1936, Les Belles Lettres, 1999, p. 26. The enthusiasm for Republican France is also well portrayed in Ariel Zeitoun's film *Le Nombril du monde* (France, 1993). We see Tunisian Jews enthusiastic about the idea of fighting for the French Republic in 1940, which was logical from their point of view. In a scene from Roman Polanski's film *The Pianist*, we see a Jewish family waiting for war to be declared against Germany.

well what was expected of him, as Grandfather Benatar and Uncle Mardoche often reminded him of the role of the Jewish People:

"Israel must rule the world, Daniel said.

—We are feared, repeated old Benatar, because we are the race of the Prophets. Daniel, repeat a little of all the great men who are of our blood" (page 18)..." Children, remember that you are Jews, that you have been chosen to increase in the world the power and glory of Israel and that you owe your emancipation to the noble French people" (page 20)..." This year will be good. Children, you will be able to conquer the world" (page 44).

"Sara trembled. Her father stroked her head." Our generation cannot yet conquer Christianity. You will be able to lay the foundations and your children will be on the ground. They will mingle with the Christians. Israel will lead the world as it should be, and we will praise the French people for what they did to liberate us" (page 126).

Little Daniel would not forget the lessons of his deceased grandfather: "Behind the body of old Benatar, carried on the shoulders of four men in the narrow streets of the *Mellah*, Daniel swore to be faithful and loyal to his grandfather's ideal. Holding back his tears, he repeated in his innermost self: 'To become one of the great ones of the earth for the glory of God's people and the good of mankind'" (page 26). Undoubtedly, Daniel had become quite ambitious, for he said: "Life is of no interest if you don't have a joystick" (page 39). Here, then, is the depth of the soul of some Moroccan Jews. Their love for France is undeniable, since that country seems to them to be a springboard to the conquest of the universe.

In 2000, *Éditions des Belles Lettres* also republished in the same collection a 1929 book by a certain Pierre Paraf, entitled *When Israel Loved*. It should be remembered that this Pierre Paraf (1893–1989) was also co-founder of the LICA (League against anti-Semitism), which at the time did not claim to also fight racism.

One novella in that anthology, *The Choir of Three Voices*, hinted at the theme of Jewish messianism through the mouth of a character. The story was set under the Roman Empire: "The Rabbi of Alexandria taught me:—There are seventy nations on earth and of those seventy nations, fifty-nine are under the yoke of the emperor. But a day will come when the seventy nations will be illuminated by the light of Israel. For it is said that our people will be a blessing to the world."

Unfortunately, anti-Semitism already existed in those times. We can imagine how the Jews were accused of all evils, past, present and future, and how they served as scapegoats for the frustrations of the

Gentile peoples: "Are we not everywhere treated as an intriguing and insidious race[144]?", wrote Pierre Paraf.

The story entitled *Marquise of Israel* confirmed this messianic mentality. In the 18th century, at the time of Voltaire and the philosophes, a character in the novel proclaimed at a worldly gathering: "Yes, the revolution will come, and I wish it with all my heart. In thirty years' time, perhaps twenty years' time, the thrones will be shaken. The tree of the philosophers will have borne its fruit. They will have undermined everything, the axe of the wise men, destroyers of an ancient world to which they owe perhaps the best of their life and thought."

We see here the undeniable apocalyptic face of messianism. This is accompanied by a tireless activism that constitutes, as we have seen, the very core of the Jewish soul: "Everywhere foolish men suffer because they do not know our law... It is throughout the world that the Eternal sends us to fulfil our mission."

The problem is that the "others" do not seem to understand the benefits that the Jews bring, so for the time being it is better to move forward on the sly: "Even if we have to change our dress and our name to spread our teachings, as the people of Holland and England do, we will march on happily in the certainty that in a few years or a few centuries our great-grandchildren will be able to take off the mask—the garb of their intact and inviolate soul—and proudly wear the true face of Israel[145]."

Clearly, Jews live in a permanent state of tension, filled with the hope that one day the Messiah will finally arrive. As Elie Wiesel put it: "I recognise that of all the traits that characterise the Jewish people, the one that strikes me most is the duty to hope[146]."

The celebrated Austrian writer Joseph Roth also expressed this absolute faith in Israel's destiny and the Jew's deep contempt for the goyim who do not understand their divine mission. Jewish children know from their earliest childhood that they belong to the chosen people; the humiliations of the little goyim cannot affect them: "The apparent cowardice of the Jew—who does not react to the stone that the boy throws at him in play, who does not want to hear the insulting cry directed at him—is, in reality, the pride of one who knows that one day he will triumph... What does he care about a pebble or the saliva of a rabid dog? The contempt felt by an Eastern Jew against the infidels is a

---

144 Pierre Paraf, *Quand Israël aima*, 1929, Les Belles Lettres, 2000, p. 98, 111

145 Pierre Paraf, *Quand Israël aima*, 1929, Les Belles Lettres, 2000, p. 72, 70

146 Elie Wiesel, *Mémoires II*, Éditions du Seuil, 1996, p. 156.

thousand times greater than that which could reach him[147]." We are warned then.

Jewish intellectuals, who continually present the chosen people as a people unjustly persecuted, are in reality advancing with a mask, as they themselves put it. For example, in October 2005, the American cartoonist Will Eisner published a comic book entitled *The Plot, a secret history of the Protocols of the Elders of Zion* to denounce the imposture represented by this document. The comic was prefaced by the great novelist Umberto Eco (author of *The Name of the Rose*), who also occasionally prefaces works dealing with the Cabala[148].

According to *Le Nouvel Observateur* magazine, Will Eisner's research "lasted twenty years" to denounce the unbearable lies of the anti-Semitic propaganda that accuses Jews of wanting to dominate the world. Will Eisner thus did a public health job, revealing the truth about these gross falsehoods to all in an accessible way: "Over the years, hundreds of books and scholarly articles have denounced the infamy of the *Protocols*. Most of the time, however, these studies are produced by academics and aimed at specialists or readers previously convinced of the fraud... The occasion presents itself to attack this propaganda head-on in more accessible language. It is my hope that this work will definitively rivet the coffin of this ghastly vampire-like imposture." We see here that while some Muslim women wear a veil, many Jewish intellectuals prefer to wear a mask.

Jewish identity

We now know that the Jewish people have a mission to fulfil. Scattered over the face of the earth, living in the midst of other peoples, Jews claim the nationality of the place where they have settled and the rights granted by the host country, while retaining their Jewishness, and often their visceral attachment to the State of Israel. This is another form of ambivalence that we always find in the mentality of Judaism and the Jewish personality, and it is no coincidence that the word "paradox" appears so frequently in the pen of these intellectuals.

In *Israel's Destiny*, the philosopher Jacob Leib Talmon confirmed that there is a Jewish uniqueness, a Jewish way of conceiving the world, a "way of thinking, feeling and behaving" that is very specific to

[147] Joseph Roth, *Judíos errantes*, Acantilado 164, Barcelona, 2008 p. 47.

[148] Umberto Eco has prefaced the book by Moshé Idel, *Mystiques messianiques, de la Kabbale au hassidisme, XIIIe—XIXe siècle*, 1998, Calmann-Lévy, 2005.

Judaism. However, Jewish identity has blurred, blurred contours. We know that it is not only religion that shapes Jewish identity, for atheistic Jews continue to declare themselves members of the chosen people. Leading Marxist doctrinaires and revolutionaries such as Karl Marx himself, Lenin (distant but plausible origin, ndt), Trostki, Rosa Luxembourg, George Lukacs or Ernest Mandel, to name but a few, were militant atheists, but whose Jewish origins were clearly transparent through the messianic character of their struggle for a "better world".

"After three and a half thousand years, it is still not possible to determine who are Jews and who are not," wrote Talmon. But there is, however, a fairly clear criterion of membership on this point, and that is that of filiation by the mother. Talmon stated: "A man of Jewish race who has lost the Jewish faith and who has rejected any religious practice does not cease to be a Jew, since anyone born of a mother of Jewish race or religion is a Jew. The individual whose father is Jewish but whose mother is not, is not recognised as a Jew, since one cannot be sure of paternity."

This explanation leads to the following conclusion: "A Jew is an individual of Jewish race or religion who has not officially embraced another religion, regardless of whether or not he practises his own. To be considered a Jew, the determining factor is blood (the Jewish mother) or the adoption of the Hebrew religion, a decision that is always equivalent to wanting to share a common destiny[149]." This does not include Jews who have converted to another religion but who continue to practise Judaism in secret.

Elie Wiesel confirmed this idea that Jews are a nation apart, and that it is convenient to consider them as foreigners living among other peoples. In the *Testament of a Murdered Jewish Poet*, he wrote explicitly: 'Between a merchant from Morocco and a chemist from Chicago, a rag-picker from Lodz and an industrialist from Lyon, a kabbalist from Safed and an intellectual from Minsk, there is a deeper kinship, more substantial because more ancient, than between two citizens of the same country, the same city and the same profession. Even when alone, a Jew is never solitary[150]."

In his *Memoirs*, he further wrote: "To be a Jew, in my opinion, was to belong to the Jewish community, in the broadest and most direct sense. It was to feel offended every time a Jew was humiliated, whatever his origin, his social status or the country where he lived. It was to react, to protest every time a Jew, even an unknown and distant

---

[149]J.-L. Talmon, *Destin d'Israël*, 1965, Calmann-Lévy, p. 137, 139, 140.

[150]Elie Wiesel, *Le Testament d'un poète juif assasiné*, 1980, Points Seuil, 1995, p.57

one, was beaten and attacked by anyone, for the simple reason that he was Jewish… That's right: as a Jewish writer I feel solidarity with my people. Their quest is my quest and their memory is my country. Everything that happens to him affects me[151]."

In the second volume of his *Memoirs,* he wrote: "The Jew is obsessed with the beginning rather than the end. His messianic dream refers to the kingdom of David. He feels closer to the prophet Elijah than to his neighbour on the landing … everything that struck his ancestors affects him. Their mourning weighs on him, their triumphs encourage him[152]."

The desire to maintain this spirit of community at all costs has for centuries encouraged Jews all over the world to live in seclusion. In *Planetary Hopes,* we had already noted, under the pen of Jacques Attali, that some Jewish communities had themselves claimed the right to ghettoise themselves in order to maintain the purity of the Jewish people against foreigners[153]. Elie Wiesel acknowledged that such secular provisions were still common at the time of the Second World War. At the time he lived with his family in Romania, in a region in the north that was later annexed by Hungary at the beginning of the conflict: "The yellow star? Well, it doesn't really bother me. It even allows me to feel more intimately connected to the Jews of the Middle Ages who wore the *wheel*[154] in the ghettos of Italy… There are stars for all prices. Those of the rich are resplendent; those of the poor are dull. Strange, but I wear mine with an inexplicable pride[155]."

In his town of Sighet, which had just been annexed by Hungary, Wiesel saw how the Hungarian gendarmes—like the Romanians—did not have the Jews in their hearts and was finally glad that a ghetto had been created to bring together all the Jews: "The Hungarian gendarmes; never enough bad things can be said about them … they carried out Eichmann's plan with a brutality and eagerness that will remain a dishonour to the Hungarian army and nation … they carried out Eichmann's plan with a brutality and eagerness that will remain a dishonour to the Hungarian army and the Hungarian nation … so that

[151]Elie Wiesel, *Mémoires, Tome I,* Éditions du Seuil, 1994, p. 212, 513.

[152]Elie Wiesel, *Memoires Tome II,* Editions du Seuil, 1996, p.46.

[153]Hervé Ryssen, *Planetary Hopes, (*2022).

[154]The wheel was a small piece of cloth whose ostentatious use was imposed on Jews as a distinctive sign of dress by the civil authorities in the Middle Ages. Cut into a ring, it is said to symbolise the 30 denarii of Judas, according to the traditional interpretation. (NdT).

[155]Elie Wiesel, *Mémoires, Tome I,* Éditions du Seuil, 1994, p. 82.

the announcement of the ghetto was almost a relief: we will be among Jews like this. As a family… I have the impression of reopening a page of medieval Jewish history. We are going to live as our ancestors lived in Italy and Spain first, and then in Germany and Poland… I consult the Jewish encyclopaedia… Surprise: I discover that in ancient times, Jewish quarters were created by the Jews themselves who feared foreign influences. This was the case with the communities of Rome, Antioch and Alexandria. It was only later that the ghetto was imposed on them under different names[156]."

Laurent Cohen's book on the writer Franz Kafka, entitled *A Jewish Reading of Franz Kafka,* gave a few insights into the customs of the Jews of the Austro-Hungarian Empire. Again we see that strong tendency towards communal isolation, even suspicion and hostility towards the natives. Kafka, who "frequented only Jews", himself gave an idea of the barrier that separated the Jewish and Christian communities in the Habsburg Empire: "No Christian member of the bodies in which my father played an active role ever set foot in the house. And it showed." Do you want to go back to the ghetto?' I was asked in discussions. I would reply: 'It is you who live in the ghetto. You just don't want to admit it—where are the Goyim? You have never invited one home[157]."

This exclusivist identity has been defined and explained by Gershom Scholem, quoted in Laurent Cohen's book to explain Kafka's feelings of identity: "There exists in the Jewish tradition a concept that is difficult to define and yet very concrete, which we call *Ahavat Israel,* "the love of the Jewish people". This concept of love for his own people, Kafka had integrated it into the core of his being … making "gratuitous love" between Jews the priority of priorities[158]." Franz Kafka "linked it with another fundamental concept of Jewish thought: *Ahdout Israel,* literally: "Unity of Israel"." It is indeed these two concepts that underpin the discourses of Elie Wiesel and Jacob Talmon, who regard Jews as foreigners living among other nations.

The obsessive preoccupation with racial purity appears in many writings of Jewish intellectuals, and is translated by the constant rejection of mixed marriages. In *Flammes juives,* for example, the writer Camille Marbo recounted how the son of a Moroccan Jewish family travelled to France in the 1920s to study at university and how he reassured his poor mother Rebecca, "fearful that her son would fall

---

156 Elie Wiesel, *Mémoires, Tome I,* Éditions du Seuil, 1994, p. 83.

157 Laurent Cohen, *Variations autour de K.,* Intertextes éditeur, Paris, 1991, p. 29.

158 Laurent Cohen, *Variations autour de K.,* Intertextes éditeur, Paris, 1991, p. 121.

in love with a Christian woman" (page 26). Fortunately, his sense of belonging to Judaism had not altered in the midst of the Goyim. On the contrary: 'He dared not tell his mother that his religious faith was dead while his enthusiastic devotion to the Jewish race grew, claiming that he would never marry "a woman who was not of our race". Rebecca wept blessing him[159]."

Camille Marbo's novel has the same pedagogical function as Jacob Talmon's book mentioned above, and reflects in the same way the deep anguish of the novelist and the philosopher to see their compatriots mixing with the goyim. The concern to preserve the purity of Israel's blood has also been expressed by Elie Wiesel, when he mentioned the misfortune of a Jewish family whose daughter had fallen in love with a Goy: "A young girl had been converted to marry a Hungarian officer. The tragedy of her shamed parents troubled me[160]."

If we want to realise the seriousness of the drama experienced by Jewish families when a child marries outside the community, we can watch Norman Jewison's beautiful film, *Fiddler on the Roof,* which describes the life of the *shtetl,* those Jewish villages in Central and Eastern Europe before the war, and which focuses precisely on the progressive weakening of Jewish tradition and the temptation for children to intermarry outside the community. Indeed, while Jewish families were gradually beginning to accept that children could reject a partner chosen by the family and the matchmaker, there was still one case where there was no compromise: exogamous marriage, considered by the parents as nothing less than the death of the child.

In a book about Jewish gangsterism in the United States in the early 20th century, American author Rich Cohen gave an account of that tradition and of one of the leading gangsters of the time, Arnold Rothstein. He was the son of a wealthy man. His father Abraham owned a textile emporium and a spinning mill. Arnold one day introduced his father to his future wife. Problem: she was not Jewish: "The older man shook his head and declared: "Well, I hope you will be happy". After the wedding, when he had pronounced the death of his son, when he covered the mirrors and read the *Kaddish*[161], that moment signified a great step forward for crime in the USA… It corresponded to Arnold's release. For Rothstein, it was the decisive breakthrough[162]."

Even today, when a member of an orthodox family marries a

[159]Camille Marbo, *Flammes juives,* 1936, Les Belles Lettres, 1999, p. 26.
[160]Elie Wiesel, *Mémoires, Tome I,* Éditions du Seuil, 1994, p. 47.
[161]*Kaddish*: the main Jewish prayer that is also recited at duels.
[162]Rich Cohen, *Yiddish Connection,* 1998, Denoël, 2000, Folio, p. 73.

gentile, the family performs the rite of *Shiva*, normally reserved for deaths. Doing *Shiva* is like declaring that the person is considered dead in every way.

In his *History of Anti-Semitism*, Leon Poliakov showed how Jewish customs of old were implacable against Jews who indulged in desires to leave the community. Rabbi Ascher ben Yehiel, who had fled Germany to take refuge in Spain where he became the rabbi of the Toledo community, did not joke about such transgressions: "He severely censured customs, and having noted with horror that sexual commerce between Jews and Christian women and vice versa was still frequent, he demanded that the noses of Jewish offenders be cut off[163]."

Let us recall here that the State of Israel, like the Orthodox Jews of the diaspora, does not allow mixed marriages. The progressive English newspaper *The Guardian* revealed some information on how the new immigrants are treated in Israel, who are called upon to replace the Palestinian labour force considered too uncooperative. In fact, a few years ago, the Hebrew state recruited around 260,000 foreigners to replace in factories and farms the Palestinians from the territories who were forbidden to stay in the Eretz Eretz. The correspondent of the British newspaper wrote: "Chinese contract workers in Israel are obliged to undertake in writing not to have any sexual contact with Israeli women—including prostitutes—and, of course, not to marry Jewish women, on pain of immediate dismissal and expulsion" ... at their own expense, of course. This mandatory clause has been confirmed by the Israeli police spokesman who sees "nothing illegal" in it.

Western cosmopolitan intellectuals, most of them standard-bearers of the State of Israel, see no contradiction in advocating immigration and a pluralistic society in the European countries where they have settled. It is another "paradox" of the Jewish spirit that distils an anti-racist discourse for others, while at the same time they are deeply racist towards their own community. The anti-racist discourse is thus a product destined solely for export.

Bernard-Henri Levy, for example, continually declares his unfailing attachment to Israel to anyone who will listen. In fact, this is how he expressed himself from Jerusalem in 2003, at a conference at the Institute of Levine Studies: "On the question of Israel, I have never changed since the time when I presented myself on the fifth day of the Six-Day War at the Israeli consulate in Paris to enlist in the Tsahal."

---

[163]Léon Poliakov, *Histoire de l'antisémitisme, Tome I*, 1981, Points Seuil, 1990, p. 328.

Bernard-Henri Levy feels "an extreme attachment to Israel… I have written a hundred times, said the philosopher, that Israel and the diaspora are like the heart and conscience of each other, that one is the support, the pillar, the source of the other—and vice versa[164]… I am a Jew, of course, because of my link with Israel. I am a Jew when, like every Jew in the world, my heart beats in unison with that of all Israelis under threat… When the whole world believes that Scud missiles are going to fall on Tel-Aviv, I come here instinctively, almost without thinking about it … because Israel remains the refuge state of the Jewish people."

But what is valid for Jews is not valid for other peoples. While extolling the Jewish people, Jewish traditions, the Jewish clan, Bernard-Henri Levy denies non-Jews the right to have feelings of communal belonging and to praise the virtues of their lineage. In fact, cosmopolitan intellectuals never hesitate to denounce—and always in the most virulent manner—the patriotic feelings of the French and Europeans in general, who are concerned about the massive arrival of immigrants from the Third World. The concerns of the "Whites" have no value for them: it is a "paranoia" to be cured, a "disease" of the mind, as Alain Minc wrote. They are "racist opinions" that should not be tolerated in a democracy. This is how Bernard-Henri Levy declares loud and clear when he is in France his intransigent opposition to all forms of "intolerance" and "fascism": "I am Jewish because of my anti-fascism, he wrote in the same text, because of my denunciations of all ideologies of the terroir, the body, race and blood… I am Jewish when, remembering that we were foreigners in Egypt, I founded the organisation SOS Racisme twenty years ago."

The discourse addressed to the Jews is therefore the exact negative of the discourse addressed to the Goyim. But in order to speak to the French, to lavish the cosmopolitan discourse on the nations, Bernard-Henri Levy is obliged, despite everything, to become a little French and wave his little tricolour flag: "I am a Jew in France. I am a Jew and a Frenchman, a Jew who loves France[165]." So it was clear, but the core of his identity remained monochromatic: "I am a Jew, I am a Jew with all the fibres of my being. I am so with my lapses, I am so because of the dietary rules I have imposed on myself… I am so because of the way I write… I am Jewish by virtue of the invisible pact that unites Jews all over the world… I am Jewish because of my messianic patience… I am a Jew because of my rejection of nationalism, the repugnance I feel for

[164]Bernard-Henri Lévy, *Récidives*, Grasset, 2004, p. 405, 408

[165]Bernard-Henri Lévy, *Récidives*, Grasset, 2004, p. 415-421.

the ideologies of rootedness… This is what Jewish thought teaches me… From Levinas, I remember that it is the plants that take root and that men are the servants of the roots and free thanks to the law. From Rosenzweig, in *The Star of Redemption,* I am left with the image of that people…" eternal traveller rooted in time and in the law". And of the Maharal of Prague[166]… I remember that a place is never holy unless it has been consecrated by a conscious act of man. And, above all, I believe that the locality of the place counts for nothing, or almost nothing, for the realisation of the Redemption… There where man is, there is the *Halacha*[167], there is the kingdom of God. A history, a law, which we do not wear glued to the soles of our shoes, but on our tongue[168]."

The land, the place of birth, the country of their childhood, to which all human beings are sentimentally attached, are therefore of no importance for Jews, who are bound only to their law, and are thus predisposed to change countries easily, to speak another language, to adapt to local customs, while maintaining their Jewish specificity within themselves. Strangers in the midst of other nations, the Jews of the Diaspora have a mission to fulfil: "I am a Jew of the *Galout*[169], wrote Levy, I am a universalist Jew… The choice of the Jewish people, for me as for Rosenzweig, means opening for all peoples the invisible and sacred doors that illuminate the Star of Redemption[170]."

In *The Star of Redemption*, Franz Rosenzweig insisted on the racial concept of Jewish identity: "Only the community of blood feels the guarantee of its eternity flowing warmly through its veins already today. Only for it alone time is not an enemy to be appeased and over which it may—it hopes, but perhaps not …—win." The eternal people "retains always the unattachment of one who goes on a journey… He is only a stranger who has settled in his own country… The sanctity of [Israel's] land preserves her from his taking possession of it when he could have done so… It compels him to concentrate all the verve of the will to be

[166]"Maharal of Prague (1520–1609) was a prominent Talmudist, Jewish mystic and philosopher who served as rabbi in the Bohemian city of Prague.

[167]*Halacha,* Jewish Law, literally "*the way to behave*" or "*the way to walk*". It includes the 613 mitzvot (commandments) and subsequent rabbinic and Talmudic law. It is the collective body of Jewish religious rules, drawn from the written and oral Torah. Orthodox Jews are those who strictly follow *Halacha*. Orthodoxy does not refer to doctrine or belief, as it is understood in Christianity. It refers to the specific behaviours and practices prescribed by the *Halacha*.

[168]Bernard-Henri Lévy, *Récidives,* Grasset, 2004, p. 413-415.

[169]*Galout* Jew: Jew of the exile, of the Diaspora. Living outside the State of Israel.

[170]Bernard-Henri Lévy, *Récidives,* Grasset, 2004, p. 384, 385

a people on a single point … on the pure and authentic point of life, on the community of blood[171]."

The American novelist Philip Roth acknowledged that "assimilation" was very superficial among Jews. Here are the words of one of his characters, the novelist Appelfeld: "I have always been fond of assimilated Jews, because it was in them that the Jewish character, and perhaps also the fate of the Jews, was most strongly concentrated[172]." When Jewish intellectuals speak of "assimilation", we must understand "social assimilation" and "social success". And indeed, Jews assimilate very quickly into the local populations.

This feeling of Jewishness always goes hand in hand with a violent and contemptuous rejection of the identity of non-Jews. This is how Guy Konopnicki allowed himself to write with flagrant insolence: "I have never found the France populated by French people that we hear so much about… All that remains is Jean-Marie Lepen and a few similar fossils to trace the foreigner to the third generation and even to the point of accusing me of not being a descendant of the Gallo-Romans or the Franks, our ancestors." And he added this indignant question: "So how many generations does it take to be French[173]?" We can now answer him properly: as many as it takes for a Jewish intellectual to abandon Judaism.

---

[171]Franz Rosenzweig, *La Estrella de la Redención*, Hermenia 43, Ediciones Sígueme, Salamanca, 1997, p. 356, 357, 358.

[172]Philip Roth, *Operation Shylock*, Debolsillo Penguin Random House, Barcelona, 2005, p. 129.

[173]Guy Konopnicki, *La Place de la nation*, Olivier Orban, 1983, p. 16, 36

PART TWO

THE COSMOPOLITAN MENTALITY

1. The Jewish Personality

The Jews feel solidarity with each other, whatever country they live in and whatever language they speak. They also have very specific character traits that all observers of Judaism have noticed in all different ages and in all latitudes. This is because their spirit is formed from an early age by reading the same texts, and because the teachings handed down by their parents are the same everywhere: the important thing is obedience to the "Law" of the Torah, that "pocket homeland", as the German poet Heinrich Heine wrote in the 19th century.

Bernard Lazare left a rather exemplary book on the subject. An anarchist socialist and supporter of Dreyfus[174], Bernard Lazare published in 1894 a book that was intended as a response to Edouard Drumont's *The Jewish France,* which had been a resounding success. The following passage gives an insight into what this "Law" can be and its universal character in Judaism: "But the Jew had something better than his god: he had his Thora—his law—and it is this law that he kept. This law, not only did he not lose it when he lost his ancestral territory, but on the contrary it strengthened his authority: he developed it and increased his power and also his virtue. When Jerusalem was destroyed, it was the law that became the bond of Israel: it lived for its law and by

[174]The Dreyfus case originated in an allegedly anti-Semitic court ruling, against a background of espionage and anti-Semitism, in which the accused was Captain Alfred Dreyfus of Alsatian Jewish origin, and which, for twelve years, from 1894 to 1906, shocked French society at the time, marking a milestone in the history of anti-Semitism. (NdT).

its law. Now this law was meticulous and formalistic; it was the most perfect manifestation of the ritual religion into which the Jewish religion had become under the influence of the doctors, an influence which can be opposed to the spiritualism of the prophets whose tradition Jesus continued. These rites, which foresaw every act of the

life, and which the Talmudists complicated to infinity, these rites moulded the Jew's brain, and everywhere—in every country—they moulded it in the same way. The Jews, though dispersed, thought in the same way in Seville and in New York, in Ancona and in Regensburg, in Troye and in Prague. They had the same feelings and the same ideas about beings and things. They looked through the same lenses. They judged according to similar principles from which they could not deviate, for there were no grave and lesser obligations in the law: they were all of equal value because they all emanated from God. All those whom the Jews drew to themselves were imprisoned in this terrible gear which crushed minds and moulded them in a uniform way[175]."

This was also what Mark Zborowski wrote in his great anthropological study of Eastern European Jewry: "A page of Talmud looks the same as it did a hundred years ago, and it looks the same in Vilna and in Shanghai. All over the world, pupils meditate on the same Torah, the same Talmud, the same Rachi commentary. The children chant in their flute-like voice the same text that opens the *Michnah... Wherever* his footsteps lead him, and as long as it is in a traditional community, the shtetl scholar will find the same studies, the same debates carried on with ardour and zeal."

We find this same uniformity and atavism in the writings of Jewish intellectuals of today as of old." In the teachings of traditional Judaism, the barriers of time are blurred and confused, wrote Zborowski. The habit of referring to ancient texts to govern the present and to modern texts to elucidate the past has forged between past and present an indestructible chain to which each scholar adds a link... This silent disdain for Western divisions of time and space affirms that the unity of tradition is more solid than the breaks in physical and temporal continuity[176]." This is precisely what some have called "the eternal Jew" *(Der ewige Jude)*.

---

[175]Bernard Lazare, *Anti-Semitism, its history and causes, (1894).* Editions La Bastille, Digital edition, 2011 p. 120, 121.

[176]Mark Zborowski, *Olam*, 1952, Plon, 1992, p. 107, 108 [See again note 109 on *midrash*].

The darkest hours[177]

The media image of the Jewish community in all the countries where it has settled is that of a persecuted nation. TV documentaries or films on the subject are countless and recurrent, so that this aspect of Judaism remains the most visible and the main specific feature of this community for the general public. It is interesting to note that the writings of Jewish intellectuals before the Second World War already reflected the same tendency to "jeremiads", something that has also been observed by different authors of our time. Shmuel Trigano was well aware of this unfortunate situation when he wrote: "Jews are often accused of wallowing in this victimising lamentation and I am the first to deplore it[178]".

This peculiarity is therefore not a consequence of the Holocaust, but a permanent disposition that is very characteristic of the Hebraic mentality. Of course, this observation in no way detracts from the horrors of war. The testimonies of Elie Wiesel and Samuel Pisar, among many others, are quite revealing in this respect. However, they tend to err on the side of sappy sentimentality and a certain egocentrism that seems to make them forget the tens of millions of other victims of the era. The atrocities committed during the war by the Nazis are undoubtedly the worst moments in the entire history of the Jewish people. Testimonies about these painful events are, fortunately, numerous enough to give us an idea of what the prisoners in the death camps had to endure. Samuel Pisar is one of these survivors of the gas chambers. Of Polish origin, he became a naturalised French citizen before eventually becoming a very wealthy American businessman. In his famous book *The Blood of Hope*, which was to become a worldwide *bestseller*, he recounted how he experienced these dramatic events as a teenager.

In Bialystok, a town in eastern Poland where he lived with his family, he managed to escape the Germans for the first time when they decided to raze the ghetto where the Jews were separated from the rest of the population: "Finally, the Nazis razed the ghetto and deported all its inhabitants. A few men and some teenagers, completely unarmed, tried to resist. Heroic and insignificant rebellion, suppressed in an atrocious manner. They killed them all." One of the fighters, Malmed,

---

[177]*Les heures les plus sombres*: an expression coined and used by the French cultural and media sphere that refers to the 1930s and the Second World War. It is a kind of reminder invoking the memory of the public whenever it is pronounced.

[178]Shmuel Trigano, *L'Idéal démocratique*... Odile Jacob, 1999, p. 43.

was savagely tortured and hanged before my eyes for having thrown a bottle of sulphuric acid in the face of an SS officer, blinding him[179]." Such a spectacle, as we can imagine, must have scarred little Samuel's conscience forever. The executioners tortured in the middle of the street, with no concern for passers-by and onlookers watching their cruel methods. But, in such circumstances, heroism also consisted in witnessing this interminable spectacle, without looking away until the fatal outcome.

Samuel Pisar faced other difficult situations during the ghetto evacuation. Here is another anecdote: "At dawn, the SS forced open the doors. They entered the hall and threw us out into the street with guns, as if we were a herd. A dark silhouette, with the skull emblem on his helmet, stood before us. — I want this! — What, sir?—said my mother. — The ring on her finger. It was her engagement ring. A small diamond surrounded by tiny rubies arranged in the shape of a heart. She tried to take it off at once, but her fingers were swollen with fatigue. The SS pulled out his bayonet:—Hurry up or I'll take my finger too! In my terror, I remembered a piece of soap that I had placed at the bottom of my suitcase. In a few seconds I pulled it out. I spat on my mother's finger, while soaping it, and the ring slipped off. I held it out to the Nazi. — Here you are, sir. In that instant I had become someone else. It was my first decision to fight for life[180]..."

Samuel and his mother had a narrow escape. We can imagine little Samuel throwing himself on his suitcase, opening it feverishly to try to save his mother. Fortunately the SS did not react at that moment by firing a burst of machine gun fire for fear of seeing the teenager pull out a weapon. But Samuel was lucky, once again.

After this episode, the Nazis deported the Jews to internment camps. Crammed into train carriages like animals, they experienced the worst horrors during the long journey to their deaths. Once again, little Samuel was to witness atrocious scenes:

"We remained for seventy-two hours locked in our carriage, without food and water... When the train stopped and the doors were opened, a good part of the occupants, about twenty of them, were dead. They had been crushed to death by their companions or had died of thirst. The mass of bruised corpses spread like lava. It was dark, and the survivors, dazed, were blinded by the light of the searchlights. An SS

[179]Samuel Pisar, *La Sangre de la esperanza*, Editorial Planeta, 1990, Barcelona, p. 42, 43.

[180]Samuel Pisar, *La Sangre de la esperanza*, Editorial Planeta, 1990, Barcelona, p. 44, 45.

cordon was accompanied by numerous police dogs. A brief order and the Molossers burst into the wagon. In the blink of an eye, some stragglers were completely torn to pieces before our horrified gaze. On the platform it was all panic, banging and screaming. Clutching my small suitcase to my chest, I reached the exit, jumping over the bodies, pushed all over the place." Here again, try to imagine the scene in more detail. Indeed, we see very well the SS and their dogs climbing into the wagon in the opposite direction, while the deportees descend from it, stepping over or stepping over numerous corpses to go to the bottom to look for the stragglers, and finally unleash their ferocious beasts on these weak beings. We can imagine the panic of the last deportees rushing out of the wagon, crashing to the ground, one on top of the other, while, inside the wagon, in the gloom, some poor wretches were probably devoured by the beasts.

Life in the camp also brought its share of extraordinary incidents, and Samuel Pisar had more than once the opportunity to demonstrate his fearlessness: "I approached an SS man on the other side of the barbed wire. He pointed his machine gun at me. I took out of my suitcase a small parcel that my mother had given me before we parted. It contained my father's watch and ring. I opened the package and showed it to the Nazi… The SS looked at the package with incredulous eyes. —Throw me that. — Yes, if it brings me water. — Throw it or I'll shoot. — No, water first. I had phrased my answer with measured stubbornness. He knew he could kill me, but then he would not get his booty because I was situated on the other side of the fence… He walked away and returned in a few minutes with a full bottle." Little David had triumphed over Goliath! But other thirsty deportees came dangerously close to take advantage of the miraculous water source: "I raised the bottle to my lips and took a long drink and then another… A clamour. Men were advancing towards me from all sides, in a compact, vociferous mass. I handed the bottle to the first one who came and jumped aside. They began to fight, the container fell to the ground and broke[181]. Then, desperate, and as if hallucinating, they got down on their knees to greedily lick up what was left: the wet earth[182]." The circumstances were truly difficult.

Little Samuel came close to death several times, and it can be said

---

[181]Samuel Pisar, *La Sangre de la esperanza*, Editorial Planeta, 1990, Barcelona, p. 53, 54.

[182]Samuel Pisar, *Le Sang de l'espoir*, Robert Laffont, 1979, p. 55-57. [*Alors, désespérés, comme hallucinés, ils s'accroupirent en léchant avidement ce qui restait: la terre humide.* In the French version].

without exaggeration that his survival in that concentration camp hell was a miracle: “Between my first camp, Maidanek, and my arrival in Auschwitz, I was selected four times. Four needle changes to life or death”: “The old, the sick, the sickly, the unwell, even the wealthy, all those in the left row were gassed before we arrived... Maidanek, as we immediately learned, was a camp of pure extermination. A dreadful pollution was a constant reminder of the approach of death. The smoke and flames given off by the tall brick chimneys, set up at the other end of the courtyard, spread across the camp the smell of bodies thrown into the crematorium ovens.”

It was there, in Maidanek, among the tens of thousands of poor people, that he met a friend of Bialystock’s. What incredible luck: “There, dressed in a striped suit like mine, with his head shaved like mine, stood Ben. His back was turned, but it was undoubtedly him. —Benek! He turned around:—Mule! I didn’t remember his eyes being so big. In a few months he had aged several years. We embraced each other in tears...” After the happiness of their reunion they vowed to go forward together: “My pact with Ben was sealed: the will to live[183].”

Samuel Pisar, who grew up in the death camps, forged his character in the midst of these harsh realities. One day, in the Auschwitz camp, he made a mistake that cost him dearly: “One day I passed one of the camp commandants without seeing him. In the evening, at roll call, the punishment was announced to me. We were all standing still in the camp, in front of the barbed wire and the observation towers. —Number 1713 will receive twenty-five lashes for disrespect. They stripped me naked and tied me up in front of my comrades. The first blows fell; the leather straps ended in lead balls that hit my groin. —One, two, three, four, five, six, seven... Whether out of a reflex of childish pride, or because I naively thought it would be a score in my favour, I didn’t let out a single groan. The SS officer who was whipping me stopped in intrigue. —Wow, tonight we have a prisoner who doesn’t feel any pain! Let’s try it another way: seven, six, five, four, three, two, one... And then again; one, two... The blows cut into my skin like knives. I didn’t react. In the ranks some of the prisoners shouted:—Howl, asshole, or you’ll burst! I received more than thirty lashes before I faded away.” Once again, little Samuel had triumphed over Goliath. He then revealed the following: “The fundamental rule that must always be observed, if you want to survive, is never to admit, or show, the slightest sign of illness or weakness. A sore throat, a dislocated leg, a

[183]Samuel Pisar, *La Sangre de la esperanza*, Editorial Planeta, 1990, Barcelona, p. 55, 56, 58, 59, 61

wound that gets infected? Impossible! The principle is implacable: the weakest must be destroyed." Samuel Pisar did not forget the lesson, for he would not mention again in his book the after-effects that this painful ordeal had left on his body.

The extermination of Europe's Jews continued unabated. The gas chamber swallowed thousands of deportees every day: "Despite the ingenuity of the Nazis, the convoys that kept pouring loads into the slaughterhouse had to reach higher and higher levels: six thousand, seven thousand and then eight thousand gassed per day. It is not enough! A higher and higher quota must be reached, up to ten thousand or more per day. The death factory must continually break its own records[184]." The productivity of the gas chamber and the efficiency of the crematoria seemed to surpass all hopes, all forecasts of the Nazi criminals.

Samuel Pisar later told us how he managed to escape the gas chamber unscathed. One day, having been "selected", he managed to get through thanks to a subterfuge that saved his life. In the waiting room, in the middle of the other convicts, he grabbed a wooden bucket full of water and a brush that were lying around and began to scrub the floor, squatting down, slowly making his way towards the exit door: "The guards, who regularly peek inside, through the open door, have seen me. But they involuntarily become my accomplices:—Hey, this part is still dirty, start again! On my knees, I keep rubbing. They give me orders; I obey… I keep crawling and scrubbing, under the mocking eyes of the watchmen who enjoy multiplying the humiliations. —Clean up this corner again, you slacker! My obedience is total. When finally, after an infinite time, I reach the steps leading to the exit, I rub each one of them with conviction, with a conviction that would soften the most fearsome of kapos[185]."

This mind-blowing testimony of truthfulness will also be taken up in another book by Samuel Pisar, *The Human Resource,* as it exemplifies Samuel Pisar's ability to "find the exit door" in any circumstance.

Samuel Pisar, still in fairly good health after those terrible years, was transferred to labour camps with his two friends Ben and Nico: "The Hitler regime had a growing shortage of industrial labour. As we were still relatively presentable, we were loaded onto a goods train, with a contingent of other prisoners, and transferred to the heart of Germany."

---

[184]Samuel Pisar, *La Sangre de la esperanza,* Editorial Planeta, 1990, Barcelona, p. 70, 71, 72

[185]Samuel Pisar, *La Sangre de la esperanza,* Editorial Planeta, 1990, Barcelona, p. 73.

They then reached the Oranienburg camp, then Sachsenhausen and finally Leonberg, near Stuttgart. There they would see their liberators. In a very symbolic way, the liberators mentioned by Samuel Pisar are personified by a large American Negro, probably the better to impress on the reader's mind the idea that the atrocities he had suffered could only have been done by white men. The image is perhaps a bit far-fetched, like Hollywood movies with their inevitable happy endings:

"...the Germans had opened fire again and I was in the middle of the firing line. Unconsciously, I kept running... I reached the armoured car. A tall black man came out of the turret and apostrophised me in an unintelligible language. I threw myself at the soldier's feet and hugged his legs. The three English words that my mother so often repeated to me when I thought of our liberation came back to me and I shouted at the top of my lungs:—*God Bless America!* The black man made me climb the turret. I was free[186]."

The Polish Jewish writer Marek Halter also wrote a few pages about the horrors of the Nazi regime. In his book *The Force for Good,* he recounted, for example, the testimony of Varian Fry, passed on to him by his friend Mary Jane Gold: One day in 1935 in Germany, a "guy" who looked like a Jew was standing next to him in a cafeteria. Marek Halter recounted: "Two Nazis came in, SS or SA, I don't remember. The Jew, the so-called Jew, was a bit nervous when he was about to take the glass. Then one of the Nazis came up and planted a knife in his hand! His hand was stuck through and stuck to the table! He screamed in pain. The Nazi retrieved the knife and walked out of the bar with his companion. Varian heard them exclaim: "It is good to have Jewish blood on the blade of a German knife! Today is a holiday! For us it is a beautiful holiday! He saw all that, that whole infamous scene[187]."

This type of testimony is not verifiable, but it probably reflects very well the perception of the events of the time by the main stakeholders.

In a book entitled *Anti-Semitic Hatred,* Serge Moati shared his evocative impressions of the atrocities of the war, inspired by Claude Lanzmann's film about the death camps. He wrote, full of resentment, against the Poles: "In *Shoah*[188], Claude Lanzmann described very well

[186]Samuel Pisar, *La Sangre de la esperanza,* Editorial Planeta, 1990, Barcelona, p. 82, 94.

[187]Marek Halter, *La force du Bien,* Robert Laffont, 1995, p. 161.

[188]*Shoah* (Hebrew for "catastrophe") is a French documentary film by director Claude Lanzmann, released in 1985 and lasting approximately ten hours. The subtitles and

this indifference, this abominable complicity of the population. When you see the glittering, rich fields around Auschwitz, when you know that the local people got rich with the gold from the teeth of the camp martyrs … that gold which they found in the earth itself and which they used to build their beautiful houses", you can only retch at the sight of those Poles." Today, some still go to sift through the soil of Auschwitz to find the remains of teeth or jewellery in the ashes. Another story is also told. During the Warsaw ghetto uprising, there was a fair in the vicinity with a carousel of flying chairs that soared through the air. Many would go up to watch the Jews burn on the other side of the ghetto wall. People went to watch Jews die on the merry-go-round. And tickets were sold at high prices on the black market[189]." All these "stories" that are "told" are indeed frightening and do not reflect well on the Poles.

The writer Elie Wiesel personally experienced the death camps. He recounted with great emotion the atrocities he saw with his own eyes: "It is like a dream, a bad dream of God, in which human beings throw living Jewish children into the flames of great pits. I reread what I have just written, and my hand trembles, my whole being trembles. I am crying, I who hardly ever cry. I see the flames and the children again, and I tell myself that crying is not enough. It took me time to convince myself that I had not been wrong[190]." What he saw is simply unbelievable; but what he heard him say is perhaps even more so. In *Words of a Foreigner*, he recounted the Babi-Yar massacres in the Ukraine, where the Germans had executed Soviets and numerous Jews: "Later, I heard from a witness that for several months the ground had not stopped shaking; and that from time to time, geysers of blood came out of it[191]."

We can relate this testimony to that left by the Nobel Prize winner Isaac Bashevis Singer in one of his novels, entitled *The Slave*, in which he recounted the unspeakable atrocities committed by the Cossacks in the 17th century:

"The Cossacks had practically razed the city to the ground, and most of its inhabitants had been slaughtered, burned or hanged. Some, however, managed to survive… The murderers had even torn up the tombstones. Not a single chapter of the Sacred Scroll, not a page of the books of the house of study had been saved… Why did this have to

---

filmed testimonies were published in a book of the same name, translated into Spanish in 2003. In France, *Shoah* is often used to refer to the Jewish Holocaust.

[189]Serge Moati, *La Haine antisémite*, Flammarion, 1991, p. 105, 106.

[190]Elie Wiesel, *Mémoires, Tome I*, Seuil, 1994, p. 102.

[191]Elie Wiesel, *Paroles d'étranger*, Seuil, 1982, p. 86.

happen to us?—asked one of the men. Josefov was a Torah home. —It was God's will," answered another. —But why? What sins had the children committed? They were buried alive… —What harm had we done to them? … Did the Creator need the help of the Cossacks to reveal His nature? Was that sufficient reason for the children to be buried alive?"

Anti-Semitism is definitely incomprehensible, both today and in the past. Will the "powers of Evil" never cease their work of destruction? As always, the executioners compete with each other to see which is more cruel to the weak and unarmed victims. Reading the novelist Isaac Bashevis Singer, we see that the Cossacks' refinement in the matter was nothing to envy that of the Germans: "Moishe Bunim was impaled. He moaned all night. Twenty Cossacks raped your sister Leah, and then they butchered her… On such a morning it was hard to believe that this was a world where children were murdered or buried alive and where the earth was still nourished by blood as in the days of Cain[192]."

As a result of a youthful trip to India, Elie Wiesel told one of his amazing stories: "A Wise Man comes to me as I leave the hotel in Bombay: 'For five rupees I will tell you your future.' I replied: 'I'll give you ten if you tell me my past'. Surprised, he asks me to write down my date of birth and some other date on a piece of paper. He takes it and turns around to do his calculations and I stand there for a moment. When he turns around again he looks startled: "I see dead bodies. A lot of dead bodies. This surprises me. He can't know what 11 April 1945 means to me. Who knew[193]! "

In his *Memoirs*, Elie Wiesel was also outraged by the disbelief of some members of the Jewish community about the testimonies of the 'survivors'. This was the case of Alfred Kazin, a literary critic "unknown in France, but with a certain reputation in the United States", who allowed himself to doubt the writings of the "great writer" Jerzy Kosinski, the author of *The Painted Bird.* A dismayed Elie Wiesel reported the ironic words Kazin had dedicated to the writer's suicide: "Jerzy Kosinski has committed suicide—sensationally, evidently—sitting in his bathtub, putting his head in a plastic bag", as if, Wiesel added, Kosinski's gesture had been "another way of self-promotion." And Alfred Kazin added in his *New Yorker article*, to Elie Wiesel's chagrin: "I have never been able to believe a word he said… He always

[192]Isaac Bashevis Singer, *The Slave,* 1962, Epublibre, digital publisher German25 (2014), p. 294, 342.

[193]Elie Wiesel, *Mémoires, Tome I,* Seuil, 1994, p. 287.

acted in public. It was probably all related to the fact that he was a Holocaust survivor."

In the second volume of his *Memoirs*, Elie Wiesel returned to the case of Jerzy Kosinski, shedding further light on the doubts his work inspired in his own community. Elie Wiesel's glowing review of *The Painted Bird had earned* him a series of insulting letters from some Jews who had known Kosinski in Poland." I was wrong, they said, to be warm to this disgraceful Jew… Apparently, his book is nothing but a jumble of fanciful lucubrations… I refuse to believe it: Disgraceful Jew, Jerzy? Impossible! Liar, him? inconceivable! … A long article in the *Village Voice* has called him an impostor. A recent biography tries to demystify him: having spent the war with his parents, he could not have lived through the atrocious experiences narrated in *The Painted Bird, nor could* he have written his books on his own. The news of his suicide—like that of Bruno Bettelheim—has shocked me[194]."

It remained true, however, that Elie Wiesel could not contain his indignation at Alfred Kazin's attitude, and at Kazin's inexcusable suspicion of the sincerity of the survivors' grief:

In the beginning," Wiesel wrote, "we saw each other or phoned each other regularly. He is a member of the literary jury founded by the survivors of Bergen-Belsen, the chairman of which is a certain Yossel: Kazin accompanies us to Belsen, then to Jerusalem, and Yossel showers him with gifts: more than comfortable hotel rooms, spending money, presents for him and his wife. He even invites him to his home. And all that this New York intellectual is able to say about that visit, in a pompous and pedantic article, is that Yossel's wife owns a luxurious flat and also an inordinately large number tattooed on her arm: as if she had had it done on purpose at Cardin[195]… Worse still: in a text where he tries to recall "what he owes" to Primo Levi and me, he writes that he would not be surprised to discover that I invented the episode of the hanging in *The Night*[196]."

A hundred pages earlier, on page 342 of the first volume of his *Memoirs*, Elie had already been forced to rectify a note by François Mauriac[197] in his *Blocs-notes*, in 1963, in which he quoted "four novels"

---

[194]Elie Wiesel, *Mémoires, Tome II*, Seuil, 1996, p. 475. The famous pedo-psychiatrist Bruno Bettelheim also committed suicide with a plastic bag over his head.

[195]Pierre Cardin: Haute couture designer, famous from the 1950s onwards.

[196]Elie Wiesel, *Mémoires, Tome I*, Seuil, 1994, p. 436.

[197]François Mauriac (1885–1970) was a French journalist, critic and writer. Winner of the Nobel Prize for literature in 1952, he is known as one of the greatest Catholic writers of the 20th century.

by Elie Wiesel: *The Night, The Dawn, The Day, The City of Luck*: "*The Night* is not a novel", Elie Wiesel emphasised for those who still doubted it. However, five pages further on, he did not hesitate to inform us about his methods of writing his books:

On a visit "in Bnei Brak, the most religious quarter of Tel-Aviv", Elie meets the old Rebbe Israel: "He asks me questions about my work. He wants to know if the stories I tell in my books are true, that is, if they really happened. I reply: "Rabbi, in literature, it is like this: there are things that are true, but which nevertheless did not happen; and things that are not true, even though they did happen". I would so much like to have received his blessing[198]."

Elie Wiesel also strongly urged Auschwitz survivors to testify, so that nothing would be forgotten." In truth, my main concern has always been for the survivors. Through writing, I tried to convince them of the necessity and possibility of giving testimony: 'Do as I did, I told them. Declare, tell, even if you have to invent a language[199]."

The famous American novelist Philip Roth spoke similarly in his 1993 novel *Operation Shylock*, where he imagined a dialogue between "Roth" and another writer, Appelfeld, author of Badenheim 1939, who also witnessed tragic events during the war:

"I have never written things as they happened… To write things as they happened is to become a slave to memory, which is only a secondary element in the creative process… The most authentic things are very easy to falsify. Reality, as you well know, is always stronger than the human imagination… The reality of the Holocaust surpassed all imagination. If I stuck to the facts, no one would believe me… I snatched "my life story" from the powerful clutches of memory, putting it in the hands of the creative laboratory… From "my life story" I had to remove the unbelievable parts, in order to get a more plausible version[200]." A little more and we might think that Samuel Pisar used the same method.

However, we can see that Elie Wiesel had preferred Nazi Germany to the Red Army: "18 January 1945: the Red Army is a few kilometres from Auschwitz… Berlin decides to evacuate the prisoners into Germany. A feverish agitation reigns in the barracks… My father comes to see me in the hospital. In the general disorder, they let him in. I told him: "The sick can stay at KB, but… —But what? And I add: "But you

---

[198]Elie Wiesel, *Mémoires, Tome I*, Seuil, 1994, p. 341, 342, 347.

[199]Elie Wiesel, *Mémoires, Tome I*, Seuil, 1994, p. 443.

[200]Philip Roth, *Operación Shylock*, Debolsillo Penguin Random House, Barcelona, 2005, p. 96, 97

can stay with me, you know—is that possible? He asks me—"Yes, it is possible". There is room. Today the surveillance is slackening. In the general back and forth everything is possible. The idea is tempting, but we reject it. We are afraid. The Germans will leave no witnesses behind them; they will kill them. All of them. Every last one. It is within the monstrous logic of their action. They will blow up everything so that the free world will not know the nature and extent of their crimes."

This is how Elie Wiesel and his father chose to march with the Germans instead of waiting for the Red Army. The sick who had stayed, contrary to the predictions of the Wiesel father and son, had not been exterminated: "What would have happened to us if we had chosen to stay? All or almost all of the sick survived, liberated by the Russians nine days later. In other words, if we had chosen to stay in the infirmary, my father would not have died of hunger and shame ten days later in Buchenwald[201]." Therefore, the sick in Auschwitz, including the poor Jews, were cared for.

Jewish sensitivity

Obviously, there is no attempt here to minimise the sufferings of the Jewish people during this tragic period. The purpose of this study focuses solely on Jewish intellectuals' perceptions of the events, and not on statistical data. It is true that Jews have been distrustful of the populations among whom they live for centuries, a distrust nourished by centuries of experience of rejection, expulsions, pogroms and humiliating laws. This instinctive, animalistic fear has not disappeared after the Second World War, on the contrary. But it is also important to understand that these manifestations of fear and mistrust also correspond to a secular tendency of the Jewish people.

Elie Wiesel expressed the wickedness of his contemporaries in the concentration camps where they gave vent to their frustrations: "Those Ukrainians who beat us, those Russians who hate us, those Poles who hurt us, those Gypsies who slap us[202]."

We will see later in this study that the analysis of anti-Semitism by Jewish intellectuals reveals an identical distrust of Hungarians, Spaniards or Latvians, who also persecuted the Jewish people at different times.

The French scholar Maurice Rheims, who was a resistance fighter

[201]Elie Wiesel, *Mémoires, Tome I*, Seuil, 1994, p. 119.

[202]Elie Wiesel, *Mémoires, Tome I*, Seuil, 1994, p. 111.

during the Second World War, himself recounted the cruelty of the men towards the persecuted Jews: "The last time I met God in person was in Drancy, in the heart of the night. French gendarmes came to warn us that at dawn they would be forced to aim and shoot at us[203]." Fortunately, Maurice Rheims emerged unscathed from this horrible ordeal.

The fact is that the Jews have always been persecuted, in all ages and under all latitudes, by all the peoples where they have settled. However, the Jewish people are fundamentally innocent of all that they are accused of, and are intrinsically incapable of evil.

In the first volume of his *Memoirs*, Elie Wiesel expounded in several paragraphs on this Jewish uniqueness. Indeed, after all the horrors of the war, the Jewish survivors showed an outstanding loftiness and nobility of soul. They did not fall into baseness and vengeance against the executioners, as ordinary Goyim would have done, but on the contrary, they generally showed great restraint and self-control. This is what Elie Wiesel wrote:

"The Germans fear us. Quite rightly too. The sight of a free Jew must fill them with apprehension, with terror... They have been mistaken. The Jewish avengers were few, and their thirst for revenge was short-lived. The Jewish prisoners had every reason to return to Germany, to invade it to break its stiff neck... But the Jews, for metaphysical and ethical reasons deeply rooted in their history, chose another way. How can one explain this absence of violence in the survivors? How can one understand this absence of murderous hatred on the part of the victims towards the executioners, the torturers of yesterday? There were no bloody reprisals. Few summary executions. No public lynchings. No collective revenge. Except for the Nuremberg trial and a few big trials (against the criminal doctors and against the *Einsatzkommandos*), nothing, almost nothing. Almost nothing. Denazification? Nothing serious really[204]."

The Jewish people's penchant for forgiveness is indeed well known to the rest of humanity, and if some elders have been dragged out of their lairs thirty, forty or sixty years after the fact to be dragged before the courts, these were only a few exceptions that highlight even more the spirit of meekness and the great tolerance of the leaders of the Jewish community.

Since Jews are a weak and extremely vulnerable people, and since they have endured too much suffering in their history, they cannot bear

---

[203]Maurice Rheims, *Une Mémoire vagabonde*, Gallimard, 1997, p. 78.

[204]Elie Wiesel, *Mémoires, Tome I*, Seuil, 1994, p. 176.

to inflict it on others without suffering painful inner torments. Just look at the frightened animal fears of Elie Wiesel, a young journalist in 1961 in front of the former Nazi Eichmann, on trial in Israel:

"I am covering the Eichmann trial. I watch it. I look at him for hours; he frightens me. Yet in his situation, in his armoured glass cage, he represents no danger. Why does he inspire such fear in me; is there an ontological evil embodied by a being who does not need to act or come out of himself to make his evil might felt[205]?"

Elie Wiesel rubs shoulders with America's high society of billionaires, but twenty years after the war, he is still trembling. This shows the extent to which fear and anguish are deeply rooted in the hearts of Jews all over the world. A few pages later in his *Memoirs*, Elie Wiesel again illustrated that intrinsic weakness of Jews, incapable of wanting or doing evil. In Israel, for example, contrary to what the false propaganda would have you believe, the Jews, victors again against the Arabs in 1967, show that characteristic greatness of soul:

"In *The Beggar of Jerusalem*, Wiesel wrote, I echo the thoughts of the rabbis and speak of the sadness felt by the victor in the face of the vanquished. And even more so before the Arab children who see in him a victor capable of doing them harm."

You have understood: if a Jew does evil, it is very much to his regret. They are not responsible, and perhaps they suffer more than their bloodied victim. These children," Wiesel continues, "I have seen them in the old city. I have passed them in Hebron. I met them in Ramallah and Nablus. I'm afraid of them. For the first time in my life, the children were afraid of me." Elie Wiesel's suffering was then inhuman, ineffable: "Victory does not prevent suffering from having existed, nor death from having ravaged. How to fight for the living without betraying the absent? "For a survivor of the death camps, the sensitivity to pain is strongest, and perhaps even more so when it comes to oneself and one's own people: "The survivor in me is both vulnerable and strong. The slightest offence hurts me and the slightest gesture of generosity moves me[206]."

This fear of a cornered animal, which was the harsh condition of the Jewish people during many centuries of persecution, Elie Wiesel translated it with a sensitivity and poetry that expressed the tragedy of Jewish existence. For example, when he applied for American citizenship a few years later, he also felt the plight of the human being under the yoke of nationality. He was shocked to learn that the FBI

---

[205]Elie Wiesel, *Mémoires, Tome I*, Seuil, 1994, p. 456.

[206]Elie Wiesel, *Mémoires, Tome I*, Seuil, 1994, p. 517, 518, 521.

wanted to interrogate him:

"A few days earlier, I received a message from the hotel concierge: I must call an FBI agent... The refugee in me is awakened. I tremble with fear. What could I have done to attract the attention of the all-powerful and all-knowing service of the terrible Edgar J. Hoover?" Clearly, this was only an administrative formality, but this testimony indicates that even in the heart of New York, the survivor of the death camps can feel in danger and tremble before the number and power of those ever potentially hostile goyim.

The Yiddish poet Heschel also wanted to express the pain of the Jewish people, as if he wanted to carry on his shoulders the pain of all humanity at war: "How can I claim my Jewishness if I remain insensitive to the pain and mourning of the men, women and children who, for years, have seen their dreams destroyed by the nightly bombardments[207]?"

The writer Marek Halter also expressed this intrinsic goodness of the Jews with the same emotion, sometimes with a slightly sappy grandiloquence: "When I write that one man can save all of humanity by doing good, it is not about the salvation of bodies but about an idea of man and humanity: that which allows hope. And hope gives us something to live for[208]."

This Jewish compassion is directed not only towards human beings, but also towards all living animals, all God's creatures, even the most insignificant insect. We find this particular Jewish sensibility in the celebrated Yiddish writer Isaac Bashevis Singer. In his novel *The Slave*, he narrated the vicissitudes of Jacob, a poor Jew in 17th century Poland, whose family was massacred in a pogrom, and who was reduced to serfdom in a mountain village, lost in the midst of stupid and violent peasants. Jacob, he, was different from other men:

"Jacob had no choice but to battle the flies and lice that attacked him and the cows. It was necessary to kill. When he went from place to place he could not avoid stepping on toads and worms, and when he picked grass he found poisonous snakes that hissed at him and he had to crush them with his stick or a stone. But every time such a thing happened, he felt like a murderer. Deep down, he reproached the Creator for forcing one creature to annihilate others. Of all the questions he asked himself about the Universe, that was the one he found most difficult to answer[209]."

---

[207]Quoted in Elie Wiesel, *Mémoires, Tome I*, Seuil, 1994, p. 382, 485.

[208]Marek Halter, *La Force du Bien*, Robert Laffont, 1995, p. 139.

[209]Isaac Bashevis Singer, *The Slave*, 1962, Epublibre, digital publisher German25

The Austrian writer Joseph Roth also had this sensitivity in spades: "The hand gesture of a waiter on the terrace of a café to kill a fly is more significant than the fate of all the customers on the terrace. The fly is free and the waiter is disappointed. Why, oh waiter, are you angry with the fly[210]?"

We have another similar image in *Oh You Human Brothers* by novelist Albert Cohen:

"My mother who was afraid of the Jew-haters, my mother who was naïve and kind, and who was made to suffer… I remember that one day, in order to tell me about the greatness of the Eternal, he explained to me that he loved even the flies, and each fly in particular, and he added: I tried to do as He did with the flies, but I couldn't, there are too many[211]."

We see here that love for all creation is deeply rooted in the heart of every Jew. To use a somewhat grandiloquent phraseology as they themselves seem to appreciate, one might say that "the Jew is love"; he has a mission to work for peace and love[212].

Samuel Pisar also has a very special awareness of the tragic fate of the Jewish people. In 1967, after the overwhelming military victory of the Jewish people over their Arab neighbours, he recounted his emotions: "One evening in 1967, on my way home from Paris, I saw on television an incredible, unthinkable spectacle: the liberation of the Wailing Wall in Jerusalem. I saw the Hebrew soldiers praying at the foot of the holy place. Suddenly, I, who have always known how to control my nerves, burst for the first time into sobs, of which my children would never have believed me capable, sobs coming from the depths of my being and from the origins of time ... the memory of what I had suffered, of what a whole people had suffered for millennia, had just broken my affective barrier before that eternal symbol of affliction and

---

(2014), p. 182, 183.

[210]Joseph Roth, article of 24 May 1921, *Berliner Börsen-Courier*, Éditions du Rocher, 2003.

[211]Albert Cohen, *Oh you, human brothers and sisters*, Editorial Losada, 2004, Madrid, p. 36.

[212]"There is an outlet for children's aggression that parents close their eyes to. Occasionally, a pig gets lost in the yard of a house. When that happens, the children of the neighbourhood gather to mistreat it. Armed with sticks, they pounce on it, chase it from one corner to another, martyr it until it squeals with rage and terror; and the pig's screaming is more reminiscent of a torture chamber than a pen: "an angry pig is as dangerous as a lion". Adults do not intervene. Cruelty is forbidden, one must have "compassion for all that lives", noisy games, racket and fuss are forbidden. But he is a pig, and as long as he does not manage to escape, he will pay for it." (Mark Zborowski, *Olam*, 1952, Plon, 1992, p. 331). There are also many other "impure" beings for the Jews.

hope[213]."

We will note here that this event, undoubtedly spectacular, perhaps made a far greater impression on Jews around the world than any victory in their host country. It would not, however, be the only time we would see Samuel Pisar weeping. In 1969, listening on the radio to General de Gaulle resign and announce his immediate departure after the referendum[214], he wrote: "I feel that a chapter of history is brutally closing. And a chapter of my life. At that moment, I discover that I am crying. I am an American citizen and I cry. With his departure, the film of my life flashes before my eyes again[215]."

This sensitivity is in fact part of the tradition. It is not a question of denying real suffering, but of taking it in its proper perspective, insofar as we understand that many Jews, consciously or not, keep alive this anguish, this inner restlessness, which contributes to nurturing in them a sense of their own Jewishness to the detriment of their integration into the rest of the population. The manifest weakness of the Jewish people, the eternal scapegoat of history, the eternal victim of man's folly, reflects a certain disposition to lamentation, which is undoubtedly one of the most visible—or audible—characteristics of Jewish uniqueness.

The great historian of anti-Semitism, Leon Poliakov, analysed the "suffering" of the Jewish people as follows: "The cult of suffering, its systematic and reasoned valorisation, its perception as divine punishment, but also as an expression of God's love, gave it a profound meaning and thus made it easier to overcome it[216]."

This is what Elie Wiesel recounted, for example, when his little sister was born: "I came home. Through the closed door, I heard my grandmother pleading with my mother: 'Don't hold back, Chilla! Chilla! You have to squeal when it hurts—and it hurts, I know it hurts[217]."

Mark Zborowski's anthropological study of Ashkenazi Jewish life in the shtetls of Eastern Europe confirmed this tendency: "The shtetl does not value holding back tears. Crying is a loyal weapon and a

---

213Samuel Pisar, *La Sangre de la esperanza (The Blood of Hope)*, Editorial Planeta, 1990, Barcelona, p.51

214On 27 April 1969, a referendum was held in France on "the draft law on the creation of regions and the renewal of the Senate. The negative result led to the resignation of President Charles de Gaulle the following day.

215Samuel Pisar, *La Resource humaine*, Jean-Claude Lattès, 1983, p. 50.

216Léon Poliakov, *Histoire de l'antisémitisme, tome I*, 1981, Points Seuil, 1990, p. 326.

217Elie Wiesel, *Mémoires, tome I*, Seuil, 1994, p. 38.

perfectly normal mode of expression whose range extends from suffering, grief, joy, anger and even the impotent rebellion of the child who dares not talk back to his parents. Tears, not being shameful, are not hidden; on the contrary, they sometimes show that one knows how to rise to the occasion… If one has to cry, one cries, and without forcing oneself." Weep now", the *zogerke* orders the women in the synagogue. During Yom Kippur celebrations, everyone weeps; the moving melody of the *chazan*[218] resembles a long sob. At certain moments, he weeps for the entire community he represents… The tears are usually associated more with emotions that are impossible to contain than with scenes of dispute. A five-year-old boy could not cry at the body of his deceased grandfather: "I had to be pinched to get the tears out." On the way back from the cemetery where his father had just been buried, a young boy stunned with grief provoked this comment: "Look Berl, he doesn't cry, he's indifferent! Immediately, I started crying non-stop". Marriages, burials and the celebration of Yom Kippur are almost obligatory occasions for crying[219]."

In his book *Wandering Jews*, the writer Joseph Roth echoed these sufferings when he described the "true and warm tradition" that prevailed in the shtetls of Central Europe. Here is a passage that reveals this very picturesque aspect of Jewish spiritual life, and which seems to unfold fully on the day of the Great Atonement:

For Yom Kippur, Roth wrote, "everyone, without distinction: the rich are as poor as the poor, for no one has anything to eat. All are sinners and all pray. A vertigo comes over them, they stagger, they become beside themselves, they whisper, they hurt themselves, they sing, they cry, they cry, heavy tears fall in streams down their old beards, and hunger has vanished by the work and grace of the pain of the soul and the eternity of the melodies…"

Jews externalise this grief during burials in a very special and, no doubt, excessive way in the eyes of Europeans. On that occasion, as Joseph Roth described it, "the corpse of the devout Jew lies in a simple wooden box, covered with a black cloth… They almost race the corpse through the streets. The preparations have lasted a day. No dead person

---

[218] The Chazan: this is the name given to the person who leads the singing in the synagogue. In addition to singing, he also leads the order of the prayers.

[219] Mark Zborowski, *Olam*, 1952, Plon, 1992, p. 322, 292. On their floor, the women are also arranged according to their social rank, from front to back. In a silken murmur, they repeat, while discreetly comparing their respective jewels, the prayers indicated to them by the *zogerke*, one of the few women who knows Hebrew. After her, they repeat each syllable, imitating each intonation. When the *zogerke* says: "Women, the hour of tears has come", they cry." (*Olam*, p. 45)

is allowed to remain in the ground for more than twenty-four hours. The wailing of those who have survived him must be heard in the whole city. Women march through the streets shouting their grief to every stranger they meet. They speak to the deceased, address him affectionate appellations, demand his forgiveness and his grace, cover themselves with reproaches, ask, perplexed, what they will do now, assure him that they no longer want to live—and all this in the middle of the street, on the road, at full speed—while in the houses indifferent faces peep out, strangers go about their business, carriages pass by, and shopkeepers attract clientele[220]."

Apparently, such noisy demonstrations seem to be quite natural for other Jews who understand that tradition must be respected. So there is nothing to be alarmed about, and only outsiders could get caught up in this game of exaggerated dramatisation. Shouting, crying and jeremiads are part and parcel of Jewish communal life.

Entrepreneurship

In 1945, after four years in the concentration camps, Samuel Pisar was 16 years old. Fortunately, he and his two comrades were in the best of health and set off without further delay in the "*business*":

"The occupation of Germany, he wrote, offered everyone attractive and fruitful possibilities. The left hand acquired in the camps, stimulated by our new and ambitious energies, was looking for a field in which to put it into practice. We quickly found it. Most of the Germans lived in abject poverty as opposed to the good-natured Americans, immersed in a solitary abundance, accompanied by enormous waste... I could not believe my eyes. We could act as intermediaries between these two worlds. For a carton of Lucky Strike cigarettes we could bring a drunken black GI and a complacent German Frau into contact." By selling the needy and frightened German women to black American men, Samuel Pisar and his friends were in a way engaging in pimping and probably also satisfying an unspeakable desire for revenge against the German people. Their cunning and cunning then bordered on racketeering, going to the limit of theft and swindling, as this testimony illustrates:

"But our real bargaining power lay in coffee, the supreme and inaccessible commodity. Ben found a position as a cook's assistant in a black American regiment and every morning, while preparing

---

[220]Joseph Roth, *Judíos errantes,* Acantilado 164, Barcelona, 2008, p. 59, 60

breakfast, he would put several hundred extra servings of coffee in the pot. Then I would arrive on my motorbike and put all the waste in my silver side-car. I would take it to our flat and there we would dry it in the oven of the old fireplace. Then we would take it to the market, in little bags of what we called "real Brazilian Bohnen coffee", in exchange for anything of value. The German population, which had been subjected to the substitute coffee regime long before the war, was prepared to make all the sacrifices it could to finally taste the aroma and flavour of "real" coffee. Then we diversified the system… Within a month we had acquired real notoriety in the town of Landsberg."

Judging by the energy these former deportees put into enjoying their victory, the aftermath inflicted in the death camps was ultimately not so profound. Admittedly, the chaos of post-war Germany offered all sorts of joys for the children of Israel. Had the situation lasted longer, there is no doubt that the three compadres would have become the "godfathers" of the region, the heads of a powerful mafia, as indeed some of their peers already were in the United States where they had made a career in gangsterism[221]:

"In exchange for a pound of second-hand coffee, we got a bottle of first-class *schnaps*. For five bottles of this liquor, plus a docile blonde, the American drivers who drove the huge tanker trucks would agree to transfer part of their gasoline load. The new activity was thriving so spectacularly that we were on the verge of rendering the entire American division stationed in the region almost non-operational… Nico had become an easy-going man who collected women and suits of the finest cut. Draped in a blue overcoat and wearing a carelessly knotted white scarf around his neck, he strolled through the city, his silhouette indolent… Years spent in the death camps had convinced me that he was immortal."

But little Samuel and his friends were again confronted with anti-Semitism and barbarism: "One morning, Nico went out on his rounds and found himself in prison. He was arrested at the home of the daughter of a former Wehrmacht general by two American policemen in white helmets who took him away in a Military Police jeep. I was shocked. A victim of Nazi persecution was once again deprived of his freedom. And to top off the provocation, the good, dear Nico was incarcerated in the same German prison that, twenty years earlier, had housed an agitator called Adolf Hitler, who had taken advantage of his detention to write *Mein Kampf* there, and I found it monstrous. I thought it was monstrous.

[221]Hervé Ryssen, *Planetary Hopes, (*2022) and *The Jewish Mafia (*2022).

What had we done, except respond effectively to the law of supply and demand[222]?"

Samuel Pisar's reaction is very symptomatic of a certain mentality that makes some swindlers believe that everything is permitted to them because of past persecutions, and that they can correct the injustices they feel they have been victims of by extra-legal self-compensatory actions. Even after years have passed, the adult Samuel Pisar does not seem to understand that his swindling and trafficking contravened the laws of the land. These protestations of innocence, proclaimed with aplomb, even when the overwhelming evidence is there, were similar, for example, to those of the murderer Pierre Goldman in the 1970s, or the swindler Jacques Crozemarie who kept in his pocket part of the funds he collected for the fight against cancer[223].

But it took more than that to impress Samuel Pisar. Incarcerated, he organised a prison revolt: "Ben and I were also arrested... I, who was sixteen years old, was locked up in a cell reserved for young German delinquents. In a few days I succeeded, without any difficulty, in creating such a climate of rebellion among the prisoners that I was put in a separate cell." Again, we see in Samuel Pisar's indignant speech the centuries-old image of the ghetto that separated the Jewish people from other nations. But his stay in prison was not to last forever. Samuel Pisar went to Australia, and then to the United States and France where he continued his business activities and became a millionaire and philanthropist." He was an American at heart[224]", he wrote. He also loved France, the homeland of human rights, where he was one of the financiers of François Mitterrand's socialist party.

Samuel Pisar's testimony is consistent with an article by Arnold Mandel, published in the Jewish community magazine *L'Arche* in November 1977: In the "ruins of Berlin" in 1945, one did indeed encounter "groups of Jewish survivors who were engaged in unorthodox, let alone *"Kasher"*, profit-making activities", wrote Arnold Mandel, specifying further that "they no longer believed that they had moral obligations."

Elie Wiesel reported that other Holocaust survivors had also become enormously rich to show the rest of mankind that life was not over: "Some have dedicated their lives to making a fortune. Normal.

---

[222]Samuel Pisar, *La Sangre de la esperanza,* Editorial Planeta, 1990, Barcelona, p. 98-102.

[223]Hervé Ryssen, *Planetary Hopes* and *The Jewish Mafia.*

[224]Samuel Pisar, *La Sangre de la esperanza,* Editorial Planeta, 1990, Barcelona, p. 102, 168.

Having lost everything, they wanted to rebuild their lives, preferably well off and have a family. Rich, often very rich, it took them many years to become aware of their mission and to take part in the fight against oblivion. It is now that they are catching up."

Wiesel then told us of the success of a friend of his, leaving us with a picturesque picture of the success of some upstart Jews: "My articles in the Yiddish press and *The Night* won me the friendship of a man named Yossel and his circle. Small in stature, overflowing with vitality, with a sparkling, mischievous eye, brimming with imagination, a lover of racy stories and heretical anecdotes, Yossel first struck me by the brilliance of his primitive language and his princely lifestyle: he lived in a luxurious flat, filled with paintings by masters. Originally from Poland, a veteran of Auschwitz and Belsen, he talked about it non-stop and without the slightest inhibition. I admit that at first it annoyed me… In painting, he showed good taste, as demonstrated by his Picasso, Chagall, Renoir and Manet[225]." To own a mansion decorated with paintings by masters worth a fortune is undoubtedly a beautiful revenge on the gas chambers.

This ability of many Jews to get rich quickly has always aroused envy in the rest of the population in all countries. This is not something new, and it does not only concern "Christians". Leon Poliakov, one of the great historians of Judaism, recounted, for example, the case of Semuel Ibn Nagrella in 11th century Muslim Al-Andalus and the hatred that his insolent fortune had aroused. Semuel Ibn Nagrella was an omnipotent minister of King Badis ben Habus of the taifa of Granada who had enraged the Muslim poet Abu Ishaq of Elvira:

"The chief of these apes has adorned his residence with precious inlays of marble; he has ordered fountains to be built from which the purest water flows, and while he makes us wait before his door, he mocks at us and our religion. If he were to say that he is as rich as you, my king, he would speak the truth; hasten to slit his throat and offer him as a burnt offering, sacrifice him, he is a fat ram! Nor spare his kinsmen and allies; they too have amassed immense treasures…"

The affair ended badly for Ibn Nagrella's family. In 1066, during a brief popular uprising, Joseph Ibn Nagrella, his son who succeeded him, was crucified by the unbridled mob and "a large number of Jews were killed; it seems that the survivors had to leave Grenada for some time[226]", Leon Poliakov pointed out. It is one of the rare examples, under the pen of a Jewish author, where the anti-Semitism of the

[225]Elie Wiesel, *Mémoires, tome I*, Seuil, 1994, p. 444.

[226]Léon Poliakov, *Histoire de l'antisémitisme, tome I*, 1981, Points Seuil, 1990, p. 104.

population is more or less explained.

This greed was also illustrated in this more contemporary example, in an article in the weekly *Le Point* of 9 February 2006 entitled: "Steven Cohen, the Wall Street Boss". Steven Cohen, the "star of the stock market", likes to maintain secrecy around him: "The real boss of Wall Street does not live in Manhattan, but is confined to a house in Greenwich (Connecticut) enclosed by a four-metre high wall. Steven Cohen, 49, hardly ever shows himself… In 2005, he pocketed 500 million dollars. What is his secret? He knows everything before anyone else. With his eyes glued to the control screens, he analyses thousands of data and gets furious when Wall Street analysts don't give him the scoop on a piece of information. The investors who entrust him with their money (4 billion dollars) pay him dearly for his services: Cohen receives 3% of the sums as management fees (against an average of 1.44%) and 35% of the profits (against an average of 19.2%)." Cohen "professes total capitalism: "You eat what you kill," he tells his *brokers*, who are paid on the basis of their skills and performance."

Jews in general certainly have the ability to enrich themselves more easily than others. Post-war Germany was undoubtedly a business-friendly terrain for those people who were more gifted in commerce and money management. The chaotic situation in Russia after the collapse of the Soviet Union, as in Germany in 1945, was a golden opportunity for many Jewish businessmen who took advantage of the situation by buying up former state industries at knock-down prices. Within a few years, they acquired most of Russia's wealth and amassed colossal fortunes, until Vladimir Putin, elected president, led a popular resistance, which some judged to be "anti-Semitic", and dismantled the "Russian mafia", which was in fact nothing more than a Jewish mafia of Russian origin. There too, liberalism was nothing more than the law of the fox in the henhouse[227].

The very long tradition of the Jews to generate profit and profit was already explained by some analysts who underlined the secular practice of usury by the Jews since Antiquity, even before the Christian era. Together with the spirit of the Talmud[228], this long experience

[227]Hervé Ryssen, *Planetary Hopes* and *The Jewish Mafia.*

[228]"For the LORD, your God, will bless you, as he has said to you, and you shall lend to many nations, and you shall not borrow from anyone; you shall rule over many nations, and they shall not rule over you." " (*Deuteronomy 15:6-8*); "As we learned in a mishnah: Rabbi Yishmael says: He who seeks to be wise should devote himself to the monetary laws, for there is no greater discipline in the Torah, for they are like a flowing well from which innovations are constantly gushing forth." (Talmud, *Berakhot 63b*) (NdT).

effectively gave them a certain advantage over others, as Bernard Lazare wrote:

"The Jew is undoubtedly better endowed than any other to achieve success... He is cool and calculating, energetic and flexible, persevering and patient, lucid and exact, and all these qualities he has inherited from his ancestors the ducat handlers and dealers. If he is engaged in commerce and finance, he benefits by his secular and atavistic education, which has not made him more intelligent, as his vanity declares, but more suited to certain functions[229]."

It is therefore not surprising that, under these conditions, Jewish intellectuals are the champions of liberalism and market deregulation, as they are better prepared and armed for the financial business they have been successfully practising for centuries.

An insolent success

The successes of Jewish financiers and businessmen are known to all, and it is well known that among the world's greatest fortunes there is a wholly disproportionate number of Jewish billionaires. In fact, Jews account for half of all billionaires (in billions) in the United States, while they represent only 2% of the total population. Already in the 19th century, the prodigious rise of the Rothschilds and the formidable power they had accumulated in a few years had raised suspicions and questions in all European countries. Barely out of the ghetto, a few Jewish financiers had risen to the top and seemed to exercise ruthless domination." Having always excelled in the race to riches, the emancipated Jews applied themselves to it with double the ardour, and the political and economic transformations of the time facilitated many spectacular promotions," wrote Poliakov.[230]

This is what Guy de Rothschild wrote in 1983 about his ancestor James de Rothschild, founder of the French branch of the family and of the famous rue Lafitte bank in 1817: "He was naturally proud. He could occasionally be imperious, even disdainful, and is known to have spoken cruelly: "Our ministers ... are like napkins. After a while, they have to be washed and left to rest, that makes them better." "

About his father, an influential man between the two world wars, he also wrote in a falsely ironic way: "My father, as is well known, was

---

[229]Bernard Lazare, *Anti-Semitism, its history and causes, (1894).* Editions La Bastille, digital ed. 2011, p. 159.

[230]Léon Poliakov, *Histoire de l'antisémitisme, tome II,* 1981, Points Seuil, 1990, p. 134.

also the regent of the Bank of France. Blum and Rothschild: France undoubtedly belonged to the Jews[231]!"

Samuel Pisar's financial success was equally impressive. His social standing brought him into contact with the greats of this world and the stars of the cinema. Pisar described with satisfaction for his readers the joys and advantages of being a wealthy and influential man: "On my way from Washington to Europe, I stopped in Lausanne. I had lunch at the home of the actor Yul Brynner, in the company of my friend the director Anatole Litvak, the divine Audrey Hepburn and the banker Loel Guinness… It is exciting to have breakfast in Paris with Catherine Deneuve or in Madrid with Ava Gardner, to discuss the contract for their next films, and then to fly to London and take part in a working lunch at the Rothschild bank." In fact, Samuel Pisar seemed to take the same satisfaction in boasting both of his own successes and those of his peers. Regarding Louis B. Mayer, he wrote Mayer, he wrote: "The emperor of American cinema, founder of the legendary Metro Goldwyn Mayer, which made and unmade Hollywood's biggest stars, proposed to me, as soon as I left Harvard, that I should act as his company's lawyer[232]."

But Samuel Pisar's achievements were not limited to show business. He was also an influential man, whose immense fortune could be useful for some political ambitions. The dinners he hosted at his home with his wife brought together the crème de la crème of the political world of the time. Samuel and Judith Pisar, American citizens, thus showed us how Jews knew how to be open and eclectic in their relations:

"With Judith, who as president of the American Cultural Centre in Paris has been able to give new impetus to relations between France and the United States and their artistic exchanges, we had fun mixing political adversaries, with the exception of the communists, in our invitations. They, too, seemed delighted with the setting. A subtle complicity was established between us: we were innocent Americans who, probably out of ignorance, did not respect borders and circles. They were too perfect products of French politeness to be offended by it. What a pleasure, and what a good memory, to see, for example, Pierre Mendès France and Michel Debré talking warmly and amicably in our living room! … And Simone Veil arguing with Jacques Chirac [Pierre Uri]… That evening, our guest of honour was Henry Kissinger. The former Secretary of State, who had symbolised the American diplomacy

---

[231]Guy de Rotschild, *Contre bonne fortune…*, Belfond, 1983, p. 75, 109.
[232]Samuel Pisar, *La Sangre de la esperanza*, Editorial Planeta, 1990, Barcelona, p. 179, 181, 175.

of the last ten years with verve, shared my concerns about the political vulnerability of Western Europe, and of France in particular... [Françoise Giroud talking at length with Jacques Attali] It was not trivial, and above all not discouraging: what a country, and what wealth[233]! "

While he knew how to mix Sephardim and Ashkenazim very well, he was apparently very careful not to mix Jews with Goyim. In this case, his taste for provocation was not so much to the detriment of his guests, who knew perfectly well that they were among them according to their own secular customs, as of his Goyim readers whom he seemed to mock with a certain disdain.

Françoise "Giroud", who was visibly a regular at Samuel Pisar's soirées, also left an interesting testimony about the worldly and media life of certain Jewish circles in France at the time. She had participated with Jean-Jacques Servan-Schreiber in the creation of the great weekly *L'Express* in 1953, becoming its director. After her death in 2003, the journalist Christine Ockrent, the wife of the former socialist minister Bernard Kouchner, published a biography based on interviews that constitutes an interesting sociological chronicle of this liberal and social-democratic Jewish diaspora. This is what the weekly *L'Express* wrote about her:

"You have to please the Queen, and everyone is doing their best to please her. We are in Versailles. Jean-Jacques reigns as absolute monarch, changing his favourite as he pleases, but she is the boss of the paper...". You can't imagine the power of *L'Express* in those days: one could enter everywhere, in all circles... It was before television"... Françoise Giroud was the head of that newspaper[234]."

This pride manifested itself on the material level in a way that had already been highlighted by the great French sociological painters of the 19th century: "From her childhood, Françoise Giroud retained a lifelong nostalgia and taste for luxury—and even displayed it in an ostentatious manner when she had access to it. Cars, shoes and tailor-made clothes, five-star hotels, the Trianon in Versailles or Eden Roc in Cap d'Antibes... Daniel Heymann confirmed: "She didn't need money, she needed luxury. An unquenchable need of which she openly boasted.

---

[233]Samuel Pisar, *La Sangre de la esperanza*, Editorial Planeta, 1990, Barcelona, p. 227." *Simone Veil discussing with Pierre Uri (instead of Jacques Chirac)" and "Françoise Giroud conversing at length with Jacques Attali"*, in the French version *Le Sang de l'espoir,* Robert Laffont, 1979, p. 260, 261.

[234]Christine Ockrent, *Françoise Giroud, une ambition française*, Fayard, Paris, 2003, p. 20-24.

It was revenge for her childhood". Jean Daniel recounted for his part, "Françoise had a passion for success and did not disdain to flaunt it." "

However, Françoise Giroud's resounding success could not be explained by her style or her literary qualities, far from it. She had benefited above all from the help of a powerful figure who had introduced her to journalism: Pierre Lazareff." The Lazareffs had reigned for many years over Paris," wrote Giroud herself, "and they introduced me to a certain Parisian society which was then brilliant and stimulating." The all-powerful owner of *Paris-Soir*, who was also the owner of *France-Soir* and *France-Dimanche*, was clearly a very influential man: ""The Lazareffs were at home at the Elysée[235], said Daisy de Galard[236]."

In her book *Private Lessons*, Françoise Giroud recounted an interesting detail of the life of this journalistic dynasty: "The Lazareffs—after the intermission of the war—had not yet established their supremacy. They never really settled anywhere. Wherever they lived, in Villennes, in Louveciennes, receiving prime ministers and first swords of all ranks, one had the feeling that after breakfast the headwaiter would dismantle the set, or that an usher would turn up for the embargo. All around him everything seemed precarious[237]." Of "Russian Jewish" origin, the Lazareffs, who had fled to New York before the war, still had those reflexes so deeply rooted in the consciousness of the chosen people.

Bernard Lazare left some very explicit lines on the inordinate pride of some of his fellows: "An energetic, dynamic and infinitely proud people, who considered themselves superior to other nations, the Jewish people wanted to be a power. They instinctively had a taste for domination because, by virtue of their origins, their religion[238] and the character of a chosen race which they had always attributed to themselves, they believed themselves to be above all others. To exercise this kind of authority, the Jews could not choose the means. Gold gave

---

[235]Elysée Palace: The official residence of the President of the French Republic.

[236]Christine Ockrent, *Françoise Giroud, une ambition française*, Fayard, Paris, 2003, p. 53, 54, 63-79.

[237]Françoise Giroud, *Leçons particulières*, Fayard, 1990, p. 140. See the film *Une étrange Affaire (*1981).

[238]On the supremacy of the Jewish nation the reader may consult the Holy Scriptures: *Genesis, 27: 29; Exodus, 19: 5, 6; Deuteronomy, 7: 6; Deuteronomy, 14: 2; Deuteronomy, 28: 1, 10; Isaiah, 40: 15; Isaiah, 42: 1–6; Isaiah, 60: 11, 12, 16; Isaiah, 61: 5, 6, 9; Psalms, 22: 27–28; Haggai, 2: 7-8; Micah, 5: 8; Jeremiah, 3: 17; Jeremiah, 10: 25; Zephaniah, 3: 19–20;* etc, etc, etc, etc.All versions at www.Bibliatodo.com. (NdT).

them the power that all political and religious laws denied them; this was the only power they could hope for. Holders of gold, they became masters of their masters, and dominated them[239]."

Jewish solidarity

It is well known and well known that Jews demonstrate among themselves a highly developed sense of solidarity. This concept, as we have already seen, is called *Ahavat Israel*, i.e." the love of the Jewish people". Although Françoise Giroud may have benefited from this tribal solidarity, hers is not an isolated case. The journalist Christine Ockrent gave us another example of this solidarity in media recruitment:

"Jean-Jacques, on the advice of his father, refused to join *Les Echos*, where sisters, cousins and partners already worked for reasons of profitability and clan spirit[240]." And when he created his own newspaper, Jean-Jacques Servan-Schreiber acted in the same way: "At the newspaper, the Servan-Schreiber family is everywhere: the mother, the wife, the brother-in-law, and also the cousin Marie-Claire who is in charge of advertising, who will soon live with Pierre Mendès France[241]." One day, Florence Malraux, André's daughter and friend of Madeleine Chapsal, Jean-Jacques Servan-Schreiber's wife, received a phone call from JJSS: "Come and serve France, your place is with us[242]! "At the age of 23, she became Françoise's assistant, with whom she shared an office. This is a good example of what Jewish solidarity can be.

Simon Nora, a tax inspector and secretary general of the National Accounts Commission, "was one of the many young people in the administration whose imagination Mendès France had managed to capture. A friend of Jean-Jacques, he had co-opted for *L'Express* many of his colleagues who were eager to put their knowledge at the service of our company—in other words, at the service of Mendès France", wrote Giroud.

"For years, I have seen Pierre Mendès France several times a week… I have worked with him around *L'Express*, I have experienced

---

239Bernard Lazare, *Anti-Semitism, its history and causes, (1894)*. Editions La Bastille, digital ed. 2011, p. 50.

240Christine Ockrent, *Françoise Giroud, une ambition française*, Fayard, Paris, 2003, p. 88, 89.

241Prime Minister during the 4th French Republic.

242Christine Ockrent, *Françoise Giroud, une ambition française*, Fayard, Paris, 2003, p. 118-120, 113.

with him all sorts of vicissitudes[243]."

In this very exclusive club, we obviously meet Elie Wiesel: "Mendès France? I ended up meeting him in New York at a reception at the Weizmann Institute[244]." We can see perfectly well that Franz Kafka was right when he reminded his peers of their ethnocentrism and lack of openness to the world of the Goyim.

But Jewish solidarity had a much broader purpose than mere professional cronyism, for we know that the weekly *L'Express* had been founded "to bring Mendès France to power", as Françoise Giroud wrote. As for the "service of France", it should be made clear: for *L'Express,* this consisted above all in denouncing the actions of the French army during the Algerian war.

Seen from the outside, this solidarity is particularly visible in the world of art, entertainment and culture, where many Jews occupy influential positions. One need only open the cultural pages of any newspaper, regardless of its democratic leanings, to see that the articles praising such and such a modern painter, flattering such and such a young writer, praising such and such a young actress or film director, are often written by Jews who support their fellow Jews. The examples are legion, and the reader will be able to verify for himself this evidence that Jewish artists and intellectuals benefit from a media sounding board to which not everyone has access. This favouritism could at best be justified if the beneficiaries were indeed more qualified than others and if their works had the merit of always being superior. We do not deny here that in music, in particular, composers and performers of Jewish origin sometimes prove to be very talented. But in painting, sculpture, literature and philosophy, it seems quite clear to us that Jewish authors and artists benefit too much from the systematic and hasty support of their peers, and this discrimination probably penalises the most talented French Goyim, who are condemned to remain in the shadows.

For example, we read in the newspapers that Franz Kafka is "the greatest German-language novelist of all time" or that Vasili Grossman's novel *Life and Fate* is the "*War and Peace* of the 20th century". At the time of this study, while collecting information, we learned by chance that the 2005 Nobel Prize for Literature had been awarded to the "English" playwright Harold Pinter, thus succeeding the "Austrian" Elfriede Jelineck[245]. The prize thus rewarded "one of the great names of contemporary English theatre". Harold Pinter seemed

[243]Françoise Giroud, *Leçons particulières,* Fayard, 1990, p. 187-189, 165

[244]Elie Wiesel, *Mémoires, tome I,* Seuil, 1994, p. 325.

[245]Hervé Ryssen, *Planetary Hopes,* (2022).

modest, however, after this triumph: "I don't know why they gave me this prize," confessed the 75-year-old playwright. The Swedish Academy, for its part, explained that it wanted to recognise the one who "in his dramas, discovers the abyss beneath the verbiage and forces a passage into the closed rooms of oppression." This single sentence is enlightening enough to understand the jury's motivations. Harold Pinter is indeed the son of a Jewish carver born in 1930 in East London:

"Exposed from an early age to anti-Semitism, he will also find himself deeply ... [blah blah blah] ... [blah blah blah]... But Harold Pinter has also written for film and television. He is the collaborator of director Joseph Losey, for whom he wrote the screenplay for *The Servant* (1963). Since the 1970s, he has taken a stand for human rights, criticising Margaret Thatcher's liberalism and US policy in Latin America. At the end of the 1980s, his work became increasingly committed to this struggle...". Well, as we can see, there is no point in going any further: we are dealing with a "committed" author, and that is clearly what is important to receive the Nobel Prize and the cheque that goes with it. The script of *The Servant*, written by Pinter, is very revealing of the cosmopolitan mentality: a young English aristocrat, presumptuous and sufficient, hires a servant for his service. The former will gradually sink into alcoholism and ruin, while the latter, very dignified, will increasingly dominate his master. This systematic tendency to reverse values and to dominate is very symptomatic of the Hebraic mentality, as we shall see below.

Here is another example of Jewish solidarity chosen among thousands: The weekly *Le Point* of 13 October 2005 published in its cultural pages an article on another playwright, Yasmina Reza:

"Yasmina Reza is the queen of contemporary theatre. Success befell her on the evening of 28 October 1994, with her play *Art*, staged by Patrick Kerbrat. A play written in a month and a half. A world tour, frenzy, packed houses, applause. From Tokyo to New York, elegant premieres, endless applause, agents in dinner jackets, good translators [sic], envious authors, and heartfelt headlines; thanks to her, French theatre shines once again. In short: the entourage and the crown of success. Moreover, she has a long silhouette like Yvonne de Galais, an Egyptian neck, an Etruscan eye, a skirt to tread the boards of Deauville, the delicate vibration of a lover's voice... Neither death nor the desolation of the heart that we sense affects her style: chaste and classy, furtive, pure, new, white, embroidered with Alençon stitch... Yasmina the loquacious ... continues Nathalie Sarraute's work". It should be noted first of all that the journalist from *Le Point* writes in rather dubious French, and that it is therefore curious that he should have a column in a weekly with a large national circulation. He can sign his article "Jacques-Pierre Amette", or whatever it is, we don't care. But as for his charming Yasmina, we do not deny her probable talent, even if the grace of her style has not been revealed to us. However, we doubt that she could have written an everlasting masterpiece in a month and a half. Although it is true that, judging by the success of a novelist like Marc Lévy, we understand that what sells best nowadays is no guarantee of quality. And in order to please the democratic crowd, one has to aim lower. Finally, we are glad that, from Nathalie Sarraute to Yasmina Reza, the Sephardim have taken over from the Ashkenazis. After all, it is only fair that everyone should have their share of the cake.

But it is not enough to write good books and plays; you have to know how to sell them. The great Elie Wiesel revealed some of the marketing methods he used for one of his publications. One day, when he met one of his old and very rich friends, a certain Kathleen, she enthusiastically offered to catapult his book to the top of the sales charts: "Excited, she called me to come to the editorial office of the *Jewish Daily Forward* (Yiddish: the *Forverts*). I was passing through New York and she invited me to meet her at the luxurious Sherry Netherlands Hotel on Fifth Avenue… If I would let her, she told me she was willing to immediately buy a thousand copies of my novel to help get it on the bestseller list[246]."

Jewish ethnic solidarity operates in many other circumstances: whether it is for the election of a minister's cabinet secretary, for the hiring of a new manager, or when it comes to the great generosity of wealthy donors to the poor in the Jewish community. But historically, this solidarity is much more 'audible' when it comes to a court case.

Of course, the Dreyfus case is well known, and it was a very famous case at the end of the 19th century, when the captain was accused of being a spy in the service of Germany. It should be remembered that the Dreyfus case followed the famous Panama scandal, in which many of the political staff of the republican regime and some important Jewish personalities had been implicated in the scandal. This new case was therefore a good opportunity to clean up its reputation at the expense of Catholics and nationalists.

A similar script would be played out again in the 1950s in the United States, with the case of the Rosenbergs. Accused of espionage on behalf of the Soviet Union, they were also supported by the

---

[246]Elie Wiesel, *Mémoires, tome I,* Seuil, 1994, p. 344.

"international media community". In his book *Anti-Semitic Hatred*, Serge Moati recalled that tragic episode in which anti-Semitism had bordered on horror:

"Julius and Ethel Rosenberg, he wrote, embodied the ideal culprits: Jews, progressives, potential double traitors. Despite an international campaign, they were convicted without evidence in 1951 and electrocuted in 1953. Strongly suspected by the ultraconservatives of being Bolshevik agents in America, the Jews were accused in Europe by Stalin and his supporters of being agents of international capitalism[247]." Once again, innocent and undefended Jews were unjustly condemned[248].

However, we are forced to recognise that "accusations" of espionage against Jews appear regularly in history. Jacques Attali recalled that these "accusations" were not new and recent: "In 1744, Emperor Maria Theresa decided to expel the Jews from Bohemia on the accusation of spying for the benefit of the Prussians." Fortunately, the unfortunates also benefited from the decisive support of their community: "Wolf Wertheimer then alerted the court providers and community leaders in Rome, Bordeaux, Bayonne, Frankfurt, Amsterdam, London and Venice. The community in Rome intervened with the Pope; those in Bordeaux and Bayonne organised collections for the expellees. At the request of the Jews around them, the King of England and the States General of the Netherlands intervened with Maria Theresa, who finally annulled the expulsion decree in exchange for the payment of 240,000 guilders for Wolf Wertheimer and his friends[249]."

In France, we also remember the case of Pierre Goldman, which caused quite a stir in the 1970s. This former communist militant, who had become a gangster, was accused of several armed robberies and the murder of two pharmacists in Paris at the end of 1969. Goldman confessed to three robberies committed with his Guadeloupean friends, but always denied the double murder of the chemist's shop on Boulevard Richard-Lenoir, despite the fact that several witnesses had reliably identified him.

His power of conviction was such that he managed to win the support not only of the Jewish community, but also of the show business

[247]Serge Moati, *La Haine antisémite*, Flammarion, 1991, p. 149.

[248]US and Soviet archives confirmed his guilt.

[249]Jacques Attali, *Los Judíos, el mundo y el dinero,* Fondo de cultura económica, 2005, Buenos Aires, p. 283. Wolf Wertheimer, a palace Jew and son of Samson Wertheimer, was Maria Theresa's banker around 1740.

world and political militancy. His former comrades who had been the leaders of the May '68 revolt, Alain Geismar and Alain Krivine, as well as his old friend Marc Kravetz, expressed their solidarity. In September 1974, Goldman was nevertheless sentenced to life imprisonment by the Paris Criminal Court. The sentence provoked great emotion in the courtroom. The crowd of Pierre Goldman's friends shouted and insulted the jurors. Pierre Goldman then dignifiedly uttered these words: " The absurdity of this sentence is, if I may say so, perfectly in keeping with my fate, with my fundamental fitness to be accused."

Pierre Mendès France, Joseph Kessel, Régis Debray, Yves Montand, Simone Signoret, Philippe Sollers, Eugène Ionesco and many others declared themselves "outraged" in a communiqué. But there was still hope, as Goldman was entitled to a second trial.

In the meantime, he wrote in prison his *Memoirs*, published in 1975, in which he claimed his innocence and did not hesitate to accuse the entire political and judicial system: "Let us not forget that in 1970, the police were hunting leftists and that, for them, I was the archetype of the leftist, an armed leftist, a leftist who had been in a guerrilla, a leftist who had been involved in crime... The time has come for me to say, here and now, that being innocent, a Jew and a friend of blacks, a far-left activist or a leftist, I have been subjected to racist, ideological, police procedures... That trial was obviously racist... I was a Jew. A Jew who also had no desire for integration or assimilation. Most of my friends were from the West Indies and this came out clearly in the discussions at the trial[250]."

For Goldman, his personal case illustrated once again the persecutions carried out against innocent Jews throughout the ages: "There was the solidarity of Jews, he wrote. Of Jews who considered themselves Jews and of Jews who did not consider themselves Jews. From communist Jews and conservative Jews. From Zionist, anti-Zionist and non-Zionist Jews. All, in this trial, had felt that they were Jews, and that I was there totally Jewish, for me, for the Jews, for the others... This purely Jewish solidarity moved me; I had for an instant an access of Jewish mysticism: I was a criminal, a thief, but falsely accused of murder, unjustly condemned, I had represented for a moment the Jews before the justice of the goyim[251]."

Evidently, the book "grazed the Goncourt prize". The second trial

---

[250]Pierre Goldman, *Souvenirs obscurs d'un Juif polonais né en France,* Points Seuil, 1975, p. 227.

[251]Pierre Goldman, *Souvenirs obscurs d'un Juif polonais né en France,* Points Seuil, 1975, p. 268, 278.

took place in Amiens in May 1976. A few days earlier, François Mitterrand had declared that he "did not believe" in Pierre Goldman's guilt. The actress Simone Signoret even came to support him at the Amiens hearing. The verdict finally came down: Pierre Goldman was found not guilty of the double murder at the pharmacy, but was sentenced to 12 years in prison for the three robberies. It was a great victory "for justice and democracy". Goldman was finally released shortly afterwards, and in 1977 he published a novel entitled *L'ordinaire mésaventure d'Archibald Rapoport (The Ordinary Mischief of Archibald Rapoport)*, in which he acknowledged in a veiled way that he was indeed guilty of the murders of which he had been accused and finally acquitted.

The hero of the novel was an outcast Jew, a mad killer, who killed policemen and magistrates. Arnold Mandel gave a brief introduction to the novel in the Jewish monthly magazine *L'Arche* in November 1977, in which he condemned in half-words the behaviour of Goldman, who was obviously identified with his novel hero and "the inadmissible slogan" that his character seemed to have made his own: "*Tov chebagoyim harog*: the best of the goyim, kill him." Next to each of his victims, Archibald placed an "*olisbos*", a kind of factitious phallus. We then learned that Archibald did not have Christianity in his heart either: "Archibald looked at his cock. It had the horrible shape of a crucifix which he wrenched furiously without any pain."

All Goldman's friends could legitimately feel cheated by his semi-confessions. Everyone had been fooled. This poise of Goldman's is another rather characteristic trait. Thirty-five years later, two books were published about the character Pierre Goldman in which it was revealed that the main alibi witness, Joel Cautric, admitted to having lied. But Pierre Goldman did not live long after his release. He was shot dead in the street in September 1979 by two men who had claimed responsibility for his act thus: "The justice of power having once again demonstrated its weaknesses and its laxity, we did what our duty demanded." For the philosopher André Glucksmann, this was necessarily an "anti-Semitic crime", as he wrote in the progressive daily *Libération* on 27 September 1979: "Pierre Goldman made a Jew out of every man". Evidently.

This is what the French Academy member Maurice Rheims wrote about Jewish solidarity: "Since my childhood, being a Jew has involved more concerns than certainties. When by chance, while reading the *Temps*, my father heard about some ugly affair or some evil crime involving a Herzog, a Behr, a Levy, and when the Dreyfus case was on our table, I remember that we all felt responsible[252]."

The neo-Kantian philosopher Hermann Cohen (1842–1916) lashed out at his fellow human beings in these terms: "Look in the mirror! That is the first step to self-criticism. That you are terribly like one another, and that the misconduct of one is therefore imputed to all of you, there is nothing to be done about it[253]…"

This is exactly what was described at the beginning of the 20th century by the famous Austrian Jew Otto Weininger, who, in analysing the very particular mentality of his fellow Jews, saw in the "solidarity" of the Jews only the manifestation of a clear communal interest:

"Anti-Semitism falsely assumes that there is a conscious agreement among Jews, and speaks of "Jewish solidarity". This is an easily understood confusion. When an accusation is made against any stranger belonging to Judaism, all Jews feel inwardly disposed in his favour, and wish, hope and seek to prove his innocence. But let it not be thought that the subject in question interests them because he is a Jewish individual, that his individual fate, because of that status, awakens in them greater pity than if he were an unjustly persecuted Aryan. No, this is not the cause. The aforementioned phenomena of involuntary partiality are due purely to the threat that might hang over Judaism, to the fear that a harmful shadow might fall over the Jews as a whole, or, to put it better, over everything connected with them, over the idea of Judaism[254]."

We understand better why the "international media community" systematically mobilises in its entirety to defend a fellow human being when he or she is caught in the meshes of the justice of the goyim.

Ethnocentrism

Jewish solidarity is also manifested by the pride they show in the work done over time by previous generations. Jewish intellectuals trumpet the historical successes of their fellow Jews in culture and science, and do not hesitate to marvel at their genius even in the most

---

[252]Maurice Rheims, *Une Mémoire vagabonde*, Gallimard, 1997, p. 81.

[253]Léon Poliakov, *Histoire des crises d'identités juives*, Austral 1994, p. 123.

[254]Otto Weininger, *Sex and Character*, Ediciones 62 s|a Barcelona, 1985, p.306." This leitmotiv always returns: "All Jews are responsible for each other". If anyone in the community fails in his duties or "jumps the fence", he then becomes a "sinner in Israel". His misconduct threatens to fall on everyone." (Mark Zborowski, *Olam*, 1952, Plon, 1992, p. 214)." The offence done against one affects others: "What happens to Israel affects me too." (*Olam*, p. 413).

dubious cases. This solidarity here takes the form of exacerbated ethnocentrism.

In the Austro-Hungarian Empire of the early 20th century, and especially in Vienna, cultural life was largely influenced by a bustling Jewish intellectual elite. In 1867, Emperor Franz-Josef, who regarded them as the most loyal subjects of his Empire, granted them perfect equality with other nationalities. Tens of thousands of Jews flocked to the capital to enrich themselves or to facilitate the studies and careers of their children. Vienna was home to writers Stefan Zweig, Joseph Roth, Karl Kraus, but also to musicians such as Arnold Schoenberg and Gustav Mahler, not forgetting, of course, the famous Sigmund Freud. Stefan Zweig and Joseph Roth left rather colourful testimonies about how these celebrities came to support each other and flatter the members of the brotherhood[255].

Guy Konopnicki embarked on the same apologetic exercise, but to praise the following generation, in the interwar Berlin of the Weimar Republic. He extolled that brilliant era with great pride and satisfaction: "The Berlin of Döblin, of Berg, of Hindemith, of Piscator, of Fritz Lang, the Berlin that was home to perhaps the most extraordinary cultural flowering of all time." In the publicist's mind, of course, this cultural flowering was due to the wonderful Jews: "Painting, music, film and literature were rarely as rich and as diverse as in Berlin during the Weimar Republic. And, as in America, or as in Paris in its heyday, there was in Berlin a whole fauna of international artists."

But Konopnicki also readily acknowledged that Berlin was not the only cultural centre of the time, as communist-held Moscow was then rivalling the German capital.

Let us listen to him waxing ecstatic about the magnificent works of his fellow Soviets: "The years of the Revolution were marked, like those of the Weimar Republic, by an extraordinary flowering of literary and artistic creation. Malevitch, Chagall, Suprematism, Futurism, Tinianov, Alexander Bloc, Maiakovski, Mandelstam, Meyerhold and many others... What an era[256]! "

This was as much as to say that without the Jews, German and Russian cultures were reduced to almost nothing. In the same way, we will understand that Konopnicki's devotion to American culture was the expression of the same communitarian tendency.

It was the same ethnocentric pride that Alfred Grosser expressed in 1989 in his book *Crime and Memory*: "The contribution of "German

---

[255]Hervé Ryssen, *Planetary Hopes*, (2022).

[256]Guy Konopnicki, *La Place de la nation,* Olivier Orban, 1983, p. 179, 184, 185.

citizens of the Israelite faith" to the cultural, scientific, medical and legal life of Weimar Germany is all the more extensive and visible that the first German republic has, alongside its many weaknesses, constituted a kind of short golden age of a culture and civilisation[257]." Here, too, we see how Jewish artists and intellectuals, and they alone, seem to bring about civilisation.

Marek Halter expressed himself in a similar way about these German and Austrian Jews fleeing Nazism. They are "the European elite": "In Marseilles, which at the time had some 15,000 Jewish inhabitants, those arriving by the thousands ended up crowded into small, filthy hotels. Among them, the European elite: Marc Chagall, Max Ernst, the children of Thomas Mann, Anna Mahler, Franz Werfel, Arthur Koestler, Hannah Arendt, Anna Seghers, Lion Feuchtwanger… A whole forsaken civilisation[258]."

This idea was also expressed by Samuel Pisar when he wrote: "The experience of the Third Reich shows us that the root of its failure was not allowing men like Albert Einstein, Thomas Mann or Willy Brandt to breathe within its borders[259]." We would point out, however, that the failure of the Third Reich was perhaps due more to the hundreds of thousands of tons of incendiary bombs that were dropped on its cities.

Generally speaking, Jews seem to regard themselves as superior to other nations, and indeed this inordinate pride appears in numerous books. In 1929, for example, Pierre Paraf already expressed this pride: "He maintained that Christianity owed the best of itself to the Jewish people, he recalled that without our holy Scriptures there would have been no Gospels, and that the Gospels, moreover, were sometimes only a pale reflection of them[260]." This was also the teaching of the philosopher Jacob Talmon, who considered the Jews to be "bearers of a superior and older civilisation[261]."

Sigmund Freud himself expounded this idea. He recognised that the people of Israel, "developed peculiar characteristics and at the same time aroused the cordial antipathy of all other peoples." For him, the "characteristic trait of the Jews which dominates their relations with other peoples" was first of all their inordinate pride. And so he described it:

"There is no doubt that the Jews have a particularly exalted opinion

---

[257] Alfred Grosser, *Le Crime et la mémoire*, Flammarion, 1989, p. 68.

[258] Marek Halter, *La force du Bien*, Robert Laffont, 1995, p. 160.

[259] Samuel Pisar, *La Sangre de la esperanza*, Editorial Planeta, 1990, Barcelona, p. 186.

[260] Pierre Paraf, *Quand Israël aima*, 1929, Les belles lettres, 2000, p. 47.

[261] J.-L. Talmon, *Destin d'Israël*, 1965, Calmann-Lévy, 1967, p. 14.

of themselves, that they consider themselves more noble, lofty and superior to others, from whom they also differ in many of their customs." Moreover, thanks to Freud, we learn that the haughtiness of the Jewish people goes back to very ancient times, since they already had the same faults in antiquity: "We know the reasons for this attitude and we know what their most secret treasure is. The Jews really consider themselves to be God's chosen people, they believe themselves to be particularly close to God, and this belief gives them their pride and their confident security. According to reliable notions, they already conducted themselves in this way in Hellenistic times, so that already then the Jewish character was perfectly shaped, and the Greeks, among whom, and next to whom they lived, reacted to the Jewish peculiarity in the same way as their present-day "guests".[262]

In the aftermath of the Second World War, press director Jean Daniel noted the danger of declaring oneself "God's chosen people", which could be perceived as an unbearable arrogance by the Goyim, and noted that the great post-war Jewish thinkers felt the need to redefine this "Choice" to protect themselves from the indignant reactions of the Gentiles: "Among the things that have surprised me most is the difficulty of the most important Jews in trying to define the Choice. Think of Martin Buber, Levinas and Leibowitz. They all say: be careful, it would make no sense for us to believe that we are superior. Choice is not given, it is deserved. In short, they spent their time destroying what Choice contains."

Martin Buber, Emmanuel Levinas, Franz Rosenzweig and Gershom Scholem "have put all their energy into redefining the term Election and that of Covenant in such a way that the Jewish people cannot claim to have the exclusivity of one or the other... According to them, God conceived for the Jews a vocation that is specific only in excellence and never in difference or superiority... Everyone can choose to become a saint, that is, a Jew... I have come to the conclusion that Jews should only retain from their Election the exhortation to be the best, and from the Covenant, the obligation to make Israel a beacon of the nations[263]." Indeed, this changes everything.

We must therefore understand that the Jews are simply "indispensable" to civilisation, and that it is inconceivable, even for a moment, that any people in the world could manage without them.

---

[262]Sigmund Freud, *Moses and monotheistic religion: three essays, Collected Works*, EpubLibre, Trad. Luis López Ballesteros y de Torres, 2001, p. 4417.

[263]Jean Daniel, *La prisión judía. Meditaciones intempestivas de un testigo*, Tusquets, Barcelona, 2007, p. 184, 163, 164, 161.

Clara Malraux, the wife of General de Gaulle's famous minister, wrote of her fellow Prussians of the Enlightenment era: "Barely freed, often temporarily, from the worst obligations and humiliations, their contribution was very valuable, undoubtedly indispensable, because it was marked by that particular openness of vision which proximity to various civilisations confers[264]."

This idea of the absolute necessity of Judaism for civilisation was in turn expressed by Martin Buber, one of the great Jewish thinkers of the 20th century. In his book entitled *Judaism*, published in 1982, he wrote: "Mankind needs Judaism, and will need it until the end of time because it is the most significant embodiment, the most exemplary representation of one of the highest aspirations of the spirit[265]."

The inescapable Jacques Attali also gave his opinion on the matter. This was his conclusion: "None of the sedentary societies could have survived without nomads who transported goods, ideas, capital between them and for that they dared to take intellectual and material risks that no sedentary would have been willing to take... The Jewish people played the role of the nomad who creates wealth for the sedentary. Thus, they fulfilled their task, to "mend the world"... Nomadism is not a superiority, but merely a specificity shared with other peoples and absolutely necessary for the survival and well-being of the sedentary." The Jews "are the key to the development of the world. There is no sedentary development without these nomads. But there is also no questioning of the established order without them[266]."

Thus, "the misfortune of the Jewish people, therefore, is a misfortune for all men", Attali wrote, adding, furthermore, following his logic, the following comment: "According to a magnificent later commentary (*Sukkah 55a*), the disappearance of the Temple is also a tragedy for non-Jews, because the Hebrews prayed for them: 'They do not know what they lost'."

The Jewish people are at the centre of humanity, and it is unimaginable that life could be conceived in any other way. The other peoples of the earth cannot exist without the Jews, not even the last tribe of the Amazon[267]. Jacques Attali's very subjective point of view did not prevent him from reminding us of the well-known rules of Judaism: "Impose a very austere morality, do not tolerate arrogance or

[264]Clara Malraux, *Rahel, Ma grande sœur...*, Edition Ramsay, Paris, 1980, p. 158.
[265]Martin Buber, *Judaïsme*, Edition Verdier pour la traduction française, 1982, p. 31.
[266]Jacques Attali, *Los Judíos, el mundo y el dinero*, Fondo de cultura económica, 2005, Buenos Aires, p. 485, 486, 489.
[267]Hervé Ryssen, *Planetary Hopes, (*2022).

immorality, so as not to create jealousy or pretexts for persecution[268]." Indeed, it was high time to say it.

A fertile imagination

Elie Wiesel's international glory is largely based on the success of his accounts of his painful experience in the concentration camps. His talent as a storyteller was also quickly recognised by the writer François Mauriac, who took him under his protective wing, as he recounted in his *Memoirs*: "Without Mauriac, what would have become of me? He watched over my "career". On each of my trips to France, I went to visit him." The two men met at a worldly reception: "I saw Mauriac in 1955 during an independence celebration at the Israeli embassy... Surprised, he insisted: 'I am happy that you invited me. I have a great interest in Israel. I like to participate in your party[269]."

In his early days, however, Elie Wiesel had to work hard to earn a living. Settled in Paris, he served as a tour guide for his fellow travellers visiting France. This anecdote is an eloquent illustration of his ability to embellish the truth:

"Miriam asks me for explanations about Paris, and I am happy to give them. Effortlessly. I improvise with a poise that still embarrasses me today... At the time, I used to embellish, invent spicy details about the history of Paris that you couldn't find in any book or novel. Why? Out of tiredness. Too many Israeli visitors insist that I show them the Louvre and Concorde, Montmartre and the Russian cabarets. At first, I do my job as a guide conscientiously: I just say what I know. But then I realise that the tourists in my charge are insatiable when it comes to Parisian culture: they want to know more. More colourful stories. The façade of Notre-Dame with its Jews in pointy hats and its blind, miserable synagogue is not enough for them[270]..." All that, they say, we have learned at school. Well, that's the end of it: I'm starting to invent an anecdote for each statue, a story for each monument. Re-inventing the past of the capital for an hour, for a morning, what harm would that do to France? One day, however, the inevitable happens: a guide, unfortunately a professional one, is in the Place de la Bastille with the small French-speaking group, listening to me gawping as I describe the events of 1789; I am fit, I know the name of the officer who first opened

[268]Jacques Attali, *Los Judíos, el mundo y el dinero,* Fondo de cultura económica, 2005, Buenos Aires, p. 122, 75, 490.

[269]Elie Wiesel, *Mémoires, tome I*, Seuil, 1994, p. 338, 326.

[270]Elie Wiesel confuses it with Strasbourg Cathedral.

the prison doors; and that of the prisoner who, on his knees, begged for mercy. In the next cell, a princess was preparing for death; she wished to die, but at the sight of the officer she changes her mind, and lo and behold, shocking her friends, she cries out her love for life and the living… I could continue to adorn thus until the next revolution were it not for the wounded animal cry of a good man unknown to us… He rushes at me, ready to tear me to pieces:" How … how dare you? I who know this city, the history of every stone, how dare you lie in my presence and make history lie? "We left him rather hastily." Take no notice," consoles one of my guests of circumstance. He's an angry madman." Another corrects him: "No way, he's jealous, it's plain as day." But Miriam loves stories. And, besides, she's beautiful[271]."

This is a good example of flight forward. But for once, the author seems to admit that his aggressor's anger may have been justified, even though his fellow men were willing to support him stubbornly against such an injustice.

As a journalist, Elie Wiesel got to know many interesting people. He met an extraordinary character, a certain Joseph Givon, who was accustomed to moving in the circles of power. Elie Wiesel was impressed by this mysterious and influential personality. His interlocutor was very prompt in his telephone communications: "I'll pick you up tomorrow at twelve o'clock sharp". Without time to answer, he has already hung up on me. Call Dov? A small voice advises me to be cautious. You never know with Givon. Tomorrow could mean next week or next year."

The man was mysterious, a bit flamboyant, and tremendously manipulative: "He holds out his invalid hand to me (I never knew why he sometimes held out his right hand and sometimes his left), says goodbye and limps away."

His secret influence on politics was nevertheless very real, as the little journalist could see: "It is he, and not the President of the Council, who decided on the location of the interview. Mendès France has only to obey! I still haven't recovered from my stupor and Givon continues: "I have asked that we have breakfast together. It's better. And more intimate"… Unfortunately, he had to leave Paris. International current affairs are calling him elsewhere, and so is history. So is history. Ho Chi Minh? Giap? Krushchov? I showered him with questions that made him shrug his shoulders: "I'm sorry, but…". It's all right, I understand: restricted area, absolutely forbidden to go in there. A matter of

[271]Elie Wiesel, *Mémoires, tome I,* Seuil, 1994, p. 271, 272.

espionage, probably. Believe it or not, he didn't take me to the Mendès France house? If he knows the president of the council, he could very well frequent the big boys of this world, couldn't he? The fact is that he disappeared from Paris... From now on, our contacts will be made exclusively by mail: letters from Warsaw, Peking, Prague, or Moscow, where he will become a film producer... The *Izvestia*[272] will publish an article denouncing his smuggling activities: arrested as a trafficker, he will be sentenced to ten years in prison." I am innocent, I would confess in a pathetic letter. The truth will triumph in the end. The truth? Under Givon's pen it seems hesitant. But it would triumph all the same. Freed—"thanks to the intervention of several Western ambassadors"—he would receive an apology from the court. Fed up with the Soviet system, he returned to Prague and then reappeared in Paris ... before settling permanently in Israel. There, he died of a heart attack. The newspapers and magazines of Tel-Aviv devoted numerous articles to him, insisting on the picturesque, bizarre and manipulative side of his character... Disbelieving and fascinated, the public was entertained by the mystery surrounding him. How to distinguish truth from fantasy in him, since he could not make it all up? Sometimes I think of him with affection. Thanks to him, I almost lived some of his adventures. Real or imaginary? It doesn't matter. Adventurers don't always tell the truth: they invent it first. Besides, didn't I have breakfast with Mendès France[273]?"Intelligence agent, film producer, smuggler, international trafficker with a full agenda of contacts, Joseph Givon was apparently a man as influential as he was discreet and mysterious. Internet search engines return only five hits on his name, and they all appear to be homonyms. But on page 325 of his *memoirs*, six pages further on, Elie Wiesel wrote: "Mendès France? I ended up meeting him in New York, during a reception at the Weizmann Institute".

But other interesting and colourful characters, real or imaginary, have crossed Elie Wiesel's path, such as this Mané Katz, with whom he seemed to have certain affinities:

"Small and bright, with surprising agility for his age, he hopped as he walked and talked. He loved to tell anecdotes (true or false) about his distant resemblance to Ben Gurion. A woman would have fallen in love with him when she mistook him for the Israeli Prime Minister. A spy is said to have offered him Arab military secrets in exchange for a certificate of good conduct towards God, who, as everyone knows, lives somewhere in Jerusalem. A thief is said to have offered him a large sum

---

[272]Izvestia: the official press organ of the Soviet regime.

[273]Elie Wiesel, *Mémoires, tome I*, Seuil, 1994, p. 313-319.

of money to gain access to the Jewish state's treasury." As soon as I reveal my true identity, they turn their backs on me," he added, laughing out loud."

That Mané Katz one day offered Elie Wiesel a valuable painting, which he ingeniously refused, finding "an exit door" in the Torah, just as Yentl did: "Citing ancient sources and references that had nothing to do with anything, drawn both from the Scriptures and from my imagination, he talked fast, for an hour or two, perhaps until dawn ...: "In the case of a judge who accepts gifts, the Bible devotes all sorts of expletives to him" Did I convince him? I don't know. The real reason for my refusal is this: I was too poor to possess works of that value. And he would not have known where to put his paintings anyway. Wanderer by taste and profession, rootless, he only owned a typewriter and a suitcase. You can't keep works of art in a suitcase[274]! "

Elie Wiesel also recounted in his *memoirs* how he narrowly escaped death. In 1955, he almost fell victim to a terrible air disaster: "In order to recover and get a change of scenery, I went to Israel. I had booked a ticket on an El Al plane, but I offered it to a friend of Bea's who had come from Montreal with her two children and could not get three seats on that flight. The plane was shot down over Bulgaria. I took the sea route[275]."

The author, who gave no further details, did not seem particularly affected by this terrible tragedy. It must be said that our searches for information about this air disaster were all fruitless. Perhaps it was a small plane, a tiny plane?

Elie Wiesel had the opportunity to travel to the Soviet Union. During the communist regime, since Stalin finally excluded the "Zionist" leadership from power after the war, Jews were not free to emigrate to Israel. The "international media community" then cried out in indignation and demanded the right for Jews to leave the Soviet Union. Elie Wiesel went there to gather more information. At Moscow airport, almost as soon as he got off the plane with his two bodyguards on his back, another bizarre episode in the life of the great writer occurred:

"The Aeroflot plane arrives. Below the gangway are the last two checks: on the right, the Intourist stewardess checks my boarding pass; on the left, an officer examines my passport. The young woman signals for me to board, but the officer shouts something to someone. Suddenly, events are rushing forward. In the blink of an eye, my two Israelis

---

[274]Elie Wiesel, *Mémoires, tome I,* Seuil, 1994, p. 321, 322.
[275]Elie Wiesel, *Mémoires, tome I,* Seuil, 1994, p. 345.

emerge at my side. One of the two grabs my plane ticket, the other snatches my passport from the officer's hands; I notice how he lifts me up like a sick man, like a bundle; they run, and I run with them, whistles, hoarse orders and shoves. I don't know how we managed to get through all the gates, all the barriers, we jumped into the embassy vehicle and rolled into the open. Why didn't the police stop us? I have no idea[276]. I will stay three days and three nights at the embassy before I get the green light. How did David manage it? He never told me, although, to tell the truth, I didn't ask him, even though the journalist in me would have liked to know. The important thing was to get out of Moscow. To regain my freedom. I return to the airport, always accompanied by my two Israeli bodyguards, and this time everything happens as if I were an ordinary tourist[277]."

In any case, there is no doubt that luck always smiled on Elie Wiesel. We have already spoken in *Planetary Hopes* about the extraordinary episode that happened to him during the Gulf War in 1991. The great writer travelled to Israel to support his community during the difficult times when Iraq, ravaged by US bombing raids, was launching its old Scud missiles on the Hebrew state with a vengeance:

"My cousin Eli Hollender is glad I came: "Come home, he says. Come to dinner. We'll wait for the Scuds together. Strange invitation, curious idea… I accept his invitation and we agree to meet. At the last minute I cancel. An unforeseen impediment. The same evening, we listen to the radio, each in turn, to the information about the missile attack that has just begun… A month later, I receive a letter from Eli in which he thanks God for my hindrance: "If you had come, we would have stayed at home instead of spending the night at our children's. Who knows what would have happened to us? And who knows what would have happened to us. A Scud fell on our house and destroyed it completely. It's a miracle you didn't come[278]."

Elie Wiesel is undoubtedly a survivor of the Gulf War. His adventure is all the more extraordinary when, by his own admission, "the Scuds made no casualties. The man who died in Bnei Brak? Cardiac arrest. Elsewhere, a woman locked herself in a cupboard and prayed psalms. The room collapsed, but the cupboard remained intact." It is just as they tell you: Israel is the land of miracles!

In the old days in the shtetls, in those Jewish villages in Central Europe at the beginning of the 20th century, Jews lived a secluded life,

---

[276]Neither do we!

[277]Elie Wiesel, *Mémoires, tome I,* Seuil, 1994, p. 495, 496.

[278]Elie Wiesel, *Mémoires, tome II,* Éditions du Seuil, 1996, p. 148.

cut off from the rest of the population. The colourful characters that made the charm and uniqueness of Jewish life were depicted by novelists and film-makers. The rabbi was evidently the central character in these small communities. For Hasidic Jews, the spiritual leader was called the *tzaddik*. This holy man sometimes had supernatural powers. Indeed, we regularly see "miracle-working rabbis" in Yiddish literature.

The matchmaker (the *shadkhn*, who could also be a matchmaker), was another important character in the shtetl. He brought the young people's parents into contact with each other, as they were completely subject to the authority of the father of the family in choosing a partner. In Jewison's beautiful film, *Fiddler on the Roof, however,* we see how these traditions were beginning to be chipped away at in the early 20th century, and how young women claimed the right to freely choose their husbands. There was also the itinerant book seller who responded to the demand of a cultured and educated population: "Illustrated books for women, holy books for men". On Friday evening, before sundown, the *shames*—the synagogue servant—could be heard roaming the streets and shouting, "Jews, to the ritual bath! "

The *schlemiel* is undoubtedly one of the two most famous characters in Yiddish human comedy. He is a simpleton, a clumsy misfit. We also see the *schlimazl*. He is the other celebrity of the shtetl: he is a loser, a wretched man on whom bad luck has taken its toll. When the *schlemiel*'s soup spills (which is inevitable), it always lands in the *schlimazl*'s trousers.

In his book *Errant Jews*, published in 1927, Joseph Roth informed us about the existence of another interesting and picturesque character in those Central European shtetls where part of the Jewish population was concentrated: the *batlen*.

"The strangest office of all is held by the East-Jewish *batlen*, a jester, a jester, a jester, a philosopher, a storyteller. In every small town there lives at least one *batlen*, who amuses the guests at weddings and christenings, sleeps in the oratory, makes up stories, listens to men quarrelling, and wracks his brains over useless things. Nobody takes him seriously. And yet he is the most serious of men. He might as well have been a dealer in feathers and coral, like the rich man who invites him to the wedding so that the others can have a laugh at his expense, but he is not. He finds it hard to run a business… Sometimes he wanders from village to village, from town to town. He does not starve, but he lives always on the brink of hunger… His stories would probably cause a sensation in Europe if they appeared in print[279]."

The profession has become more prestigious since the departure of the shtetl. The "*batlen*" no longer lives in squalor and destitution. He no longer travels the muddy roads from village to village, but frequents airports assiduously, hopping from continent to continent to preach the good word and tell extraordinary stories. In volume II of his *Memoirs*, Elie Wiesel wrote: "For thirty years I have travelled the continents to the point of exhaustion: by dint of speaking at conferences I have reached the point where I cannot bear the sound of my voice... I saw myself travelling the Earth, going from town to town, from country to country, like the madman in Rabbi Nahman's tales, reminding men of what they are capable of, for good and for evil, and drawing their eyes upon the innumerable ghosts crowded around us[280]."

A surprising plasticity

The Jews adopt the habits and customs, sometimes even the religion, of the countries where they settle with remarkable mimicry, but always retaining their Jewish individuality. Within a few years, they speak the local language of the natives and blend into the population. But this assimilation, as we have seen, is often only apparent. For centuries, the Jewish people have learned to live in secret; and from an early age, the young Jew learns to respect the secrets of Israel and to convince anyone who will listen that Jews are "men like other men", and that they only want to integrate.

Jacques Le Rider argued that in the Austrian Empire at the beginning of the 20th century, Viennese Jews were de-Judaised, and that in a way it was the anti-Semitism of the environment that forced them to return to their community of origin: they were "assimilated into German culture, and most would have considered their Jewishness as a pious family memory, as a strictly private matter, if a society in crisis had not forced them to define themselves[281]." Thus we can deduce that

---

[279]Joseph Roth, *Judíos errantes,* Acantilado 164, Barcelona, 2008 p. 63, 64. Mark Zborowski, in *Olam,* gave the same description of the character, but with the name "*badkhn*" ("kh" is pronounced like the Spanish j, it would be *badjn* instead of *batlen*): "The *badkhn* is at once actor, poet, composer, singer and reporter. But this is only true of a great *badkhn,* for sometimes they have to be content with a local person who amuses them for the occasion. But the high-flying jester enjoys real fame and is much in demand, so that he is constantly travelling from one end of the country to the other." (Mark Zborowski, *Olam,* Plon, 1992, p. 266).

[280]Elie Wiesel, *Mémoires, tome II,* Éditions du Seuil, 1996, p. 214, 530.

[281]Jacques Le Rider, *Arthur Schnitzler,* Éd. Belin, 2003, p. 201

anti-Semitism can be useful for the leaders of Jewish communities who feared, above all, intermarriage and complete assimilation." Thus, we can deduce that anti-Semitism can be useful for the heads of Jewish communities who fear intermarriage and complete assimilation above all.

The writer Joseph Roth observed the situation of the Jews in the interwar Weimar Republic and reported the same thing: "The German Jews, despite all kinds of threatening anti-Semitic symptoms, felt themselves to be pure Germans; or at best, on the great festivals, Jewish Germans." For him, the assimilation of the Jews into the European world was undoubtedly successful: "The Jews are themselves Europeans. The Jewish governor of Palestine is undoubtedly an Englishman. And probably more English than Jewish[282]."

Recently, in the daily *Actualité juive*, in December 2005, we were able to read statements along the same lines, but with the added impudence of certain Jewish intellectuals who are inclined to supplant the autochthonous. This "*chutzpah*" allowed Albert Siboni to state the following: Jews with "their dispersion, their diversity and their numerous contacts, have been, in a way, the first Europeans."

But this is once again a discourse reserved for export, for otherwise, everything that can be read makes it clear that Jewish intellectuals have nothing in common with the Goyim, be they European or Muslim.

Alain Minc's view on this was rather curious and reflected the "squatter" mentality of moving into the landlord's house and claiming the place for oneself. Let us listen to this liberal intellectual talk about the deep, traditional, wasp (*White Anglo Saxon Protestant*) United States that has been removed from power and left to a gang of unscrupulous careerists: "In the United States of the 1980s, the Wasps have lost their monopoly on power. President Carter's Georgians, President Reagan's Californians: close associates who would have seemed too exotic for the Morgenthau and Hopkins of the 1940s. With their exoticism they have brought a different world view. Was Kissinger the last of Europe's sons in charge of American policy?"For Alain Minc, the real "wasp" Americans of European origin are the Morgenthau, Hopkins and Kissinger, while the newcomers, the "Georgians" and "Californians" who represent the new power-hungry conquerors, are still somewhat foreigners in this deep America. The real wasps, according to Minc, are the Jews. This is exactly the *chutzpah*

[282]Joseph Roth, *Judíos errantes*, Acantilado 164, Barcelona, 2008, p. 9, 38

characteristic of the Hebraic mentality, i.e. that extraordinary chutzpah that allows them to say anything to keep hammering their propaganda. This mentality consists of inverting all established truths and defending the exact opposite views.

Alain Minc pretended to ask himself: "Where are the Harvard or MIT professors of European culture still to be found in the most influential circles? What residual positions do the last Wasp[283] manage to occupy?" By way of reply, we could suggest to Alain Minc: "Whatever the "Californians" want to leave them! "For it is common knowledge that the "Californians", so present in George Bush's entourage, plan to dominate the world and, as the novelist Norman Mailer so aptly put it, they intend to make "a takeover bid for the planet[284]". Who will protect us from the voracity of the "Californians"?

Jews therefore have special dispositions to adapt and assimilate to the peoples where they have chosen to settle. However, it is a matter of measuring the depth of assimilation of those who continue to claim Judaism.

In 1952, Elie Wiesel was then a promising young journalist, commissioned by the Israeli daily *Yedioth Ahronoth to* cover the first official negotiations between West Germany and Israel in the Netherlands:

"Only four journalists have been accredited by the two delegations: Sam Jaffe for the Jewish Telegraphic Agency; Marc Rosen, editor of the official organ of the Jewish community in Düsseldorf; Alfred Wolfmann, representative of Berlin radio, and myself, the only correspondent for an Israeli newspaper." Elie Wiesel instinctively experienced a strong distrust of the German journalist and refused to have any kind of relationship with him:

"Relations between Wolfmann and me are non-existent. You don't fraternise with an officer who swore allegiance to Hitler. However, I sometimes watch him out of the corner of my eye: he is not lacking in intelligence or finesse. Moreover, he knows his trade inside out. His analyses are insightful, often fair… Judged satisfactory by both sides, the conference ends and our little group separates. Alfred holds out his hand to me, but I pull away. He pouts: "I thought the war was over between our two peoples". I don't deign to answer him."

The next day at his hotel, Elie Wiesel received an unexpected visitor: "A knock on the door wakes me up early in the morning. Who is it? A man's voice answers, but I don't recognise it. I open the door:

---

[283]Alain Minc, *La Grande illusion*, Grasset, 1989, p. 25.

[284]Hervé Ryssen, *Planetary Hopes*, (2022).

it's Alfred Wolfmann: "But what do you ... what do you want? Annoyed, I repeat my question. He gestures to come in, but I forbid him to enter: "Go away. I don't want to see you. Not in my room, not anywhere." He smiles, and his haughty smile drives me out of my mind. He shrugs and leaves, scornful." A few weeks later, someone rings the doorbell of my Parisian flat: "He's at it again, and again he wants to come in. I'm about to throw him out when he starts talking to me ... in Hebrew. Stupefied, I fall from the clouds...". I lied to you. I was never a Wehrmacht officer. I am a Jew..." I feel like grabbing him and shaking him: "Are you making fun of me? I am a Jew, he repeats." A Jew has the right to lie, doesn't he? Understand me, in Palestine they make fun of me because I was a "*Yékké*", that is to say a German Jew... They took me for a well-educated idiot, an educated imbecile who can be easily fooled... I wanted to show you that I could fool you as long as I wanted to."

In short, the four journalists selected to cover the negotiations between Israel and Germany were Jewish. But in the end it doesn't matter, they were true professionals doing their jobs honestly.

For all his "finesse" and "intelligence", Alfred Wolfmann succumbed to the after-effects of the painful experience of the Holocaust. Like many of his peers, he plunged into a rather severe depression that brought him to a fateful end: "By dint of fighting the Nazi resurgence in his country," explained Elie Wiesel, "he began to fear it until he fell ill. Paranoid, he felt it necessary to be constantly armed. He saw Nazis everywhere. In the street, in front of his house. We phoned each other frequently. I tried to calm him down, to cheer him up... The next day, he shot himself in the head[285]."

Alfred Wolfmann had been hiding his true identity for years, and finally he could no longer endure this double life. It is indeed useful not to always reveal one's true nature if one wants to live and prosper in the midst of potentially hostile people. But it must be tiresome and exhausting at times, and it must be admitted that suicides are quite frequent among Elie Wiesel's acquaintances.

Here is another anecdote from the *Memoirs* of the great man, which shows how the children of Israel know how to change their appearance in order to blend into the masses. The journalist Elie Wiesel was now due to embark from Marseilles for Brazil to report on the unacceptable actions of the Catholic Church:

"The Catholic Church is reportedly engaged in suspicious

---

[285]Elie Wiesel, *Mémoires, tome I,* Seuil, 1994, p. 264-269.

missionary activity in Israel, especially with Jews recently arrived from Eastern Europe. They are poor, disillusioned, and the emissaries from Rome offer them a visa to Brazil, the price of the trip and two hundred dollars on condition that they convert to Catholicism." Come and see", Dov suggests to me. I agree. For a good story, a real reporter would go to the ends of unexplored planets. Arriving in Sao Paolo, "I turn to a group of passengers and learn with astonishment that some thirty or forty Israeli emigrants have made the crossing in third or fourth class… I approach them and find them dismayed, angry and desperate: they are forbidden to disembark…" We are sorry," reply the officials, "your visas have been cancelled. We are only obeying orders."

Elie Wiesel then preached to those renegades: "But what an idea, what an idea to abandon not only the land but also the people of Israel for a little money, a visa and a passage on a ship. Are you so desperate and unhappy? How is it possible that Jews like you, with your past, have been able to accept to convert? Your ancestors chose death by sword or fire rather than renounce the faith of their people, of our people, and you have consented for a trip to Brazil? "They protest: "Hey, watch out! Don't call us renegades! We have not renounced our faith! The God of Israel is still our God." But didn't you pledge to convert?" Pledged? Who's talking about pledging? We have pledged, yes, we have pledged, so what? You can't pledge anymore?"… "We are not traitors of our people… We are good Jews[286]".

This is another amusing anecdote. In 1957, Elie Wiesel was travelling around the United States with two friends. They decide to visit an Indian reservation in Arizona:

"The man who greets us under his tent decorated with feathers and other tribal insignia could work in feature films. His stride is slow and dignified. He is tall, straight, impassive, majestic. Wrinkled, angular face; bushy eyebrows, measured gestures. He explains to us the Indian

---

[286]Elie Wiesel, *Mémoires, tome I,* Seuil, 1994, p. 300-304." Jews may swear falsely by using double-meaning phrases, or any subterfuge." (Talmud, *Schabbouth Hag., 6d*). Moreover, on the eve of Yom Kippur, the feast of atonement for sins, the most solemn of Jewish holidays, the religious celebration begins with the recitation of *Kol Nidré*: "All pledges, restrictions, oaths, oaths, excommunications, renunciations, and any synonyms, by which we have pledged, sworn, or by which we have excommunicated or restricted ourselves; from the present Yom Kippurim until the following Yom Kippurim, which is for our benefit, (as to all of them), we repudiate them. They are all undone, abandoned, cancelled, annulled and invalidated, of no force and effect. Our promises are no longer promises, and our prohibitions are no longer prohibitions, and our oaths are no longer oaths." The content of the *Kol Nidré* prayer appears in the Talmud in the Book of *Nedarim 23 a-23b*. Vows and promises are not valid, as long as one remembers that at the time of pronouncing them.

conception of life and death, and we listen attentively to his every word. Respectful, he inspires respect. At the end, he asks us to sign his golden book. Tourist imperative. Dov gives me the scoop. I don't know why, but I sign in Hebrew. The Indian honours me with a vigorous nod: "*Sholem Alei'hem*" (Yiddish: good morning or peace be upon you). Despite not having touched them, Dov and Lea almost collapse. First with astonishment, then with laughter. Our guest turned out to be Jewish. Originally from Galicia and a survivor of the concentration camps, he emigrated to Mexico. But business did not go well for him, so he decided to make a living by becoming an Indian. Indian by day and Jew by night[287]."

In a book about Jewish communist activists in Central and Eastern Europe, *The Revolutionary Yiddishland*, we can note a passage that is very similar to the above anecdote: "A Galitzian Jew, member of the communist party, Shlomo Strauss is mobilised in 1939 in the Polish army. Wounded during the German invasion, he was taken prisoner and interned in a camp. When he learns that the prisoners are to be divided according to national origin, he decides to forge a new identity for himself: from now on he will be called Timofei Marko, the natural son of a Ukrainian washerwoman. He grows a long Cossack moustache[288]."

Let's cross the ocean again to look at the world of those terrible American gangsters of the 1920s and that mafia that was not only Sicilian. Police repression began to seriously shake their positions with the nomination of an upright and "incorruptible" judge: Tom Dewey. It was he who conducted the first major trial against the Mafia in 1933 and brought down Waxey Gordon. Dutch Schultz was next on the list. His real name was actually Arthur Flegenheimer, Rich Cohen pointed out in his book *Yiddish Connection*, in which he also explained the tactics the killer would adopt to get away with it:

"In 1935, after evidence was again gathered against him, Schultz's lawyers obtained a change of venue so that the trial took place in Malone, New York State. One church. One small street. A single traffic light… He set up shop in a small hotel, introduced himself to locals he didn't know, made donations at local charity sales, wore very simple suits… He was seen at small church meetings, at neighborhood parties, at bingo games. A week before the trial, he went to a local church and converted to Catholicism. He was not the first Jew to try to pass himself off as a provincial type by abjuring his faith. By the time the jury had

---

[287]Elie Wiesel, *Mémoires, tome I*, Seuil, 1994, p. 385, 386.

[288]Alain Brossat, Sylvia Klingberg, *Le Yiddishland révolutionnaire*, Balland, 1983, p. 187.

to deliberate, Schultz had deceived and corrupted the whole town. There is a picture of him, taken just after the exculpatory verdict, with the big grin of a little boy who has just rigged his election as class deputy." In this tough guy world, there's no room for donkeys," he told reporters[289]."

We can mention in this chapter the story of the Marranos, those Spanish Jews who had converted to Catholicism in order to escape the general expulsion[290]. On 31 March 1492, Ferdinand and Isabella signed the edict expelling the Jews from Spain, requiring them to leave the country by 31 July." In vain they offered the treasury immense sums of money", wrote Leon Poliakov. Baptism in extremis was then the only remedy that allowed them to stay. Fifty thousand Jews converted to Catholicism, but 150,000 preferred exile.

Most of them moved to Portugal and prospered. King Manuel I then forced them to convert officially, leaving them the possibility to "Judaise" openly. Baptism was enough for civil peace. But this truce did not last, and Manuel I, who was seeking a marriage alliance with Spain, instituted an inquisition like the Spanish one in 1497, which forced the Jews to emigrate. Many of them settled in Turkey, mainly in the city of Thessaloniki (now in Greece), where they soon reaffirmed their Judaism. Others, like the family of the famous Spinoza, settled in Protestant Holland.

---

[289]Rich Cohen, *Yiddish Connection*, 1998, Denoël, 200, Folio, p. 283

[290]The phenomenon was already old: "But after 1391, when the pressure on the Jews became more violent, whole communities embraced the Christian faith. Most of the neophytes eagerly took advantage of their new position. They thronged in their hundreds and thousands to places from which they had previously been excluded by their faith. They entered forbidden professions and the quiet cloisters of universities. They conquered important positions in the State and even penetrated the sanctum sanctorum of the Church. Their power increased with their wealth, and many could aspire to be admitted to the oldest and most aristocratic families in Spain… A near contemporary Italian observed that Jewish converts practically ruled Spain, while their secret adherence to Judaism was ruining the Christian faith. A wedge of hatred inevitably drove the relations of old and new Christians apart. The neophytes were known as marranos (probably "the reprobate" or "the swine"). They were despised for their triumphs, for their pride, for their cynical adherence to Catholic practices. While the masses viewed the triumphs of the new Christians with grim bitterness, the clergy denounced their disloyalty and insincerity. They suspected the truth that most of the converts were still Jews at heart, that forced conversion had not extirpated the heritage of centuries. Tens of thousands of the new Christians outwardly submitted, mechanically went to church, mumbled prayers, performed rites and observed customs. But the spirit had not been converted." In Abram Leon Sachar, *History of the Jews, Ch. XVI (The Marranos and the Inquisition)*, trans. of the 2nd American ed. revised to 1940, Ediciones Ercilla, Santiago de Chile, 1945, p. 276, 277.

As for the fifty thousand Spanish Jews who converted to Catholicism, they went to mass every Sunday, respected the feasts of the Christian calendar, but in reality continued to practise Judaism in secret. With the spread of the Inquisition, many in turn emigrated to Portugal, fleeing again from there to America, Brazil, Mexico and Peru, where some became rich in the slave trade or in the famous silver mines of Potosi.

Le Monde des livres of 27 September 2001 published a review of Nathan Wachtel's book, *La Foi du souvenir (The Faith of Memory),* which dealt with the Marranos of Spanish America: "Rich or poor, they were caught by the long arm of the Inquisition which came to persecute on the other side of the Atlantic those suspected of secretly Judaising. The trials, which were recorded in the inquisitorial archives, enabled Nathan Wachtel to find their traces: "They confessed, most of them repented under heavy pressure, but they persisted, inventing innumerable tricks, codes, signs, simulations, although, after successive arrests, they ended up being condemned to perish as *"relaps*[291] "". From the portraits that have come down to us, common ways of acting and thinking emerge: a preference for endogamous alliances, a variable background of beliefs and customs, and this uniformly shared "valuing of secrecy"." The Jews are indeed a people who love secrecy.

Wherever they settled, the Marranos faithfully conformed to all Catholic rites, went to mass and confession, and could rightly boast of "living very Christian lives". This was what the historian Leon Poliakov wrote about those Portuguese Marranos who had chosen to settle in Holland:

"Their camouflage was so perfect that Josephus of Rosheim, the "regent" of the Jews of Germany who visited the great marrano centre of Anverso in 1536, was even able to write: "It is a country where there are no Jews"."

The truth, however, was entirely different, and it erupted during the religious conflicts. The Jews were so deeply imbued with the Catholic way of life, Poliakov wrote, that "later, in the Protestant Netherlands, they did not reveal their quality of secret Jews until they were threatened with expulsion for being Catholic[292]."

Leon Poliakov also cited the example of a great "Spanish" Lord of the mid-15th century. A statesman and reputed jurist, Pedro de la Caballería was in reality a marrano:

"According to the inquisitorial archives, wrote Poliakov, he had

[291]Relaps (adjective and noun): to fall back into heresy after having abjured it.

[292]Léon Poliakov, *Histoire de l'antisémitisme I*, 1981, Points Seuil, 1990, p. 200.

entrusted himself to a Jewish lawyer who reportedly asked him, "Sir, how could you become a Christian, you who are so well versed in our Law?" To which "Mr Peter" replied: "You fool, what could I have become with the Torah but a rabbi? Now, thanks to the little hanged one (Jesus), I receive all kinds of honours, I lead the whole city of Saragossa, and I make it tremble. Who prevents me, when I wish, from fasting on Kippur and observing your feasts? When I was a Jew, I dared not break the barriers of the Sabbath, and now, I do whatever I please[293]."

While the case of the Spanish and Portuguese Marranos is well known, that of the Dunmehs and the Frankists is less well known. Here we must go back to the origin of these two sects. We have seen in the first part of this book that messianism, through the Kabbalah, was a reaction to the expulsion of the Jews from Spain, in the sense that grandiose perspectives were opened up to them, which nourished their hopes and comforted them in the face of the adversities they were going through. The mysticism of the Kabbalah had strongly influenced and marked religious circles, but also the entire Jewish community, contributing extensively to the spread of messianic hopes. It took some time, however, before Jewish messianism took shape among the chosen people and was finally embodied in a human figure. This occurred during the year 1665, when Shabtai Tzvi provoked an outburst of messianism that began in Palestine and spread throughout the Diaspora. This Sabbatean phenomenon, wrote Gershom Scholem, "remains one of the most astonishing enigmas of Jewish history[294]." Whichever way you look at it, Sabbateanism represented a crisis of tradition.

Shabtai Tzvi was a descendant of Spanish Jews who had been expelled in 1492. He lived in the Jewish community of Smyrne, Turkey, and must have been quite gifted, for at the age of eighteen he was teaching Kabbalah to groups of young students. He also displayed an extraordinary imagination in his Kabbalistic interpretations. From the beginning of his career, the charismatic character of his personality was evident. He would soon attract crowds of people whom he would persuade that he was indeed the Messiah, giving rise to numerous rumours. Legends sprang up around him and caused messianism to spread rapidly and contagiously. News of Shabtai Tzvi and the spirit he had generated spread throughout Europe like wildfire.

The Kabbalah had prophesied that the year 1648 would mark the beginning of the Messianic era. But the Jews were quickly

---

[293]Léon Poliakov, *Histoire de l'antisémitisme I*, 1981, Points Seuil, 1990, p. 157.

[294]Gershom Scholem, *Le Messianisme juif*, 1971, Calmann-Lévy, 1974, p. 115, 116.

disillusioned, for the year 1648 was for the Eastern Jews one of the worst moments in their history. Indeed, instead of the Messiah, it was Bogdan Chmielnicki who showed up with his Cossacks to put down a revolt of the Jewish communities against the Poles, wreaking terrible havoc on them. Far from calming tempers, the news from Poland provoked an upsurge of messianic frenzy; and since the year 1648 had not brought redemption, Shabtai Tzvi pinned his hopes on another date: 1666 at last! This date, paradoxically, was not drawn from Jewish Kabbalah, but was based on Christian calculations from the Book of Revelation. The year 1666—this time for sure!—would mark the beginning of the millennium. What had hitherto been a hope and a dream was to become a reality: proof that the Jews had not suffered in vain for so many centuries.

1666 became the year of the Redemption. The Jews of Poland rose up in great hope, especially after the terrible persecutions they had suffered. Some abandoned their homes and possessions, refused to work and proclaimed that the Messiah was coming to take them on a cloud to Jerusalem. Others fasted for days, even denying food to their young children.

Shabtai Tzvi was to begin his work of redemption by dethroning the sultan of Turkey, who then reigned over the Holy Land. Two days before the year 1666, he had the audacity (the famous *chutzpah*) to go to Constantinople to ask Sultan Ibrahim to hand over the throne to him. And what was bound to happen happened: he was imprisoned in a fortress in Gallipoli." But he had such powerful supporters that the prison was transformed into a royal residence where Jews from all over the world flocked to bring him gifts. He had become the spiritual leader of hundreds of thousands of people[295]."

The Turks then devised a plan to render the Sabbatean movement ineffective. Interestingly, it was proposed by a Jewish advisor to the sultan. Shabtai Tzvi was then put in the dilemma of choosing between death and public conversion to Islam." He was allowed to feign his conversion, but the act had to be public," wrote David Bakan. In November 1666, towards the end of the year of redemption, Shabtai Tzvi converted to Islam with great pomp and ceremony. He received a Muslim name, Mehmet Effendi, and was appointed chaplain to the sultan with a generous salary before going into exile in Albania.

This caused great consternation among Jews around the world, as was to be expected, although the authors are not very prolix about it.

[295]David Bakan, *Freud et la tradition mystique juive*, 1963, Payot, 2001, p. 120.

But even though the great messianic ferment had subsided, the idea continued to warm some spirits[296]. A Lithuanian named Zadok prophesied that the year 1695 would be the true date of the coming of the Messiah. A Kabbalist, Hayim Malakh, taught that Shabtai Tzvi was indeed the Messiah, but that like Moses, who had prevented the Jews from entering the Promised Land for forty years, one had to wait forty years, from 1666 to 1706, before the redemption would be fulfilled. It would be 1706! In 1700, Hayim Malakh led a caravan of 1300 people to the Holy Land to welcome the Messiah. About a thousand of them survived the gruelling journey." Disappointed by the vain waiting, some became Christians, some Muslims, some returned to Poland to spread unrealistic mystical stories[297]."

The Sabbatean movement thus continued, in fits and starts, in the form of a Jewish sect, despite the efforts of the rabbis to stifle it. The collapse of the movement had naturally led to great suspicion and distrust of the exacerbated messianism of the Kabbalah. Against the Sabbateans who endangered Jewish communities, the rabbis did not hesitate to launch the *herem* (excommunication).

It was in this context that the Dunmeh sect was born in Thessaloniki. After the death of Shabtai Tzvi in 1676, hundreds of families in Salonica converted to Islam in 1683 to follow the example of their Messiah. Other more restricted groups did the same in Adrianople and Istanbul. The Sabbatean movement then took shape in Islam with that sect of voluntary Marranos, called Dunmeh (meaning "apostate" in Turkish)." Doubly apostate, wrote Leon Poliakov, since they were apostate to both Islam and Judaism and, consequently, equally despised by both sides. To the ten commandments of Moses, the sect substituted the eighteen rules of Shabtai Tzvi. The second rule commanded belief in Shabtai Tzvi ("the true Redeemer; there is no salvation apart from him"); the sixteenth and seventeenth stipulated that all the customs of Islam were to be followed ("whatever is seen from without, must be observed"), but one should not enter into marriage or alliance with the Turks ("for they are an abomination, and their wives are reptiles")[298]."

This echoes some statements by Bernard-Henri Levy, who defines himself as a good Frenchman, more French than the French, and at the same time claims to be Jewish on all four sides, depending on the circumstances.

---

[296]See translator's note in Annex VI. 1.

[297]David Bakan, *Freud et la tradition mystique juive*, 1963, Payot, 2001, p. 124.

[298]Léon Poliakov, *Histoire de l'antisémitisme I*, 1981, Points Seuil, 1990, p. 218, 219.

Indeed, Gershom Scholem admitted that, under these conditions, it was legitimate for the Goyim to be suspicious of the sincerity of the Jews: 'Although the Turkish authorities welcomed these collective conversions to Islam and had high hopes for the Jews of Turkey, they quickly had to realise that these were by no means genuine converts." Scholem further specified that "most of the dunmeh families ... were in the habit of secretly giving their children Hebrew and Judeo-Spanish names and surnames, apart from their official Turkish names and surnames."

Apparently, the sect had not yet been extinguished until recently: "Recently, Scholem wrote, members of the Dunmeh intelligentsia have revealed their names in private interviews with Jewish visitors. With a knowing glance they have scribbled them in Hebrew on their Turkish business cards[299]."

The journalist Françoise Giroud, the "queen of journalism", felt linked to the Dunmeh sect. Born France Gourdji in Geneva, she was the second daughter of Salih Gourdji and Elda Fragi, both Turkish and Sephardic Jews. Born in Baghdad, he had become a journalist before setting up the Ottoman Telegraph Agency in Istanbul. He had to flee Turkey at the beginning of the First World War "because of his libertarian ideas and his opposition to the alliance with Germany" and was later to lead several missions for the Allied intelligence services. Some would rightly speak of "treason" in favour of the enemy, and if the man had been arrested by the Turkish authorities, we bet that the whole community would have leapt to his defence against such an injustice.

"My maternal grandfather had the title of pacha, a non-hereditary title of nobility. My father was a bey." Christine Ockrent took up Françoise's confessions, but was surprised by her interlocutor's visible discomfort on this subject: "One day I let her know my surprise about her reticence about the Turkish part of her history", and finally she confessed her family's origins: "My father is probably descended from a *deunmeh* family, that is to say from one of the five hundred Sephardic families converted to Islam in the 17th century. The wealthy and active deumnés [or deunmeh, donmeh] were the first in the Turkish world to open up to secular, liberal and national ideas[300]."

The Young Turk movement, the Kemalist revolution and Western

[299]Gershom Scholem, *Le Messianisme juif*, 1971, Calmann-Lévy, 1974, p. 229, 239, 240.

[300]Christine Ockrent, *Françoise Giroud, une ambition française*, Fayard, Paris, 2003, p. 40-42.

secularism in Turkey have their origins here. This is what Gershom Scholem stated in turn: The Dunmehs "have contributed numerous members to the intelligentsia of the Young Turks... They played an important role in the beginnings of the Union and Progress Committee, an organisation of the Young Turk movement which originated in Thessaloniki... We have proof that David Bey, one of the three ministers of the first Young Turk government and an important leader of the Young Turk party, was a Dunmeh[301]."

This is also what the highly influential press director and notable intellectual Alexandre Adler said at a conference on 14 March 2005 at the Itshak Rabin Centre: "It will not surprise you if I tell you that I have many Donmeh friends, i.e. disciples of Shabtai Tzvi, and that I find them quite extraordinary... If there had not been so many Donmehs among the Turkish elites at the end of the 19th and beginning of the 20th century, there would not have been Kemalism. The "great Donmehs" have been "at the forefront of school reform in Turkey" and have created "the first modern high schools such as Mustafa Kemal's high school in Thessaloniki, where he studied". Of course, Turkish Islamists claim that Kemal was himself a Donmeh, but this is false. Instead, his close associates and friends were widely Donmeh[302]."

It is thanks to the influence of these Donmeh Jews, falsely converted to Islam, that the alliance between Turkey and Israel can be explained, Adler explained: "If there had been no Donmeh as foreign minister during the first thirty years of secular Turkey—they still account for 40 percent of Turkey's ambassadors in the world and all of Turkey's ambassadors to the United States since the 1950s—Turkey would undoubtedly not be an ally of Israel."

But in the case of Françoise Giroud, we have no doubt that she was a true Frenchwoman, "perfectly integrated": her mother Elda wanted in fact to educate them in this way: "Elda wanted to make her daughters perfect little Frenchwomen. They would therefore be baptised, learn catechism and go to boarding school at the Institut Molière... Giroud would later write—but no one is there to confirm this—that her mother had secretly converted to Catholicism around the age of thirty... She would insist throughout the war on insisting that she did not feel affected or worried, either for herself or for her daughters, by the anti-Semitic Vichy laws. The yellow star did not go with them, it was not their history, their community or family[303]."

---

[301]Gershom Scholem, *Le Messianisme juif*, 1971, Calmann-Lévy, 1974 p. 235. 235

[302]http://www.beit-haverim.com/anoter/ConfAdler0305.htm

[303]Christine Ockrent, *Françoise Giroud, une ambition française*, Fayard, Paris, 2003,

And so it was that, imbued with these patriotic feelings and unconditional love for France and the French, Françoise and her sister committed themselves to the Resistance against the Nazis. Just as, as we have already seen, she would recount all her memories at the worldly dinners organised by Samuel Pisar, along with all the other "Resistance fighters".

The Sabbatean movement did not only concern the Ottoman Empire. While there were many who came from Poland to join them in the 17th century, there were still many more who stayed in Poland to follow the path laid out by another radical Messiah, Jacob Frank.

Jacob Frank was born in 1726 in Korolovka, on the border of Podolia, in western Ukraine and Moldova. His father was a Sabbatean who had been expelled from the community where he was a rabbi. He was a poorly educated man, but endowed with great physical strength and imagination. He was most likely a "psychopath, a personality with an underdeveloped Overself", wrote David Bakan. He travelled here and there as a peddler, preaching Kabbalah, posing as a healer, dispensing religious and medical aids. For the Polish rabbis, the individual in question embodied the devil in person:

"It is said that he engaged in banditry with his disciples, that he had cut a Torah scroll to make shoes for his friends, and that he had stolen a *shofar*[304] and taught some gentile children to play it."

He considered himself the reincarnation of Shabtai Tzvi and gave new impetus to the Sabbatean movement. In 1755, Frank appeared in Podolia to reinvigorate the decaying Sabbatean groups. In his new doctrine, he put forward the principle of the Holy Trinity: he distinguished God, who had incarnated in Shabtai Tzvi, from his replica or female part, the Shechinah, attributing to himself the role of Messiah. He rejected the teachings of the Talmud and declared that only the Zohar was sacred. The idea of a God who was both male and female served as a pretext for religious practices of a sexual nature, such as the exchange of women. It proclaimed that the Law was dead; that the yoke of the old Torah had been broken; the yoke of the Law was only valid for an unredeemed world where the Messiah had not yet appeared. The new redemption and the revelation it brought was such that all things, including evil, were now sanctified. It was this reasoning that formed the basis of the doctrine of Evil.

---

p. 50, 51.

[304]A ram's horn that serves as a trumpet during great religious ceremonies. The sound of the shofar is used to shake the listener to the core, to provoke an awakening, an alarm (NdT).

"The doctrine of Evil, wrote David Bakan, rested on the thesis that the divine sparks had been scattered and that men had to let themselves be carried away by sin to reunite them. The idea of sanctified sin became predominant, salvation would come through sin; out of the excess of sin would emerge a world where there would be none. Frank had declared: "I am come to take out of the world all the laws and ordinances hitherto in force[305]."

The Frankists "glorified sin as a path to redemption", wrote David Bakan, adding this precision: "The conception of evil as a divine manifestation has never been completely rejected[306]."

Gershom Scholem wrote that the movement represented a "revolt against the stagnant orthodoxy and fanatical obscurantism of the rabbis[307]." This revolutionary nature of Jacob Frank's doctrine was also confirmed by Martin Buber: "Holy sin becomes a system, men must rush into sin in order to snatch the divine sparks from it… The yoke of the old Torah is broken, it was only valid for the unredeemed world[308]."

The Frankists, heretical Jews, were excommunicated (declared *herem*) by the rabbis and the rabbis responded by attacking the Talmud, "saying that it was false and evil." David Bakan referred to the serious accusations of the Frankists against the rabbis: "They even accused the Talmud of forcing the use of Christian blood and testified that Jews perpetrated ritual crimes[309]."

Frank's career reached its apogee in November 1759, when, following the example of Shabtai Tzvi[310], he and all his disciples were converted in great pomp and ceremony. At first, the Poles were no more discerning than the Turks, and the Sabbateans were sponsored by members of the Polish nobility from whom the newly baptised took their names or surnames.

A good number of them became nobility in this way. Jacob Frank held court in Offenbach near Frankfurt until his death in 1791. The sect he founded had become a particularly radical branch of the Sabbateans, but this time with a Catholic façade.

305David Bakan, *Freud et la tradition mystique juive*, 1963, Payot, 2001, p. 130, 131. See translator's note in Annex VI. 2.

306David Bakan, *Freud et la tradition mystique juive*, 1963, Payot, 2001, p. 209.

307Gershom Scholem, *Le Messianisme juif*, 1971, Calmann-Lévy, 1974, p. 256.

308See translator's note in Annex VI. 3.

309David Bakan, *Freud et la tradition mystique juive*, 1963, Payot, 2001, p. 132.

310"Abraham Cardoso said of Shabtai Tzvi that he had to disguise himself, like a spy who enters the enemy camp in order to fulfil his mission." In Gershom Scholem, *Le Messianisme juif*, 1971, Les Belles Lettres, 2020 p. 296.

If the Dunmehs favoured the progressive movement of the Young Turks at the beginning of the 20th century, the Sabbateans and other Frankists also played an important role in the spread of liberal ideas in Europe at the end of the 18th century[311]." After the French Revolution, explained David Bakan, the Sabbatean groups that still existed within Judaism promoted and supported movements in favour of reform, liberalism and the Enlightenment[312]."

Gershom Scholem thus recounted the life of one Moses Dobruska (1751–1793), in a book entitled *From Frankism to Jacobinism*. Moses Dobruska was a mysterious character. He was born in a Moravian ghetto. Raised as an orthodox Jew, he later became a follower of the heretical cabalistic sect of the Frankists in which he played an active role. A Hebrew-speaking writer, he converted to Catholicism, was ennobled by the Emperor of Austria and took the name Franz Thomas von Schönfeld. In Vienna, he frequented enlightened nationalist circles while secretly a member of esoteric Freemasonry. He left the Austrian capital in 1792 and settled in Strasbourg, then in Paris, under the name of Junius Fey, where he became an active member of the Jacobin Club. In 1793, he published a *Social Philosophy*, which was naturally a vibrant apology for Jacobin ideas. Finally, the fatal outcome was to come: "Engaged in financial intrigues, accused—without proof [naturally]—of being an Austrian agent, he was guillotined at the age of 40, on 4 April 1791, in the company of the heads of the Dantonist faction[313]", we read on the book's title page. In short: this Junius Frey was a revolutionary who acted in secret without revealing his true allegiances and who rubbed shoulders with the greats of this world, as well as being a financial racketeer accused without proof of being a spy. We can say that Gershom Scholem has indeed chosen a representative

[311]"Relations between the two sects in Thessaloniki and Warsaw had to be maintained until the end of the 19th century. I personally knew of a case that went back even after 1920. A Dunmeh visiting Vienna revealed to a Jewish friend that his group was closely connected with some apparently very Catholic families in Warsaw. (Gershom Scholem, *Le Messianisme juif*, 1971, Calmann-Lévy, 1974, p. 241).

[312]David Bakan, *Freud et la tradition mystique juive*, 1963, Payot, 2001, p. 125. See translator's note in Annex VI. 4.

[313]Georges-Jacques Danton was a lawyer and politician who played a decisive role during the French Revolution. He is considered by some historians, along with Mirabeau, to be the main force behind the fall of the Ancien Régime and the establishment of the First French Republic. He was an early leader of the Jacobins Club alongside Robespierre and one of the first members of the Committee of Public Salvation. He was eventually arrested on the latter's orders and condemned to the guillotine on charges of corruption and mercy towards the enemies of the Revolution. (NdT).

case.

This plasticity seems to predispose some Jews to espionage, and it must be acknowledged that "accusations" of this kind frequently appear in the pages of newspapers. Historian Leon Poliakov protested against such ignoble accusations, and defended the usual scapegoat thesis: "At the dawn of the 20th century, tensions between nations were becoming increasingly dramatic, and Jews were the first designated victims, regarded by the populations as 'spies' of the enemy. This kind of belief was in force on both sides of the Rhine..." However, on the same page, a few lines further down, Poliakov cited the case of this English citizen, Ignace Trebitsch: "He began his adventurous career by getting himself elected, under the name of Lincoln, to the British House of Commons, while at the same time spying for Germany. He was eventually discovered and took refuge there, before finally moving on to China, where he became a Buddhist monk, this time spying for Japan[314]..."

At the beginning of his work on the Bolshevik Revolution (*Two Hundred Years Together*, 2003), the much celebrated Soviet dissident Solzhenitsyn cited the rather similar case of a certain Gruzenberg. The man had lived in England and the United States. In 1919 he held the post of Consul General of the Soviet Union in Mexico (a country on which the revolutionaries had their eyes); in the same year, he was seen holding sessions in the central organs of the Komintern. He then served in Sweden, then in Scotland, where he was arrested. He surfaced again a little later in China in 1923 under the name of Borodine, with a whole gang of spies, where he became the "chief political adviser to the Executive Committee of the Kuomintang", a post which enabled him to further the careers of Mao-Tse-Tung and Zhou-Enlai. However, Chiang-Kai-Shek suspected him of subversive activities and expelled him from China in 1927. He then returned to the Soviet Union where he became editor-in-chief of the Soviet Information Bureau. He was finally shot in 1951.

We see, then, with what surprising plasticity some Jews can change their identity and adopt the most unexpected disguises. Pure German, newly landed Catholic Brazilian, old Indian chief, moustachioed Cossack, gangster turned charity sister, Spanish or Dutch Catholic, Turkish Muslim Pacha, Polish aristocrat, Jacobin revolutionary, Buddhist monk or Chinese conspirator, the disguises of these Jews are always provisional and are no more than a mask that they will discard

[314]Léon Poliakov, *Histoire des crises d'identité juives*, Austral, 1994, p. 141. Poliakov also quoted Puchkine, speaking "of the inseparable notions of Jew and spy." (*Histoire de l'antisémitisme, tome II,* Points Seuil, 1990, p. 312, 313).

when the time is right[315].

Solzhenitsyn recalled here the reflections of the Zionist leader Jabotinsky, who said at the beginning of the 20th century: "When the Jew assimilates into a foreign culture, one should not trust the depth and consistency of the transformation. An assimilated Jew gives in at the first push, abandons the borrowed culture without the slightest resistance as soon as he is convinced that his reign is over[316]."

This is what made the English "brilliant anti-conformist critic" Henry Mencken say in 1920: "They think in Yiddish and write in English." And Poliakov even quoted Joseph Goebbels, who had realised that: "When a Jew speaks German, he is lying! [317]"

Having understood the dominant features of Jewish identity, one can better grasp the true nature of the discourses of some cosmopolitan intellectuals, who assure us that they are "perfectly assimilated" in order to propagate their universal message to the Goyim. After the publication of Bernard-Henri Lévy's book, *The French Ideology*, in 1981, the intellectual and academic Raymond Aron was alarmed at how insulting the book could be to the French, and urged the philosopher to restrain his contempt so as not to fuel anti-Semitism[318]. The philosopher Levy replied in these terms:

"You have read me too well, I am sure, to ignore that it is as a Frenchman and as a Frenchman that, like any other French philosopher, I have risked this research on black France[319]." It is indeed simpler, and above all less risky, to carry the beret and the *baguette*[320] under one's arm to spit and vomit on deep France and its terroir. It is a very practical position, since it allows one to reject in advance all those who dare to make an anti-Semitic reply.

In his book *Wandering Jews*, Joseph Roth offered another valuable testimony to this characteristic plasticity, which also refers to Jewish patronymic names:

"The lack of piety of the Jews towards their names is not surprising. With a lightness that is astonishing, Jews change their

---

[315]The Jews disguise themselves during the Purim festival. The beautiful Esther had disguised her identity until she arrived at the king's bedside in order to convince him to get rid of the enemies of the Jews. The massacre of 75 000 Persians is celebrated by the Jews every year since then.

[316] Alexandre Solzhenitsyn, *Deux siècles ensemble, tome II*, Fayard, p. 550.

[317] Léon Poliakov, *Histoire de l'antisémitisme II*, 1981, Points Seuil, 1990, p. 425, 244.

[318] Read in Hervé Ryssen, *Planetary Hopes, (*2022).

[319] Bernard-Henri Lévy, *Questions de principe, deux*, Grasset, 1986, p. 306.

[320]Typical French loaf of bread (NdT).

names, the name of their parents, the sound of which, to a European spirit, always has at least a sentimental value. For the Jews, the name has no value, because it is simply not their name. The Jews, the Oriental Jews, have no name. They carry forced pseudonyms. Their real name is that by which on Sabbath and holidays they are called in the Torah: their proper Jewish name and that of their father. The surnames, however, from Goldenberg to Hescheles, are imposed names. Governments have ordered Jews to accept names. Are they their own? If someone is called Nachman and transforms his first name into the European Norbert, is not Norbert the disguise, the pseudonym? Is it more than mimicry? Does the chameleon feel pity for the colours to which he is continually forced to change? In the United States, the Jew writes Greenboom instead of Grünbaum. He is not bothered by the changed vowels[321]."

Guy Konopnicki confirmed these frequent forgeries: "Although I was born a few years after the war, my identity was transcribed in a family book that was notoriously falsified in 1940 and is still valid today. It was on the basis of that document that I received my identity card. So the fashionable equation between identity and authenticity

---

321 Joseph Roth, *Judíos errantes,* Acantilado 164, Barcelona, 2008, p. 109. ["The obligation to bear a patronymic surname appeared with the edict of tolerance promulgated by Joseph II in 1787, in the regions of Habsburg obedience, after the partition of Poland. It was gradually imposed in all the other regions throughout the 19th century." (Marc Zborowski, *Olam,* 1952, Plon, p. 422). Joseph Roth went on to explain that Jews who wanted to cross borders often gave false information in order to obtain their identity papers, as this information had the advantage of being more credible to customs officers and the police. Joseph Roth put the matter in a somewhat convoluted and misrepresentative way: "Such names cause difficulties for the police. The police don't like difficulties—and if only it were only the names! But the dates of birth don't add up either… How did he get across the border? Without a passport? With a false one? Moreover, it turns out that he is not called what he is called, and although he presents himself under so many names, which in itself implies that they are false, they are also probably false from an objective point of view. The man who appears on the papers, on the registration card, does not share the same identity as the man who has just arrived. What can be done? Should he be locked up? In that case, the one who is locked up is not the real one. Should he be expelled? In that case, the one expelled is an impostor. But if he is sent back to his point of origin to bring back new documents in the proper way, with undeniable names, the one sent back is not, in any case, only the authentic one, but the impostor is eventually turned into an authentic one. It is thus returned once, twice, three times, until the Jew realises that he has nothing left to do but to provide false data in order to pass for the real thing… The police have made the Oriental Jew come up with the excellent idea of concealing his real and true—though muddled—personal circumstances… Everyone is amazed at the ability of the Jews to provide false data, but no one is amazed at the clumsy demands of the police." In Joseph Roth, *Judíos errantes,* Acantilado 164, Barcelona, 2008, p. 74, 75. Note the Talmudic-inspired *pilpul* in this argument (see note 416). (NdT)].

leaves me dumbfounded[322]."

The writer Marek Halter, for example, also had a false identity, as a report in the newspaper *Le Point* of 28 April 2005 showed. Everything about the character was false. His identity is false, his date of birth is false, his genealogy is false, and his whole biography is largely false[323].

Jewish humour

The plasticity of the Jewish personality is undoubtedly one of the main ingredients of Jewish humour. Combined with a fearlessness that can be seen in any situation, it is an explosive mixture that can cause hilarity when it is devoid of malice and political purpose. In the opposite case, we then see that famous "impudence" which has always been denounced by all observers of Judaism.

This form of Jewish humour was well exemplified in Roberto Benigni's film, *Life is Beautiful*: We are in pre-war Fascist Italy. Our hero is an amusing and brilliant histrion who is in love with a young woman he wants to seduce at all costs. Going one day to the school where she is a governess, he learns by chance that an academy inspector is due to arrive at the same moment. She decides to take advantage of the situation and impersonate him. She immediately metamorphoses, enters the classroom where all the school staff are waiting for her, greets everyone with a handshake like an inspector and improvises a totally delirious speech in front of the pupils and teachers, which has the expected effect on the young governess, who looks at her with admiration and wide-eyed amazement.

Another scene in the film is very revealing of this unbridled audacity: the beautiful governess must unfortunately marry a fascist, who is evidently a rude character. During the wedding dinner, where all the dignitaries of the region are gathered in a magnificent mansion, our Roberto, who has devised a plan to abduct the beauty, has no other idea than to ride into the great reception hall on a white horse, thus convincing the young bride to follow him on his mad adventure in front of a stupefied audience.

A third scene is even more extravagant: a prisoner of the Germans, he now arrives at a concentration camp with his young son, whom he wants to calm down at all costs, and whom he makes him believe that it is all a big game. Barely settled in the barracks with the bunk beds,

---

[322] Guy Konopnicki, *La Place de la nation*, Olivier Orban, 1983, p. 14.

[323] Hervé Ryssen, *Planetary Hopes*, (2022).

the commandant enters accompanied by soldiers to shout out the instructions and the camp's very strict rules. No offence will be tolerated! But he needs a translator." Who speaks German?" Our Roberto seized the opportunity. Evidently he doesn't speak a word of German, and after each sentence of the commandant, he translates for the Italian prisoners the rules of a completely stupid game, a game of hide and seek in which you must score points and not get caught if you want to win the first prize: a real tank! Mission accomplished in the end, because his son will believe in the trickery to the end and will conscientiously obey his father in order to earn the points and win the big prize.

This truly amusing scene shows very well the plasticity of the Jewish personality. It also illustrates that tendency not to back down from anything, to metamorphose, to disguise oneself as anything to achieve one's ends. Stubbornness, audacity and plasticity are the basis of that famous Jewish humour.

The scandal

But this boldness, which Jews know how to use in many situations, does not always provoke hilarity. Unfortunately, this character trait can provoke hostility from those who feel hurt by what they see as irony and mockery of their values.

We have already seen some predispositions of the cosmopolitan spirit to say, write or do things that can often be seen as grossly impudent, as far removed from reality as they are from our social norms. This theme appears in all observers, in all those who describe Judaism. And it is precisely these "provocations", conscious or not, that have always exacerbated latent anti-Semitism.

Otto Weininger noted in 1902 with regard to his former fellow Jews: "The Jew does not believe that there is anything true and immutable, holy and invulnerable. That is why he is eminently frivolous and makes fun of everything; he does not believe in the Christianity of any Christian, and still less in the honesty of a Jew's baptism[324]."

This is nothing new, for this irony and this tendency to ridicule the faith of Christians had already been felt as a kind of insolence by authors in the Middle Ages. Thus, at the time of Charlemagne, the Archbishop of Lyon Agobard had made this Jewish singularity the title

324 Otto Weininger, *Sex and Character*, Ediciones Península, Edicions 62 s|a, Barcelona, 1985, p. 317.

of his treatise: *De Insolentia judaeorum*: "On the insolence of the Jews". It is a pity that Leon Poliakov did not mention this book in his monumental *History of Anti-Semitism*, as it is one of the factors explaining the problem. It should be stressed, however, that there are constants in history that go back quite far in time. Indeed, it is striking to note that the characteristics we observe today in our contemporaries are also those noted by the analysts of very distant times.

But insolence is only one aspect of that boldness, which is one of the characteristic features of Judaism. In philosophical or political matters, the Jew is someone who is "daring". In fact, they are perfectly aware of that faculty, which they call "*chutzpah*", and which naturally leads them to formulate the most outlandish theories, to construct entirely new systems of thought, to ask for an audience with the pope, to want to dethrone the sultan, or to invest hundreds of millions of dollars in a gigantic project.

We have already seen how the "Messiah" Shabtai Tzvi travelled to Istanbul imagining that he could dethrone the sultan. We find something similar in the novelist Philip Roth, when he imagines himself negotiating with the Pope: "When Philip Roth and the Pope meet and solve all our problems[325]?"

The father of the Zionist idea, Theodore Herzl, was also madly bold in laying the foundations of the ideology of what was to become the state of Israel. His contemporaries were often sceptical about his plans to create a Jewish state in Palestine. But it is often overlooked that before becoming the champion of Zionism, the man who had observed that the integration of Jews into European societies was impossible, had considered the possibility of converting all Jews en masse so that they would disappear: "He wanted to address Pope Leo XIII, to ask for his protection. In 1893, he wanted to organise a solemn conversion of all the Jews of Vienna in St. Stephen's Cathedral, and in 1895, he still wrote in his diary: "Otherwise, if I wanted to be something, I would be a Prussian nobleman with old roots[326]"." We shall return later to this kind of inner conflict of personality and identity, which is another of the many manifestations of the ambivalence of Judaism.

In his *History of Jewish Identity Crises*, Leon Poliakov cited the case of Benjamin Disraeli, who was for a time in the 19th century the Prime Minister of England. He had set out his programme of political action in three novels: *Coningsby, Sybil* and *Tancred*, which some saw

---

[325] Philip Roth, *Operation Shylock*, Debolsillo Penguin Random House, Barcelona, 2005, p. 186.

[326] Léon Poliakov, *Histoire des crises d'identité juives*, Austral, 1994, p. 145.

as a provocation in the face of the English Empire: "He claimed to belong to the chosen people," wrote Poliakov, "and therefore demanded favourable treatment and political promotion for his co-religionists. He justified this claim in such a way as to cause scandal. Disraeli elevated the "Semites" to the status of "nature's aristocracy"."

These impudent remarks earned him many attacks and pullazings: "Thomas Carlyle, the illustrious critic, was indignant at such "Jewish quackery", and wondered "how long John Bull will allow that absurd ape to dance on his belly?" But these verbal attacks did not prevent him from being elected to the House of Commons: on the contrary, in 1847 he made a speech in the same House to demand the admission of Jews[327]."

Leon Poliakov brought us another interesting testimony, coming from the philosopher Solomon Maimon. He was born in Poland in 1754, and was influenced by the German philosopher Moses Mendelssohn and the philosophy of the Enlightenment[328]. Provocative and sceptical, he mocked his own peers who still lived in those communities that had been governed for centuries by rabbinical laws. Solomon Maimon amusingly mocked the Talmud and some of its rationales: "For example, how many white hairs can a red-haired cow have before it is still considered red-haired?" or "Is it permissible to kill a louse or a flea on the Sabbath?"

But it is true that Solomon Maimon was somewhat at odds with his own community. As a rationalist Jew, he had an instinctive distrust of the "mystics" of Hasidism. Leon Poliakov recounted the following anecdote: "Having attended a party at the house of Dov Baer, the leader of the Hasidic sect, he was immediately displeased: this 'Master', on learning that the wife of one of the faithful had given birth to a girl, ordered the unfortunate man to be whipped, which was immediately executed. Solomon Maimon severely judged this sect, highlighting its most caricatured features: "Eager to pass themselves off as true cynics,

---

[327] Léon Poliakov, *Histoire des crises d'identité juives*, Austral, 1994, p. 97.

[328]Moses Mendelssohn was the founder of the Jewish intellectual movement called *Haskalah*, which in Hebrew means enlightenment or enlightenment, and which sought the integration of Jews into European society through a certain openness and political reform of Judaism. Mirabeau, a Freemason and famous leader of the French Revolution, wrote in 1787 a work entitled: *On Moses Mendelssohn, on the political reform of the Jews*. Several authors confirm that Mirabeau was the main link between German Illuminism and French Freemasonry. In fact, Mirabeau wrote several pages on the Illuminati in his work *On the Prussian Monarchy* and recorded his great knowledge of that country in his *Secret History of the Berlin Court*. On these issues and Freemasonry read Alberto León Cebrián, *Las Revoluciones masónicas*, Bubok, 2015. (NdT).

some of them sinned against the rules of decency, ran around in the buff with their simple attributes and satisfied their natural needs in public, etc.[329]"

Cosmopolitan spirits have an unfathomable contempt for everything that has to do with "sedentary" and "rootedness". And this contempt leads them to the conviction that they can make those they are trying to deceive fall into line. Thus, we heard the intellectual and essayist Alain Minc say that immigrants were "slightly more numerous today than fifteen years ago" and that they represented "a smaller part of the population than in the 1930s[330]." In the same vein, Daniel Cohn-Bendit had declared that "to curb xenophobia, the best thing to do would be to increase, rather than reduce, the number of foreigners[331]." And with the same formidable impudence, he also said: "In Germany, as in France, there is nothing better than a closed border to increase the number of foreigners and transform temporary emigration into permanent settlement[332]." Indeed, there is no shortage of such closed borders in Europe.

Chutzpah has a political purpose here: it is about achieving one's goals at any cost, and anything goes to fool people who want to be convinced to accept the borderless society. Any slightly educated and observant reader can legitimately think that these intellectuals have the gift of making people look like fools and arousing anger. But in a democracy, the pressure of the media system is such that it prevents the uninformed from realising the absurdity of such arguments made by intellectuals who strut their stuff on every television set.

Although the cosmopolitan spirit rejects the idea of the frontier and militates tirelessly for its disappearance, we know that it is first and foremost a politico-religious plan, which has no other aim than to work for the establishment of the global Empire and to hasten the coming of the Messiah. We have noticed the double-speak of the Jewish intellectuals, which consists in inciting others to disavow their traditions, while they preserve and cultivate the traditional values of Judaism.

However, to dwell on this point of the phenomenon would undoubtedly be superficial. We must understand that this mentality corresponds precisely to its own value system. For Jewish identity is, in reality, fundamentally fluctuating, ambiguous and ambivalent, despite

[329] Léon Poliakov, *Histoire des crises d'identité juives*, Austral, 1994, p. 55.

[330] Alain Minc, *La Vengeance des nations*, Grasset, 1990, p. 11.

[331] Daniel Cohn-Bendit, *Xénophobies*, Hamburg, 1992, Grasset, 1998, p. 43–45.

[332] Guy Sorman, *Waiting for the Barbarians*, Seix Barral, 1993, Barcelona, p. 31.

all the professions of faith of Jewish thinkers who thus seek to reassure themselves and justify their "mission". Although embodied in a chosen people whose ethnic boundaries are rather vague, Judaism is thus above all an idea that disdains terrestrial, intellectual or social boundaries[333]. The Jewish personality is always on the edge, always bordering on the boundaries, always with one foot on each side, but never touching the ground.

"The Jew is the eraser of boundaries. He is the polar opposite of the aristocrat, for the fundamental principle of aristocracy is the strict observance of all boundaries between men... To this must be attributed the lack of manners in his relations with others and the lack of social tact."

Otto Weininger noted another aspect of this fundamental ambivalence of the Jewish personality: "Servility has disappeared, giving way to its ever-accompanying reverse, insolence—both are alternative functions of the will in the same individual[334]."

Jewish audacity is also a reason for the success of some members of the Jewish community, especially in business, but also a cause of tension and conflict because of the misunderstanding that can arise when insolence is openly tinged with contempt for the Goyim. [335]The murderer Pierre Goldman, for example, did not hesitate to take advantage of the credulity of the Goyim to escape conviction by playing the "scapegoat" of a "racist" justice system and a "racist" state.

The swindler Jacques Crozemarie, president of the League against cancer, who only handed over 26% of the money donated by the French, also showed this phenomenal brazenness in 1996 when he declared to the television cameras: "I would be a criminal if I had pocketed something, but look at my representation fees, they are nil! I don't even get reimbursed for the restaurant bills! "(*Secrets d'actualité* television programme of 26 March 2006). He even went so far as to question the competence of the magistrates of the Court of Auditors." They don't know how to count! "In court, during the trial, "he berated the president, accusing her of doing nothing against cancer[336]".

The best way to get out of a tight spot is, of course, to deny reality,

---

333 "They are obsessed with abstraction', explained Danny Balint, a young skinhead, who was in fact a Jew who had become violently anti-Semitic. See Henry Bean's film *Danny Balint* (USA, 2001).

334 Otto Weininger, *Sex and Character*, Ediciones Península, Ediciones 62 s|a, Barcelona, 1985, p. 307, 308, 310.

335 The "scapegoat" is a very important biblical figure in Judaism.

336 On Crozemarie, read *Planetary Hopes and The Jewish Mafia*.

to lie through one's teeth with unquestionable aplomb. The philosopher André Glucksmann explained on 1 April 2006 on a popular television programme (*Tout le monde en parle*) that during the war he had seen his mother lie to the authorities with aplomb. That "insolence", he declared—a term he himself used—was a lesson he never forgot.

This monumental brazenness reached its peak in an extraordinary scam in 2005, reported in the 7 October issue of the daily *Libération*. On 25 July, just after the deadly attacks in London, the manager of a bank branch received a call from a man posing as the bank's president, Jean-Paul Bailly: "The DGSE[337] has asked us to help," he told her. Terrorists are preparing an attack in Paris and are going to withdraw money from your branch. A DGSE agent is going to call you. Do whatever he asks you to do."

An hour later, "Jean-Paul from the French services" telephones the head of the bank branch, gives her a code name, "Martine", demands confidentiality and sends poor Martine on her first mission: "Your phone line is not secure. You must get a mobile phone that will only be used for our communications. This is a number that you will call to give yours." Martine runs to buy a mobile, then leaves her number on Jean-Paul's answering machine. He calls her back: "Whatever happens, you must keep this mobile switched on day and night".

According to one of the investigators, Gilbert C. bombards Martine with continuous calls, some forty in two days. He floods her with information about the DGSE's work to thwart an imminent attack. He calls her at all hours, even at night, to such an extent that Martine no longer sleeps." If she doesn't answer quickly enough, he tells her off. If she hesitates, he beats her. He keeps telling her: 'Above all, don't talk to anyone about this. He pushes her to the limit. Martine is a wreck."

Once well conditioned, Martine will obey everything, persuaded that she is "working for the nation". Jean-Paul then orders her: "Turn on the computer. Tell me the names of the five biggest clients of your branch." Martine complies. According to the investigations, the fraudster then names one of the five names at random as the financier of an imminent attack and warns that someone is going to withdraw 500,000 euros from that account that evening. But the branch manager announces that there are only 350,000 euros in the account. Jean-Paul was furious: "You're really not operational at all! "Martine cries, empties all the drawers and drawers, and finally gets 8,000 euros more. Jean-Paul finally gives in and accepts the 358,000 euros: "Now, go buy

[337] French Intelligence Service (NdT).

a suitcase. I'll call you back." After buying the suitcase, Martine receives a call from Jean-Paul: "Before giving the money to the client, we must magnetise the banknotes to trace the entire terrorist financing circuit and disrupt the entire network. Take a taxi..." Then he orders her to get out at a café in the Place de la Nation: "Do you see my agents? —No." Martine sees nothing." OK, they are well hidden, they work well. Sit on the terrace."

A few minutes later, she calls back: "Go down to the toilet and lock yourself in." Martine goes down to the toilet. He calls her back: "An officer will knock three times on the bathroom door, give him the suitcase, go back to the terrace and wait ten minutes for us to return it." Knock knock knock." Martine, hand over the suitcase," says Shirley, an accomplice of Gilbert C., who ends up taking the loot.

Martine then returned to the terrace of the café and waited... She waited several hours before realising and admitting the facts as they were. Exhausted, she presented herself to the judicial police on 28 July, after three days of "terrible psychological manipulation". The first investigations by the judicial police who traced the telephone number led them to "a number in England based in Israel" and made it possible to stop around twenty similar attempts at fraud in August 2005 by warning the bankers in time.

Gilbert C. then invented a variant in September that earned him much more, getting bankers to make "international transfers" into accounts supposedly used by terrorists." With his phenomenal gab, the journalist wrote, and his way of persuading bankers that they were serving their country in the fight against Al-Qaeda, the "mastermind" Gilbert managed to get millions transferred into the accounts of shell companies set up in Hong Kong by his front men. On 28 September, a bank disbursed \$2.5 million in Switzerland and \$2.72 million in Hong Kong. Alerted by a suspicious banker, the Judicial Police blocked the funds. In contrast, two transfers totalling 7.25 million euros were transferred on 29 September to accounts in Estonia and immediately deposited by the "Gilbert gang"."

Gilbert C., 40, and his brother Simon, 38, both born in Paris, now live as refugees in Israel. From his hiding place, Gilbert C. had the cheek to taunt the judicial police on the phone: "I'm not going back, I'm not going to give up, I'm protected by Israel". After reading the account of this scam, everyone will agree that the commonly used word "cheek" is now a bit mild to describe these actions. Unless, of course, it is another form of the famous Jewish humour[338].

The best explanation for this phenomenon seems to be of a religious and moral nature. Indeed, we know that in certain mystical Christian sects of the Middle Ages, the followers, the "chosen ones", imagined themselves to be above the law, believing that they too were "allowed to do anything". These anarchistic manifestations can be described as "antinomian", if "antinomism" is understood as a movement of liberation from the law (nomos). Generally speaking, all beliefs or doctrines that diminish or deny the importance of moral rules for those who have attained "perfection" can be categorised under this name.

There were also antinomian currents throughout the history of Christianity. At the time of the Protestant Reformation, for example, there arose properly antinomian sects, such as the Anabaptists of Münster in the 16th century. This phenomenon, which spread within Christianity, was in reality, according to Gershom Scholem, a copy of Jewish messianism:

"The political messianism and millenarianism that developed important religious currents within Christianity is a replica of Jewish messianism, Scholem wrote. We know how firmly these movements were condemned by the orthodoxy of both Catholicism and Protestantism. From the point of view of the facts, the reproach was undoubtedly quite justified." This situation was explained, Scholem continued, because " revolutionary messianism and millenarianism, such as always appeared, for example, in the Taborites, the Anabaptists or in the radical wing of the Puritans, " has " drawn its inspiration mainly from the Old Testament and not from Christian sources."

In fact, in Christianity, redemption, which has already taken place, has in a way calmed the spirits, while on the contrary, "anti-Noma tendencies are always latent in the utopian messianism[339] " present in Judaism. And this is perhaps an important point to understand the mentality of some Jews today who behave in some cases politically, financially or intellectually as if they felt themselves to be above the laws of this world[340].

---

[338] It was actually Gilbert Chiki (read *The Jewish Mafia*, Hervé Ryssen).

[339] Gershom Scholem, *Le Messianisme juif*, 1971, Calmann-Lévy, 1974, p. 42, 48, 49. See again Annex VI. 2

[340] On scams: Hervé Ryssen, *The Planetary Hopes, (*2022) and *The Jewish Mafia*, (*2022*)

Contempt for the goy

The Yiddish novelist Isaac Bashevis Singer was born in 1904 near Warsaw into a Hasidic family. He emigrated to the United States in 1935 and was awarded the Nobel Prize for literature in 1978 in recognition of his entire body of work in which he described the life of Central European Jews. In his novel *The Slave*, published in 1962, he gave us an insight into the way Jews might see the world of the Goyim. It tells the story of Jacob, a poor Jew in 17th century Poland who was sold into slavery to a peasant in the mountains after pogroms destroyed his community.

In the midst of these peasants, Jacob never renounced his Judaism: "The highlanders had wanted to marry him off to one of their daughters, build him a hut and make him a member of the village, but Jacob had refused to renounce the Jewish religion." This is how Isaac Bashevis Singer described the Polish peasant women of the time:

"They chased him night and day. Attracted by his tall figure, they provoked him, chatting, laughing and behaving almost like animals. They relieved themselves in his presence without the slightest restraint, and continually rolled up their skirts to show him insect bites on their thighs and hips. Jacob behaved as if he were deaf and blind, and he did so not only because fornication was a mortal sin, but because these women were impure, had lice in their clothes and were always dishevelled; many had pimples and stitches on their faces, ate rodents and bird carrion. Some of them could hardly speak, grunted like animals, gesticulated with their hands, shrieked and laughed like fools[341]."

But the master's daughter, Wanda, was nevertheless a peasant girl different from the others." Compared to those savages, Wanda, the widowed daughter of Jan Bzik, looked like a city lady... At twenty-five, she was taller than most women. Blonde and blue-eyed, her complexion was fair and her features were harmonious." All the peasants were assiduous in their pursuit of her.

Evidently, Wanda fell in love with the slave who was more educated and finer than those rude and crude peasants: "She fell in love with the slave as soon as she saw him ..., the attraction he exerted on the young woman did not diminish, and she waited impatiently for the night to come. The people of the village murmured. The women

[341] In Judaism, the Jewish man is the *homo locuens,* the one who speaks. Bernard-Henri Lévy, in his book on *Daniel Pearl,* shows the Islamists "hissing" like snakes (JMB).

laughed and made sardonic remarks. It was said that the slave had bewitched her."

The only creature worthy of respect among these Poles was thus promised to the Jew, despite the reluctance the latter might have against the village goyim: "In the village there were plenty of cripples, boys and girls with goitres, with deformed heads or disfigured by birthmarks. There were also mute, epileptics and strange types with six fingers on each hand or on each foot." It must be said that the members of Wanda's family were not worth much more than the rest of the peasants: "The hut stank, her family behaved as if they were animals. It had not occurred to any of them that they could bathe in the stream that ran in front of the house[342]."

Jacob, however, could not marry a woman of the goyim without great internal suffering. He was well aware of "the Talmudic law, according to which any member of the community is authorised to kill a man who cohabits with a gentile, [although] it could only be applied after a warning, and provided that there were witnesses to the adultery[343]." However, "he sinned enough by eating the bread of the Gentiles. His soul tolerated no more impurity."

Moreover, the situation was complicated by the fact that "the Jewish law forbade Gentiles to convert for reasons outside the faith." Despite all these difficulties, he had to admit things as they were: "Satan had become arrogant …, asked him to become a pagan among the pagans and ordered him to marry Wanda or at least to sleep with her."

That Polish society was really repulsive. Watch the priest enter the village tavern: "The tavern was almost in ruins. The roof was broken and the walls were covered with fungus… There was no pavement. One of the customers got up and went to urinate in a corner, on a pile of rubbish. Zagayek's daughter laughed, showing her toothless gums… There were loud footsteps, grunts and snorts. Dziobak, the priest, entered the tavern. He was a short, broad-shouldered man… His eyes were green like frizzy grapes, his eyebrows like brushes, his nose thick and mottled with black, and his chin sunken. Dziobak wore his cassock covered with stains. He walked with a stooped, limping gait, leaning on two thick canes. The priests are shaved, this one's face had black hair, thick and coarse like bristles… Dziobak had a hollow voice that seemed to come out of his chest as if from the bottom of a barrel—Yes, one

342 Isaac Bashevis Singer, *The Slave*, 1962, Epublibre, digital publisher German25 (2014), p. 35, 45, 46, 64, 97, 98

343 The Talmud also says: "Heretics, informers and apostates are to be lowered into a pit and forgotten there." (*Avodah Zarah, 26b*)

needs a drink to burn the devil." Listen next to the priest Dziobak spreading hatred against the poor Jews: "He opened up

his frog's mouth, exposing a long black tooth." The tavern keeper filled him in on the conversation before his arrival: "We were talking about the Jew that Jan Bzik has in the mountains. Dziobak was furious. —I'd like to know why there's so much talk. Go upstairs and send him away at once in the name of God[344]."

Reading Isaac Bashevis, it seems that all Poles were equally disgusting. The nobles did not seem to be worth more than the peasants or the priests: "They were always drunk. The peasants kissed their feet and, in return, received a few blows with the whip. The girls would come home with bloody shirts, and after nine months they would give birth to bastards."

Jacob had nothing in common with that human rabble. He was a Jew, and, like all Jews, he was educated, intelligent and full of finesse." To occupy his time he would enumerate the two hundred and forty-eight commandments and the three hundred and sixty-five prohibitions contained in the Torah. Although he did not know them by heart, his years of exile had taught him that human memory is very miserly." So he went to the mountain and began to engrave on the rock the six hundred and thirteen prescriptions of the Law: "It was slow work. On the rock he engraved phrases, fragments of phrases and single words. The Torah had not disappeared. It remained hidden in the recesses of his mind."

His thoughts were profound, far removed from the preoccupations of those vulgar Poles: "He now noticed things that had escaped him before, and that one law of the Torah generated a dozen laws of the Mishnah, and five dozen of the Gemara; in the more recent commentaries, the laws were as numerous as the sands of the desert[345]."

Unfortunately, ever since he had gone to the mountain with Jan Bzik's flock, Jacob had been forced to meet the other shepherds. One day they came to him to invite him to drink and dance with them: "The man drooled, stammered and slurred his speech. His comrades were drunk and laughing and shouting incoherently, holding their stomachs in their hands and rolling on the ground... These people stank; their smell was a mixture of sweat and urine with the stench of something nameless, as if their bodies were rotting in life. Jacob had to hold his

---

344 Isaac Bashevis Singer, *The Slave,* 1962, Epublibre, digital publisher German25 (2014), p. 117, 131, 147, 147, 163, 108, 112

345 Isaac Bashevis Singer, *The Slave,* 1962, Epublibre, digital publisher German25 (2014), p. 119, 325.

nose, while the girls laughed until tears came to their eyes. The men leaned against each other and uttered barking cries." In a clearing where Jacob was brought, "drunken musicians played drums, flutes, a ram's horn... The audience, however, was too intoxicated to do anything but roll on the ground, grunt like pigs, lick the earth and mutter at the stones. Many lay like corpses..." Well," he said to himself, "I've seen it now. These are the abominations that moved God to demand the annihilation of whole peoples"... But suddenly, as he looked at the rabble, he realised that there were forms of corruption that could only be cleansed by fire. Thousands of years of idolatry were manifest in these savages. In their eyes, dilated and reddened, Baal, Ashtoreth and Moloch were peeping out."

Of course, these early Christians behaved like beasts: "The shepherd who had given him the drink shrieked. —Give him more. Let the Jew drink. Fill his glass. -Let him eat pork," shouted another. He foamed at the mouth and cursed... His comrades swore with laughter and uttered threats. —Murderer of God! Jew! Tender! "

"A few steps away, a shepherd jumped on a girl, but he was too drunk to do anything. They both writhed and struggled like dog and bitch. Those around them guffawed, spat, blew and whipped at the couple."

Jacob was far superior to these subhuman people: "He held with the Almighty a constant debate: How long will the heathen continue to rule the world, while the scandal and darkness of Egypt prevail?"

Yet the image of Wanda haunted him day and night." Though he knew it was all Satan's trickery, Jacob thought of her all day long, unable to control his desire. He was ashamed to desire a gentile in this way, but the more he tried to stifle his desire, the more it grew." Isaac Singer was then going to pick that beautiful flower from the dunghill on which it grew, for we must take what is beautiful from those filthy goyim: "Jacob awoke shivering, opened his eyes, and found Wanda lying beside him on the straw. Although the air in the stable was cold, he felt the warmth of her body. Wanda pressed against him and brushed her lips against his cheek." And Wanda would eventually say to him, "Take me to your Jews. I want to be your wife and give you a child... Where you go, I will go. Your people shall be my people. Your God will be my God."

It is good, and it is sensible for goyim to renounce their families and traditions. But entering Judaism is only possible for docile and obedient goyim women: "But you must not become one of us because you love me, but because you have faith in God." To which Wanda replied: "I do, Jacob, I do. But you must teach me. Without you I am blind[346]."

On Christmas Day there was one man short of the full number of diners, but Jacob stubbornly refused: "Jacob was adamant. It was not kosher food; it was all idolatry, and it was better to die than to take part in such ceremonies[347]. He stayed in the barn and ate dry bread, as usual[348]. Wanda was hurt that he was isolating himself and hiding from the others. The girls made fun of him, and also of her, since Jacob was her lover. The mother spoke plainly of the need to get rid of the accursed Jew who had brought disgrace to the family. Wanda took extra precautions to visit him at night, for she knew the men wanted to harm him[349]. They planned to take him out of the barn and force him to eat pork…"

However, the story ended rather badly. Jacob managed to extirpate Wanda from his community; the two of them settled in a small town in Pilitz, where Sara—"her very name showed that she had converted to Judaism"—pretended to be deaf and dumb so that her origins would not be suspected." If he told the truth, Sara and he would be burned at the stake."

But the pains of childbirth would make it impossible for Sara to hold back her screams. The other women were stunned by what they thought was a deaf and dumb woman: "Do the dumb cry out? Do they cry out in pain? Sara cried and screamed, but did not speak." Indeed, Sara was crying, screaming, and then even raving … in Polish: "The speaker is a dybbuk. -A dybbuk has entered Sara, shouted a voice in the dark street… Who are you, how did you get into Sara's body?—asked a woman, addressing the dybbuk… Bring the rabbi! shouted a woman. He will take the dybbuk out of her[350]."

Poor Sarah would die in childbirth[351]. Jacob managed to escape, going into exile in Palestine with the baby. Twenty years later, he

---

[346] Isaac Bashevis Singer, *The Slave*, 1962, Epublibre, digital publisher German25 (2014), p. 167, 50, 183, 200, 204, 237

[347] Talmud, *Iore Dea (112, 1)*: "Avoid eating with Christians, it generates familiarity."

[348]Talmud, *Gittin (62a)*: "A Jew may not enter a gentile's house on a holiday and greet him, for it appears that he is blessing him in honour of his holiday."

[349]Attention! To strike a Jew is like slapping God himself in the face" (*Sanhedrin, 58b*)." It was again the madness of Kafka saying that "he who strikes a Jew strikes humanity"." Bernard-Henri Lévy, *Le Testament de Dieu*, Grasset, 1979, p. 181.

[350] Isaac Bashevis Singer, *The Slave*, 1962, Epublibre, digital publisher German25 (2014), p. 634, 491, 602, 609, 612, 615.

[351]Talmud, *Orach Cahiim (330, 2)*: "We do not help a non-Jewish woman to give birth on Shabbat, even by doing something that does not involve the desecration of Shabbat."

returned to Pilitz to be buried next to Sarah. His son became a teacher at a yeshiva in Jerusalem.

The famous novelist Philip Roth summed up in a few lines the contempt and spirit of revenge that ooze from the pen of American Jewish intellectuals such as Appelfeld, Bernard Malamud, Norman Mailer and Saul Below: ""The word *goy* came up… It was the word his father turned to from time to time to define irreversible stupidity". The gentile with whom the Jews in your books share the world, Roth said, addressing Appelfeld, is often the embodiment not only of that irreversible stupidity, but also of threatening and primitive social behaviour; the *goy* is a drunkard who beats his wife; the *goy is* a half-wild, uncouth and brutal fellow, unable to control himself… In other cases, Roth noted, the *goy* is described in terms of a pedestrian spirit … brimming with health. *Enviable* health. As Cattails' mother says of her half-gentle son: "He's not like me, he's not frightened. A different, calmer blood runs through his veins." "

But "the most one-sided portrait of the *goy* in American narrative is in Bernard Malamud's *The Clerk*. The *goy is* Frank Alpine, the vagabond who ransacks the poor grocery shop of a Jew, Bober, and then attempts to rape Bober's devoted daughter." Eventually, the aforementioned would end up "abjuring *goy* bestiality." In *The Victim*, Saul Below's second novel, the hero, a New York Jew, is pursued by Allbee. He is "a gentle misfit and alcoholic, no less a scoundrel and a crook than Alpine," wrote Philip Roth, who added about Norman Mailer:

"We all know that in Mailer the sexual sadist is called Sergius O'Shaugnessny, and the one who kills his wife is Stephen Rojack, and the unrepentant murderer is not called Lepke Buchalter, but Gary Gilmore[352]."

Let us recall here Albert Memmi's statement: "Jewish identity is in general much more present than is believed in the behaviour and thinking, even in the confessions, of most Jews[353]." So when a Jew writes a novel, we must understand that he is also sending us a message.

The spirit of revenge

We have already seen, through film productions, that the

[352] Philip Roth, *Operation Shylock*, Debolsillo Penguin Random House, Barcelona, 2005, p. 243, 244.
[353] Albert Memmi, in the endnote of David Bakan's book, *Freud et la tradition mystique juive*, 1963, Payot, 2001, p. 342.

cosmopolitan spirits are not only moved by generous ideas of Peace and Love, but that their universal enterprise takes the form of a tireless planetary propaganda which reveals a rather characteristic spirit of revenge. Revenge is indeed a dominant feature of the cosmopolitan spirit for reasons that we can symbolically trace back to the destruction of Solomon's Temple in Jerusalem. Naturally, this feeling of revenge appears frequently in literature.

Les Éditions des Belles lettres reprinted in 2000, in the collection *L'Arbre de Judée*, a book by Pierre Paraf, an author we have already mentioned above. In that collection of novels entitled *When Israel Loved*, Paraf told the story of General von Morderburg, illustrating quite well this mentality animated by pride and revenge.

General von Morderburg has led a quiet and discreet life since 1918. At the age of seventy-five, he is retired from the Prussian army. As a young officer, he had once married Countess Josepha von Neuendorff: "To tell the truth, this marriage had not failed to arouse in the young captain certain doubts and uneasiness. Josepha's mother had been born Goldschroeder and, as such, was she not descended from a family of Jews from Poland...?"

His son, Lieutenant Fritz von Morderburg, was "a tall young man with black eyebrows." He "had always shown a different character from his schoolmates. A strange nostalgia animated him, though he himself did not sense his origin… Whence came those bloodier lips, those larger pupils, and those eyes whose depths reflected seas more voluptuous than those of Pomerania? Where did he get those airs of a dispossessed king which he dragged unwillingly through the old castle park, into the austere rectitude of the barracks, and even into the disciplined sumptuousness of Potsdam and Berlin; where did he get that disturbing tendency to sympathise too much with the sufferings and aspirations of his soldiers which made his superiors say: "The young baron is an ideologue? His parents had neither the interest nor the possibility of delving into this mystery. Fritz was strong, gentle and loyal: what did it matter to them?

The reader has already guessed: Fritz knew nothing of his distant origins, which secretly gave him that instinctive superiority over the Prussian military brutes around him. Life went on without drama in this aristocratic family, until the day the son informed his parents that he wanted to marry a foreigner, a Russian Jewess: Rachel Davidova. His father, curt and authoritarian, did not accept this ill-fated marriage and judged his son "unworthy to wear the uniform and unworthy to be a German." The general brutally pronounced his sentence: ""Our son is dead ... no one in the castle must speak his name. Let him become a dancer or a prostitute, if he pleases! Fritz von Morderburg has disappeared from this world". In the castle chapel the baroness prayed for a long time. The general heard at night the sound of her stifled sobs."

As we can see, the Prussian traditions were not tolerant. This rigidity was evidently accompanied by a most odious anti-Semitism, as Pierre Paraf imagined it: The general "could conceive of no greater pride than to be, perhaps of all the generals of the Reich commanding an army, the only one never to have let a Jew pass the castle fences."

Fritz eventually died during the war. A 1916 letter written by his beloved Rachel effectively revealed his unarmed nature: "A poet, the general thought indignantly; that was what was missing for our poor son! A pacifist, a humanitarian, growled the general sadly. A true soldier may be afraid. But he avoids confessing it[354]! "

It seems that the memory of his son did not soften the Prussian baron's stony heart. It was only after Rachel Davidova presented herself at the castle with a letter that Fritz had written before his death that the general felt remorse and realised how tragic the situation was. In fact, reading the letter, he realised that Fritz had renounced the German Reich and joined the Austrian army under a false name. The drama was that under this name he served under his own father, and that his father, not recognising him, sent him to die at the front. General Morderburg was then depressed by the news: "Our Fritz is dead. He is dead because of me... I am his murderer. I killed him twice. First by expelling him from the castle, and then, later, on that March morning eight years ago, by appointing him, without having recognised him, to occupy a trench at Verdun."

Fritz's true humanistic nature came out in him before he died. This is what he wrote to Rachel, his son's beloved: "Israel, whose voice I was prevented from hearing for so long, Israel, you who have awakened in my soul, on that day, your victory will be near. And you, dear Rachel, your parents from the ghetto will not have suffered in vain[355]! "In reality, it was evidently the author who expressed himself in this way.

The punishment inflicted by the novelist on this reactionary general was quite severe, for he had him kill his own son. The days passed slowly for the old couple who had been struck down by fate. The punishment was harsh enough; cruel even. But Pierre Paraf's fertile imagination had other tortures in store.

General von Morderburg ended up a lonely widower. One day, the

---

[354] Pierre Paraf, *Quand Israël aima*, 1929, Les Belles Lettres, 2000, p. 138-149, 169.

[355] Pierre Paraf, *Quand Israël aima*, 1929, Les Belles Lettres, 2000, p. 196.

municipality asked him to preside over the unveiling of a monument in honour of the war dead. But overwhelmed by doubts and scruples, locked up in his loneliness and suffering for so long, he judged himself unworthy of such an honour and politely declined. Such an attitude would provoke the indignation of the population and create a scandal. The case was discussed in the military hierarchy, and the Reich government decided to abolish his pacifist general's pension." Nature takes advantage of it to perfidiously take her revenge," added Pierre Paraf kindly, who seemed to continue the tale of his personal revenge thus: "When the general crosses, solitary and sombre, the streets of Pommernberg, the mayor avoids greeting him"; the children mock him, "his poverty moves no one."

Alone and desperate, he finally wrote to Rachel Davidova: "Madam, even though you are Jewish and Jews do not like us very much, I beg you, in memory of the lieutenant, to take the train to Pommernberg to comfort a poor father and tell him that his Fritz loved him in spite of everything… And perhaps Herr Baron will leave you the castle to reward you when he dies. In his burning cheeks, General von Morderburg felt the tears flowing. This interminable eleventh chapter of this book is simply titled: "The victory of Israel: *The Victory of Israel*. The old general died in his bed." Israel had loved. Israel had won[356]."

This "anti-racist" story could have ended with those words, but no! A final chapter was still needed to quench the thirst for revenge that was welling up in Pierre Paraf's imagination. Indeed, Fritz was not dead! Although badly wounded and mutilated, he was still alive. There he was at the old general's funeral, in the wagon beside Rachel. During the funeral procession through the streets of the village, the general was booed to his grave. Young people shouted: "Down with Morderburg! Long live Germany! And they spat three times with contempt."

In his final ordeal, the general had only a miserable hearse. In addition, the patriotic hatred of the populace was mercilessly inflicted upon him. But then, an extraordinary scene took place, like an apparition which impressed the imagination of the people: "The mutilated, surly and elusive man, who had hitherto remained motionless, rose from the little carriage, tearing off the woollen cloth which covered his face. The attendants were petrified, believing that he was going to speak. But Fritz contented himself with raising his eyes towards them, and the expression in his eyes was such that the trembling

[356] Pierre Paraf, *Quand Israël aima*, 1929, Les Belles Lettres, 2000, p. 204, 217, 229.

women crossed themselves, the young men fell silent and lowered their heads, and the men returned to their homes in fright[357]."

You get the picture: that crowd of stupid, dumb, dumbed-down *goyim* had just realised who the new master was. The style is a bit grandiloquent, but the story has the merit of revealing the background of the cosmopolitan spirit. In Hebrew, these motivations are summed up with the following formula: "*Laassoth nekama bagoïm*"; "To take revenge on the Gentiles[358]."

Rage and the passion to destroy

The Florentine writer Giovani Papini (1881–1956) was "one of the most brilliant writers of his time". Seduced in his youth by Marinetti's Futurism, he would end up following the example of many Jews by sincerely converting to Catholicism. In a novel entitled *Gog*, published by Flammarion in 1932, Papini summarised in a condensed form the anti-Semitic thinking of his time through the monologue of a strange character, a certain Ben Roubi, who appeared for a job interview. This text, written by a Jewish intellectual, is a key document for understanding Jewish identity crises:

---

[357]"The language of the eyes is of great importance in everyday life—they always mean something… You can devour or murder with your eyes…" My brother rightly said that he would a hundred times rather have his eyes hammered out by our mother than receive a single glance from our father." The weight of the glance is immense in a culture where the evil eye is a constant threat." (Mark Zborowski, *Olam*, 1952, Plon, 1992, p. 324).

[358]While this account is nothing more than a revealingly convoluted fiction, these motivations can sometimes be revealed more clearly in the wake of real and tragic historical events. Just listen to Joseph Roth, in his book *Wandering Jews*, published in 1937, as a warning: "An anathema of the rabbis has been hanging over Spain ever since the Jews had to leave that country… Perhaps I may be permitted at this point to refer to the most terrible event of recent years, and precisely in connection with my reports on the anathema which, after the expulsion of the Jews from Spain, was pronounced by the rabbis: the Spanish Civil War. Few readers will probably know the version according to which *jerem*, the great anathema, was to expire this year. Needless to say, I do not have the right to allow myself to establish a clear relationship between the metaphysical and the very cruel reality. But I do have the right to refer to these, to say the least, shocking facts. I do not want to take for granted the formulation that just when the anathema expires, the greatest catastrophe Spain has ever known begins. I just want to point out this—certainly more than curious—simultaneity; and that verse of the Fathers, which goes like this: "The judgement of the Lord dawns every hour, here below and there above". Sometimes centuries pass, but the judgment is unfailing." This is a way of warning us, with exquisite tact, that revenge is a dish best served cold. In Joseph Roth, *Judíos errantes*, Acantilado 164, Barcelona, 2008, p. 99, 123, 124. Regarding the Spanish Civil War and the role of the Jews, read *El Fanatismo judío*. (NdT).

"What could the Jew, trampled and sullied with gargages, do to avenge himself on his enemies? To demean, degrade, unmask, dissolve the ideals of the *Goyim*, to destroy the values by which Christianity claims to subsist. And, indeed, on the face of it, the Jewish intelligentsia has done nothing in a century but sully and undermine your beliefs, the pillars that support the edifice of your thought. From the moment the Jews have been able to write freely, your whole spiritual scaffolding threatens to collapse.

"German Romanticism had created Idealism and rehabilitated Catholicism: suddenly a little Jew from Düsseldorf, Heine, bursts in and uses his jovial and malignant inspiration to mock the Romantics, the Idealists and the Catholics.

"Men have always believed that politics, morality, religion and art are higher manifestations of the spirit, that they have nothing to do with the purse and the stomach; along comes a Jew from Treves, Marx, and shows that all these very idealistic things grow in the muck and dung of low economics.

"Everyone imagines that the man of genius is a divine being, and the criminal a monster; then a Jew of Verona, Lombroso, comes along and shows you clearly that genius is a half-mad epileptic, and that criminals are nothing but the manifestation of the atavisms of our ancestors, and that they are therefore our next of kin.

"At the end of the 19th century, the Europe of Tolstoy, of Ibsen, of Dostoevsky, of Nietzsche, of Verlaine, boasted of being one of the great epochs of humanity; a Jew from Budapest, Max Nordau, appears, mocking them and explaining that your famous poets and writers are degenerates, and that your civilisation is based on lies.

"Each of us is persuaded that he is, as a rule, a normal and moral person: here comes a Jew from Freiberg in Moravia, Sigmund Freud, and discovers that, inside the most virtuous and distinguished gentleman, there lurks an inverted, an incestuous and a murderer.

"Since the times of courtly love and the Platonic troubadours, we have been accustomed to consider woman as an idol, as a vessel of perfection; a Jew from Vienna, Weininger, intervenes and demonstrates scientifically and dialectically that woman is an ignoble and repugnant being, an abyss of filth and baseness.

"Intellectuals, philosophers and so on, have always held intelligence to be the only means of attaining the truth whose pursuit is man's greatest glory; along comes a Jew from Paris, Bergson, and, with his subtle and brilliant analyses, overturns the primacy of the intellect, dismantles the age-old edifice of Platonism, and concludes that conceptual thought is incapable of embracing reality.

"Religions are almost universally regarded as the result of an admirable collaboration between God and the highest faculty possessed by the human being; but a Jew from Saint-Germain-en-Laye, Solomon Reinach, contrives to show that religions are simply a redoubt of primitive savage taboos, of systems of prohibitions with variable ideological superstructures.

"We thought we were living peacefully in a solid and ordered universe, based on time and space considered distinct and absolute; along comes a Jew from Ulm, Einstein, and establishes that time and space are the same thing, that absolute space does not exist and, like time, that everything is based on perpetual relativity and that the edifice of the old physics, the pride of modern science, has been destroyed.

"Scientific rationalism was sure that it had conquered thought and had found the key to reality; a Jew from Lublin, Meyerson, appeared to dispel this illusion as well: rational laws are never completely adapted to reality, for there is always an irreducible and rebellious residue that defies the supposed triumph of reasoning reason. And one could go on.

"And I do not speak of politics, where the dictator Bismark has as his antagonist the Jew Lassalle, where Gladstone sees the Jew Disraeli beat him again and again, where Cavour has as his right-hand man the Jew Artom, Clemenceau, the Jew Mandel, and Lenin, the Jew Trotsky. Notice how I did not highlight obscure second-rank names. Intellectual Europe today is, to a large extent, under the sway, or, if you prefer, under the spell of the great Jews I have quoted.

"Whether German or French, Italian or Polish, poets or mathematicians, anthropologists or philosophers, they all have a common trait, a common goal: to call into question the accepted truth, to lower what is above, to sully what seems pure, to shake and shatter what seems solid, to stone what is respected. This dissolving effect of the poisons we have been distilling for centuries is the great Jewish vengeance on the Greek, Latin and Christian world. The Greeks mocked us, the Romans decimated and dispersed us, the Christians tortured and despoiled us, but we, too weak to avenge ourselves by force, have carried out a tenacious and corrosive offensive against the pillars on which rests the civilisation born in Plato's Athens and the Rome of emperors and popes. Our revenge is at hand.

"As capitalists, we dominate the financial markets at a time when the economic sphere is almost everything. As thinkers, we dominate intellectual markets, gradually undermining old beliefs, sacred or profane, revealed religions as well as secular religions.

"The Jew unites within himself the two most fearful extremes; despot in the realm of matter, anarchist in the realm of the spirit. In the economic order, you are our servants, and in the intellectual order, our victims. The people who were accused of immolating a God wanted in turn to immolate the idols of intelligence and sentiment, and to force you to kneel before the most powerful idol, the only one left: Money. Our humiliation, from the slavery of Babylon to the defeat of Bar-Kojba, from the ghettos of the Middle Ages to the French Revolution, our humiliation is at last well paid, and the outcast among the peoples can now sing the hymn of a double victory!

"...In speaking thus, little Ben Roubi had become a little excited: his eyes sparkled in their sockets; his slender hands cleaved the air; his voice, weak at first, became higher-pitched. He realised he had spoken too much and suddenly fell silent. There was a long silence. At the end, Dr. Ben Roubi, in a shy, soft voice, asked me: "Could you advance me a thousand francs on my fee? I have a suit to make and I would like to pay off some small debts I have"... When he received his cheque, he looked at me with a smile that was meant to be fine: "Don't take at face value the paradoxes I spouted this afternoon. Jews are like that: we like to talk too much; and, when we go on, we talk, talk, talk ... and we always end up offending someone. If I have offended you in any way, please forgive me[359]"."

This undoubtedly anti-Semitic text can perhaps be explained by Giovanni Papini's resentment against his former community. He must surely be included in the long list of Jews who suffered from this famous "self-hatred", and who professed anti-Semitism in order to free themselves from their heavy burden. Curiously enough, Papini even went so far as to splash his invectives on poor Otto Weininger, whose heart was already wounded and broken enough. But beyond these considerations, it is true that we seem to see in this extraordinarily explicit text the same statements as in Alain Minc, Viviane Forrester, Camille Marbo or Pierre Paraf, in which the humiliation of the enemy always precedes the "final victory".

Evil

The image of the Jew has always been negative in the European world until recently. If it was able to evolve in a much more positive direction during the 20th century, it seems that this was only possible

---

[359] Giovanni Papini, *Gog*, Flammarion, 1932, p. 75-79

thanks to the power of the media, which has imposed the image of the persecuted Jew in the minds of Westerners. In his great *History of Anti-Semitism*, Leon Poliakov recalled that at the beginning of the Renaissance Christians were horrified by Jews. Poliakov gave, for example, the testimony of a bourgeois at the end of the 15th century who explained the persecution of the Jews in his own way:

"The Jews are harshly punished from time to time. But they do not suffer innocently, they suffer because of their wickedness: because they cheat the people and ruin the countryside with their usury and their secret murders, as everyone knows. That is why they are so persecuted and not because they are innocent. There is no people more wicked, more cunning, more avaricious, more shameless, more boisterous, more venomous, more choleric, more deceitful and ignominious[360]."

In the following century, William Shakespeare popularised in his plays a particularly negative image of the Jew, embodied in all his harshness by the character of Shylock. The American novelist Philip Roth recently despaired of "the genuine loathing of the Jews that moved Shakespeare", and how he had made Shylock a rapacious, ruthless and unfeeling usurer, who went so far as to take human flesh from his debtor to collect the sums he had borrowed. In Shakespeare's play, in fact, we see him sharpening his knife to remove the pound of flesh from Antonio's chest.

"For audiences all over the world, Shylock is the incarnation of the Jew... That brutal, repellent, villainous Jew, twisted by hatred and revenge, who has become our double, in the eyes of the enlightened conscience of the West... Do you remember the first thing Shylock says? Do you remember those three words? What Jew would be able to forget them? What Christian would be able to forgive them? "Three thousand ducats"... Those repellent and hateful Jews ... whose persistence as villains, both in history and in the theatre, is unparalleled; the hook-nosed moneylender, the selfish, miserable, money-mad degenerate, the Jew who meets with his own kind in the *synagogue* to plot the death of virtuous Christians... That is the Jew of Europe, the one the English threw out in 1290, the one the Spanish expelled in 1492, the one the Poles terrorised, the one the Russians decimated, the one the Germans incinerated, the one the British and Americans rejected as the crematorium ovens roared in Treblinka[361]."

Philip Roth surely knew that Shakespeare's Shylock was staged in

[360] Léon Poliakov, *Histoire de l'antisémitisme, Tome I,* Points Seuil, 1990, p. 360, 361.

[361] Philip Roth, *Operación Shylock,* Debolsillo Penguin Random House, Barcelona, 2005, p. 316, 317, 318

1600, and therefore could in no way influence the rulers of the preceding centuries to motivate the expulsion of the undesirables.

Another famous 20th century American novelist left an interesting personal testimony. In his biography, *Turns of Time*, Arthur Miller, described his maternal grandfather, Louis Barnett, as follows: "He had owned a flourishing business in the 1920s, yet he had gradually acquired a reputation for direct action. He would invite the union leaders of his labour contingent to climb to the top of a staircase and while talking to them in the most judicious manner, he would give them a hard shove so that their heads would collide and he would throw the astonished individuals down the stairs." This is how he described the Jews he met in his environment: "the mean, money-mad *cloakies*, the Jews who were only interested in business[362]."

The philosopher Jacob Talmon confirmed this hardness of character of some of their fellows: "It is beyond doubt that the excessive vehemence of the Jews, typical of the constant need of marginal minorities to justify their independence by an assertion of themselves, has an ambivalent polarity: besides an idealistic vocation for the things of the spirit, we see in the Jews a particularly hard, sharp and unscrupulous kind of egoism[363]."

It would be false, however, to think that this harshness only manifests itself against the *goyim*. Philip Roth, in *Operation Shylock*, bitterly lamented this communal specificity:

Why is it that we Jews treat each other with so little regard? Why do we Jews, when we are among ourselves, lose the courtesy that is normal in all coexistence? Why do we have to magnify every offence? Why must there be fighting every time there is provocation? ... The lack of love of the Jews for their Jewish comrades," said Smilesbuger, "is the cause of much suffering among our people. The animosity, the ridicule, the pure and simple hatred of one Jew for another... Why? Why, where is our tolerance and forgiveness, when it comes to our neighbours, why is there so much division among Jews? ... Because of the festering hatred that Jews have for each other... Fierce quarrels, verbal insults, malicious backbiting, scornful gossip, jeers and jeers, destructive criticism, constant complaints, condemnation, contempt... Who has put it into the heads of the Jews that one must always be talking, if not shouting or making jokes at someone's expense, or picking apart the faults of one's best friend over the telephone for a whole afternoon?"

---

362 Arthur Miller, *Vueltas al tiempo*, Tusquets, Barcelona, 1999, p. 15, 27

363 J.-L. Talmon, *Destin d'Israël*, 1965, Calmann-Lévy, 1967, p. 32.

This slander has a name: *loshon hora*. Philip Roth pointed here to the pathological dimension of the thing. Those Jews who could not stop badmouthing turned to Freud, wrote Philip Roth:

"To Freud the verbally incontinent Jews flocked like sheep, and to Freud they spouted *loshon hora* that had not left the mouths of Jews since the destruction of the Second Temple[364]... Now: it might be argued, with some cynicism, that saying *loshon hora* is what makes Jews Jewish, and that nothing more Jewishly Jewish can be conceived than what Freud prescribed in his practice to his Jewish patients."

"If a saint of tolerance ... went so far as to congratulate himself on his own deafness, because he no longer had to listen to *thehon hora*, imagine what damage he could do to the frightened mind of the average Jew," observed Philip Roth. The novelist, who dreamed of seeing "Jews no longer free from the turbulence of their own disorders" and who would not "slander and despise their Jewish comrades", despaired of seeing his people mend their ways: "If for one moment of time there were not a single word of *loshon hora* in the mouth of any Jew... If, all at once, the Jews of the whole world decided to shut their mouths for one second... But given the impossibility of even one second of Jewish silence, what hope is left for our people?"

But in Israel, the situation is not much different than in the diaspora." The *loshon hora* is a hundred times worse in Eretz Yisroel, a thousand times worse in Eretz Yisroel than it was in Poland... In Poland there was anti-Semitism, which at least forced us to silence the faults of Jewish comrades in the presence of the goyim. But here, without having to worry about the *goyim*, you put gates on the camp... They think of something that can generate hatred: they say it. They think of something that might generate resentment: they say it. A joke at someone's expense? They tell it, they put it in writing, they include it in the next news programme[365]."

Isaac Bashevis Singer also put these words into the mouth of his character in his novel *The Slave*: "No," he finally said, "speaking ill of others cannot be as serious a sin as eating pork, or else no one would dare to do it... It is easier not to eat pork than to master the tongue[366]."

In another of his novels, *The Destuction of Kreshev*, Isaac Bashevis

---

[364] *Loshon hora*: literally "tongue of evil": evil speaking, viper's tongue, slander, evil tongue. The second Temple was destroyed by the Roman legions of Titus.

[365] Philip Roth, *Operation Shylock*, Debolsillo Penguin Random House, Barcelona, 2005, p. 383–390.

[366] Isaac Bashevis Singer, *The Slave*, 1962, Epublibre, digital publisher German25 (2014), p. 440, 441.

Singer presented another testimony to the harshness of the Jews in the shtetls of Central Europe. Shloimele's wife, Lisa, guilty of adultery with the coachman, was to pay dearly for her and her lover's lapse: "According to the sentence, the sinners were to walk through all the streets of the village, stopping in front of every house to have every man and woman spit on them and throw dirt on them. The procession started at the rabbi's house and went on its way until it reached the houses of the most wretched members of the community." Everyone ran to meet the culprits. The women raged against Lisa: "It was obvious that the ladies of the burial society had taken great pains to bring the daughter of a noble and wealthy family to the highest degree of shame and degradation... The women ... came out of their homes to injure the sinners with shouting, wailing, cursing and raised fists... Although they had been warned not to use violence, several women pinched her and abused her. One woman emptied a bucket of urine on her, another stoned her with chicken entrails, and between them they covered her with all kinds of filth[367]."

So we can understand that hospitality towards foreigners is not their strong point either; as they say: "after all this time you'd know..."." These were the opinions of three Jewish personalities regarding the hypothetical reception of extraterrestrials in their community. Their answers to this rather far-fetched question are nevertheless interesting and evocative of this mentality that is hopelessly closed to *goyim* and foreigners. The *Courier international* newspaper of July 1997 translated the article from the Israeli daily *Jerusalem Report*: "What if Martians existed? Would the laws in the Torah that apply to non-Jews also apply to intelligent non-humans? "Here are the answers of these "great Jewish thinkers" on the subject:

Harold Schuweis is a rabbi in California. To the question: "What would be the Jewish reaction to first contact," he replied:"... Take, for example, the raging debate over the true meaning of Leviticus XIX, 18: "Love your neighbour as yourself". In our community, numerous authorities affirm that "your neighbour" means "your fellow Jew", others wish to limit the meaning of "your fellow Jew" to Jews who are "brothers in respect of the faith". This is the point some of us have come to today; so what can green-blooded aliens expect?"

Moshe David Tendler is a rabbi, professor of microbiology at Yeshiva University in New York. To the question: "Could extraterrestrials convert to Judaism", he replied: "Someone asked me

---

[367] Isaac Bashevis Singer, *The Destruction of Kreshev,* 1958, Folio, 1997 p. 84, 85. Translation free PDF version, The Destruction *of Kreshev* p. 28, 29.

one day what would happen if we were able to programme a computer to be able to choose, and it wanted to convert to Judaism. I replied that we should first take it to the *mikveh* (ritual bath), which would cause a short circuit." Indeed, it is extremely difficult for a goy, almost impossible, to be accepted into the Jewish community. It is more feasible for a *shiksa*[368].

Robert Sheckley, a multi-award-winning science-fiction author, responded: "What would the discovery of extraterrestrial life mean for Judaism? I would not be surprised, he replied, if extraterrestrials landing on earth one day were prone to anti-Semitism. My first reaction would be to say: I knew it! I always felt that there was something in us that was stuck in creation. For a Jew it would be a wonderful thing, something worth being ostracised for. If we realised that the whole Universe hates us, that would make us an even more exceptional people."

Hatred of the "others

Certainly, Jews take pleasure in cultivating their uniqueness. But for them, the cult of "memory" carries with it a strong sense of revenge, as we have seen in literary and cinematic productions. We also see that since the destruction of Germany in 1945, Jews are not given to forgiveness: more than fifty years after the events, they continue to persecute those responsible and to bring old people to court. We know that Elie Wiesel has worked continuously to perpetuate the memory of the Holocaust in the survivors of the gas chambers. In a style that was always a little grandiloquent and bombastic, he wrote: "The memory of silence, he said to them, I celebrate it; but the silence of memory, I challenge it[369]." The memory, the remembrance of past sufferings and adversities are indeed a powerful communal mortar which enables the bonds of blood to be maintained: "Zakhor," "Remember! "says the Bible.

The case goes back a long way. We saw with Abravanel how the Jews never really digested the destruction of the temple, and how they intend to take revenge on any adversary who rejects the Law of Israel, personified in the Bible by the name of Amalek. This is how Marek Halter wrote: "Remember what Amalek did to you… Don't forget it…", the Bible repeated to me one hundred and sixty-nine times. Even if I

[368] *Shiksa*: pejorative term for a goy woman.

[369] Elie Wiesel, *Mémoires, tome I*, Seuil, 1994, p. 443.

wanted to, how could I forget, when history has never let me forget?" "Forgive? But "why would we forgive those who repent so little and so rarely of their monstrous crimes?" wondered Vladimir Jankelevitch[370]."

The academic Maurice Rheims confirmed this mentality: "Of course, there is a time for forgiveness. But then, I remember the mark of the ghetto, the bonfires, the pogroms. Hating is not very Christian. But I'm not a Christian either. It would be good if I consulted with the cardinal, my cardinal, the academic. Holy man, he had to train hard to achieve absolution. As far as I am concerned, in this world, I do not forgive[371]."

A minor novelist like Boris Schreiber managed to express this even more vehemently. Born in Berlin in 1924 to a Jewish émigré family, he lived as a nomad between France and the United States. In *The Torn Torn Sun*, he expressed his feelings about the Latvian criminals operating during the Bolshevik regime in revolutionary Russia. About the famous Pole Dzerjinski who distinguished himself during the repression, Boris Schreiber wrote:

"His staff was mainly composed of Poles. For dirty work, investigations, arrests and summary executions, he recruited Latvians. Mainly Latvians. In Moscow, in those years, we trembled before the Latvians. They wore a cap, dressed in a short leather jacket and with a revolver in their belts. Those bands of Latvians arriving in cars at night, commanded by a man as sensitive as Robespierre… —When I think what we have survived! Latvia, who is now playing the victim? Let it die! Let it die now! The Latvians, murderers with the Bolsheviks, murderers with the Nazis, and the imbecile West that pities them, that spoils them! Blow them up, that's what they have to do! "

Boris Schreiber's rages against the Latvians obviously have the advantage of silencing the overwhelming responsibility of the Jewish revolutionaries for the atrocities committed during that period, as Solzhenitsyn demonstrated. But Boris Schreiber's hatred was not only limited to the Latvians. Indeed, he did not seem to appreciate "that ignoble Poland" either:

"In these countries, he wrote, there is only one consensus: hatred of Jews." It is true that Jews are better seen in France than in Poland: "At least in France, we are calm: it's the West, it's civilisation… Here, we are anonymous. Who knows our religion here? But in Poland, as in all the countries of the East, it is impossible to be anonymous. Everyone

[370]Marek Halter, *La force du Bien*, Robert Laffont, 1995, p. 215, 110

[371]Maurice Rheims, *Une Mémoire vagabonde*, Gallimard, 1997, p. 69.

recognises the Jews[372]." The ideal, indeed, is to be able to act without being recognised or identified.

Guy Konopnicki was also originally from Poland; and he didn't seem to particularly appreciate the inhabitants of that country either: "I had been told that my family came from a city in the East where the Jews wore beards, spoke Yiddish ... that they called that country Poland and that it inspired more revulsion than nostalgia[373]."

Nor, however, should one think that Guy Konopnicki considers the French better than the Poles. Although France welcomed him and his family, it does not deserve more gratitude than other European peoples, judging by the words of thanks he wrote in the epigraph to his book *The Place of the Nation, in* which he mentioned those who deserved his esteem and to whom he dedicated his book:

To the Senegalese of the Road of the Ladies[374], to the Arabs of Monte Cassino, to Michel Manouchian and Max Rayman, to the German, Italian and Spanish anti-fascists, to the foreign Jews arrested by the French police" and also to "Stendhal, who preferred to live in Italy, and of course to my German-born Austrian-Polish Jewish mother, a real French beret seller: "To Stendhal, who preferred to live in Italy, and naturally, to my Austro-Polish Jewish mother born in Germany and a real French beret seller, and finally to my father, who gave this country forty-nine years of work plus four years of resistance without receiving the same pension as Maurice Papon[375]." For him, France, which had taken him in, did not deserve any consideration.

Pierre Paraf also expressed this instinctive distrust of Jews and their aversion to foreigners through the mouths of some of his novel characters:

"The *chazan*[376] gravely thrust his sententious commandments in my face: "Never forget, he said to me, that you are a good Jew, and distrust the *goy*, even when he is in the coffin ... and above all, do not forget to put *mezuzot*[377] in every room where you are going to live, to

---

[372]Boris Schreiber, *Le Tournesol déchiré*, Éd. François Bourin, 1991, p. 185, 293.

[373]Guy Konopnicki, *La Place de la nation*, Olivier Orban, 1983, p. 13.

[374]Road leading to the front at Verdun during World War I. (NdT)

[375]Maurice Papon: was a French politician and senior civil servant who held various positions in the administration between 1931 and 1981. In 1981, the newspaper *Le canard enchaîné* denounced Papon's documented collaboration with the Nazis while he was an official of the Vichy regime and his involvement in the persecution of Jews during World War II, for which he was prosecuted and sentenced to prison as a war criminal in 1998. (NdT)

[376] Chazan: one who recites in the synagogue.

[377]Mezuzot are small pouches containing two verses of the Pentateuch, fixed vertically

put tefillin on your arms and on your forehead[378], and beware of touching under any pretext a crucifix[379]".."

Crucifixes and the Catholic religion are, in fact, the object of great aversion. We were able to see how cosmopolitan film-makers had made numerous propaganda films on the subject with the sole purpose of ridiculing and defiling Catholicism, as well as arousing contempt and abhorrence of this religion. The philosopher Jacob Talmon confirmed that the most influential Jews had worked for the secularisation of European societies. The establishment of the Republic in France in 1870 naturally represented a great step forward: "The Jews of modern times have everywhere advocated, if not the separation of Church and State, at least the right to freedom of conscience, and have called for the secularisation of politics and political life[380]."

More recently, we have seen how in other European countries that are less de-Christianised than France, the action of influential Jews has remained the same. Thus, Amos Luzzatto, president of the Union of Jewish communities in Italy, called at the end of August 2005 for the removal of all crucifixes and Catholic objects from public places, considering that these symbols were offensive to other religions[381].

Pierre Paraf, who was co-founder of the League against anti-Semitism (today Lycra), and Jacob Talmon, were even more explicit in their words, clearly expressing their hatred of the Catholic religion and the secular revenge that was planned against Christian civilisation: "So many of our brothers with the mark of the ghetto groan under the Christian lash. Glory be to God! Jerusalem will one day reunite them; they will have their revenge like all the disinherited[382]! "This is exactly what Jacob Talmon wrote: "The Jews have a long-standing bloody score to settle with the Christian West[383]." This is also the "true face of Israel".

In his *History of Anti-Semitism*, Leon Poliakov mentioned the famous case of the philosopher Baruch Spinoza, who made recriminations against his own community. In the *Theological-Political Treatise*, Spinoza wrote: "That the Jews should have subsisted for so

---

to the doorframes of homes.

378Tefillin, from tefila, prayer. Phylacteries: small leather wrappings containing strips of parchment with passages from the Bible that Jews wear tied to their left arm and forehead during certain prayers. (NdT).

379Pierre Paraf, *Quand Israël aima*, 1929, Les Belles lettres, 2000, p. 26.

380J-L. Talmon, *Destin d'Israël*, 1965, Calmann-Lévy, p. 152.

381Read in Emmanuel Ratier's letter, *Faits et Documents (*1 September 2005).

382Pierre Paraf, *Quand Israël aima*, 1929, Les Belles lettres, 2000, p. 19.

383J-L. Talmon, *Destin d'Israël*, 1965, Calmann-Lévy, p. 18.

many years dispersed and without a State, is not at all strange, since they have separated themselves from all nations, to the point of arousing against themselves the hatred of all nations." (Chapter III)

Spinoza further wrote: "The love of the Hebrews for the fatherland was therefore not mere love, but piety, which, together with hatred of other nations, was fostered and nourished by daily worship, to the point of becoming a second nature. Indeed, the daily worship was not only totally different (from which it followed that the Hebrews were absolutely unique and completely isolated from the rest), but also totally contrary ... a permanent hatred, which took root within them more than any other, since it was a hatred born of a great piety or devotion[384] "(Chapter XVII). Spinoza was evidently excommunicated, repudiated by his community in 1656.

Two hundred years later, another great thinker of Jewish origin, Karl Marx, would say something similar in his writings of 1843: "Mankind must emancipate itself from Judaism... It is not the Jews that must be killed, but Yahweh, their God. There is no religion that celebrates hatred so much as Judaism."

---

[384]Léon Poliakov, *Histoire de l'antisémitisme, Tome I,* Points Seuil, 1990, p. 226. Baruch Spinoza, *Tratado teológico-político,* Altaya, 1997, Barcelona, p. 132, 371.

2. Anti-Semitism

In the opening pages of his book on the causes of anti-Semitism, Bernard Lazare identified the problem raised by the presence of Jews in a foreign society: "Anti-Semitism has flourished everywhere and at all times," he observed. The Jews "have been, successively and equally, maltreated and hated by the Alexandrians and the Romans, the Persians and the Arabs, the Turks and the Christian nations … the Jewish race has been the object of the hatred of all the peoples among whom it has settled. Since the enemies of the Jews belonged to the most diverse races, lived in countries far removed from one another, were governed by different laws and ruled by opposite principles, had neither the same mode of life nor the same customs, and were animated by dissimilar spirits which did not enable them to judge alike of all things, it is necessary, therefore, that the general causes of anti-Semitism have always resided in Israel itself and not in those who have combated it[385]."

But Jewish intellectuals are not all as honest as Bernard Lazare. The latter figures, along with a few others, as an exception on the fringes of Judaism, if not outright rejected by his community and accused of suffering from "self-hatred".

Inexplicable anti-Semitism

The Jews are well aware that they are a people apart and have always been rejected by others. At all times and in all latitudes. But anti-Semitism is for them a phenomenon that is difficult to explain, judging by what we have read.

Elie Wiesel spoke at the beginning of his *Memoirs* of the persecution suffered by Jews in Romania, the country of his childhood, during the interwar period: "Every time the anti-Semitic "Iron Guard" raised its head, it wrote, we lowered ours. Graffiti would appear on the walls: "Zsidans (Jews) in Palestine!" Rascals with faces unhinged with hatred would pounce on Jews in the streets, tearing out their beards and their hair. The "*kuzists*", as they called themselves, were Romanian

[385]Bernard Lazare, *Anti-Semitism, its history and causes*, (1894). Editions La Bastille, Digital Edition, 2011, p. 5, 6, 7

Nazis. Savages thirsting for Jewish blood, they could improvise a full-fledged pogrom if they wanted nothing more."

There is nothing to explain this hatred in Elie Wiesel's text, apart from grotesque explanations: "We lived in terror, he wrote. We could never know: the enemies were capable of anything. Even imputing ritual murders to us. I remember a sad song my mother used to sing: the one about Tiszaeszlár. A Jew recounted his sorrows: accused of having slit the throat of a Christian child for ritual reasons, he cried out: "Damn our enemies who claim that Jews need blood to practise their religion! He went through these adversities without surprise, almost without suffering, wrote Elie Wiesel. I was not far from thinking to myself: it's their problem, not ours."

Apparently, however, these permanent tensions could raise painful questions: "During the darkest periods, when the threat had been hanging over the community for too long, I asked myself simple, if not simplistic, naïve, childish questions: Why do they hate us? Why do they persecute us? Why do they torture and torment us? Why so much persecution, so much oppression? What have we done to men that they want to hurt us so much? I confided in my Masters, also in my friends. We tried to understand. The only answer of my Masters was to make us read and reread the Bible, the prophets, the martyriological literature. Rooted in suffering, but anchored in defiance, Jewish history describes a permanent conflict between us and others. Since Abraham, we have been on one side and the whole world on the other. Hence the animosity we attract upon ourselves."

But these answers, which were certainly not enough, did not appease Elie Wiesel's spirit: "The survival of my people continued to perplex me," he wrote, "just as the perennial hatred against them continued to intrigue me[386]".

Reading Elie Wiesel, it seems that the persecutions to which the Jews of Central Europe were subjected were declared unpredictably, totally incoherently, according to the mood of the occupying invader:

During the First World War," he wrote, "the German army came to the rescue of the Jews who, under Russian occupation, were beaten, mocked, oppressed by the savage Cossacks, whose mentality and religious traditions were nourished by anti-Semitism. After their departure, our region experienced a period of calm. The German officers were polite, helpful and cultivated[387]." But this was indeed only a short period of calm, for soon the Germans also began to persecute

[386]Elie Wiesel, *Mémoires,* tome I, Seuil, 1994, p. 30-32.

[387]Elie Wiesel, *Mémoires,* tome I, Seuil, 1994, p. 42.

the Jews, for reasons as yet completely unknown: probably because they needed a "scapegoat".

In his book *Anti-Semitic Hatred*, published in 1991, Serge Moati provided us with testimonies which coincided with the above. Questioned by the journalist, the lawyer Hajdenberg, who was responsible for the Jewish Renaissance in the 1970s in France, asked the same question: "If a child were to ask me: 'Why is there so much resentment against the Jews', I would be unable to give him a reasonable, objective explanation." The reasons for anti-Semitism "are so complex, so irrational, that no objective data can combat them[388]."

The writer Maurice Rheims of the Académie française also saw no rational cause for anti-Semitism. In *A Vagabond Memory*, he mentioned the persecutions in terms of the scapegoat theory, which was ultimately the only possible explanation for him. Thus, humanity would need "the Jews, men and women to beat their bad moods upon, easy to persecute, torture, massacre and accuse of the seven deadly sins. Perhaps that is the reason the Lord made the Jews[389]." The explanation is perhaps a little short, but we have no doubt that it will amply satisfy the few readers of Maurice Rheims.

Cardinal Jean-Marie Lustiger (Aaron Lustiger) also looked for the causes of the phenomenon, but could not find a valid explanation: "I spoke to anti-Semites in the past, he said; I tried. I tried to understand them. I think I saw through what mental mechanisms they came to these extreme, horrible conclusions in which they indulged—but I never understood why… The real mystery is the informer, the betrayer, the torturer, the executioner, the agent of extermination of the system[390]."

The press director Jean Daniel also failed to elucidate this "mystery". In his work entitled *The Age of Ruptures*, he acknowledged that the "chosen people" often had to pay the price of this choice: "I know perfectly well that the price of choice is persecution and that this price is terrifying. This choice-persecution pairing is unbearable to me. This couple contains, in my opinion, the whole Jewish mystery. I mean that this mystery, when it besieges me, veils my thoughts instead of enriching them… Where are these people if not in persecution? No one has ever succeeded in defining it[391]."

This is what the French philosopher André Glucksmann told us in his book *The Discourse of Hatred*, published in 2004: "Hatred of the

[388]Serge Moati, *La Haine antisémite*, Flammarion, 1991, p. 195.

[389]Maurice Rheims, *Une Mémoire vagabonde*, Gallimard, 1997, p. 66.

[390]Marek Halter, *La force du Bien*, Robert Laffont, 1995, p. 214.

[391]Jean Daniel, *L'Ère des ruptures*, Grasset, 1979, p. 113.

Jews is the enigma of all enigmas. This destructive passion crosses the millennia, takes various forms, is continually reborn from the ashes of the various fanaticisms that motivate it… For the anti-Semite, the object of his aversion remains a UFO. He does not know of whom or what he is talking about… The Jew is by no means the cause of anti-Semitism; one must analyse this passion for and by itself, as if this Jew that he persecutes without knowing him did not exist… Two millennia that the Jew has been a source of discomfort. Two millennia of being a living question for the whole world. Two millennia of innocence, having nothing to do with anything[392]."

The great Jewish philosopher Emmanuel Levinas, Bernard-Henri Levy's spiritual master, provided a luminous explanation of the strange phenomenon of anti-Semitism. According to Levinas, anti-Semitism is "the repugnance towards the unknown of the psyche of the other, towards the mystery of his interiority or, beyond all agglomeration and all organisation into an organism, towards the pure proximity of the other human being, that is to say, towards sociability itself[393]." A bit complicated for us to understand, to tell the truth.

But let Jean-Michel Salanskis interpret the thought of the great philosopher:

"Emmanuel Levinas said that, through Hitlerism, the Jews had been exterminated as the "indiscernible other", as people known for making a difference, but whose difference, precisely, was no longer manifested by any character, thus making it impossible to locate them. He interpreted Hitler's hatred of the Jews as the secret hatred of the other man in general that the Nazis had brought to the surface beneath the veneer of civilisation[394]."

Here at last is the missing explanation to our intellectual puzzle. It is indeed the only valid explanation, for there is no doubt that one cannot rationally hate only Jews, but men in general.

This was also what the Nobel laureate Elie Wiesel told us, for whom anti-Semites are the enemies of all mankind. It is simply impossible that individuals can rationally be hostile to Jews, and only to Jews, because there is no reason for it:

"It is so and nothing can be done about it, he wrote: the enemy of

---

[392]André Glucksmann, *Le Discours de la haine*, Plon, 2004, p. 73, 86, 88." Never forget that the anti-Semite, by definition, does not know what he is talking about." (Stéphnae Zagdanski, *De l'Antisémitisme*, Climats, 1995, 2006, p. 35).

[393]Emmanuel Levinas, *L'au-delà du verset*, Minuit, 1982, p. 223, quoted by Jean-Michel Salanskis, *Extermination, loi, Israël*, Les Belles Lettres, 2003, p. 140.

[394]Jean-Michel Salanskis, *Extermination, loi, Israël*, Les Belles Lettres, 2003, p. 72.

the Jews is the enemy of humanity. And conversely. By killing Jews, the murderer kills more than Jews. He starts with the Jews, but then he will inevitably take it out on the other ethnic groups, religions or social groups… By killing the Jews, the murderers undertook the murder of the whole of humanity[395]."

Clara Malraux's analysis was in complete agreement on this point: "Persecution is less hard to bear when one knows that it is totally and absolutely unjustified and that, as a result, the enemy becomes the enemy of humanity[396]."

We must therefore start from the intrinsic innocence of the Jews if we are to understand their way of perceiving events. This means that to kill a Jew, innocent by nature, is to attack any innocent person or any other community; and is therefore to define oneself as an enemy of humanity. But there is also another, more classical, interpretation, which starts from the postulate that the Jews define themselves as the only true humanity; the other nations would be, according to a well-known Talmudic formula, nothing more than "the seed of cattle".

Clara Malraux (née Goldschmidt) was the wife of the famous writer André Malraux, who was also General de Gaulle's Minister of Culture. Analysing German society after the fall of Napoleon, she pointed out how the Jews still endured many hardships, sometimes even pogroms: "Wandering hither and thither, expelled from Austria to be massacred in Poland, mistreated in every possible way in a spiteful Germany. In the Prussia of Frederick II, only two gates were open to the Jews; to cross them they had to pay a fee, the amount of which was voluntarily the same as that of a head of cattle… All this despite the fact that Frederick II had taken some benevolent measures in favour of those unfortunates."

Clara Malraux also noted with regret that animosity against Jews had not ceased after the Napoleonic troops had entered Germany." As early as 1816, anti-Semitic demonstrations broke out. In 1819, there was a pogrom in all its horror, with beatings, injuries, and looting of shops."

Clearly there is no valid explanation for the persecution of these "innocents". However, not all Jews in Berlin were treated so harshly, since, for example, the famous Rahel Levin received in her salon the most prestigious society of her time: Goethe, Hegel, Beethoven and the poet Heinrich Heine were guests whom she treated with familiarity and

---

[395]Elie Wiesel, *Mémoires, tome II,* Éditions du Seuil, 1996, p. 72, 319.

[396]Clara Malraux, *Rahel, Ma grande sœur… Un salon littéraire à Berlin au temps du Romantisme,* Editions Ramsay, Paris, 1980, p. 15.

whom she "influenced[397]". Rahel's father, wrote Clara Malraux, "was one of the tolerated Jews. He had the dual function of goldsmith and banker." So things were not so bad, at least for some Jews who were able to get rich and prosper comfortably.

But it is true that the common people did not seem to appreciate the chosen people as much as the Berlin aristocracy. Clara Malraux's book reported on some of the recriminations levelled against them. Jews were considered as "guilty, criminals, murderers, adulterers and sinners, who should not be admitted to the guilds of good and loyal merchants."

Perhaps we have here the beginning of an explanation for this strange phenomenon that runs through the history of all mankind … mankind! On page 136, we read that the murder of a writer who did not seem to please the people of Israel had provoked in response a series of repressive measures: the "murder … of Kotzbue, a mediocre writer, a spy in the service of Russia … enabled the rulers to take the most infamous measures against the Jews, among others[398]." We began to see more clearly into the matter. All we had to do was to put the events in order.

In *Crime and Memory*, published in 1989, the writer Alfred Grosser also wondered about the anti-Semitic phenomenon: "That in Germany, and later outside Germany, members and bearers of a civilisation born of centuries of cultural progress have been destroyed, that philosophers, composers, architects and Nobel Prize winners of all kinds have been regarded as subhuman—this is something that is such a scandal for the spirit that a singularity results from this very scandal[399]."

For Alfred Grosser, the Jews are perfectly innocent of any reproach: "It is wrong to speak of Jewish-Christian reconciliation, as the churches still too often claim. I really don't see why the Jews should be forgiven by the Christians", he wrote on page 236.

And yet, a few pages further on, Alfred Grosset himself presented some explanations by referring to the anti-Semitic words of a certain "Father Bailly", who wrote in 1890: "A man of heart wrote to us: 'Would it not be necessary to make a petition to be signed by all Frenchmen who wish to throw off the yoke that oppresses them and to ask parliament: 1— That Jews should not be allowed to have two

[397]Clara Malraux, *Rahel, Ma grande sœur… Un salon littéraire à Berlin au temps du Romantisme*, Editions Ramsay, Paris, 1980, p. 13-17.

[398]"The Goyim who attempt to discover the secrets of the Law of Israel commit a crime punishable by death." (*Sanhedrin, 59a*)

[399]Alfred Grosser, *Le Crime et la mémoire*, Flammarion, 1989, p. 75.

nationalities and should return to the status of foreigners in France? 2- That foreigners who disturb the peace of the country and sow discord among the various classes of citizens by stirring up hatred and division, be expelled from France" (page 59).

The anti-Semitism of the time was clearly perceptible in the "reactionary" newspapers. Thus, in its March-May 1898 issue, *Catholic Sociology* published an article entitled: "The Jewish question considered from the point of view of race and customs", in which one could read: "Fools, fools, and writers sold out to the Jews try to move us with the fate of the Jews. Their misfortunes have been the just punishment for their abominable behaviour…" (page 60)." (page 60).

M. Grosser's ellipses conceal from the reader the causes of the animosity that his fellow human beings seem to have aroused. This could have been a starting point for an explanation. But perhaps M. Grosser preferred to follow the example of Elie Wiesel, who wrote frankly at the beginning of his *Memoirs*:

"I want to warn you that I intend to omit certain events: those that concern my private life and that of others, and those that threaten to embarrass friends or acquaintances and, in general, those whose revelation could harm the Jewish people[400]." All in all, this is a good answer.

Jews and Communism

In his book entitled *Anti-Semitic Hatred*, the journalist Serge Moati gave the floor to a number of anti-Semitic personalities from different fields in an attempt to better understand the nature of their delirium. In Russia, he questioned Valery Liemelianov. The historical founder of the Pamiat ("memory") movement, "closely linked to anti-Zionist movements in Arab countries", now lives in Moscow. He explained[401]:

"Since 1917, the KGB had been staffed by Jews. The gulag, described by Solzhenitsyn, was created by Jews, namely by the Jew Trotsky and the Jew Smirnov. Solzhenitsyn accuses Stalin instead of attacking the Jews. The syphilitic Lenin was nothing but a puppet in their hands… In seventy-three years of communism, the Jews have liquidated here a hundred million people, of whom thirty-seven million in the times of the syphilitic Lenin… The Jews crush the other nationalities, they enjoy considerable privileges. Although their share

[400]Elie Wiesel, *Mémoires, tome I*, Éditions du Seuil, 1994, p. 28.

[401]Serge Moati used the verb "to belch" here, but this changes nothing to the facts stated.

of the population is only 0.69%, they invade all the key positions in society: administration, culture, economy, politics, religion… The Jews seized power in 1917. The entire elite of the revolution was composed of Jews[402]."

In the early 1990s, the Pamiat movement was led by Dmitry Vassiliev, the best known and most popular of Russia's nationalist leaders. He had this to say:

"Who made the revolution? Nobody but the Jews. Trotsky, Zinoviev, Kamenev, Lenin—all Jews! They have killed the Tsar. They have destroyed the Church. Socialism is not a Russian concept, it is a foreign concept. Marx was baptised, but he was a Jew." He added: "I have been fighting Zionism for more than fifteen years. Since I started, I lost my job. Since then, the secret services have been after me. The press has been covering me with opprobrium."

These two testimonies, which revealed a truth that was all too horrific, could not go without a counterbalancing response. Serge Moati thus hastened to counter these statements and to draw the reader's attention to the crimes of the Stalinist period:

"The Red Tsar Stalin would be fiercely anti-Semitic. He would exterminate a large part of the Jewish intellectual elite. He would have Yiddish-language writers shot and would wipe out all Jewish culture. A genocide of the spirit under the most implausible pretexts. In January 1949, he launched the first of a long series of anti-Jewish campaigns. On 12 August 1953, 24 Jewish writers and artists were to be shot. During the course of a five-year plan, from 1948 to 1953, Stalin had 238 writers, 106 actors, 19 musicians, 87 painters and sculptors disappeared. All Jews… Fortunately, Stalin's death on 5 March 1953 put an end to this grim operation[403]."

But Stalin's sudden anti-Semitism, which manifested itself after the Second World War, should not obscure the overwhelming responsibility of very many fanatical Jews for the appalling atrocities committed during the first thirty years of the regime. If we do the math, Stalin's sudden anti-Semitism after the war is quite laughable compared to the endless martyrdom of the Russian people. In fact, Stalin's own death itself remains unexplained.

Serge Moati then dealt with anti-Semitism in Poland in the 1980s, after forty years of communism. But he was not alarmed to be confronted with the same accusations levelled by Russian anti-Semites. For example, one of his journalist correspondents confessed to him:

[402]Serge Moati, *La Haine antisémite*, Flammarion, 1991, p. 127.

[403]Serge Moati, *La Haine antisémite*, Flammarion, 1991, p. 135-137, 131.

"Today, the general atmosphere of furious anti-communism is tinged with strong anti-Semitism. Jews are accused of having run the Stalinist apparatus. This is easily explained: a good number of Jewish intellectuals, refugees in the Soviet Union to escape Nazism, returned after the Liberation in Red Army boxcars to take over the reins of their country. It is true that a large number of sincerely communist Jews have tried to build socialism."

There was nothing reprehensible about this enterprise, for after all, "communism has embodied the great dream of modernity." Proletarian internationalism had been "conceived and felt as an apotheosis of modernity."

That the liberating theory of humanity may have engendered a bloody dictatorship is a secondary issue, for it was in the name of the ideal that the revolutionary experience allowed the limits of the human being to be exceeded. The end justifies the means.

Gabriel Meretik, a French journalist of Polish Jewish origin, justified this speech thus: "All the Polish elites have been decimated, and the Soviets have relied on the Jewish Communists, cosmopolitan and internationalist, devoted to the Cause. They were loyal and grateful to the Moscow regime which had enabled them to escape from the Nazi extermination camps. They therefore put themselves at the service of that utopia, one of the noblest that these Polish Jews could imagine: happiness and equality for all on earth."

But clearly, the fact is that many Poles did not perceive events in this way, and all Gabriel "Meretik's" contrivances of language to denigrate the "purity" of the nation will not change anything. Indeed, he explained that "Poles experienced communism as a cancer transplanted by the Russians with the help of the Jews into the body of a healthy and pure nation."

For want of denying the evidence, Serge Moati's conclusion on this chapter was to seduce the reader with the horrors of anti-Semitism, a bit like those harrowing soundtracks that enhance the horror of television documentaries on the Second World War, even if the images are sometimes simply trivial: "In short, it is the return of the old themes, barely updated. In Poland, the last peasant society in Eastern Europe where land has not been nationalised, the Jew is always perceived as the cosmopolitan creature of the evil city, destroyer of traditional values."

This allowed him to stand up and say: "You always hear the same refrain: the Jews are the masters of international finance and the press. They want to buy Poland in order to enslave it… The Jews, perfect scapegoats, have been the ritual target of an improbable nation whose territory has not ceased, over the centuries, to be disputed, invaded, chopped up and occupied by foreign powers[404]…" But we must insist and ask Mr. Moati if it is true that "many Jews" have played a leading role in the appalling crimes committed under the Soviet regime. Yes or no, Mr. Moati?

But, after all, all that is now far away from us, and the most important thing is that yesterday's enemies can forgive and reconcile. In this case, the weakest had to take the first step. On 20 May 1991, Lech Walesa, the new president of the Polish Republic, on an official visit to Israel, spoke these words from the rostrum of the Knesset: "There are among the Poles people who harmed you. Here in Israel, in the cradle of your culture and your renaissance, I ask for your forgiveness." But Serge Moati remained suspicious about this Polish repentance: "Lech Walesa came to seek absolution in the land of Israel. Will this solemn and collective 'forgiveness' begged before the Jewish people be enough? Only the Polish people have the answer[405]."

What did Serge Moati mean by that rhetorical question, other than: "Will that be enough to quench the hatred and thirst for revenge of the chosen people against Poland?"

The question now is how long it will take for a representative of the Jewish community to apologise to the peoples of Europe for the tens of millions of victims of communism for which Jewish doctrinaires and officials are directly responsible.

Anti-Semitism in Central Europe has been analysed by another French intellectual. In 1990, immediately after the fall of communism, essayist Guy Sorman investigated the origins of anti-Semitism in Hungary in his book entitled *Exiting Socialism*: "Why this anti-Semitic obsession of the Hungarians," he wrote. Indeed, it never ceased. In the 1930s, the Budapest *intelligentsia* was divided between the "Jewish camp" and its enemies; any further debate was secondary. It was in Hungary that the first anti-Jewish laws were adopted in 1938—earlier than in Germany."

Sorman reversed the situation, holding the communists responsible for the resurgence of anti-Semitism: "After the war, the communists wanted to make people believe that the entire population had resisted Nazism. So there was no collective soul-searching, no catharsis, no explanation. The question was not asked; like all uncomfortable questions in a communist society, it was taboo for forty years. Once the

---

[404]Serge Moati, *La Haine antisemite*, Flammarion, 1991, p. 99-106.

[405]Serge Moati, *La Haine antisemite*, Flammarion, 1991, p. 121.

communists left the Jewish question resurfaces publicly[406]."

The perceptive reader realises here to what extent the Hungarian communists played a perverse role in knowingly concealing Hungarian anti-Semitism during the war, in order to exalt the victory against fascism. A few lines later, however, Guy Sorman was obliged to mention, very succinctly, the role of Jews—of many Jews—in the atrocities committed in the brief communist republic established for 133 days under the presidency of Bela Kun, as well as the role of very many Jews in the administration of the new communist regime established in 1948[407]:

"Some find "objective justifications" of a historical-political nature for this permanent anti-Semitism. It was Jewish intellectuals who introduced communism into Hungary: Bela Kun, head of the 1918 Commune, was a Bolshevik and a Jew; Rakosi, head of the 1948 Stalinist government, was also a Jew."

Guy Sorman responded to these vile accusations with great ease: "It is nowadays Jewish intellectuals—Giörgy Konrad, Janos Kis—who represent the most uncompromising liberalism. They are the ones who demand privatisations, at the risk of putting the least qualified workers out of work."

Guy Sorman thus went off on a tangent, arguing that the anti-Semitic accusations were unfounded simply because the Jews were both Bolshevik leaders and fierce militants of liberalism. In reality, there is nothing contradictory in this, for the two systems work together for the dissolution of nations and for the advent of the global empire so dear to the children of Israel. The democratic ideal would ultimately prove far more effective than the rigidity of the communist systems in dissolving ethnically homogeneous peoples and favouring the great universal miscegenation. It is not surprising, therefore, to see how most Jewish intellectuals have operated their mutation with such ease. This was precisely the subject of our previous book, *Planetary Hopes*.

However, there was still a certain bitterness in the hearts of Hungarians towards those responsible for the ignominies committed during the communist regime; a resentment that could effectively be described as "anti-Semitic", and which can only be increased by the shameless denials of the main parties involved.

For Sorman, as the reader will understand, anti-Semitism has no serious justification, and the Jews are returning to the country to contribute all their genius and inexhaustible creativity, without which

---

[406]Guy Sorman, *Sortir du socialisme*, Fayard, 1990, p. 250.

[407]On Hungary: *Planetary Hopes* and *Jewish Fanaticism*.

Hungary would remain a rearguard country:

"It should be noted here that, in a general way, the return of Jewish intellectuals constituted the ferment of cultural and political life in the whole of Central Europe," Sorman wrote. Since the Jews are innocent of all that they are reproached for, the problem can only come from the Hungarians, whose ambiguous identity would be the cause of their aggressiveness: "Intellectuals who lapse into anti-Semitism, Sorman wrote, seem especially to defend the Hungarian national identity precisely because it is imperceptible."

This tendency to blame their own faults on the Jewish people is not peculiar to the Hungarians. Guy Sorman reminded us that this defect also affected the Spaniards who expelled the Jews and the Moors in 1492: "This obsession with Magyar blood purity goes back to the same delusion as that of the Spaniards in the 15th century, when they expelled the Moors. Like the Spaniards of that time, today's Hungarians are of mixed blood: Hungary was crossed for centuries by invaders from Asia, occupied by the Ottomans (just as Spain was by the Arabs), colonised by the Germans, the Slavs, the Jews, the Serbs. In reality, Hungary is Hungarian only in its language."

As you will have understood, it is the lack of self-identity that made the Hungarians and Spaniards aggressive against the Jews. The invention of the scapegoat," continued Guy Sorman, "serves to consolidate the unity of the social group, without which it would explode into pieces... Hatred of the Jews would therefore be dramatically consubstantial to Hungary because it is difficult to be Hungarian: uncertain identity[408]! "

But unfortunately, anti-Semitism did not only develop in Hungary and Spain. Another famous French liberal essayist, Alain Minc, took the pulse of Polish anti-Semitism after the fall of communism, pretending not to take seriously the overwhelming responsibility of "very many Jews" for the tragedy of communism. His irony even led him to mock the Polish anti-Semitism that still exists today, despite the fact that the number of Jews in Poland today is derisory. For Alain Minc, the anti-Semitism of the victims of communism is obviously just as ridiculous as the old Christian anti-Semitism that it seems to have replaced.

Communism, Minc wrote, acts here as a "second original sin", for "the death of Christ no longer fulfils its divine office. The establishment of communism in 1947 by the Jews: here is the opportunity to stir up hatred against the Jewish people for a long time to come! A clear anti-

[408]Guy Sorman, *Sortir du socialisme*, Fayard, 1990, p. 251.

Semitism in the streets, in conversations, in slogans and in the old refrain, which is still being repeated: apparent cosmopolitanism, abuse of power, economic privileges, trafficking… Nothing is lacking in this Poland, always at the forefront of progress. An anti-Semitism that is finally crystal clear and pure, because there are no more Jews[409]".

The crass stupidity of the Poles is obvious. Alain Minc's analysis, which noted the presence of anti-Semitism without Jews, could however be interpreted differently. One could simply understand that Poles have a bad memory of the presence of Jews in their country. That would be another plausible explanation.

The truth is that Poland was for a long time in European history the only country to welcome Jews, who had been expelled from everywhere since the Middle Ages. They were expelled from England in 1290, from France in 1306, and then radically in 1394. They were expelled from Spain in 1492, from Russia, from Austria and from all the German states at one point. But Casimir the Great, King of Poland (1310–1370), had granted them the right to settle and live in his kingdom according to his laws[410]. This is why the Jewish population was so large in Poland before the Second World War.

Poland's progressive decline from the 17th century onwards led to its dismemberment by its neighbours and eventually to its disappearance. Poland, weakened, was effectively dismembered first in 1772 by Prussia, Russia and Austria, and then again in 1792, disappearing from the maps of Europe in 1795. After a short-lived revival under Napoleon, Poland reappeared only in 1918 after the First World War. It would probably be interesting to study in parallel the situation in Spain, which began its Golden Age precisely after the expulsion of 1492.

In a chapter of his book symptomatically entitled *Jewish Identity, Human Identity,* Raphaël Draï dealt with the Bolshevik revolution, going on at length about the pogroms committed against the Jews from 1919 onwards: "The Jews were reduced to the status of insects" (p. 388). According to Raphaël Draï, these pogroms "explained certain adherents to the revolution." Here again, we must point out the error of interpretation, and specify, as Solzhenitsyn had shown in his book *Two Hundred Years Together (1795–1995),* published in 2003, that these pogroms took place during the civil war, and that they were in some

[409]Alain Minc, *La Vengeance des nations*, Grasset, 1990, p. 43.

[410]King Casimir had a Jewish mistress named Esterka." The inhabitants of Kraków had been complaining about their Jews since 1369". (Mark Zborowski, *Olam*, 1952, Plon, 1992, p. 445)

way a response to the massive presence of Jews in the Bolshevik regime. This manifest difficulty in discussing the role of their fellow Jews in the Bolshevik adventure was apparent in the somewhat caricatured way in which the events were presented on page 392: "The revolt of the Spartacists," wrote Draï, "bloodily repressed, pillories the revolutionaries described as 'of Jewish origin' like Rosa Luxemburg. In a general way, the Jews are declared responsible for the defeat of the Reich[411]."

The term "qualified" used here is eminently representative of a whole mentality. So it was time for Raphaël Draï to move on quickly to another chapter: "1933: The Jews trapped in the Law"; "1935: The racial laws." After all, the role of victim is more comfortable than that of executioner.

The problem is that by denying the evidence, Jewish intellectuals not only lose all credibility, but also arouse legitimate suspicion about other, seemingly grotesque and "delusional" accusations against their fellow Jews from the Middle Ages to the present day. Surely it would be wiser to acknowledge their participation in the massacres. After all, error is human.

Going off the deep end

The clear difference between the media image of the Jewish community and the more prosaic realities forces cosmopolitan intellectuals to maintain a rather sophisticated discourse in order to deal with sometimes awkward questions. Fortunately, on television and radio, journalists and the politicians who serve as their interlocutors are polite enough not to question community representatives on sensitive subjects, such as the role of Jewish traders in slavery and the slave trade, the responsibility of Bolshevik leaders in the atrocities of the Russian revolution, the role of certain influential men in triggering the war in Iraq, Serbia, Afghanistan and perhaps soon in Iran. There are also situations in which one prefers to dilute a sensitive issue under other more trivial considerations.

Pierre Birnbaum, professor of political sociology at the University of Paris I, is the author of a book published in 1993 entitled *France for the French, A History of Nationalist Hatred*. For him, as for other cosmopolitan authors, the patriotic sentiments of the native French[412]

---

[411]Raphaël Draï, *Identité juive, identité humaine*, Armand Colin 1995.

[412]*Français de souche* in the text: an expression used in France to refer to the "root"

indicate a "pusillanimity", as Alain Minc would say, and a very despicable pettiness. The cosmopolitan intellectual's feeling of superiority, once again, is very clearly perceptible in the way he analyses the situation:

France for the French," wrote Pierre Birnbaum, "is the rallying cry that is tirelessly repeated at all times, in Paris as in many provincial towns and even in sleepy little villages, by angry nationalist demonstrators… This slogan demonstrates an identitarian tension, a rejection of universal citizenship."

It should be noted that Mr. Birnbaum did not express himself as a cosmopolitan intellectual, but as a "perfectly integrated" Frenchman. However, when it comes to explaining the anti-Semitism of the population, and the accusations specifically directed against the Jewish community, one has no choice but to "beat around the bush". If we start from the premise that Jews are by nature innocent, as they themselves repeat, "anti-Semitic" accusations against them cannot have any rational basis. To the cosmopolitan mentality, such accusations are gross errors, an attack on all humanity, or at least on all the "scapegoats" of society. Thus, Jews are never the only victims, which is very reassuring for them. On the other hand, the accusations are grossly exaggerated in order to ridicule them:

"The most distant history, wrote Pierre Birnbaum, shows that in the most distant and diverse provinces of the country there was a rejection of the presence of the Jews similar to that of those other beings considered equally evil and dangerous, such as lepers and witches: at certain times, their persecution was frequent, sometimes leading to direct expulsion, imprisonment or pogroms… This openly declared hatred in the name of the Catholic identity of French society was also directed against the equally intolerable Protestants; and, until well into the contemporary period, one heard them continually defending and vindicating Saint-Bartholomew[413]; something which Protestants and Jews, and soon also Muslims, should take very much into account in the light of facts which are amply confirming all fears[414]."

This kind of intellectual subterfuge was also seen, for example, in

---

indigenous French, as opposed to the *Français de branche*, the "branch" French, from recent immigration. (NdT).

[413]The St. Bartholomew's Massacre was the murder of Huguenots (French Protestants of Calvinist doctrine) during France's wars of religion in the 16th century. It began on the night of 23–24 August 1572 in Paris, and spread for months throughout the country. (NdT).

[414]Pierre Birnbaum, *La France aux Français, Histoire des haines nationalistes,* Éd. Seuil, Paris, 1993, p. 14, 16

the response of the famous press director Jean Daniel to a writer who had made headlines in 2000 when he was outraged by the "over-representation" of Jews on a public radio programme. Renaud Camus, a left-wing writer who had been proving his respectability for years, had written the following in his newspaper *Campaign of France*: "Five participants and what proportion of non-Jews? Very small, if not non-existent. Well, this seems to me, not exactly scandalous perhaps, but exaggerated, and out of place, incorrect. And no, I am not anti-Semitic, and yes, I consider the Jewish race to have made one of the highest spiritual, intellectual and artistic contributions to mankind ever… But no, I do not think it is appropriate that a talk show, prepared and announced in advance, i.e. official, about integration in our country, on a public service broadcaster, should be held exclusively among Jewish journalists and intellectuals or those of Jewish origin… I think I have the right to say so. And if I don't, I say it anyway. I say it in the name of this French culture and civilisation of ancient roots which are mine, and whose achievements through the centuries are more than respectable and of which I regret to hear hardly any more in the country which was theirs."

These words, perfectly justified, had given rise to the traditional "commotion within the community". The media scandal was such that the publisher Fayard had to withdraw the book from sale before reissuing it without the incriminating passages. Numerous personalities had nevertheless defended the writer, denouncing a veritable lynching.

Jean Daniel was going to give his opinion in this polemic by approaching the question in the same way as his colleague Pierre Birnbaum, that is to say with that deep contempt that the cosmopolitan feels towards the indigenous. The first step was to exaggerate the accusation out of all proportion in order to make it lose credibility. Then, the next step was to "make a mess of things" by placing the accused in the middle of a group of "scapegoats" (witches, lepers, homosexuals, women, immigrants, gypsies, Protestants, proletarians, etc.) in order to dilute them into an anonymous mass. Jean Daniel carried out this work conscientiously before concluding with outrageous accusations against the accuser:

This exasperation at the predominantly Jewish composition of *France Culture*'s "chat show", he wrote, "this distrustful, antipathetic and traditionally French mood reveals a very specific mentality. What does the expression "over-representation" mean? First of all, there are over- and under-representations, but of whom? Of the communities that make up French society? Would it be appropriate—according to parity and politically correct thinking—for each of the communities to be equally represented, if not by provinces, at least by religions? Would the Muslims and blacks who recently declared themselves misrepresented on television and radio be legitimised in this way? This may or may not be regretted. Would this extension of parity between men and women to all categories be to the detriment of merit and skills? ... It is said, it can be said, or will be said: there are too many blacks in football teams, too many West Indians in nurses, too many Catalans in rugby teams, too many Corsicans in customs teams, etc. But this obviously does not have the same meaning as pointing out that there are too many Albanians in the mafia, too many gypsy car thieves, too many North Africans and blacks in prisons, too many Protestant managers in banking—and too many Jews in the media. Is that over-representation? And if so, where is the danger in a society so plural, so multi-confessional and so multi-ethnic? Who can still be, without suffering from the blindness of hatred, nostalgic for that pure Catholic France, in a Europe safe from the Moors and the Saracens? ... In reality, I fear that Mr Renaud Camus is a genuine anti-Semite, and, if I may say so, an anti-Semite in good company. I am sure he has excellent Jewish friends and is loyal to them. But believe me, he is thoroughly anti-Semitic. In cases like his-so peaceful-I doubt that he can be cured[415]."

In truth, Jean Daniel pretended to believe that the accusations were directed against the Jews, when the heart of the matter lay in the partiality or impartiality of Jewish intellectuals. He pretended not to understand this and cleverly evaded the issue.

Such a natural inclination to "muddle the waters", to muddle the situation and to bamboozle the adversary is observed in the majority of cosmopolitan intellectuals all over the world, as we saw in *The Planetary Hopes*. This homogeneity of thought can only be explained by the common basis of Jewish intellectual training: that is, the exhaustive study of the Torah from an early age, and later of the Talmud, as well as a long practice of *pilpul*, i.e. those oratorical combats in which contradictors compete with tortuous ingenuity to impose their point of view. It is indeed in the art of reasoning that the intellectual superiority of Ashkenazi Jews is most fully expressed. For want of being the "people of the book", i.e. of great literature, the Jewish people are the people of the Talmudic *pilpul*, i.e. of pure intelligence and intellectual contortion[416].

---

[415]Jean Daniel Bensaid, *Soleils d'hiver*, Grasset, Poche, 2000, p. 337, 323

[416]"*The name pilpul,* discussion, literally pepper, is often given to Talmudic studies because of their piquancy, richness and the stimulation experienced in them. They excel

At the end of the 19th century, the anti-Semitic writer Edouard Drumont had already noted this tendency of certain cosmopolitan intellectuals to skilfully evade awkward questions. After a series of financial scandals involving several personalities of Jewish origin, among others, Edouard Drumont imagined this illustrative dialogue at the beginning of his book entitled *Jewish France in the face of opinion*:

"It is impossible to make oneself understood by this fake deaf man who is determined not to hear anything and who ends up getting into someone else's bed. Israel thus amuses himself by playing with us with words and interrupted dialogues.

—How is it possible that in just a few years almost the entire fortune of France has been concentrated in a few Jewish hands?

—Would you, in the name of the prejudices of another age, prevent us from worshipping the God of Jacob, from celebrating Yom Kippur and Pesach?

—You have fallen like a plague of locusts upon this unfortunate country. You have ruined it, you have bled it, you have reduced it to misery, you have organised the most terrible financial exploitation the world has ever beheld.

—Is it the festival of Sukkot that bothers you? Sukkot, the poetic feast of foliage… Come on, live in your own time, let everyone have freedom of conscience.

—The German Jews whom you have introduced in all the ministries, in the prefectures, in the Council of State, are ruthless persecutors; they vilify everything that our fathers respected, they threw our crucifixes into the rubbish dumps, they attack our heroic Sisters of Charity!

—The principles of tolerance proclaimed in 1789! That is all there is! It is the glory of Israel for having defended those doctrines. Dear and good Israel! Israel beacon of the nations! Israel is the champion of Humanity; he desires the good of all peoples …, that is why he takes it

---

above all in comparing various interpretations, in imagining all possible, imaginable and impossible aspects of a hypothetical problem and, by ingenious intellectual manoeuvring, in solving what seems insoluble. Acuity, knowledge, imagination, memory, logic, subtlety, everything possible is done to solve a Talmudic question. The ideal solution is the *khidesh*, an original synthesis hitherto unheard of. This intellectual performance is a pleasure for the one who performs it and for those who listen to it. There is a joy in exercising one's thinking with strength and skill, in showing one's fluency at this level of elevation and abstraction. When two established scholars begin a "racy" debate, an admiring circle gathers around them, silently awaiting each retort, even at the cost, in passing, of discussing this or that subtlety with one of the two, engaging in a new argument." (Mark Zborowski, *Olam*, 1952, Plon, 1992, p. 89).

from them.

Under these conditions, as you will understand, no serious discussion is possible. You are asking Mr de Rothschild. You want to know, by virtue of your rights as a citizen, what work he has produced in exchange for the prodigious sums of money he has received. Mr. de Rothschild has gone outside. In his place, it is Mr. Frank who comes forward; a very honest man, a decent scientist who talks to you about religion when you talk to him about political economy, and who answers you with platitudes about Progress when you ask him about the outrages of his co-religionists[417]."

We do not judge here whether Drumont's accusations were well-founded or not, although they were probably excessive and even frankly delusional. Instead, we are interested in the behaviour of the accused character, in the role of the slippery eel, insofar as it is effectively a caricature of what we saw in Pierre Birnbaum and Jean Daniel.

In his *History of Anti-Semitism*, Leon Poliakov provided us with some interesting testimonies about the image of Jews in Christian plays of the 14th century, in which "the unfathomable perfidy of the Jews" was described in unkind words.

"The wide range of epithets used to describe them may give an idea of this tendency," wrote Poliakov: "false Jews", "false thieves", "false unbelievers", "evil and felonious Jews", "perverse Jews", "treacherous Jews", "false and perverse nation", "false scoundrels"[418] "." Already there was clearly a certain mutual incomprehension.

The mirror of the anti-Semite

In the introduction to his novel *In the Crosshairs* (preface to 1984), the famous American writer Arthur Miller also denied any Jewish specificity when it came to answering the accusations of anti-Semites. There is no more "chosen people", no more "mission" to be fulfilled to save humanity. The Jews are people like any others, like the Chinese, for example, who are also accused of wanting to dominate their neighbours:

"I was amused to hear in Bangkok descriptions of the local Chinese exactly the same as those that circulated in the West, and no doubt still

[417]Edouard Drumond, *La France juive devant l'opinion*, Marpon & Flammarion éditeurs, Paris, 1886, p. 25, 26.

[418]Léon Poliakov, *Histoire de l'antisémitisme I*, 1981, Points Seuil, 1990, p. 305.

circulate, about the Jews." The Chinese are only loyal to each other. They are very intelligent, they study harder in school, they always try to be first in their studies. There are a lot of Chinese bankers in Thailand, too many; the truth is that it has been a real mistake to give the Chinese Thai citizenship because they have secretly taken control of the banking system. Moreover, they are China's spies or will be in times of war. What they really want is a revolution in Thailand (even if they are bankers and capitalists) so that we will end up depending on China"." As can be understood, the accusations directed against the Jews simply indicated a certain natural envy of the common people, always ready to express their frustrations and resentment against a scapegoat minority. In fact, the same identitarian reaction existed in Cambodia against the Vietnamese, Arthur Miller explained: "Many of these same contradictory reflections applied to the Vietnamese who had resided in Cambodia for generations; they too were more industrious than the natives, were of dubious loyalty, were about to become spies for Communist Vietnam, even if they were fervent capitalists, and so on. These examples reveal two striking similarities: the Chinese in Thailand and the Vietnamese in Cambodia were often merchants, shop and small house owners, peddlers, and many were teachers and lawyers or intellectuals, enviable in a rural country."

Arthur Miller's conclusion was however rather Talmudic, a twisted fallacy that amounts in the end to accusing the accuser:

"The anti-Semitic mind sees the Jew as the bearer of the very alienation, the indiscriminate exploitation, which the people fear and resent. I will only add, Miller wrote, that they fear this alienation because they feel it in themselves as a hopelessly anti-social individualism, deprived of a sense of belonging, which belies the fervent desire to be a useful part of the mythical whole, the sublime national essence. They often seem to fear the Jew as they fear reality. And perhaps this is why there is no real end to anti-Semitic sentiments. Seeing oneself, contemplating one's own image in the mirror of reality and the ugliness of the world, does not offer the slightest consolation[419]..."

We recognise here the same reasoning of Guy Sorman, when he explained that Spanish and Hungarian anti-Semitism were due to the lack of identity of these two peoples, or that of Alain Minc about Polish "purity". Clearly, again, the problem lies not with the Jews but with their accusers.

---

[419]Arthur Miller, *En el punto de mira*, Tusquets Editores, Barcelona, p. 15, 16

Philosopher Jacob Leib Talmon made the same analysis when he wrote in *Israel's Destiny*: "When we look at the question, we are often struck by the fact that a large number of the accusations levelled by anti-Semites at the heads of Jews actually apply to the anti-Semites themselves[420]." Indeed, "it is very striking".

Anti-Semites all over the world are therefore uniquely inclined to transpose their own faults on the Jews. This was also expressed by Clara Malraux: "In recent years, the manifestations of anti-Semitism have been analysed, as have its psychological causes: the need of the non-Jew to feel superior in order to reassure himself, the need to blame others for his own faults, the latter being the pariahs or scapegoats, or—and I am more inclined towards this hypothesis, as it would better explain the focus of the phenomenon on the "Children of the Book"—the hatred of the father[421]?"

This explanation was in turn found in the famous Viennese writer of the early 20th century, Arthur Schnitzler, who explained to his readers the roots of anti-Semitism: "His novel *In the Open Field*, published in 1908, and his play *Professor Bernhardi*, which premiered in Berlin in 1912, show that no social class is free from the scourge of anti-Semitism," wrote his biographer Jacques Le Rider.

Here is how Schnitzler, through his character, perceived the anti-Semitism of Austrian society at the time: "Moved by the love of humanity and truth, Bernhardi has acted according to his professional conscience as a doctor and according to the ethical principles of compassion and humanity. But because he is a Jew, he has become an enemy of the people. This is the diabolical transmutation of values that anti-Semitism operates: the Jewish victim becomes the enemy of the people, while the anti-Semitic aggressor sees himself as the victim. Even when he is released from prison after an unjust conviction, Bernhardi finds no one to ask for his forgiveness. On the contrary, it is he, once again, who must make himself forgiven for having been the cause of the whole "[422] affair"."

For Schnitzler, in fact, the Jews, inspired by love for humanity, are in any case innocent of what the anti-Semites might reproach them for. The latter are therefore the ones who try to turn the situation to their advantage "in a diabolical way". Needless to say.

---

[420]J.-L. Talmon, *Destin d'Israël*, 1965, Calmann-Lévy, p. 79.
[421]Clara Malraux, *Rahel, Ma grande sœur...*, Edition Ramsay, Paris, 1980, p. 21, 22
[422]Jacques Le Rider, *Arthur Schnitzler*, Belin, 2003, p. 195, 211, 212

Anti-Semitic paranoia

Analyses of anti-Semitism always lead logically to the mental disorder of goyim overwhelmed by incomprehensible hatred. Anti-Semitism would be first and foremost a form of paranoia.

So, to those who accuse Jews of constituting a "lobby" that wields enormous influence over French MPs and within the European Parliament, Pierre Birnbaum can give a poignant reply:

"Unlike the powerful transnational lobbies that operate freely in Brussels and maintain standing armies of agents in the city to defend their interests, the Jews could not organise themselves in this way and, moreover, would be deprived of potential allies. In a Europe of almost 450 million people, they represent about 1.5 million individuals who are separated by almost everything: language, culture, religious practices, behaviour and values. They hardly have any representatives who alone are incapable of advancing a cause, let alone imposing a point of view... They approach this new European stage in their long history on this continent with anguish... Their presence in Brussels is one of the most discreet and modest. They have only three or four permanent representatives who are powerless to make themselves heard by institutions that are already overwhelmed with requests[423]."

Thus we see that the accusations of the anti-Semites about the alleged financial power of the Jews and their influence as a constituted pressure group are totally unfounded. Journalist Serge Moati's book on *anti-Semitic hatred* presented a converging testimony of an important personality. It was Abraham Foxman, the historic president of the ADL (Anti Defamation League), the most important anti-racist organisation in the United States, whose words echoed those of Pierre Birnbaum:

"There is often talk of the "Jewish lobby", but Jews have only forty-eight representatives in Congress... The "Jewish lobby" does not exist. That word belongs to anti-Semitic terminology. Nobody says there is a Christian lobby when it is known that there are Christian lobbies everywhere[424]." So we are more relaxed.

However, on 12 January 2006, the weekly *Le Point* published a report on the Abramoff scandal that had shaken the US political world.

---

[423]Pierre Birnbaum, *Prier pour l'Etat, les Juifs, l'alliance royale et la démocratie*, Calmann-Lévy, 2005, p. 178-180. [On 16 February 2012, the European Jewish Parliament was inaugurated in Strasbourg, in the same building as the European Parliament. It is composed of 120 representatives from 47 countries, some not members of the European Union and even from outside the continent itself].

[424]Serge Moati, *La Haine antisemite*, Flammarion, 1991, p. 158.

"Jack Abramoff, a brilliant 46-year-old lobbyist close to Republican circles, was for a long time one of the most powerful figures on *K Street*, the street of lobbies. He has just pleaded guilty to racketeering, tax fraud and active corruption. Since then, the political world has been abuzz that Abramoff has agreed to cooperate with the justice system to negotiate a reduced sentence. It is feared that he will reveal the names of the parliamentarians he bribed in exchange for favours for his clients. There is talk of between 12 and 60 congressmen being implicated, one of the biggest scandals in the history of Congress. Abramoff's main clients were Indian tribes who owned casinos and whom he gleefully swindled. He billed them huge fees and imposed on them a public relations firm owned by a business partner of his ... while hiding the fact that he also collected money from the anti-gambling lobby. Abramoff has lined his pockets (82 million dollars), even though he redistributed the money from the Indians to the MPs: dinners, his luxury restaurant, trips to golf courses in Scotland, jobs for the wives... Abramoff and his clients have contributed $4.4 million to the election campaigns of more than 250 representatives since 1999. Forty of them—including some eminent Republican figures and several Democrats, such as Hillary Clinton—have rushed to donate the corrupt lobbyist's contributions to charity."

But let us not spend more time on such trifles, and let us rather look with Leon Polyakov at the manifestations of anti-Semitic madness. In his monumental *History of Anti-Semitism*, the great historian exposed the pathological nature of German anti-Semitism after the defeat of 1918. For him, the explanation was quite simple: the Germans fell prey to a well-known malady—the persecution syndrome—which can drive its sufferers to total insanity:

"The day after the October revolution, the declarations of some responsible for Germany's destiny bordered on delirium because, according to them, "an undetermined number of Bolsheviks were of Jewish origin... This delirious tendency was accentuated when it became clear that Germany had lost the war." According to Leon Poliakov, General Ludendorff himself, the leader of the Tannemberg victory in 1914, after having been the strategist who led the Central Powers between 1916 and 1918, "fell into the most complete anti-Jewish madness", and into the "delirium of persecution".

Apparently, the disease was contagious, as Churchill also suffered from the same delirium. At the end of 1919, he justified the anti-Bolshevik crusade in a speech in the House of Commons in which he lambasted, according to Poliakov, "the most formidable sect in the world". He even elaborated on his ideas in an article published on 8 February 1920 entitled *Zionism against Bolshevism*. Churchill's description of "international Jews" and other "Jewish terrorists", in Churchill's terms, "bordered on delirium", Poliakov wrote, for "the most frenzied anti-Semites could take advantage of it[425]."

Anti-Semitic madness

The Jewish vicissitudes that regularly make the news before being immediately silenced do not prevent cosmopolitan intellectuals from railing against what they consider to be the obsessive delusions of anti-Semites. In *The Guilt of the Jews*, Guy Konopnicki wrote, for example:

"One never moves innocently from the denunciation of capitalism to the denunciation of hidden financial powers hatching a global plot. All those who repeat this obsession are merely expressing the most ordinary anti-Semitism. The slip may be unintentional, unconscious, but it is the very stuff of delirium[426]."

Konopnicki thus agreed with Abraham Foxman, who had pointed out the central problem of the question of anti-Semitism by finally revealing it to be nothing more than "the disease of the non-Jewish brain". Abraham Foxman recounted a dialogue he had during one of his travels which demonstrated the perverse nature of anti-Semitism and the difficulty of understanding its logic:

"A few months ago I went to Moscow. I met some Muscovites. One evening, one of them asked me: 'Why does anti-Semitism exist? I answered: "That is a question you have to answer because anti-Semitism is a disease of the non-Jewish brain, not of the Jewish brain. We are just victims. Tell us, you, why does anti-Semitism exist? And there was silence."

Indeed, many cosmopolitan intellectuals come to this conclusion. Serge Moati, for example, in his book *Anti-Semitic Hatred*, provided another testimony to the same effect. Renée Neher, a native of Alsace, "extremely patriotic", therefore very French, who lived through the Second World War and the German invasion ... and who "has lived in Israel since 1971" (another "paradox") declared:

"Like any disease, anti-Semitism experiences periods of crisis and remission, but there is no cure for this terrible disease[427]."

---

[425]Léon Poliakov, *Histoire de l'antisémitisme II*, 1981, Points Seuil, 1990, p. 409.
[426]Guy Konopnicki, *La Faute des Juifs*, Balland, 2002, p. 128, 69
[427]Serge Moati, *La Haine antisémite*, Flammarion, 1991, p. 158, 165.

Michel Winock, historian and professor at the Institute of Political Science in Paris, whose works are authoritative, analysed the question in the same way: "Anti-Semitism is not only a moral monstrosity and intellectual ineptitude; it is the instrument of reactionary policies, it is, beyond the notions of right and left, a summary of all racisms, the negation of pluralistic society, the imbecilic exaltation of the national self and finally one of the germs of totalitarian barbarism[428]."

All human beings can suffer from this terrible disease, and not only Europeans. So we heard Elie Wiesel on French television, on the talk show *Tout le monde en parle* on 6 May 2006, declare about Iran and Iranian President Ahmadinejad: "Iran's religious leader is a madman, I mean pathologically ill; he is mad as hell." And he added logically: "His bomb does not threaten Israel, it threatens the whole world." You have understood; all those who oppose the projects of the Jews are "madmen" whom the Western world has a duty to fight.

The essayist Raphaël Draï analysed the anti-Semitic madness through the myth of the Jews' desire for world domination, disseminated by the famous text *The Protocols of the Elders of Zion,* which would eventually become "the background of Western consciousness". The "diabolical transmutation" described above, which consists for the anti-Semite in transposing all his faults on the Jews in order to rid himself of them, must in fact be analysed from the point of view of psychiatry.

Anti-Semitic hatred, explained Raphaël Draï, has "taken on a diabolical mythology: *The Protocols of the Elders of Zion...* The main objectives of the plan have already been exposed and denounced, so it is now appropriate to consider the psychopathological aspect of the document... The assertions it contains are not only crude and misleading. They constitute what is called in clinical psychopathology a denial... In other words, the denial by the author of the false document should draw our attention to the psychic inversion revealed by that document... The reading of that letter reveals a clinical document on the psychopathology of dehumanising anti-Semitism. The anti-Semite attributes to the Jews intentions which he himself has against them; intentions which he cannot directly confess... This is the mental mechanism which we find in all false documents of the same kind and with the same intention... The political and social intentions of these writings are clear... The psychopathological dimension of such constructions should attract and retain our attention... The Jews staged

---

[428]Michel Winock, *Edouard Drumond et Cie, antisémitisme et fascisme en France,* Seuil, Paris, 1982, p. 64-66.

are projective Jews; the "Judaised" image is characteristic of anti-Semitic delusions[429]."

It is therefore clear: it is the anti-Semites who project their faults and shortcomings onto the Jews, who are always the victims and scapegoats.

The psychopathological factor of anti-Semitism was highlighted in a book by the famous American writer Philip Roth, albeit in a mocking way. In his novel *Operation Shylock,* he imagined an anti-Semitic nurse trying to heal herself in an association: "I am a recovering anti-Semite. I was saved by the A.S.A.

—What is A.S.A.?

—Anti-Semites Anonymous. The rescue group founded by Philip…"

"Anti-Semitism ran in my family… It's one of the topics we used to discuss at A.S.A. meetings. Well, what difference does it make why we have it, what we have to do is admit that we have it, and help each other, and get rid of it."

Here are the ten dogmas of Anti-Semites Anonymous imagined by Philip Roth:

"1. We recognise that we are prejudiced and hateful people who are powerless to control.

2. We recognise that it is not the Jews who have harmed us, but we who hold the Jews responsible for our ills as well as those of the world in general. It is we who harm the Jews by believing such a thing.

3. A Jew may have his faults, like any other human being, but the ones we have to deal with frankly here are the ones we have: paranoia, sadism, negativism, destructiveness, envy.

4. Our monetary problems do not originate with the Jews, but with ourselves.

5. Our work problems do not originate with the Jews, but with ourselves (and the same goes for sexual, marital and communication problems with others).

6. Anti-Semitism is a way of refusing to admit reality, of not wanting to reflect honestly on our own persons and the society around us.

7. Insofar as they manifest their inability to control their hatred, anti-Semites are not like other people. We realise that the slightest anti-Semitic stain on our behaviour jeopardises our chances of healing.

8. Helping others to detoxify is the cornerstone of our recovery.

---

[429]Raphaël Draï, *Identité juive, identité humaine*, A. Colin, 1995, p. 390-392.

Nothing immunises more against the disease of anti-Semitism than working intensively with other anti-Semites.

9. We are not scientists, we are not interested in the reason why we have contracted this terrible disease: we all agree that we have it and that we must help each other to recognise that we have it and that we must help each other to get rid of it.

10. Within the A.S.A. fraternity, we do our utmost to subdue Jew-hatred in all its manifestations[430]."

Point number 9 is undoubtedly the most revealing. Clearly not of the symptoms of the "anti-Semitic disease", but of the cosmopolitan mentality. It is useless to look for the causes of anti-Semitism. There are no causes of anti-Semitism. There can be no causes of anti-Semitism, except, of course, the prejudices of another age transmitted by the Catholic religion:

"But let's see, why did I start hating Jews? Because they didn't have to put up with all that nonsense from Christians... It all started in my Christian days, but it got stronger in the hospital. Now thanks to A.S.A., I see clearly my other reasons for hatred. I hated their cohesion. Their superiority. What the Gentiles call their greed. Their paranoia and their defensiveness, always treading very carefully, always using tactics, always using their intelligence... Jews got on my nerves just because they were Jews. So that's what I got from Christians... Catholicism penetrates to the very depths. And even the insanity and stupidity goes deep down. God! Jesus Christ! ... Do you know what Philip said to me when I told him about Walter Sweeney praying, prostrate on his knees, and dying of starvation? "Christianity," he said." Gentile delights" [*goyishe nakhès*[431]]. And he spat on the ground[432]." Evidently, Mr. Roth is not an adherent of the Catholic religion.

Apparently the atmosphere in this hospital run by Jewish doctors and surgeons had generated a certain resentment in the Goyim nurses: "But in this hospital, with so many Jewish doctors and sick people, and visiting relatives, and crying and murmuring, and Jewish shouting...", the nurses could get irritated. Fortunately, the good doctor Aharon had decided to take care of them: "Tomorrow night bring another anti-Semite with you, perhaps another nurse who in her heart of hearts is

---

[430]Philip Roth, *Operación Shylock*, Debolsillo Penguin Random House, Barcelona, 2005, p. 101, 106, 115, 116

[431]In the original version, in a derogatory and mocking tone: "Delicacies for gentiles" or "It is good for the goyim" (NdT).

[432]Philip Roth, *Operación Shylock*, Debolsillo Penguin Random House, Barcelona, 2005, p. 264, 265, 266, 267

aware of the harm that anti-Semitism is doing her... The only shield against your hatred is the recovery programme that ... we have set up in this hospital ... the anti-Semite, like the alcoholic, can only be cured by another anti-Semite."

Good old Aharon takes care of his patients carefully: "That's perfect," said Aharon, amused, without taking his eyes off my marginal glosses to the Ten Dogmas, "You're going to rewrite what he writes." Although the good doctor was sometimes a little insolent: "Isn't it enough for him to have just one anti-Semite? Does he need to have all the anti-Semites of the world around him, begging for his Jewish forgiveness, confessing their gentile rottenness, proclaiming that he is a superior being and they are trash? *Tell me your unholy secrets of infidels*[433]*, girls!* That's what the Jews really get off on[434]..."

Reading these words we understand better why political opponents were locked up in psychiatric hospitals in the Stalinist regimes of the USSR and Eastern Europe[435].

Psychoanalysis of the anti-Semite

Norman Cohn took the analysis even further. In his *The Myth of the Jewish World Conspiracy: A Case Study in Collective Psychopathology*, published in 1966, Norman Cohn conducted a true psychoanalysis of the anti-Semite and came to the same conclusion as other cosmopolitan researchers: anti-Semitism is the fruit of a "diabolical transmutation".

Regarding the "myth of the Jewish world conspiracy", Norman Cohn wrote: "After reflecting on these questions, I hypothesised ten years ago that the ideas propagated about the Jews correspond to unconscious negative projections, that is, to a mental mechanism by which some human beings attribute to others their own anarchic tendencies which they refuse to recognise. More specifically, he argued that, in this form of anti-Semitism, Jews, as a collective, represent for the subconscious both the "bad" son, i.e. the rebellious son[436], and the "bad" father, i.e. the father who can potentially torture, punish and kill.

---

[433]*Goyim* in the French version.

[434]Philip Roth, *Operation Shylock*, Debolsillo Penguin Random House, Barcelona, 2005, p. 119, 120, 122

[435]Perhaps it comes from a very old religious explanation: "According to the rabbis, the disciples of Amalek are compared to a madman who pretends to throw himself into a bath of boiling water to cool it down" (JMB).

[436]The "evil son" is another biblical figure.

Later, I learned that several professional psychoanalysts had, long before me, formulated exactly the same hypothesis[437]. This work convinced me that it was a remarkably fertile hypothesis."

Norman Cohn continued: "Several psychoanalysts have claimed that because they reject the God of the Christians, the Jews represent for some of them the rebellious children, the 'bad ones'—hence the patricidal ones. This means that in all ages it was very easy and tempting for them to transform the Jews into scapegoats for the unconscious resentments they might feel towards both their father and their God... But the subconscious tends to associate the Jew more closely with the "bad" father than with the "bad" son. This is best understood by noting how the historical relationship of European Christianity with the Jewish people inevitably leads the latter to assume the role of collective father figure." In fact, the history of the Jewish people recounted in the Old Testament preceded the birth of Christianity, both heir and rival of the Jewish people.

The jealous, ruthless and cruel God of the Old Testament underpins this psychoanalysis: "Probably the most important point, wrote Norman Cohn, is that, unlike the Christian God who combines the attributes of father and son, the God of the Jews is the father alone: a father ... who appears as tyrannical as he is ruthless. Thus, Jews living in Christian lands were the perfect target for the Oedipal projections associated with the "bad" father."

For Norman Cohn, anti-Semitism can therefore be explained, psychoanalytically, on the basis of the figure of "a small child who both loves and hates his father" but who wants to kill him." This feeling is quickly repressed in the subconscious, but still seeks a way out... The figure of the bad father becomes an implacable oppressor, filled with the merciless hatred and destructive fury that the child feels in reality without daring to recognise it completely. This is how the young child elaborates, on the basis of his own destructive drive and his own feelings of guilt, a vengeful parental figure of monstrous cruelty. An all-powerful being who tortures, mutilates and devours, and next to whom, if compared, the real father seems harmless however harsh he may be imagined to be."

"The Sages of Zion, Norman Cohn continued, are evidently such

---

[437]E.g. R.M. Loewenstein, *Psychanalyse de l'antisémitisme*, Paris, 1951; H. Loeblowitz-Lennard, *The Jew as symbol*, in *The Psychoanalytic Quarterly*, vol. XVII (1948), and more recently B. Grunberger, Der Antisemit und der Oedipuskomple, in Psyche (Stuttgart, August 1962). Grunberger, *Der Antisemit und der Oedipuskomple*, in *Psyche* (Stuttgart), August 1962.

parental figures. This stands out both from their name and from the treatment they inflict upon the nations, a treatment which, to all appearances, may be compared to that which the 'evil' father inflicts upon his son. They suck the blood and life-force of nations, and use it for their sinister purposes; they inflict on peoples torture and death by provoking wars."

From the point of view of psychoanalysis, the Hitlerian phenomenon is explained in the same way: "The worst crimes were committed against the father embodied by the Jew whom Hitler identified with the "bad" father… When fanatical anti-Semites are subjected to psychological tests, an abnormally intense hatred for parental figures who appear sometimes threatening and sometimes mutilated or murdered comes to light[438]."

The psychoanalyst Ernst Simmel, reflecting in 1946 on the extreme forms of Nazi anti-Semitism, had already noted: "The process of group formation, when it occurs under pathological conditions, can lead to collective obsessions, or, rather, to a collective psychosis. That clinical syndrome: aggressive and unlimited destructiveness under the effects of an illusion, with complete denial of reality is known as psychosis; it is a paranoid form of schizophrenia[439]."

Finally, Norman Cohn concluded his analysis as follows: "These groups possess another specificity which makes them similar to paranoid schizophrenics: a megalomaniacal sense of their mission … a one-sided struggle against an imaginary conspiracy… What they believe to be their enemy is nothing but their own externalised destructiveness. Moreover, their imaginary enemy seems to them all the more terrible because their unconscious feelings of guilt are all the greater. For these feelings of guilt, far from fading away, torment them relentlessly. They originate in the child's murderous impulses towards his parents, which are then tremendously strengthened by the actual crimes perpetrated by the adult. But instead of being perceived in the form of guilt, they are denied and repressed in the subconscious. Consequently, they are perceived in the form of a vague danger, as a threat, bringing forth the blind fear of seeing the victims, i.e. the murdered parents in imagination and the real parental surrogates murdered in reality, rise up to exact retribution… When men perceive, even dimly, that a great injustice has been done, and when they feel that

[438]Norman Cohn, *Histoire d'un mythe, La "Conspiration" juive et les protocoles des sages de Sion,* 1967, Folio, p. 254, 255, 257, 261, 262, 265.
[439]Ernst Simmel, *Antisemitism: a social disease,* Éd. Simmel, New York, 1946, p. 39, quoted by Norman Cohn.

they lack the generosity or courage to protest, they unfailingly take the blame on the victims, thus relieving their own conscience." *The Protocols of the Elders of Zion* ultimately represents "an aberrant worldview, based on childish fears and hatreds."

After this refreshing reading, we now understand that Evil is deeply rooted within the goyim. But nevertheless, we seem to hear in this discourse some terms that sound familiar: "a megalomaniacal sense of their mission", an "imaginary conspiracy", paranoia, an "externalised destructiveness": a little more and we would almost have the impression that this psychoanalysis of the anti-Semite and the oedipal language that accompanies it might allow Jewish intellectuals to describe freely at last what they hide within themselves.

PART THREE

PSYCHOPATHOLOGY OF JUDAISM

1. Jewish neurosis

Role reversal

In reality, and judging from what we have read, this tendency to reverse roles, to turn situations upside down, and finally to project their own "oedipal conflicts" onto others, seems more like a symptom of a mental disorder characteristic of Jewish intellectuals.

Take the case of the writer Arthur Miller, for example. Born in New York in 1915, he was—naturally—"one of the greatest playwrights of our time". President of the Pen Club, an international writers' association, he received the *Pulitzer* Prize in 1949, twice the *New York Drama Critics Circle* Award, and once the prestigious *Tony Award*.

In his first novel, *In the Crosshairs*, we read on the cover: "In 1945, Arthur Miller dares to attack a taboo subject: the presence of a latent but real anti-Semitism in American society." In his 1984 introduction, Miller explained that in the 1930s anti-Semitism was spreading insidiously in New York: "The city throbbed with hatred." But even if we wanted to know why or the causes of this phenomenon, Miller insisted rather on the manifestations of this phenomenon, once again led by Catholics. Coughlin's radio programmes in particular: "Father Coughlin, a priest from Michigan, had hosted a weekly radio programme on CBS since 1926 that was widely listened to throughout the country. He encouraged anti-Semitism with his inflammatory speeches and was often dubbed 'the Father of Hate Radio'."

The sadistic perversity of the priests was unheard of, for the "existence among Catholic priests of militants devoted to the task and pleasure of stirring up hatred of the Jews" was notorious. In the face of these affronts to the people of Israel, always a victim and always persecuted for no reason, Arthur Miller confessed afterwards: "I cannot reread this novel without evoking the sense of urgency with which I wrote it ... anti-Semitism in America was a closed subject, if not forbidden for fiction. The mere act of putting words to paper was a relief[440]."

The imaginary hero of the novel *In the Crosshairs* is called Newman. He is "a clean-cut, well-groomed New Yorker, descended from an English family whose roots go back to the 19th century". Newman is a true American WASP, proud to be one who considers himself "of higher and purer stock." But contrary to his certainties, he will one day discover that his prejudices about Jews were in fact nothing more than ideas he unconsciously harboured against himself. During a job interview with a woman, Newman "learned for the first time in his life that the reason for his silence was not politeness. It was guilt, because both the evil nature of the Jews and their infinite capacity for deception and the sensual appetite for women revealed in their dark circles under their eyes and their dark complexion were simply a reflection of his own desires, the desires he attributed to them. He knew it how perhaps he would never know it again, because in that moment the woman's eyes had made him a Jew, and because it was his own monstrous desire that prevented him from defending himself."

Suddenly, his life was turned upside down. Newman was in for a real nightmare. He couldn't understand how those new glasses he was wearing made his nose stick out, and how everyone now thought he was a Jew. His boss became suspicious of him and he was transferred to another department where he didn't have to face the public and customers.

All this despite the fact that he was an American of good descent and frequented anti-Semitic gatherings. But then again, his new physiognomy played a trick on him. One of the participants, an expert in recognising Jews, suddenly drew the attention of the room to the intruder, and in complete hysterics shouted: "He's a Jew! —By God Almighty, can't you see he's a Jew?" Naturally, Newman exclaimed: "I'm not! —I'm not a Jew, you bloody fools, I'm not!" but his protests did nothing to prevent the crowd of piss-headed, stubborn Catholics from forcibly ejecting him from the hall.

---

440 Arthur Miller, *Focus,* 1945, Buchet-Chastel, 2002, p. 7, 9, 14, 10 and *En el punto de mira,* Fábula-Tusquet, Barcelona, p. 12.

When telling a co-worker about his misfortune, he asked him: "What I don't understand is how such a number of people can go to such extremes against the Jews… I don't understand how they can feel excited to the point of going to a meeting to study how to get rid of the Jews. That they don't like it is one thing. But to go to work, to go to such lengths… I don't understand. What's the explanation? —They're not very smart, for the most part," replied Newman, arching his eyebrows[441]."

Clearly, Arthur Miller was speaking here through his characters: he did not understand the manifestations of anti-Semitism. For him they were an enigma[442].

But Newman was to experience even more misfortunes. They followed one after the other and he could do nothing about it. In his neighbourhood, some people smashed his face "because for them, he was a Jew and therefore guilty." Soon he felt all the evil looks of the cruel goyim who hate Jews for no reason: "The people and the city surrounded him with their watchful eyes, he no longer felt anonymous in the streets or in public places." Poor Newman became paranoid. Now he felt the torments of the poor, persecuted and innocent Jews in his own flesh. His neighbour, M. Finkielstein, was also beaten up for no reason by evil goyim armed with baseball bats, guys from the "Christian Front gang": "All right, you Hebrew bastards. This was the warm-up. Come on boys[443]." So, when he finally decides to report to the police, Newman has to surrender to the evidence and declare that he is being persecuted because he is a Jew!

This indigent script and the writer's unrelieved style should not be given much importance. The author does not need it to be considered "a marvellous literary genius". Instead, the underlying idea of this story is very symptomatic of that underlying tendency to reverse roles that we see in many other texts.

But this tendency to turn situations around manifests itself above all through the projection onto the goyim of the unconscious guilt deeply rooted within the personality of Jewish intellectuals. We suspect that this responds to their need to get rid of their own "oedipal conflicts".

Thus, for example, this projective inversion is detectable in the

[441]Arthur Miller, *In the Crosshairs,* Fábula-Tusquet, Barcelona, p. 54, 55, 191, 192, 196, 197

[442]"We don't understand it", like Shmuel Trigo, Alexandre Adler, Emmanuel Levinas, Stefan Zweig, Sigmund Freud, etc, read in Hervé Ryssen, *Planetary Hopes,* (2022).

[443]Arthur Miller, *In the Crosshairs,* Fábula-Tusquet, Barcelona, p. 217, 241

story we saw earlier by Pierre Paraf, *General von Morderburg*. Tough and authoritarian, we saw how this Prussian general judged his son "unworthy to wear the uniform, unworthy to be a German". And how, when the latter decided to marry a young Jewish girl, the stubborn and intolerant general pronounced his sentence: "Our son is dead ... no one in the castle must speak his name. Let him become a dancer or a prostitute, if he pleases! Fritz von Morderburg has disappeared from this world."

In fact, this brutal and irrevocable reaction, whereby parents disown their children and consider them dead as soon as they decide to marry outside the community, is a typically Jewish, not Prussian, tradition. It is known that when a member of an orthodox family marries a gentile, the Jewish family gathers to pronounce an oath, the *shib'ah*. This rite is usually performed when a person dies. To *shib'ah* is to declare that a person is considered dead in every way. Norman Jewison's film, *Fiddler on the Roof*, shows very well how this paternal reaction is part of the oldest Jewish tradition. Pierre Paraf attributed it to his Prussian general in order to discredit him more strongly.

This instinctive tendency to attribute one's own "unconscious" guilt feelings to others can also be observed in the famous philosopher Bernard-Henri Lévy. In his 2004 book, *Reincidences, he* attributed the concept of a "chosen people" to certain European nations that may indeed have had a very specific claim to this concept at some point in their history. However, this concept of "chosen people" can only degenerate into criminal madness among the European peoples: "France, the chosen nation... Germany, the chosen nation... How many chosen nations Levinas murmured with dread and a pensive air... Perhaps the Jewish nation is, in fact, the least chosen of all... Perhaps this concept of the chosen nation is the matrix of the crime, the source of the recurrent hatred against the Jews and what they represent—namely the rejection, precisely, of this idea of choice perceived, from his point of view, as the height of idolatry[444]." This reflection expressed in this way by Bernard-Henri Lévy was quite laughable, all the more so when in his book he delighted in describing the special "mission" of the ... chosen people! But we know that Jewish intellectuals like to handle paradoxes. Their ideas are seemingly paradoxical, but, in reality, they reflect a foolproof *chutzpah* and a persistent tendency to inversion[445].

---

[444]Bernard-henri Lévy, *Récidives*, Grasset, 2004, p. 457.

[445]"We have already noted, in their doctrine of the apostate Messiah, that the Sabbateans were not afraid of paradoxes." (Gershom Scholem, *Le Messianisme juif*, 1971,

Even the famous “jeremiad”, so characteristic of the cosmopolitan spirit, as well as the image of the “martyr”, may have been projected onto the “others” as if they were congenital defects to be got rid of. A second-rate writer like Bernard Cohen denounced Christians in his book, *Thou shalt not rejoice, the return of the Puritans*: “Jeremiad, as a moralising prophecy, has become a system of thought and power. The black-clad preachers have been joined by politicians, analysts, scientists[446]...”

The accusations of the planetary intellectuals against their adversaries do indeed seem to indicate a pathological projection of their own guilt. This grid of textual analysis undoubtedly provides a better understanding of Norman Cohn’s analysis of the “paranoid schizophrenia” of anti-Semites, which has also been endorsed by other eminent Jewish thinkers. This “persecution syndrome” which would characterise anti-Semites could, however, very well apply to the usual reactions of some Jewish intellectuals.

Let us listen to Elie Wiesel, for example, who in 1974 published articles reflecting his anxieties about the resurgence of anti-Semitism: “I published an article in the *New York Times* and *Le Figaro* entitled “Why I am afraid”... Signs have appeared, and they are disturbing. The revolting spectacle of an international assembly in delirium, celebrating

---

Calmann-Lévy, 1974, p. 169).

“Dialogues, quotations, witticisms, laughter, discoveries, anecdotes, conversations, eulogies, theories, stories, encounters, interpretations, digressions, demonstrations, fantasies, metamorphoses, ellipses, variations, contradictions, parables, judgements, sarcasms, paradoxes: this sparkling multitude of phrases, dense but logical, of a logic that turns back on itself, forms what we traditionally call in Hebrew, a *Midrash* [see note 109].” In Stéphane Zagdanski, *De l’Antisémitisme*, Climats, 1995, 2006, p. 21. In the Talmud (*Erubin, 13b*), it is said of Rabbi Meir: “He declares pure what is impure and proves it; and he declares impure what is pure and proves it.” [At this point, we invite readers to discover for themselves the *midrashim* of some contemporary rabbis published on digital platforms (Youtube, Bitchute, Odysee). For example: Rabbi Yosef Mizrachi, Rabbi Alon Anava, Rabbi Abraham Benhaim, Rabbi Yekutiel Fish, Rabbi Cahn, Rabbanit Kineret Sarah Cohen, Rabbi Rav Zamir Cohen, Rabbi Rod Reuven Bryant, Rabbi Rav Ron Chaya, Rabbi Rav Avidgor Miller, Rabbi Yaron Reuven, Rabbi Michael Laitman, Rabbi Michael Danielov, Rebbetzin Tziporah Heller, Rabbi Mendel Sasonkin, Rabbi Rav Touitou, Rabbi Rav Raphael Pinto, Rabbi Lawrence Hajioff, Rabbi Tovia Singer, etc., etc. The *chutzpah*, self-satisfaction and hostility towards the gentile world that they convey in their speeches is simply astounding. We recommend in turn the outreach work of the American publicist Adam Green and his online information channel *KnowMoreNews.org*, which collects these comments and warns about these issues].

[446]Bernard Cohen, *Tu ne jouiras point, le retour des puritains*, Albin Michel, 1992, p. 51.

a spokesman for terror[447]. The speeches, the votes against Israel. The dramatic loneliness of this people with a universal vocation. An Arab king offers his guests deluxe editions of the infamous *Protocols of the Elders of Zion*. Desecrated cemeteries in France and Germany. Press campaigns in Soviet Russia. The retro wave that trivialises our suffering and the anti-Zionist, anti-Jewish pamphlets that distort our hopes. One would have to be blind not to recognise it: Jew-hatred is back in fashion[448]."

There is undoubtedly a tendency among Jewish intellectuals to over-dramatise and systematise what is perceived as 'environmental anti-Semitism'. These lines by Samuel Pisar, written in 1983, further illustrated the feeling of persecution that seems to animate Jews, whatever the era: "The recent explosion of bombs in the big cities, the anti-Semitic graffiti, the desecration of schools and cemeteries, are the same ones that have shaken my childhood, destroyed my world… We will be vigilant, watching for the faintest sound of the monster's footsteps… Our enemies are already watching us tirelessly. To them, we will always be guilty. Guilty of being Jews in Israel, of being Jews elsewhere, of being Jews. Guilty, depending, of being capitalists or of being Bolsheviks. Guilty in Europe of having been slaughtered like sheep, and guilty in Israel of having taken up arms so as not to be sheep again. Guilty, indeed, of continuing to exist[449]."

There is no shortage of contradictions within the discourse of Jewish intellectuals. We saw this earlier in the works of Alfred Grosser and Clara Malraux where they questioned the causes of anti-Semitism. But they are equally present in authors such as Jacques Attali, Daniel Cohn-Bendit or Shmuel Trigano[450], for example. These intellectuals back up their demonstrations by pointing to all sorts of "paradoxes", which is a very convenient way of avoiding explanations. The philosopher Jacob Talmon provided an interesting testimony on the ease with which some Jewish intellectuals could affirm, sometimes in the same book, one thing and its opposite depending on the circumstances.

In the nineteenth century, after the French Revolution and the emancipation of Jews in most of Europe, the Jewish people had realised the importance of these changes and had taken full advantage of the

[447] Yasser Arafat, the Palestinian President before the United Nations General Assembly.

[448] Elie Wiesel, *Mémoires, tome II,* Seuil, 1996, p. 97.

[449] Samuel Pisar, *La Ressource humaine*, Jean-Claude Lattès, 1983, p. 250-251.

[450] See Jacques Attali's analysis of the "ghettoisation" of Jews; Daniel Cohn-Bendit's on immigration in Europe; Shmuel Trigano on the role of Jews in the USSR, in Hervé Ryssen, *Planetary Hopes*, (2022).

new situation. Talmon wrote: "Around 1850, the Prague correspondent of the *Jewish Chronicle* was proud to announce to the newspaper in London that, according to statistics, the number of Jewish students at the old university was proportionately much greater than that of Jews in the Habsburg Empire. He then listed some signs of the superior standard of living of the Jewish population to that of the Gentiles around them. They earned more money and were able to climb the social ladder more quickly. One need only recall how Disraeli proudly boasted that he belonged to the "pure race of the elect", and how he said he was glad that it would one day conquer the world. The press was completely in the hands of the Jews. They constituted a dominant group in all sectors of the national economy, and were penetrating the world of the arts and sciences. Disraeli predicted that the world would shortly be at their feet."

But the Gentiles would not be so easily enslaved, and they began to react to this invasion and the continued attacks on the foundations of their civilisation. This defensive reaction is today commonly referred to as "anti-Semitism". And it was precisely this upsurge of anti-Semitism that caused the "conquering" Jews to change their strategy. Jacob Talmon's writing on this subject was quite revealing of the adaptability of Jewish intellectuals:

"They had realised that many Gentiles did not see the sudden success of the newly emancipated Jews as confirmation of the beneficent principle of the race open to all talents... Shortly afterwards, Jewish authors were to rack their brains to prove just the opposite[451]."

Thus, from that day on, Jewish intellectuals no longer boasted of wanting to dominate the world, as the English Prime Minister Disraeli claimed, but on the contrary proclaimed to the world that the Jews were poor, weak and persecuted. However, one need only scratch the surface a little and read a few books reserved for the community to realise that there are other, less confessable dispositions.

We now know that the Jews' desire for world domination, as set out in *The Protocols of the Elders of Zion*, is a "terrifying imposture in the guise of a vampire", as the cartoonist Will Eisner put it. For we must understand clearly: it is not the Jews who want to dominate the world, but supremacist Nazis, fundamentalist Christians or fanatical Muslims, if not the Church of Scientology or the Moon sect.

The famous American writer Norman Mailer, for example, asserted in his book *Why Are We at War* that the only people responsible

[451]J.-L. Talmon, *Destin d'Israël*, 1965, Calmann-Lévy, 1967, p. 50.

for the US war against Iraq in 2003 were the neo-conservative Christians who influenced American politics. They had got their revenge: “A year after the fall of the Soviet Union, there were many on the American right, the early flag-waving conservatives, who thought that this was an extraordinary opportunity. America could take over the world… Subsequently, the Clinton administration did not take up that dream of world domination, and perhaps that is one of the reasons for the intense and even violent hatred that so many right-wing groups felt during those eight years. Had it not been for Clinton, the United States might be ruling the world… After 9/11, jingoistic conservatives felt victorious. They could try to take over the world[452].”

But when we look at the number of ultra-Zionist personalities who have been involved in successive US administrations, it becomes clear, once again, that this Jewish intellectual has projected onto the “others” the wiles of his congeners[453]. And we are well aware that it was not the first time that very influential Zionist personalities expressed their warmongering ardour against recalcitrant peoples who did not want to taste the benefits of plural democracy and the consumer society[454].

Viviane Forrester’s speech, which we saw in another chapter, revealed this same projection syndrome. Let us recall her words tending to blame Europeans: “Spoliation, massacres and genocides… The aptitude of Westerners to manage, erase and conceal what makes them uncomfortable… In the name of their supremacy, with an innate sense of arrogance and the certainty of a natural superiority that justifies their universal arrogance[455].”

When one reads the Old Testament and looks in parallel at the policy of the Hebrew state since its birth, one can also legitimately think that these accusations apply equally to the Jewish people. As for the art of “hiding what makes them uncomfortable”, we will once again recall the overwhelming responsibilities of many Jews for the thirty million Russian and Ukrainian victims, swept under the carpet by Jewish intellectuals all over the world, and for which, despite their perceptible

---

[452]Norman Mailer, *Why are we at war?*, Editorial Anagrama, 2003, Barcelona, p. 68, 69, 70

[453]“The pain of being a Jew is that you feel responsible for everything that other Jews do. For to be a Jew is to live with the echo of a thousand years of alienation. Defending my people is as difficult for me as criticising them. I am not at ease with myself when I talk about Israel or the Jews.” Norman Mailer, *Why Are We at War?* Editorial Anagrama, 2003, Barcelona, p. 103–104. (NdT).

[454]On President George Bush Jr.’s entourage and warmongering politicians: Hervé Ryssen, *Planetary Hopes*, (2022) and *Jewish Fanaticism*, (2019).

[455]Viviane Forrester, *Le Crime occidental*, Fayard, 2004, p. 57, 65.

embarrassment in this respect, we still await an apology.

This is what the Russian novelist Vasili Grossman wrote for his part: "Anti-Semitism is a mirror reflecting the shortcomings of individuals, social structures and state systems. Tell me what you accuse a Jew of and I will tell you what you are guilty of. National Socialism, by accusing the Jewish people it had itself invented of racism, a lust for world domination and a cosmopolitan indifference to the German nation, was projecting onto the Jews its own traits[456]."

The pathological inversion was also evident in a passage from a book by Theodor Lessing, published in 1930, in which the author extolled the merits of one of his peers who also managed to dismantle anti-Semitism: "The Dutch Zionist Fritz Bernstein has masterfully explained the idea that the hatred of a people does not owe its existence to historical facts, but is rather an essentially psychological fact… He demonstrates with solid and sound arguments that there is not first a hateful object, prior to hatred, but that there is a prior need to hate which invents and generates the things hated."

Theodor Lessing provided further scientific arguments to back up his discourse: Indeed, following James and Lange's theory, "we do not cry because we are sad, but we are sad because we must cry. We do not have internal secretions because we are angry, in love or enthusiastic, but the other way round: it is the need for internal secretions that usually provokes anger, love and enthusiasm[457]." Isn't this "great"?

This systematic reversal of values and roles is not recent, judging by the old traditions of yesteryear. The gracious Pope Leo X, for example, who was fond of spectacles, allowed Jewish races to be organised every year for the people of Rome to enjoy themselves. As he was very short-sighted, he would go up to the balconies to catch a glimpse of the spectacle, rejoicing in the popular merriment. During carnivals, the Roman people thus mocked the customs of the Jews and their mania for taking it all in and doing it all backwards. A rabbi was mocked by riding through the streets of the city on a donkey, but upside down, the rabbi holding the tail of the donkey with his hands. But this was in ancient times, when Europeans had not yet been enlightened by the "Age of Enlightenment".

---

[456]Vasili Grossman, *Life and Destiny*, Galaxia Gutenberg, 2007, Barcelona, p. 362.

[457]Theodor Lessing, *La Haine de soi, le refus d'être juif*, 1930, Berg international, 1990, p. 159.

The mirror of Judaism

Jewish intellectuals who analyse anti-Semitism not only project onto their opponents characteristics that seem, indeed, to apply to themselves in the first place. Through coded language, they assert the superiority of the Jewish spirit modelled, as Leon Poliakov so aptly put it, on "the most acrobatic reasoning of the Talmud[458]". The knowledgeable reader can thus enjoy the ingenuity of the author and the credulity of naive readers who read the text literally. It is important to know in this respect that the mysteries of Jewish Kabbalah are based precisely on deciphering the "hidden meaning" of the Torah texts and their interpretations[459].

Jewish intellectuals have long been able to convey messages in their writings that ordinary people are unable to perceive. This aptitude is easy to understand when one considers that, for centuries, Jews could not openly combat Catholicism or Islam without risking severe punishment. They therefore adapted to the circumstances, and became accustomed to expressing in a veiled manner what they really thought.

This was the case, for example, with the Talmud, a book that medieval Christians regarded as the main source of Jewish hatred of Christianity. The book was expurgated from the 16th century onwards of the most offensive passages against Christ and Christians, thus avoiding giving rise to criticism and accusations. From then on, there was a tacit agreement that the passages left blank would be taught orally. Copies of the book were in any case scarce enough, as well as being written in Hebrew, not to alarm the population.

This was what Leon Poliakov wrote about Baruch (Benedict) Spinoza, the famous philosopher who used to insidiously spread religious doubt among his readers. Let us recall here that Spinoza was a Marrano, i.e. a Jew disguised as a Catholic:

"In the background, Spinoza, like a good and subtle Talmudist, speaks, at the same time as his explicit language, a second esoteric language; he pretends to want to demonstrate an idea, but he manages

---

[458]Léon Poliakov, *Histoire de l'antisémitisme, Tome I,* 1981, Points Seuil, 1990, p. 314.

[459]"The mystical formula of this system of interpretation is called PaRDeS. A word composed from the initial letters of Pechat, Remez, Derash and Sod which mean and correspond to: interpretation in the literal sense, interpretation in the allegorical sense, interpretation in the sense of the commentary and interpretation in the secret sense." (Mark Zborowski, *Olam,* 1952, Plon, 1992, p. 421). [P for *pesat,* the literal sense; R for *remez,* the allegorical sense; D for *derasah,* the Talmudic and aggadic interpretation; S for *sod,* the mystical sense. In Gershom Scholem, *La Cábala y su simbolismo,* Siglo XXI Editores, Madrid, 2009, p. 69].

to use certain arguments and to quote certain texts, in such a way that the reader discovers another very different idea, another consequence; and it is this second idea that Spinoza really wanted to demonstrate. He is, in the philosopher Wolfson's expression, the implicit Baruch, i.e. the unbelieving Jew, disguised behind the explicit Benedict, i.e. the Jesus-admiring Marrano. On a still deeper level, Spinoza's language is that of unsatisfied or frustrated love; we detect in him resentment towards the synagogue that rejected him[460]."

In effect, with these contortions, Spinoza was trying to ingratiate himself with his own community, which judged his ideas harshly, as did the Christians. In the end, Spinoza's deviant speeches did not prevent him from being excommunicated by the rabbis and expelled from the Jewish community.

This make-up of the texts is still perceptible in many contemporary authors. We see how Gershom Scholem himself is caught 'red-handed' in a passage in his book on *Jewish Messianism*, in which he quoted a passage from the Talmud (*Sanhedrin, 91b*): 'The only difference between today's world and the time of the Messiah is Israel's submission to the nations', Scholem wrote.

But, evidently, the correct phrase is "the submission of the nations to Israel", as we read elsewhere. The procedure here is a little crude, but it is clearly sufficient for goyim readers. The reversal of terms is due to the fact that the book, though a matter for specialists, is nevertheless disseminated to the general public, and some caution is necessary nonetheless.

In another passage, Gershom Scholem quoted an aphorism from the Zohar: "The messiah will not come until Esau has shed all his tears[461]." Scholem pointed out that "Esau's tears are the same tears that, according to Genesis, XXVII, 38, Esau shed when Jacob tricked him to get Isaac's blessing."

But we know very well that in the texts of Judaism the name "Esau" is a veiled designation for "Christendom". It is therefore "Christendom" that must shed all its tears so that redemption can finally come. And Scholem added: "Penetrating aphorisms of this kind are legion."

Here is an extraordinary and astonishing text by the Austrian writer Joseph Roth, the famous author of *Radetsky's March*. In a 1934 story

---

[460]Léon Poliakov, *Histoire de l'antisémitisme, Tome I,* 1981, Points Seuil, 1990, p. 226, 227.

[461]Gershom Scholem, *Le Messianisme juif,* 1971, Calmann_Lévy, 1974, p. 45, 57, 65. Read in translator's note in Annex V.

entitled *The Antichrist,* Joseph Roth warned his readers against the wiles of the Evil One and taught us to recognise him behind his disguises. He wrote in the epigraph: "I have written this book as a warning so that the Antichrist may be known in whatever form he appears:

Antichrist "makes himself most clearly known in the fact that he transforms into vulgar something that is noble in its essence. The meaning of his existence and his actions is precisely to profane the sacred, to demean the noble, to distort the upright, and to disfigure the beautiful. Not content with having granted itself power over the essentially vulgar—for that too is part of the earthly world—it seeks to extend its dominion over the noble. But since the noble would never submit to his discipline unless it ceased to be noble, the first thing he does is to turn it into evil. The devil resembles a violent king whose country is barren and who, in order to conquer the flourishing nations around him, begins by transforming them into wastelands in order to make them resemble his own... The Antichrist ... has the power to desertify a flowery land while he blinds us so that we believe the desert to be, justly, a flourishing garden. And while he is engaged in annihilation, we believe that he builds. When it gives us stones, we think it gives us bread. The poison in his cup has for us the taste of a fountain of life[462]."

The Antichrist's plan to subvert the nations is as follows: "Cunning as he is, he began by seducing not the rebels but, first and foremost, the keepers of the old. Not those who desired renewal, but those called to maintain the old. At first he took up residence in churches, and then in the houses of lords. For that is his method, and in that he can be known without equivocation; and it is a mistake, a mistake of the world, to believe that he is recognised for inciting and instigating the humiliated and enslaved. That would be foolishness, and Antichrist is cunning. He does not stir the oppressed people to revolt, but seduces the masters to oppress. He does not make rebels, but tyrants. And once he has introduced tyranny, he knows that rebellion will come of its own accord. In this way he wins doubly, for in a way he forces the righteous, who would otherwise resist him, into his service. He does not, for example, persuade the servants to become masters, but begins by enslaving them. Then—once they have entered his service—he forces them into bondage to the powerless, the poor, the industrious, the humble and the righteous. Then the poor and humble spontaneously become indignant

[462]Joseph Roth, *El Anticristo,* Ediciones Capitán Swing, Polifonías, Madrid, 2013, p. 49, 50.

against the violence; and the intelligent and the righteous are compelled to become indignant against folly and injustice, and it is they who put arms into the hands of the poor. And so they must, for they are righteous. Therefore, it is false to tell the world that the Antichrist leads the indignant. On the contrary, he seduces the guardians of the establishment. By his nature it is not as easy for him to approach those who suffer as it is for the powerful." In the same way, the Antichrist "also made the priests liars before pushing believers to deny God… The deniers of God—or, as they call themselves, atheists—do not deny God, but the false image of God that has been handed down to them," wrote Joseph Roth.

But make no mistake, it is not the Jews that Joseph Roth is referring to, but the anti-Semites: "Therefore, whoever believes in Jesus Christ and hates, despises or simply belittles the Jews, his earthly bosom, is a brother of Antichrist… You are possessed by Antichrist… You envy them because they get earthly goods. That is the truth. You want all earthly goods for yourselves. The Antichrist is among you and within you."

With characteristic aplomb, the famous "*chutzpah*" to which we are accustomed, Joseph Roth then explained to us what a good Christian should be like, while warning us against sheep going astray and giving his guidelines for the right management of the Church. Thus he concluded his demonstration:

"But the false Christians despise, hate or despise the bosom of their salvation, that is, the Jews. For the Jews are the earthly bosom of Jesus Christ. Whoever does not appreciate the Jews does not appreciate Jesus Christ either. The Christian appreciates the Jews. Whoever despises or belittles them is not a Christian and mocks God Himself… But he who, on his own account, wants to take revenge on the Jews in the name of God as if he were their representative, so to speak, errs and commits a mortal sin… Whoever hates the Jews is a heathen, and not a Christian. Whoever is capable of hating—whoever he may be—is a heathen and not a Christian. And he who thinks he is a Christian because he is not a Jew is doubly and trebly a heathen. Let him be expelled from the community of Christians! And if the Church does not expel him, God Himself will expel him[463]."

Contrary to the worst anti-Semitic prejudices, we must believe that Jews are poor, vulnerable and harmless beings: "Then a weak man came to see me; he was one of those who are today the weakest victims of the

---

[463]Joseph Roth, *El Anticristo*, Ediciones Capitán Swing, Polifonías, Madrid, 2013, p. 115, 116, 186, 183, 184

powerful, that is, a Jew."

And it would also be good to show a little more respect for him: "We Jews, too, once had a house. But in our books it was written that the stranger was to be in our house as a relative. And we all kept this commandment. And we even passed it on to the strangers, who learned from us that it is much better to give hospitality than to enjoy it[464]." The Jewish tradition of hospitality is indeed well known to all.

A few pages further on, Joseph Roth warned us once again against any temptation to oppose the Jews: "God alone has the right to punish the Jews. But God Himself hates men who hate the Jews... You, anti-Semite, are the right hand and the magic wand of the Antichrist."

Nor should we think that there is the slightest hint of pride or megalomania in these lines on the part of the Jewish writer. It would be an anti-Semitic opinion to think so, an affront to the entire Jewish people, and, moreover, a grave error of interpretation: "The ancient Jews claimed to be God's chosen people. But to what end did they say so? In order to beget the Redeemer, Jesus Christ, who died on the cross for all the people of the world. In reality, the pride of the Jews was humility[465]." It is really a relief to read that. We are much more at ease then.

We may legitimately think that Joseph Roth took a malevolent pleasure in sowing confusion by reversing the roles. For in reality, it seems to be the Jews, and not the anti-Semites, who, according to him, would embody the Antichrist. The author did indeed drop a crude hint in one passage of the book when he suggested that the Antichrist had "organised a war between Russia and Japan" and was in the habit of "robbing men dead" (pp. 62–63). Now, it is publicly known that Japan's 1905 war against Russia was largely financed by the very wealthy American businessman Jacob Schiff, out of hatred for Tsarism. Jacques Attali confirmed the key role of Jewish financiers in that war: "Max Warburg and Jacob Schiff then became Japan's main financiers. Schiff even made a triumphant trip to the archipelago, to the great fury of the Russians[466]."

---

[464]"Foreigners are in our house as they are in their own", declared President François Mitterrand, who was very well "surrounded".

[465]Joseph Roth, *El Anticristo*, Ediciones Capitán Swing, Polifonías, Madrid, 2013, p. 212, 213, 216, 217, 182.

[466]Jacques Attali, *Los judíos, el mundo y el dinero*, Fondo de cultura económica, 2005, Buenos Aires, p. 378.

[Numerous other sources confirm this: "Mr. Schiff on numerous occasions refused to participate in loans to Russia, and used his great influence to prevent Russia's entry into the money markets of America, solely because of the Russian government's

As for the looting of corpses on battlefields, it was a centuries-old tradition of Eastern European Jews[467] that soldiers across the continent, who saw their black silhouettes leaning over corpses after the battle, used to call the "crows".

For Joseph Roth, this work therefore had not only a combative value, intended to erase any trace of anti-Semitism from the *goy's mind. It* also had an escape valve function: Joseph Roth reversed the roles to express in a veiled way the neurosis of Judaism and the temptation of some Jews to identify with the Antichrist and the Devil. It is interesting to note in this regard that for Christians the work of "Satan", the Adversary, consists precisely in systematically inverting all established values. But for these Jewish intellectuals, it is perhaps only a simple, slightly sick intellectual game, probably the result of a serious neurosis.

The novelist Isaac Bashevis Singer illustrated this "diabolical" tendency in Judaism, spread above all by the Sabbatean heresy. In *The Destruction of Kreshev*, he recounted the misfortunes of a young Jewish woman who had unknowingly married a Jew who was apparently correct in all respects, but who turned out in reality to be an adherent of the doctrine of Shabtai Tzvi:

"Although the false Messiah was long dead, the secret cult of his followers was maintained in many countries. They met in fairs and markets, recognised each other by secret signs, and were thus safe from the wrath of other Jews who would have excommunicated them. Many rabbis, teachers, ritual slaughterers and other apparently respectable people belonged to this sect. Some posed as miracle-workers, and went from town to town distributing amulets in which they had inserted not the holy name of God, but impure names of dogs and evil spirits, Lilith and Asmodeus, as well as the name of Shabtai Tzvi himself. All this they accomplished with such cunning, that only the members of the brotherhood could appreciate their work. They took great satisfaction in deceiving the pious and spreading evil[468]."

---

mistreatment of the Jews. Japanese Finance Minister Bakatani claimed that when Japan, undertaking to negotiate a £10 million loan in London during the spring of 1904, found it difficult to secure that amount, "Mr. Schiff in a single conversation with Mr. Takahashi alone offered to underwrite half of the loan we needed". He concluded with the statement: "The amount of our loan underwritten by Mr Schiff, from the first to the fifth issue, totals £39,250,000". Cyrus Adler, *Jacob Henry Schiff, A Biographical Sketch*, The New York American Jewish Committee, New York, New York, 1921, p. 16, 15, quoted in Alberto Léon Cebrián, *The Banking Revolutions*, 2017, p. 228].

[467] Hervé Ryssen, *Planetary Hopes*, (2022), (note 817).

[468] Isaac Bashevis Singer, *The Destruction of Kreshev*, 1958, Folio, 1997, p. 53, 54. Translation free PDF version, *The Destruction of Kreshev* p. 17.

The heretical Jew was finally discovered: "He explained how he had joined the ranks of the cult of Shabtai Tzvi while still a child, how he had studied alongside his fellow disciples, how he had been taught that an excess of degradation meant greater holiness and that, the more odious the wickedness, the nearer one is to the day of redemption[469]."

In another of his novels, *The Slave*, Isaac Bashevis Singer described some Sabbatean practices in a small 17th century village in Poland: "At the time of Sabbetai Zeví, the false Messiah who later put on the fez and became a Mohammedan, Pilitz was divided. The community excommunicated his followers, who in turn publicly cursed the rabbi and the elders. The men not only insulted each other, but attacked each other. Some members of the sect tore the roof off their houses, packed their belongings in barrels and boots, and set out to flee to the Land of Israel. Others turned to Kabbalah, tried to draw wine from the walls or to create doves by the arcane powers of the Book of Creation. Some abandoned the Torah, believing that with the coming of the Messiah the law would be nullified. Others thought they found in the Bible hints that the way of redemption lay in evil, and they indulged in all kinds of abominations. There was in Pilitz a teacher who possessed such a vivid imagination, that while praying with his shawl and phylacteries, he thought he was copulating, and even ejaculated. The accursed sect considered this so great a feat that they elected him chief... They were united not only by the illusion that Sabbetai Zeví would return and rebuild Jerusalem, but also by interest. They formed associations, traded and favoured each other and intrigued against their enemies. If one of them was accused of swindling, his friends would testify on his behalf and try to frame another. They soon became rich and powerful. In their meetings they mocked the righteous and remarked how easy it was to cheat them[470]."

Sabbatean doctrine, in fact, encouraged the reversal of all established values, including those of Talmudic Judaism. We know from Gershom Scholem that the Sabbateans, although fiercely opposed by the rabbis, had nevertheless secretly achieved a pre-eminent position in the Jewish communities of Central Europe, and that many rabbis even secretly practised their rites of inversion, which called for going against the principles of the Torah.

"To acknowledge the Sabbateanism of eminent rabbis in

---

[469]Isaac Bashevis Singer, *The Destruction of Kreshev*, 1958, Folio, 1997, p. 74 Free PDF translation, *The Destruction of Kreshev* p. 24.

[470]Isaac Bashevis Singer, *The Slave*, 1962, Epublibre, digital publisher German25 (2014), p. 762–765. (See translator's note in Annex VI. 2).

Jerusalem, Adrianople, Constantinople, Smyrna, Prague, Hamburg or Berlin, would have been … to openly expose the integrity of a body of men who were always supposed to be learned and courageous defenders of the Jewish tradition, wrote Scholem. It is not surprising that investigations which might have uncovered heretical, not to say downright licentious, views in the most unexpected places were instinctively avoided… Not only did most of the families who were part of the Sabbatean movement in Western and Central Europe subsequently remain within the Jewish fold, but many of their descendants, especially in Austria, rose, in the course of the nineteenth century, to important positions: renowned intellectuals, great financiers or highly connected political men. Obviously, it was not to be expected that these personalities would be willing to allow their "compromised" heritage to be "discovered". Because of their positions in the Jewish community, it is not surprising that their wishes were listened to… I can hardly conceal my opinion that the movement was much wider than has hitherto been generally admitted… The sources in our possession, scanty as they are, make it very clear that the number of Sabbatean rabbis was much larger than has been generally estimated, larger even than was believed by Rabbi Jacob Emden who was fervently anti-Sabbatean and who was always accused of exaggeration[471]."

Although we cannot disentangle in this study what is currently Sabbatean or properly Talmudic in the spirit of the Jews, it would be interesting to investigate further in order to better understand the nature of this spirit of inversion which we find in many intellectuals. Is it the consequence of a "malicious", not to say frankly "demonic" spirit, or the manifestation of a neurosis? Or both at the same time? For the benefit of the doubt, we will accept for the time being, and until proven otherwise, the less convincing thesis.

The projection of their feelings of guilt onto the rest of humanity even leads some cosmopolitan thinkers to project onto "anti-Semites" their own aptitude for accusatory inversion, in the belief that they are ridding themselves of this burden. Taking their pathological case as a generality, they accuse their adversaries of the same psychological defects, the same implausible intellectual contortions of which they themselves are capable. We can now better understand Raphaël Draï's analysis of *The Protocols of the Elders of Zion*, as set out above:

"...it is now appropriate to consider the psychopathological aspect"

---

[471]Gershom Scholem, *Le Messianisme juif*, 1971, Calmann-Lévy, 1974, p. 142-144.

and" ... the psychic inversion revealed by this document... The anti-Semite attributes to the Jews intentions which he himself has against them; intentions which he cannot directly confess... The psychopathological dimension of such constructions must attract and retain attention... The Jews put on stage are projective Jews; the "Judaised" image is characteristic of anti-Semitic delusions[472]."

In *Anti-Semitic Hatred*, Serge Moati shared with his readers an even more eloquent testimony about the specific psychopathology of the Jewish intellectual. Here is the extraordinary conclusion of his book, in which the author, after having interviewed anti-Semites from all over the world, expressed what he really thought, revealing a part of his subconscious. Like the other Jewish intellectuals, and despite his exhaustive research, he claimed that he still did not understand the causes of anti-Semitism. But at this point in our study, this is no longer important. Let us listen to him speak:

"I have wanted to delve into the belly of the beast, and I have come up against the Mystery. I have unpacked the facts, I have listened a lot, I have tried to bring to light what I dare not call 'reasons', and yet, as in the dark initiatory tales, the Mystery remains before me, hidden, sealed, buried, deeply crouched in the consciences. The Mystery of anti-Semitism. I have collided with hatred. But the question is still there, stubborn. It knows how to resist all analyses... Anti-Semitism is truly a baleful passion that sweeps away all the dykes of reason and submerges all those who fall victim to it. From Paris to Warsaw, from Moscow to Chicago, I met again and again the same crazy words born in dark dreams. The anti-Semite says the same thing everywhere. He stutters the same speech in all languages. The anti-Semite is possessed by something beyond him and that is certainly what he suggests when he says: "I can't help it!" It sounds almost like an excuse. Insatiable search for the Jew on the part of the anti-Semite. Searching for the Jew, evicting him, rounding him up, raging, going back and starting again, imagining him everywhere, even where he is no longer there and where he never was. To invent the Jew when necessary, at convenience, where he can still serve, and, in truth, he can always serve.

The anti-Semite is a hypochondriac. He declares himself sick of Jews, but he eats them, he fucks Jews, he injects them intravenously into the poor man, otherwise the poor man dies, otherwise the poor man no longer exists. The Jew cements his identity. For him, without a Jew,

---

[472]Raphaël Draï, *Identité juive, identité humaine,* Armand Colin 1995, p. 390-392.

there is no salvation. So, after having killed them, he reinvents them all. For pleasure. To live or to try to live. The Jews are really necessary to him. During this journey, I confess, I came close, I have to confess, to suffering from the same evil. I saw the anti-Semite everywhere, in my nightmares at night or in my daytime fantasies. Behind anodyne words, or beyond harmless allusions. I was out of tune, I was harassing, I was policing the subconscious of others. I had to put an end to all that. But now, however, nothing will ever seem as trivial as before, because I have lived the everyday life of hatred. Mine and that of others.

I have felt that the subconscious of the anti-Semite overflows, subject to eruptions that make him reel. The anti-Semite hesitates and the evil that comes out of him is infinitely beyond him. Nothing satisfies his hunger and thirst, his rage and hatred. It drags him along in its mad carousel. He is its slave for ever, chained and captive…

You have heard, because I also met him, the never satiated hatred of some "enlightened" people who would not pass for folklore if history had not taught us to be strongly suspicious of madmen and their delusions… I wanted to see him closer, face to face, the one who hates me. And I was afraid. Not of the black birds passing by, but of the reflection in their faces of our common humanity. As if the anti-Semite was and still is, beyond the murder he fantasises about or has already committed, fears or desires, beyond the mirror that brought him closer, a brother in spite of everything, yes, a broken and wounded brother … the executioner cried and it was again my fault, always my fault. He told me his hatred and I heard his complaint. The executioner sobbed on my shoulder and seemed to tell me in his cruel and sad child's voice:"… Let me kill you, I have to live. I have no memory, you have one. I don't know who I am, while you have the oldest identity in the world. I hate your memory, I hate your memories, I hate your God and the pretence he has given you… I hate you because you hog my air. Because you enjoy so much and I enjoy so little. Hey Jew! Love me, I who want to kill you. Bless me for wanting to kill you. Love me, and make me you. Give me this world that is denied to me. Jew, Jew, give me the world." Crazy I was! That was the long lament I heard, that dark cry coming from the origins, a fear so ancient and irrational, so childish, and, as it were, so stupid, so monstrously stupid. I, today, have heard the anti-Semite. I am no longer afraid of him. I know his weakness… I pity him, yes, the same pity as the frail sick, but that is no reason not to fight him. With all our strength. With reason. And the subconscious. With education, with civic and moral progress, certainly…

I have wanted to dig into the belly of the beast. I have done it. At the end of this almost initiatory journey, my hands are full of blood. Among the viscera, hidden and concealed, was a very dirty mirror. I wiped the mirror with my saliva. And I shuddered: that face glimpsed in the centre of the darkness, at the end of the evil, was mine. I saw myself in the very heart of the beast's dream. It was feeding on my face, regurgitating it, devouring it. In destroying the monster, I broke the mirror. My face was broken. A new face will be born. One day. Enigma. Mystery in the form of a provisional conclusion. Enigma. Like a Jewish story, so I'm told."

The pathological dimension is very clearly perceptible here, and Serge Moati also made a very interesting confession at the end of the text, when he explained that, in this mirror found in the entrails of the "beast", it was his face that he saw, and not that of the anti-Semite. We now invite the reader to reread this text, but this time exchanging the terms "Jews" and "anti-Semites", in order to understand the problem we are facing.

We'll leave you for a moment before continuing…

So what, isn't it astonishing and overwhelming? The last conclusion of Serge Moati's book corresponded to an abrupt recovery after the delirium through which he had unwisely unburdened himself. The messianic Jew was finally recovering and reasserting his eternal mission, though evidently too heavy for such fragile minds:

"Today, I feel a strong sense of pride in belonging to a unique people that I love and respect. In its diversity and its dispersion, in its misfortunes, in its stubbornness and in its hopes. A people, my people, who are so much like humanity in their precarious struggle with each other, and with God… My people, who like me, entangled in their mission that is too heavy for them, are brave and headstrong. I love my people, here and everywhere. I love and defend them. Here, in Israel, everywhere. That's right, the proximity of the anti-Semite has only strengthened my own identity. His hatred has helped me, and I return it: he smells of death and I love love love. Thank you, my father, for having given me a Jewish birth … tomorrow I will no longer be a Jew by chance. I have challenged and fought the demons and I want to defeat them again and again. I have a Hebrew name that my father gave me: Haïm, it means life. It also means Victory. Victor is the name of my son. Victory[473]…"

[473]Serge Moati, *La Haine antisémite,* Flammarion, 1991, p. 228-232.

Jewish obsession

The Jewish intellectual seems to be literally obsessed with his Jewish identity, and the emancipation of European Jews during the 19th century did not really solve anything, as Jews seem to be always struggling between the two perfectly antinomian options of real integration into European society and fidelity to Judaism.

On this phenomenon, it may be interesting to quote here the philosopher Hannah Arendt, who wrote in 1951 about those Central European Jews who had left their shtetls at the end of the 19th century, to live in Vienna and Berlin, before settling in Paris or New York: "The result was that their private lives, their decisions and feelings became the very centre of their "Jewishness". And the more the fact of Jewish birth lost its religious, national and socio-economic significance, the more obsessive Jewishness became; Jews were obsessed by it as one might be obsessed by a physical defect or advantage, and devoted to it as one might be devoted to a vice[474]."

The early 20th century Viennese novelist Arthur Schnitzler transcribed quite well the enigmatic and obsessive character of the "Jewish question" that tormented him: "It was not possible for a Jew, he wrote, especially if he was a public man, to forget that he was a Jew, for others did not forget, neither the Christians, nor, still less, the Jews. There was no alternative but to pass for insensitive, overbearing and arrogant, or for touchy, timid and subject to persecution mania." His biographer, Jacques Le Rider, wrote of the novelist: "A reading of Schnitzler's monumental intimate diary, written from his adolescence

---

[474]Hannah Arendt, *Los orígenes del totalitarismo*, Taurus-Santillana, 1998, Madrid, p. 88. [Secularisation, therefore, finally determined that paradox, so decisive for the psychology of modern Jewry, whereby Jewish assimilation in its liquidation of national consciousness, in its transformation from a national religion into a confessional denomination and in its way of responding to the national consciousness, in its transformation from a national religion into a confessional denomination and in its way of responding to the cold and ambiguous demands of state and society with equally ambiguous resources and psychological tricks—engendered a very real Jewish chauvinism, if by chauvinism we mean the perverted nationalism in which "the individual is himself what he worships; the individual is his own ideal and even his own idol". Where Jews were educated, secularised and assimilated under the ambiguous conditions of society and state in Western and Central Europe, they lost that measure of political responsibility which their origin implied and which Jewish notables had always felt, albeit in the form of privilege and domination. Jewish origin, without religious and political connotations, became everywhere a psychological quality, became "Jewishness" and from then on could only be considered within the categories of virtue or vice." In *The Origins of Totalitarianism, Anti-Semitism*, p. 81, 88].

until 1931, shows how turning his Jewish identity over in his mind was for him an exercise he repeated indefinitely[475]."

The case of Franz Kafka was entirely similar. This is what Laurent Cohen wrote about him, noting this "illness" specific to Judaism: "Kafka no longer appears to us as a "classic" case of a sick Jew but, on the contrary, as a man obsessed with a quest for identity." He hated himself not for being Jewish, but for not being Jewish enough," the excellent biographer Ernst Pawel rightly wrote... He simply did not believe that assimilation could provide Jews with more than a thin veneer, under which, come hell or high water, they would remain themselves. Kafka "could not get used to the idea" of "getting caught up in the neurotic game of assimilation". Kafka, like many Jews, "is definitely a prisoner of his identity", wrote Laurent Cohen." How, as a supporter of the collectivist Zionist enterprise, could he write in 1923 such a depressing text as *The Work*? When we approach it, we are terrified by such a paranoid cult of enclosure[476]." This is another confirmation of a certain paranoia that is very specific to Judaism.

For the French Jews of *La Belle Époque*, the novelist Marcel Proust left a social portrait that staged two emblematic characters tortured by these two identity alternatives. Here is what Leon Poliakov wrote about this in his *History of Jewish Identity Crises*: "The double figure of Charles Swann and Albert Bloch exemplifies the two sides: Swann, a man of good taste, a scholar, a friend of the Prince of Wales, who had erased all traces of Semitic belonging in him, became sympathetic to the Jews at the end of his life, becoming a committed *dreyfusard477*, and resembling "an old Hebrew"." Albert Bloch, on the other hand, is a "pedantic young Jew, seeking by all means his integration into the better society", and, as Proust described him, "a badly educated, neurotic, snobbish[478]."

With the triumphant globalism of the late second millennium, the messianic era so long awaited by many Jews seemed to be opening up: borders were disappearing, hated white peoples were dissolving, and the entire Western world seemed at last to be "pacified". However, while some Jewish intellectuals or financiers firmly believed that "this time would be the good one", it was to be expected that the coming of the *Messiah* would not succeed in calming all spirits.

The novelist Philip Roth echoed this obsession through one of his

---

[475]Jacques Le Rider, *Arthur Schnitzler*, Belin, 2003, p. 202, 203

[476]Laurent Cohen, *Variations autour de K*, Intertextes, Paris, 1991, p. 15, 47, 50, 132.

[477]Supporters of Captain Alfred Dreyfus (see note 174). (NdT).

[478]Léon Poliakov, *Histoires des crises d'identité juives*, Austral, 1994, p. 83.

characters who could not turn the page and forget about "that subject":

"In short, then, George, he lectured me on the subject which I do not really remember having chosen to follow me thus, like a shadow, from the cradle to the grave; the subject whose obsessive enquiry I have always felt could be left for another day; the subject whose persistent intrusion into all affairs, great and small, one did not always know how to handle; the invasive, omnipresent, nagging theme, in which were encapsulated the most serious problem and the most startling experience of my life, and which, in spite of all honourable attempts to resist its spell, was now showing itself to be the irrational force that had driven my life to this point; the theme which, judging by what I was hearing, could not be considered exclusively mine either... The subject which answers to the name of *Jew479*."

The Jewish obsession is here perfectly expressed in what is neurotic for an intellectual. The problem lies in the fact that many Jews are precisely such "intellectuals", because of the traditional importance given to study in Judaism, mainly the study of the Torah and Talmud[480]. It is in that sense, indeed, that one can legitimately recognise that Jews are "the people of the book", or rather "of the books": the Torah, the Talmud, and the Zohar.

The philosopher Jacob Talmon also mentioned the obsession of the Jewish intellectual: "His painful and obsessive self-consciousness stands between him and the world[481]", he wrote.

In a lecture on 14 March 2005, the influential press director Alexandre Adler expressed the same conclusion: "Judaism is a very complicated thing, and, at the same time, it is from time to time an obsessive neurosis[482]."

Another outstanding French intellectual, Edgar Morin, gave a similarly divided picture of his identity in the daily *Libération* of 13 May 2004: "French, Mediterranean, Jewish, universalist, European, secular... These are what I call my concentric identities", he wrote. Born in Paris into a Jewish emigrant family (his father Vidal Nahoum was a Marrano from Thessaloniki), the sociologist of Sephardic culture also feels he is the spiritual son of Spinoza, "because he rejected the

---

[479]Philip Roth, *Operation Shylock*, Debolsillo Penguin Random House, Barcelona, 2005, p. 149.

[480]"... nine hours a day of machine learning required of three year olds in the Khéider." (Mark Zborowski, *Olam*, 1952, Plon, 1992, p. 15). The Kheider is the traditional primary schools whose purpose is to teach children the basics of Judaism and Hebrew.

[481]J.-L. Talmon, *Destin d'Israël*, 1965, Calmann-Lévy, 1967, p. 15.

[482]http://www.beit-haverim.com/anoter/ConfAdler0305.htm

idea of a chosen people". He therefore places himself somewhat on the fringes of the community and curiously declares himself "a non-Jewish Jew, a non-Jewish Jew." As you can see, it is not at all easy to be a Jew.

The list would be very long if we were to publish all the anguished testimonies of Jewish intellectuals. Bernard-Henri Levy himself, the man who struts his stuff on television sets, could not completely hide this "obsessive Jewishness". Nor did he deny that, with such a burden, some Jewish intellectuals could be seduced by the temptation to renege.

Albert Cohen's novel, *Bella del Señor*, was for him symptomatic of this ambivalence of Diaspora Jewry. One can read the book, Levy wrote, "as an allegory of Jewishness in the West": "Readers of the book remember, I am sure, that extraordinary scene ... in which we see the prince of gentility, Solal the Magnificent, the Grand Duke of the SDN [League of Nations], talking on equal terms with the greatest, and, at the same time, nurturing and protecting in his basement a sort of "court of Miracles[483] "composed of scrofulous, sickly, outlawed Jews, unrepresented in the world where he is one of the kings and whom he is compelled to visit secretly at night."

But by turning away from his people, Solal turned his back on the Law. By driving his character to suicide, explained Bernard-Henri Levy, Albert Cohen wanted to imply that: "Israel will never be reconciled with the Christian West." According to the philosopher, Albert Cohen's novel "showed the temptation to renege, the temptation, as Solal says at one point, to "monkey around" with Christians and be more Christian than Christians... One can read this novel as the great novel of contemporary neo-Marranism, Levy continued, the great novel that proclaims the suffering of the neo-Marran: *goy* on the outside, Jew on the inside; living by day in the world and returning at night to his inner ghetto[484]."

And let us not forget that, in other passages of his works, Bernard-Henri Lévy declared himself to be "French", more French than he was, impossible! Let us recall what he replied to Raymond Aron in 1981, when the latter was alarmed to see Lévy vomit page after page, in the most outrageous way, about France and French culture: "You have read me too well, I am sure, to ignore that it is as a Frenchman and as a Frenchman that, like any other French philosopher, I have risked this research on black France[485]."

---

[483]*La cour des Miracles*: French expression referring to the slums and shantytowns of ancien régime Paris.

[484]Bernard-Henri Lévy, *Récidives*, Grasset, 2004, p. 397, 391

[485]Bernard-Henri Lévy, *Questions de principe, deux*, Grasset, 1986, p. 306. See also in

In short, it is very practical to be a Jew." I am a Jew when I feel like it[486]", said former socialist minister Bernard Kouchner. This allows them to make apologies for everything deviant, dissident and renegade, and then complain about discrimination when they are caught red-handed.

Symptoms of madness

Jewish neurosis is, for example, very evident in the novel *A Jew on the Run* by Laurent Sagalovitch. The newspaper *Le Monde* of 2 September 2005 reviewed the novel, emphasising the pathological and tragic character of the hero's life, very similar to that of the author: He wants to "go far away. Far away from what? Away from here. From this mouldy France which bores him and which he deeply loathes. Just like Simon Sagalovitch, the character in his latest novel."

Simon is 31 years old." His neurotic sister is sleeping with a goy who is a bit of a fool." During the *Passover* dinner, Simon announces to his parents that he has decided to leave France and move to Canada: "This country is too small, too petty, too petty, too self-interested"." All right, Simon, *Mazal tov,* get out of this "mouldy" France!

To his girlfriend who wishes to have a child with him, he says: "Why do you want my semen, which suffers from obvious signs of traumatic distress and which according to my psychoanalyst is due to a metaphysical incompatibility with the universe, not to mention God's silence during the Holocaust, as well as the current nuclear threat posed by North Korea, Iran, Syria and Pakistan? How do you want me to father a child who will be either autistic, manic-depressive, hyperactive, vegetative, idiotic and uneducated? a son who will one day come to me and say, "Daddy, I love you very much, but you annoy the hell out of me! "

Simon Sagalovitch finally settles in Canada." But then boredom strikes again. And the eternal question: To leave again, but where to? Away. Away from what?" Without realising it, I had contracted the curse of the wandering Jew, never at ease anywhere, always in search of a paradise that exists only in children's books."

The laudatory comments we could read on the internet insisted rather on the ridiculousness of the story: "The journey of the hypochondriac Sagalovitch to Vancouver promises to lovers of Jewish

---

Hervé Ryssen, *Les Expectations planetariennes, (*2022).

[486]Daniel Cohn-Bendit, Bernard Kouchner, *Quand tu seras président,* Robert Laffont, 2004, p. 347.

stories, family neuroses, football, whisky or Lorazepam, one of the tastiest cocktails of the new literary season." The hero "carries with him his nostalgia for the great Saint-Étienne Greens football team, his mistrust of the goyim, his strong sense of maladjustment and a jubilant bad faith. As soon as he lands in Canada, he hooks up with a Dutch beauty (optimistic, relaxed and a heavy cannabis smoker). With her he will discover the charms of the libertarian but hygienist society of the city of Vancouver."

It is true that, although they tend to "distrust the Goyim", Jews do appreciate "Dutch beauties", and, as we have seen in film and literature, the only thing that Jews seem to really appreciate about European peoples is the beauty of their women. But even in this matter, Jews seem to find it difficult to abstract from their Jewishness. The acclaimed novelist Philip Roth wrote thus in *Operation Shylock*:

"I myself dated a girl who had been married to a Jew. The most anti-Semitic people in the world are those who have been married to a Jew or a Jewess. They all tell you the same thing: they are a bunch of fools. I know a girl who lived with a Jew for eight or nine years. In all that time, they never had more than fifteen or sixteen good fucks, because the guy never relaxed enough. He was always so obsessed with his Jewishness that he had to find himself a *shiksa* to fuck to his heart's content. Not to mention the way his parents treated her like a freshly shat shit. The mother who bore them, the amount of problems Jews have. They do nothing but whine[487]."

The *Nouvel Observateur* journalist Colette Mainguy did not seem to be very sane either, judging by what she wrote on the cover of her novel *The Jewess (*2001): "I rediscovered my Jewishness after five years of psychoanalysis. For so long I had been having recurring Germanic dreams. The Germans are chasing me. They machine-gun me and then I die under a tarpaulin in a lorry travelling through the Vercors. I am arrested in the round-ups of Jews; I reproach my mother for having abandoned me in a camp; I am a journalist and I tell what ghetto life is like before they lock me up in it; I give fellatio to Nazis, the Gestapo knocks on my door. I always run away. My hiding places are always dark cellars, sordid wardrobes or terrifying labyrinths; one night, I confront my sister Beth. She is the head of the Gestapo in a concentration camp." Apparently, those five years of psychoanalysis were not enough to exorcise the evil.

We also read in the press about the pathological case of Philippe

---

[487]Philip Roth, *Operation Shylock*, Debolsillo Penguin Random House, Barcelona, 2005, p. 296.

Zamour, 41, a judge for 10 years, who had been caught masturbating during a court hearing in Angoulême (Charente). The man was arrested, suspended from his post and charged with the offence of "sexual exhibitionism". Before this incident, Philippe Zamour had already received therapeutic care, as he used to go shopping dressed as a woman or imitate Johny Hallyday[488] in the corridors of the courthouse. According to Reuters, on 28 September 2005, Zamour was dismissed on medical grounds, and the judge was declared irresponsible for his actions by psychiatrists, who diagnosed and declared him nothing less than "schizophrenic". Under these circumstances, the Superior Council of the Judiciary considered that it was not possible to sanction the accused.

This example is highly anecdotal, but we can nevertheless consider it to reflect a very real phenomenon. What is more surprising is that, as far as we know, no really comprehensive research has been carried out and published on the specific pathologies of Jewish identity, no serious study is available to the general public. The "problem" is however of stature, judging from what we could read elsewhere about other personalities.

The writer Joseph Roth was also directly affected by Jewish neurosis, as his own wife suffered from severe mental problems. Even a Hasidic miracle-working rabbi tried to heal her in vain: "He himself, Joseph Roth, an enlightened, agnostic Jew, before converting (really or fictionally) to Catholicism, consulted a miracle-working "rabbi" for his wife Friedl, who was suffering from schizophrenia, the outcome of which was fatal[489]."

Elie Wiesel was quite critical of the Yiddish writer Isaac Bashevis Singer. Probably because the latter received the Nobel Prize for literature and occupied a pre-eminent position that Elie Wiesel secretly envied: "He didn't like me," wrote Wiesel in his *memoirs*, "and why not admit it, it was reciprocal." Elie Wiesel also reproached Bashevis for

---

[488]Famous French rocker. Generational idol. He has been considered an icon in the French-speaking world since the beginning of his career. For some, he is the French equivalent of Elvis Presley.

[489]Joseph Roth, *Juifs en errance,* 1927, Seuil, 1986, p. 29. ["For the Hasidim, the miracle-working rabbi is the mediator between man and God. Enlightened Jews have no need of any mediator. They even consider it a sin to believe in an earthly power that would be able to anticipate God's decisions... Nevertheless, many Jews, even if they are not Hasidic, are unable to escape the miraculous atmosphere surrounding a rabbi, to the extent that there are unbelieving Jews who, in difficult situations, turn to the rabbi in order to find comfort and help." Joseph Roth, *Judíos errantes,* Acantilado 164, Barcelona, 2008, p. 46].

"distorting the image of the Eastern European Jew", complaining "that his heroes were often ugly, morally insane, charming but disturbed, wise but perverse. Is it possible that Polish Jews were all sex maniacs? Is it conceivable that a rabbi devoted to God and His Law would only think of committing adultery on the night of Yom Kippur[490]?"

But Isaac Bashevis Singer is not labelled by his community as one of those Jews suffering from "self-hatred", and perhaps he simply described realistically what he had seen.

Irène Némirovsky is a well-known novelist in France who received the Renaudot Prize posthumously. She was born in Kiev in 1903 into a family of bankers. In her novel *The Dogs and the Wolves,* which seemed to be partly an autobiography, she described a Ukrainian Jewish family who settled in France after the First World War. Harry Sinner, the banker's son, was to marry a Frenchwoman: Laurence Delarcher, from the old Delarcher banking family. He was, wrote Irene Nemirovsky, "the Jewish type. Fragile, intelligent and sad. Can he like those rosy, blond girls? " In that he resembled his uncles who managed the bank, and who were like him, "men of short stature, oily complexion, sharp features and restless eyes."

For Harry Sinner, "like all Jews ... the specific defects of his race scandalised him in a much more marked and painful way than they did the Christians. And that tenacious energy, that almost savage need to get what was wanted, that blind disregard for what others might think, all these were classified in his mind under one label: 'Jewish impudence'." He was marked by "the curse of a race that could not stand still, and tries endlessly and in vain to be stronger than God Himself[491]."

Ada, a small but less affluent Jewess among his kin, was in love with him. Her husband Ben then had an understandable fit of jealousy. The silence had to be broken: "His rage erupted in curses, insults, shouts... The phrases came out of his mouth in a mixture of Yiddish and Russian. Harry could hardly understand them, and to him, there was something repulsive and grotesque about those oaths, those outbursts, those roars of hatred. At that moment he remembered the loathing on Laurence's face when he had called him hysterical. The frenzy, the bellowing, the rushing invocations of an avenging god were out of another world.

—May you die before me!—howled Ben—May your corpse be

[490]Elie Wiesel, *Mémoires, Tome I,* Seuil, 1994, p. 462, 463.

[491]Irène Némirovsky, *Los perros y los lobos,* Ediciones Salamandra, 2016, Barcelona, p. 94, 114, 130, 122

torn to pieces! May you find no rest, no sleep, no peaceful death! May your offspring be cursed! Damn your children!

—Shut up! —Harry shouted vehemently, "We're not in a Ukrainian ghetto!

—If you only knew how much I hate you...! You look down on us, you despise us, you want nothing to do with the Jewish rabble[492]! "

Attacks of rage are always impressive in this community where mental imbalances are manifestly more frequent than one might think. Regarding Irène Némirovsky herself, Pierre Birnbaum wrote: "Her wandering denotes her complete disorder, nay, her neurosis, her perpetual agitation which accentuates even more her strangeness[493]."

Franz Kafka was well aware of this specific neurosis of the Jewish intellectual. Many Jews who had left their *shtetl* to settle in Vienna had decided to convert to Catholicism in an attempt to free themselves from this tyranny. But conversion did not, however, soothe their tormented spirits: they had to wait for the next generation. Kafka wrote one day to his friends Brod and Welsch: "But what atrocious Jewish forces are stirring until they burst inside a baptised Jew. They only calm down and dissipate in the Christian children of the Christian mother[494]."

In 1886, in his famous book on the Jewish community in France, Edward Drumont had already noted this particular problem of the children of Israel who were beginning to flock to France from the ghettos of central Europe: "Neurosis, that is the relentless disease of the Jews," wrote Drumont. In this long persecuted people, always living in constant anguish and incessant conspiracies, then shaken by the fever of speculation, exercising only professions of a cerebral nature, the nervous system has finally become completely altered. In Prussia, the proportion of alienated people is much stronger among the Israelites than among the Catholics."

The American writer Philip Roth expressed the Jewish neurosis quite evocatively, always through his gruesome characters: "For he is a spoiled Jewish boy. The spoiled Jewish boyfriend of the no less spoiled *shiksa*. A wild, hysterical animal, that's what he is. And that's what I am. That's what we both are[495]", he wrote.

---

[492]Irène Némirovsky, *Los perros y los lobos*, Ediciones Salamandra, 2016, Barcelona p. 159, 160

[493]Pierre Birnbaum, *Un Mythe politique: la république juive*, Fayard, 1988, p. 134.

[494]Laurent Cohen, *Variations autour de K...*, Intertextes éditeur, Paris, 1991, p. 49.

[495]Philip Roth, *Operación Shylock*, Debolsillo Penguin Random House, Barcelona, 2005, p. 268. Translation by Ramón Buenaventura, 1996. [From the French translation

Apparently, the writer must have suffered "a few months earlier a horrifying nervous breakdown" which led him "in a moment of extreme disorientation to wonder if he really is ... suffering from one of those hallucinatory episodes whose utter verisimilitude had brought him to the verge of suicide the previous summer. His control over himself begins to seem as slight as his influence over the other Philip Roth, whom, in fact, he refuses to regard as "the other Philip Roth" or "the impostor" or "the double"..." Indeed, there is a split personality of "Philip Roth" in this novel, where the hero also bears the author's name. Philip Roth is the centre of the world.

"His great motivation. His labile personality. The hysterical monomania. The pack of lies, the suffering, the illness, the horrifying pride in the fact that he is 'indistinguishable'... The result is someone who tries to be real, without even knowing approximately how to achieve it, someone who has no idea how to be fictitious—and to pass himself off, convincingly, as someone he is not... His artifice is false to the marrow, it is a hysterical caricature of the art of illusionism, a hyperbole fuelled by perversity (perhaps even madness), it is exaggeration made an inventive principle..."

In another chapter of the novel, Roth portrayed a Jewish personality type embodied by one of the characters as follows: "Yes, Smilesburger is my typical Jew, what 'Jew' means to me, my best model. Negativism born of experience [*Worldly Negativism*]. Seductive verbosity. Intellectual veneration. Hatred. Lying. Distrust. Practicality. Sincerity [*Authenticity*]. Intelligence. Malice. [*Evilness*]. Comedy. Stamina. The theatre. Injury. The damage [*The dejection*][496]."

But two other phrases from Philip Roth's pen hold our attention and seem to us much more important for understanding the depths of the Jewish personality. The first is the author's confession that he despaired of ever finding inner peace: "I will never be free from this tendency to exaggeration, from the unbearable siege of confusion... I will never be free from myself... I will live forever in the abode of Ambiguity[497]." And the second is this: "To be a Jew is to invoke an unhinged and choleric father. To invoke an unhinged and violent father,

in the text: *"Un maldito pequeño judío completamente chiflado. The damned little completely crazy Jew of the damned completely crazy shiksa, her damned boyfriend, a madman, an animal, a hysteric, that's what he is. That's what I am. That's what we are."* Philip Roth, *Opération Shylock*, 1993, Gallimard, 1995, p. 271].

[496]Philip Roth, *Operation Shylock*, Debolsillo Penguin Random House, Barcelona, 2005, p. 277, 281, 283, 455, 456 [*From the French translation in the text*].

[497]Philip Roth, *Operation Shylock*, Debolsillo Penguin Random House, Barcelona, 2005, p. 354.

and so we Jews have been, for three thousand years, just as unhinged[498]."

And so it is that we touch on the two points which form, in our opinion, the root of the problem: the "ambiguity", or ambivalence, which forms the basis of the identity of the Jewish intellectual; and the question of the Father, which has lasted "for three thousand years", and which is the key to Jewish neurosis, as Sigmund Freud had correctly diagnosed it when analysing his own personal case.

Pierre Paraf magnificently illustrated this ambivalence through a kind of sublimation in a passage of his novel:

"A people of usurers and hedonists... A people of bloody destroyers who know only hatred. People of the pound of flesh, of the Talmudic *pilpul*, of exhausted intelligence and parched senses. Bent backs, stiff necks and lousy beards.

—Not at all. A people of lovers, whose star-flowered sky holds the scented dream of Saron roses and Galilean lilies, persevering bearers of a message that is but a love letter to mankind. God-loving people, pale people of unsatisfied tenderness, burnt by more fires than the world ever kindled[499]."

In religious life, we can also observe that kind of spiritual schizophrenia that reigns in the soul of the pious Jew when he turns to his God, moving abruptly from desperate implorations to the most familiar reproaches, to finally prostrate himself humbly. This is how Joseph Roth described it in *Wandering Jews*:

"In God's house they are not strangers as guests, but as in their own home. They do not pay him an official visit, but gather three times a day around his rich, poor, holy tables. At prayer they are indignant against God, cry to heaven, complain of his rigour, and, in God's house, take God to court, and then confess that they have sinned, that all the punishments were just, and that they want to be better. There is no people who have such a relationship with God[500]."

This reminds us of the figure of Golum, that unfortunate creature in *The Lord of the Rings* who seems to suffer from this pathological ambivalence, when he goes from secret hatred and desire for revenge to the most exaggerated manifestations of weakness in an attempt to pity his fellow sufferers, and who we then see with his eyes illuminated by

---

[498]Philip Roth, *Operation Shylock,* Debolsillo Penguin Random House, Barcelona, 2005, p. 125.

[499]Pierre Paraf, *Quand Israël aima,* 1929, Les belles lettres, 2000, p. 8.

[500]Joseph Roth, *Judíos errantes,* Acantilado 164, Barcelona, 2008, p. 45.

a messianic faith that should lead him to the empire of the world[501].

The ambivalence of the thinking of Jewish intellectuals is a reflection of the deep inner suffering and recurrent doubt they carry about the legitimacy of the "mission" of the Jewish people. The Jewish soul, always on the borderline between two antagonistic concepts, seems only to be able to assert itself in this constant effort to rid itself of the existential vacillation that is constitutive of the essence of Judaism. The Jews assert their messianic faith all the more strongly that they live in the anguish of their ambiguity and in the doubts aroused by the general hostility that has always been raised against them throughout history.

Under these circumstances, Jewish mysticism, embodied by Hasidism, can be seen as an attempt at ecstatic liberation. Appearing in the 18th century, this religious movement, which eventually brought together a large majority of the inhabitants of the *shtetl,* was first a reaction to the anguish and suffering of Polish and Ukrainian Jews after the pogroms perpetrated by Bogdan Khmelnitsky's Cossacks. Likewise, we have already seen how the moral basis of Jewish life had been shaken by the messianic fervour brought about by the "false Messiah" Shabtai Tzvi. The rabbinic reaction against this emotional current "consisted in raising the hedge around the Torah even higher with new supplementary rules," wrote Mark Zborowski." The Talmudic literati strengthened their grip, bringing the mass of the *proste502* under the yoke of innumerable precepts which they were incapable of understanding: the people of the *shtetl* had only the choice between *pilpul* and blind obedience. Wandering preachers, the *maggidim,* promised the worst torments of hell for any transgression of a *mitzvah503*. The *proste* faced alone the image of a vengeful God, jealous guardian of His covenant who left no hope for the transgressor."

The Hasidic movement first presented itself as "the revolt of the unlearned" against rabbinic authority. Its first leader was Israel ben Eliezer, Ba'al Shem Tov, the Teacher of the Divine Name, also called Besht[504]. Far from the austere and threatening speeches of the

---

[501]On the golum analogy, see Hervé Ryssen, *Planetary Hopes, (*2022).

[502]*Proste* is a Yiddish word used by Ashkenazis to indicate that a person or something is poor, vulgar or of low class.

[503]The commandments, these are the 613 biblical precepts of the Torah.

[504]"Bal Shem Tov laid down his axe. He got into a car and set off across Poland. Knocking at the doors of the synagogues, he shouted:—'Hey, what are you doing with your foreheads to the ground? I bring you the word of the Eternal, rise up and dance,

maggidim, the Hasidic leaders preached hope, mercy and love, rather than vengeance and punishment. Like the other Sabbatean movements, Hasidism met with violent resistance from the rabbinic literati and the upper classes of the *shtetl*: "The *misnagdim*[505] were ready for anything, even denunciation, imprisonment and ostracism," wrote Zborowski. There was a time when marriage to a member of the other group was considered just as reprehensible as marriage to a non-Jew.

The two streams eventually coexisted, but never merged. The court of the tzaddik, or *rebbe*, the religious leader of Hasidic Jews, remained the place of comfort and support for the humble. However, after a period of absolute rejection of instruction, Hasidism progressively opened its interpretation to the ancient written tradition and to scholarly research, and henceforth, scholar and ignoramus, artisan and rabbi, *proste* and *sheyne*, all "went to the *rebe*" for help or a few encouraging words, while the rabbi, the *rov*, remained the one to be consulted for the interpretation of the Law which regulated all the details of the *shtetl's* life. The two socio-religious groups, Hasidic and rabbinic, eventually coexisted in complementarity." The two words, *Hasidim* and *Mishnagdi*, which formerly designated two hostile camps, became the epithets of two types of personalities. The *Hasid* is the zealot, fiery and affectionate; the *Mishnagdi* is cold, sceptical and of lukewarm enthusiasm[506]."

Joseph Roth left a striking testimony about the religious practices of the Hasidic Jews: "That strength was not only that of a fanatical faith. It was, to be sure, a health whose blossoming came from the religious. The Hasidim held hands, danced in a circle, broke the ring to clap their hands, moved their heads in rhythm to the left and right, held the Torah scrolls and turned them round and round like girls, pressing them to their breasts, kissing them and weeping with joy. There was an erotic concupiscence in that dance. I was deeply moved that a whole people

---

eat, drink, smoke, sing! Let your spirit rest: it is parched with ergotiating, but your heart is fresh; listen to its impulses. Close the Talmud! What is it? At best, an old-fashioned gibberish of outmoded scholars. Here is the last cry: the Zohar, the book of splendour; open it and read it! Almost all of Israel listened to Bal Shem Tov, reading the *Fol Zohar*. And they began to pray, dancing, eating, drinking, smoking, singing. It was the birth of Hasidism. And out of Hasidism came miracles. And Bal Shem Tov, called El Balshem, the woodcutter of the Maramures, was the first miraculous rabbi." Recreation by Albert London in *The Wandering Jew Has Arrived*, Editorial Melusina, 2012, p. 60, 61. Ba'al Shem literally means "one who possesses mastery of God's name, who is able to employ it". (NdT).

[505]Misnaged, misnagdim (plural) (misnagdíes in English): the opponents of Hasidism.

[506]Mark Zborowski, *Olam*, 1952, Plon, 1992, p. 170–176. [On sectarian drift and its channelling, and in particular within Judaism, see in translator's note Annex IV. 4]

should offer their sensual voluptuousness to their God, that from the book of the most severe laws they should make their beloved, and that they should no longer know how to separate bodily desire from spiritual joy, but should unite the two. It was the ardour of zeal and devotional fervour. Dance was a divine office, and prayer, a sensual excess[507]."

Elie Wiesel also studied Kabbalah in his youth, reveling in the pleasures of the 'occult knowledge' inherited from Hasidism: 'For an adolescent eager for knowledge and illusions, Kabbalah offers the most stimulating, the most romantic, the most attractive." This is how he described these practices: "ascetic exercises, fiery and magical litanies, falling into the torments of the abyss in the hope of rising again to dizzying heights." But it was a dangerous game to be wary of: "I would wake up sweaty, out of breath. I was delirious, I didn't know when I was dreaming or when I was lucid; I didn't know who I was or where I was. Sitting on the floor, banging his head against the wall, my Master seemed desperate; sobs shook his whole body. I felt at that moment that madness was stalking us both. But I was determined to continue our quest. Whatever it took[508]."

The writer Arthur Miller left an interesting concordant testimony in his memoirs. When he was still a small boy, his great-grandfather took him with him to the synagogue one day, leaving him in a secluded corner where he was not supposed to see the ceremony.

"I heard the men begin to sing. Not in unison, like a choir, but a range of different melodies sweetly intoned by a dozen or more voices. I heard a muffled tapping, and then more tapping and deeper tapping, and the voices grew louder ... and the tapping grew faster... I saw something most astonishing: about fifteen old men, hunched over and completely covered by their respective taled, all of them with their feet encased in white socks, were dancing. I held my breath in panic. One of them had to be the great-grandfather and I was seeing the forbidden. But what exactly was forbidden, perhaps to find myself in such an undignified situation! Perhaps that, in a hidden and mysterious way, they were happy, even though they were old. For I had never heard such music as that, so crazy and impulsive, and everyone danced without any consonance with the rest, only facing the outer darkness[509]..."

No wonder that observers of other times assimilated these crazy sarabandes to the witches' Sabbath. We are a far cry from the genuine folk dances or the Viennese waltz, which undoubtedly better reflect the

[507]Joseph Roth, *Judíos errantes*, Acantilado 164, Barcelona, 2008, p. 56, 57

[508]Elie Wiesel, *Mémoires, tome I*, Seuil, 1994, p. 49, 50, 53, 57.

[509]Arthur Miller, *Vueltas al tiempo*, Tusquets, Barcelona, 1999, p. 46.

simplicity, grace and harmony of European culture since Ancient Greece.

Inferiority complex

This is first of all a physical complex due to the deficiencies generated by long inbreeding. As their Law forbids marriages outside their community, inbreeding is very high and was probably even higher in the Jews of the shtetls. By the end of the 19th century, Zionist Jews, who rejected dissolution into European society and planned to build a Jewish state in Palestine, had realised the seriousness of a certain physical degeneration of the Jewish people. This is what Jacques Le Rider wrote about it:

"The early Zionists, especially Theodor Herzl, spoke with sometimes merciless harshness about assimilated Jews who, in their view, had abandoned Jewish tradition and adopted the most objectionable behaviours of their society—but also sometimes with contemptuous severity towards the culturally "backward" and physically "degenerate" Jews of the ghetto in the cities of Central and Eastern Europe or the shtetls of Galicia[510]."

More recently, Philip Roth also spoke with a "merciless harshness" about these physical defects on the part of the Jewish community, to such an extent that the novelist seemed to be settling scores with his community. Some of his words are truly insulting. On page 291 of his book, he also made a revisionist speech under the pretext of giving the floor to one of his anti-Semitic characters. But although Philip Roth sometimes seems to have a twisted and deranged mind, we cannot say that he belongs to that class of Jews afflicted with "self-hatred", for in many other passages of his works he expresses his messianic faith in the mission of the Jewish people. Again, we must note here the ambivalence of the thought.

"A guy at the NIH who is a friend of mine did a study of a whole group of rabbis. About twenty or twenty-five years ago. And he came to the conclusion that they have diseases that are specific to Jews. It's because of inbreeding, because they've been mixing with each other for centuries. There are nine diseases specific to Jews that affect children… One of them is Down's syndrome. But they always hide the people who have it. Because, of course, you know, all Jews are geniuses. They all play the violin. Or they are nuclear physicists. Or, of course, of course,

---

[510]Jacques Le Rider, *Arthur Schnitzler*, Éd. Belin, 2003, p. 199

Wall Street geniuses (*chuckle. laughter*). The ones they never say a word about are the ones who come out idiots, because of inbreeding. They're all like jackasses. Always having kids between them… Jews have this thing called Paget's disease. People don't usually know about it. Look at Ted Koppel. And others like him. Woody Allen, that cantankerous prick, who's just falling down from being an asshole. Or Mike Wallace. Their bones thicken and their legs twist. Women have what's called the Hebrew hump. Their nails harden. Like stones. Their chins are slack. Just look at the old beans, they all have a slack chin, like mentally retarded people. That's why they hate us so much, because it doesn't happen to us. Because we are still so tender. Maybe we put on a little weight. But so tender. You know what a Jew is. An Arab born in Poland. They get huge… Jews are all very ugly. With that nose, etcetera… Like Kissinger. Huge. Big nose, big features. And that's why they don't like us. Just look at Philip Roth. A full-on ugly guy. Asshole from head to toe… What a piece of shit. The guy was so out with the *shiksas,* he got his hands on a waitress, a mental case, divorced with two kids, and he thought she was a piece of work. Dumb ass. Now he's returning to the Jewish fold, because he wants to be awarded the Nobel prize[511]."

It must be admitted here that some Jews sometimes know how to laugh at themselves with a rather amusing acidity. Obviously, this kind of humour is not everyone's cup of tea, but we have seen in the first part of this book that the scorn and sarcasm of some intellectuals could often go against the goyim, so we think it is only fair to redress the balance a little.

In a book written in a similar style, very much in vogue in today's literature, Rich Cohen told the story of those "American" gangsters between the wars. Everyone has heard of Al Capone and the Italian Mafia. What is less well known is that the main hitmen who wreaked terror in the big American cities of the time were Jewish gangsters. In his book *Yiddish Connection*, published in 1998, Rich Cohen described what some of these heroes, secretly haloed by Hollywood, looked like[512]:

"At that time in Brownsville, power was in the hands of the Shapiro brothers, whose family was originally from the Ukraine. The

---

[511]Philip Roth, *Operación Shylock*, Debolsillo Penguin Random House, Barcelona, 2005, p. 295, 292, 293

[512]On the "American" mafia of the 1920s–1930s, and on the "Russian" mafia of the 1990s: Hervé Ryssen, *Planetary Hopes (*2005), (2022) and *The Jewish Mafia (*2008), (2019).

eldest, Meyer, had been born in the neighbourhood, a lanky boy who persevered into adulthood with obesity. Everything about him was fat: fat eyes, a fat nose, fat ears, a fat mouth… The brothers owned some fifteen brothels in the underworld. Like the Jewish bosses of Odessa in 19th century Russia, they terrorised shopkeepers and merchants."

This was Abraham Reles, or Abe Reles, the "Kid", another figure of the time whose family originated in Galicia, southern Poland: "In time, Reles became a leader. Even though he was barely over six feet tall, something about him commanded respect… He spoke slowly, with a throaty voice, with a lisp. He had a curious gait: in the street, he looked like a man trying to pull his shoes forward by shaking his feet."

Reles later dethroned the Shapiro brothers in Brooklyn. With his crew, he had a career-high eighty-five kills.

In his early days, "the first person the Kid recruited was Martin Goldstein… Marty was shy, but the Kid discovered something special about him. If his shyness was put to the test, he could be driven out of his wits, put into a psychotic crisis state. That's why he was called Bugsy—because he was a bit crazy, and that was a quality you always saw in some gangsters… He had the same small-mouthed way of talking, of walking like a duck, the same tough-guy attitude as the film stars."

"Although there were already numerous established Jewish gangsters in existence years before mid-century, the first to achieve true fame was Monk Eastman. His real name was Edward Osterman… Monk was monstrous, of a monstrosity rarely seen any more—typical of the 19th century… His pockmarked face bore the marks of smallpox… His ears were like cabbage leaves, his flat nose was reduced to its minimum expression, his mouth was grim, notched… To anyone who saw him suddenly appear on an underworld street, he must have embodied death in person[513]."

These physical characteristics obviously do not apply to all Jews. But nevertheless, hereditary defects are sufficiently serious and widespread in the Jewish population to be the subject of scientific study. The American doctor Richard Goodman, who worked on the genetic diseases of the Jewish people, published a study on the subject in 1979, which established that there were more than a hundred hereditary diseases in Jews[514]. These deficiencies are 20% more frequent in Ashkenazi Jews from Eastern Europe, who represent 82% of all Jews

[513]Rich Cohen, *Yiddish Connection,* 1998, Folio, 2000, p. 31, 41, 42, 66

[514]Richard Goodman, *Genetic disorders among the jewish people,* Hopkins university Press, 1979.

in the world (Sephardim, the Jews of the Mediterranean world, represent the remaining 18%). His study also established that there is no genetic deficiency peculiar to the Caucasian race, and only one in the black race. All these diseases have their origin in neurological deficiencies affecting the nervous system and the brain. These can only be explained by inbreeding and intermarriage, which is typical of the ethnic withdrawal in which the Jewish people lived for centuries.

Tay-Sachs disease is the best known. It affects children. The child appears normal up to the age of six, but then becomes indolent, apathetic, amorphous. His movements become jerky, until he can no longer hold his head upright. The eyes become fixed. The child becomes blind in adolescence. The skull hypertrophies and the hands swell. More than 90% of the sufferers of this disease are Jewish. It is reported in one Jewish child out of 3600, but one Jew out of 27 is a carrier of this genetic trait. This frequency obliges Jews to undergo diagnostic tests before marriage.

Abetalipoproteinaemia or Bassen-Kornzweig syndrome (ABL 1): This disease affects newborns before their first birthday. The baby cannot grow or gain weight, suffers from diarrhoea and vomiting. Their vision is also affected, to the point of total blindness. Muscles weaken. In most cases, the patient dies of cardiac arrest before the age of thirty.

Blum's syndrome: Individuals with Blum's syndrome are characterised by a very small stature, a deficiency of the immune system, and a predisposition to cancer. They have a high voice. Individuals with this disease die before the age of 16. These traits are found in one Jew out of 120, but affect most Jews to a lesser extent.

Familial dysautonomia only affects individuals of Jewish origin. The individual may be abnormally small in stature and has the following symptoms: vomiting, swallowing difficulties, unsteady gait, muscle spasms in the arms and head movements, articulation difficulties, with a very particular nasal sonority, diffuse suffering and hyperactivity. The disease is reported in one Jew out of 10 000 but the gene is present in 18 Jews out of 1000.

Gaucher disease declares itself in adolescents: bones fracture easily, especially the hip. There are severe bone pains that can last for several weeks. Yellowing of the skin is observed. This disease affects on average one Jew out of 2500. Death occurs before the age of 45.

Mucolipidosis type IV is characterised by mental and physical degeneration and blindness. It affects children who can pronounce only a few words and respond weakly to verbal stimuli. They are unable to walk or feed themselves. They usually do not live beyond the age of ten.

Niemann-Pick disease: vomiting, skin lesions, skin becomes thick and yellowish-brown, loss of mental and physical functions. Death occurs before the age of four. This disease affects one Jew in twenty thousand, and the deficient gene is in one Jew in 100.

Primary torsion dystonia: it manifests itself at around the age of ten years and is manifested by involuntary, bizarre seizures of the feet, legs, head and torso. The disease affects one Jew out of 17,000 and the gene is found in one Jew out of 130. The disease is not fatal but does not allow for a very normal life.

PTA Deficiency: abnormal blood loss after a cut or operation, abnormal bleeding without external damage. The disease affects one Jew in 12 000 and the gene is present in one Jew in 56.

Spongy degeneration of the central nervous system, or Canavan disease, is a disease that begins in the third month of life. The patient cannot hold his head, he suffers from spasms. The head increases in size; the patient ends up blind. Most of them die before the age of four. The origin of the disease has never been determined, but 80% of the patients are Ashkenazi Jews.

There is a clinic in the United States that specialises in the treatment of these diseases affecting individuals of Jewish origin. Readers who want more information on this problem can consult the website of the Chicago for Jewish Genetic Disorder: *www.Jewish-geneticscenter.org*

The American writer Arthur Miller left a symptomatic testimony in his autobiography. This is what he wrote about his maternal grandfather, Louis Barnett:

"Like Samuel, my father's father, Louis came from the Polish village of Radomizl and it is likely that they were distantly related. I always thought so because they looked so much alike. They were both very fair-skinned, unflappable fellows, although grandfather Samuel, despite a noticeable curvature of the spine, was a small man whose wife and children, unusually for the time, were over six feet tall." Consanguinity does indeed explain the frequent physiognomic similarities.

On the paternal side, things were no better: "My mother ... a mistake of nature according to them, since she was the only brunette connected with that fabulous family. They were an unusually close-knit clan and only married people who looked like them. To tell the truth, one of my most beautiful cousins married a carnal uncle of hers, despite the rabbi's warnings, and although they lived in love for years, holding hands together and never tiring of contemplating each other, I think guilt eventually found its way into her, she withered in a strange way shortly after her fortieth birthday, from something no one could diagnose then, and died a wreck, hairless, half blind from some inner cataclysm, without suffering any known illness[515]."

As for the father, Arthur Miller described him quite well in this simple sentence: "When my mother told him in 1940 that I was going to marry a gentile girl, he said nothing, but as she waited for a reply at the other end of the ten-foot-six-inch Brooklyn living room, he picked up a thick alarm clock that someone had left on a nearby table and threw it at her, narrowly missing her daughter's head." Apparently, Jews don't particularly want to marry their children to goyim. After all, it is their right.

This inferiority complex, which we also see in Sigmund Freud, is also of an artistic and intellectual nature. Since ancient times, the production of Europeans in this field has been brilliant and infinitely richer than that of the Jews, and one need only compare, for example, the splendid image of our villas, cathedrals and palaces with that of the muddy alleys of the shtetls of Central Europe to get an idea. Indeed, since their departure from the ghetto in the 19th century, many Jews have not ceased in their quest to make up for lost time, so that products stamped with the Community trademark have long since invaded bookshops and cinemas, while all sorts of contemporary art sculptures, more or less crazy, adorn the squares of large cities. In fact, genius is hailed and press articles and advertising multiply to welcome any "product" coming out of the brain of a son of Israel.

This characteristic communal enthusiasm, relayed throughout the media system, is the main manifestation of that famous Jewish solidarity that often provokes some unease and tension among some eclipsed, if more gifted, artists. This hype reflects, perhaps once again, a certain inferiority complex[516]. And since we already know the tendency of some Jewish intellectuals towards inversion, it is not surprising to hear some of them accuse the "anti-Semites" of being envious of the supposed genius of the chosen people.

This is what the Russian writer Vassily Grossman—the "Tolstoy of the 20th century"—wrote in his novel *Life and Fate*: "Anti-Semitism is the expression of a lack of talent, of the inability to win in a contest fought with the same weapons; and this applies to all fields, science as well as commerce, craftsmanship, painting. Anti-Semitism is the

---

[515]Arthur Miller, *Vueltas al tiempo,* Tusquets, Barcelona, 1999, p. 14, 15, 19, 20

[516]Hervé Ryssen, *Planetary Hopes, (*2022).

measure of human mediocrity… But this is only one aspect of anti-Semitism. Anti-Semitism is the expression of the lack of culture among the masses of the people, who are incapable of analysing the real causes of their poverty and suffering. Uneducated people see the Jews as the cause of their misfortunes instead of the social structure and the state. But even the anti-Semitism of the masses is only one aspect of this. Anti-Semitism is the measure of the religious prejudice which is latent in the lower strata of society… It only testifies that there are idiots, envious and unsuccessful people in the world[517]."

But it is also true that other Jewish authors have recognised the shortcomings of their community: The philosopher Jacob Talmon agreed when he wrote the following in *Israel's Destiny*: "Jewish writers have been eminent biographers (André Maurois and Stefan Zweig). They have described in an extremely stimulating way the complexities and dilemmas of contemporary man's situation (Arthur Koestler, Arthur Miller and Ilya Ehrenbourg)… But, although their works are moving and stimulating, they cannot be said to be great literature[518]."

The indispensable Philip Roth expressed himself on this issue in his novel *Operation Shylock*, through his anti-Semitic character, and in a rather popular, if not downright vulgar, style:

"Jews have a tendency to isolate themselves from all other social groups. Then, when they find themselves in trouble, everything turns to them for help. And what reason is there to help them? The Jews came out of the ghetto, in Europe, in Napoleon's time. They were liberated, and, my goodness, what a way to spread. Once they get control of something, they don't let go of it. They took control of music with Schoenberg. But they've never written any music worth a fart. Hollywood[519]. Another good fart. Why? Because they took control. It is said that the Jews created Hollywood. Jews aren't creative. What did they create? Nothing. In painting, Pissarro. You have to read Wagner, how he goes on about the Jews. All their art is pure superficiality. They don't assimilate into the culture of the country they live in. They have a superficial popularity, like Herman Wouk, or like the one with the faggots, or like Mailer's dumbed-down blowhard, but it never lasts, because it is not linked to the cultural roots of the society. Who is their standard-bearer? Saul Bellow. And what a bird, he falls down with sadness, doesn't he? (*Chuckles*)… And Roth? A fucking wanker, all the

---

[517]Vasili Grossman, *Life and Destiny*, Galaxia Gutenberg, 2007, Barcelona, p. 362, 363, 364.

[518]J.-L. Talmon, *Destin d'Israël*, 1965, Calmann-Lévy, 1967, p. 33.

[519]On Hollywood: Hervé Ryssen, *Planetary Hopes, (*2022).

time shaking his cock, locked in the bathroom, hale, manita, hale, manita. Arthur Miller, another one like that. Let's see if it's not true that he looks like a garbage man, like a guy who runs a rubbish dump. It's just that they look like shit, man, really bad. Longer than a day without bread… The cultural production of the Jews has always been very low, very low… Maybe they do have their own cultural institutions, but they never produce anything. All you have to do is analyse the shit. On TV, everything vulgar is signed by a Jew[520]."

Philip Roth thus expressed in a somewhat brutal way the same opinion as Spinoza and some others[521], but his text at least has the merit of being lucid. Obviously, he does not write like Chateaubriand, Victor Hugo or Louis Ferdinand Céline. In this, the Jews cannot compete with the Goyim.

Self-hatred

The "mission" of the Jewish people may seem rather heavy for a people already marked by its secular heritage. So heavy and unwelcome that it is perfectly understandable that many Jews, throughout history, have preferred to turn away from this condition, which many have considered "inhuman".

The French scholar Maurice Rheims wrote about his "Jewishness": "The burden is heavy, hereditary, full of misfortunes, opprobrium, persecutions. Good luck or bad luck[522]?"

In studying the life of Jewish writers in Vienna at the beginning of the 20th century, Jacques Le Rider wrote about the writer Berthold Stauber and his novel *Vienna at Twilight*, in which he described the anti-Semitism of his time: "He lives his Jewishness as a curse and often falls simply and plainly into Jewish anti-Semitism[523]."

Otto Weininger was a writer of outstanding drive and integrity. Born in 1880 in the Vienna of Arthur Schnitzler, Stefan Zweig, Kafka and Sigmund Freud, he wrote only one book, in 1902, but it remains for posterity one of the most terrible testimonies to the suffering and torment that Judaism can inflict on its members. Otto Weininger showed surprising precocity and converted to Protestantism at the age of 22. But in contrast to many converts in those days who converted to

---

[520]Philip Roth, *Operation Shylock*, Debolsillo Penguin Random House, Barcelona, 2005, p. 294, 295.

[521]On Spinoza, Hervé Ryssen, *Planetary Hopes*, (2022).

[522]Maurice Rheims, *Une Mémoire vagabonde*, Gallimard, 1997, p. 67.

[523]Jacques Le Rider, *Arthur Schnitzler*, Belin, 2003, p. 200

Christianity with an eye to careerism, Weininger was a sincere convert. And for a good reason: the "mission" of the chosen people seemed to him a monstrosity in which he wanted no part.

He published *Sex and Character* at the age of 23, before committing suicide in October 1903. The famous "self-hatred" manifested itself there with a certain vigour, as is shown by some of the passages we have selected and arranged:

"But why does the orthodox slave of Jehovah change so quickly and easily into a materialist, into a freethinker?" Indeed, it must be said that: "The Jews have also been those who have most readily accepted a mechanical-materialist conception of the world." They are the champions of the economic ideologies of history, Marxism and liberalism. For them, matter determines all their actions.

Here Weininger seemed to adopt the words of Karl Marx in his writings of 1843: "Because he does not believe in anything, he takes refuge in material things, and this alone is the reason for his craving for money. In it he seeks a reality and pretends that "business" convinces him that existence has an end. The only real value he recognises is therefore the money "earned".

The young writer explained these dispositions by the lack of transcendence of the Jewish religion: "Their way of worshipping God has little to do with true religion", "the Jew is not the religious man of whom we have so often been told, but the irreligious man", wrote Weininger. Consequently, the action of the Jews has only an earthly purpose:

"Judaism, in the broadest sense, is that tendency whereby science can be reduced to a means to an end, to the exclusion of all that is transcendental. The Aryan feels the need to understand and derive all phenomena, as a devaluation of the world, and realises that it is precisely the inscrutable that gives existence its value. The Jew is not the least afraid of secrets, because he does not sense them. All his efforts are limited to seeing the world in the simplest and most commonplace way possible[524]."

In order to better understand the lack of transcendence emphasised by Otto Weininger, we can mention some further readings. Mark Zborowski's research on the religion and customs of Central European Jews is a reference book in this respect:

"The Covenant sealed between the Creator and his creature is a contract. He who is a member of the people who signed it may feel

---

[524]Otto Weininger, *Sex and Character,* 1902, Ediciones 62 s|a, 1985, Barcelona, Barcelona, p. 321, 311, 319, 310

entitled to expect and claim the rewards promised in return for respect of the clauses. But it is an ambiguous pact. On the one hand, there is a certain equality between the contracting parties, in terms of reciprocal rights and duties. But on the other hand, it is an agreement between a strong and a weak party, which to a large extent implies a relationship of subordination. This inequality entitles the elected People to implore help, for the strong has obligations towards the weak[525]."

Otto Weininger perhaps probed the question more deeply and intimately: "Shall I have to explain at length why the Jew lacks ardour in his faith and why the Jewish religion is the only one that does not try to make proselytes, to the extent that for the Jews themselves it is an enigma, which makes them smile in bewilderment, the cause that maintains Judaism? Must it be repeated that the Jewish religion is not a doctrine of the essence and object of life, but a historical tradition which can be summed up in the passage through the Red Sea and which culminates in the thanksgiving of the cowardly fugitives to a mighty saviour? Truly the Jew is the irreligious man who is cut off from all beliefs. He does not affirm himself and with him the world, whose essence lies in religion. All faith is heroic, but the Jew knows neither courage nor fear."

After reading these lines, we can admit that the author had definitively detached himself from the Jewish religion. Even so, Otto Weininger's onslaught went far beyond simple religious criticism, describing the personality of the Jews as shaped by a common culture. The parallel he drew between "the Jew" and "the woman" might seem surprising at first glance:

"Their similarity is based above all on the fact that they believe little in themselves. But women believe in others, in man, in the child, in 'love'; they have a centre of gravity, though it is outside them. The Jew believes in nothing, neither in himself nor in others; he does not find support in strangers, nor does he even extend his roots towards them, as does the woman. The instability of his dwelling, his profound incomprehension for real estate and his preference for movable capital seem to be symbolic… To cite an analogy with women, we will recall that Jews prefer movable property[526]."

Following on from this comparison, Weininger further pointed out this difference between "the Aryan" and "the Jew", terms which were

---

[525]Mark Zborowski, *Olam,* 1952, Plon, 1992, p. 198. (In the same sense as Weininger and Zborowski, see translator's note in Annex VII).

[526]Otto Weininger, *Sex and Character*, 1902, Ediciones 62 s|a, 1985, Barcelona, p. 319, 317, 302.

very much in vogue and used in his time. Whereas for the Aryan the principle of good and the principle of evil are distinct from each other, “in the Aryan man the principle of good and evil of religious philosophy are united, and at the same time widely separated; in him his good demon and his evil demon fight. In the Jew, almost as in the woman, good and evil are not yet completely differentiated[527].”

But “the congruence between Judaism and femininity seems to be complete as soon as one begins to think of the Jews’ infinite capacity for mutation. Their great talent for journalism, the “mobility” of the Jewish spirit, the rootlessness of their thoughts, might it not be possible to affirm of Jews, as of women, that precisely because they are nothing they can become everything?”

Weininger was thus pointing out something that we could also observe about the ambivalence of Jewish feelings and thoughts, as well as the plasticity of the Jewish personality. In stating bluntly that “the Jew is nothing”, he actually meant by this abrupt formula that the Jewish personality is based on a shifting foundation of ambiguities and doubts, which generate a pathological kind of literary hyperactivity that serves as an outlet, even if it sometimes falls into a misplaced excess.

Jewish arrogance’, wrote Weininger, ’also finds its further explanation in the lack of self-consciousness and in the enormous need to exaggerate the value of one’s own personality by lowering that of those around them. Hence their feminine ambition for titles, even though their ancestors long predate the most ancient aristocracies, an ambition which goes hand in hand with their desire to boast about something. This desire is expressed by her frequent appearance in the best boxes of the theatres, by the paintings that adorn her salons, by her friendships with Christians and by her dedication to science. But, at the same time, the Jewish incomprehension for everything aristocratic[528].”

Israeli writer Avraham Yehoshua had an interesting reaction that revealed this Jewish ambiguity. Reacting in the *Metro newspaper* of 21 September 2005 to the words of Greek conductor Mikis Theodorakis, who had declared that “all evil in this world comes from the Jews”, he

---

[527]“The individual perceives himself on the basis of the principles of the shtetl, as a field where forces oppose each other. There is always a good and a bad side, just as ‘a stick always has two ends’. This constant interplay between good and evil is not experienced as an internal conflict, any more than family disputes are seen as quarrels. It is seen as normal for the two aspects of a personality to search endlessly for a compromise, with neither trying to eliminate the other for good in order to occupy all the space.” (Mark Zborowski, *Olam*, 1952, Plon, 1992, p. 402).

[528]Otto Weininger, *Sex and Character*, 1902, Ediciones 62 s|a, 1985, Barcelona, p. 306, 316, 304.

explained anti-Semitism by "the elusiveness" of Jewish identity, adding matter-of-factly that it could "be the source of the worst fantasies."

The doubt concomitant with ambiguity was expressed by Arthur Miller in his autobiography when he wrote about his play *The Witches of Salem*, set in the American colonies of the 17th century. He had this to say about the English Puritans: "Those New Englanders ... were possible *Ur-Hebrews*, with identical furious idealism, identical dedication to God, identical tendency to legalistic narrowness, identical passion for pure and intellectually subtle polemic. God was driving them as mad as the Jews who were trying to maintain their exclusive and immaculate vessel of faith in Him[529]." Doubt and ambiguity are indeed constitutive of the Jewish personality, which are generators of madness and chaotic creativity.

Otto Weininger continued his analysis and noted a certain predisposition for scorn and sarcasm, which also stems from the above reflections: "He never manages to take himself seriously, and naturally does not take other individuals or anything else seriously either… The Jew does not believe that there is anything true and unchanging, holy and invulnerable. That is why he is eminently frivolous and makes fun of everything… Satire is at bottom intolerant, and therefore corresponds best to the typical nature of the Jew, as well as to that of the woman. Both Jews and women lack humour, but like mockery… It is this lack of depth that also explains the absence of truly great men among the Jews, and constitutes the cause that Judaism, like women, is denied genius… The specific type of intelligence attributed to both Jews and women is, on the one hand, the cautious vigilance of a great egoism, and, on the other, the infinite capacity of adaptation of both to external ends whatever they may be[530]…"

But, "totally deprived of one belief, the Jews could not have persisted and maintained themselves, and this belief is the confused, obscure and yet desperately certain feeling that something must happen to Judaism and in Judaism. This something is the Messiah, the Saviour of Judaism is the Saviour of the Jews[531]… The hope of Judaism is

---

[529]Arthur Miller, *Vueltas al tiempo*, Tusquets, Barcelona, 1999, p. 50. *Ur-hebreos*: *ur* is a German prefix indicating antiquity and pre-eminence. It would be equivalent to say proto-Hebrews.

[530]Otto Weininger, *Sex and Character*, 1902, Ediciones 62 s|a, 1985, Barcelona, Barcelona, p. 317, 315, 312, 313

[531]Let us recall the words of Guy Konopnicki quoted above: "Something is appearing, something that surpasses us and escapes us… Something is growing that is nothing like the revolutions foreseen by the bearded men of the last century, nor the triumphant progress announced at the time of the Enlightenment. Something impalpable that is

identifiable with the permanent possibility that from its species will emerge the great victor, the founder of religions. This is the unconscious significance of all messianic hopes in the Jewish tradition[532]."

The inherent hope of Jewish messianism is indeed the dominant idea that structures the Jewish personality in such a way that the whole edifice would collapse if the Messiah actually arrived. David Banon perfectly described this mental universe that feeds permanent frustration, cerebral agitation and drives the individual to exacerbated activism:

"In its essence, it is the aspiration for the impossible. Messianic tension is a feverish waiting, a restless hope that knows neither repose nor repose… Messianic tension makes the Jewish people live always expectant of the imminence of a radical transformation of life on the face of the earth… Redemption is always near, but if it were to come it would be immediately questioned in the name of the very absolute demand that it claims to bring about"." The redemption promised at the end of time sustains a reality which is always beyond the existing, and which, therefore, will never be achieved. But man must constantly aspire to it. The Messiah is always the one who must one day come … but the one who finally appears can only be a false Messiah[533]."

Weininger's parallel between "the Jew" and "the woman" became perhaps even more significant through his analysis of the social evolution of modern society, so critical of "patriarchy" and paternal authority in all its forms[534]: "In our days we see Judaism at the highest level it has reached since the time of Herod. The modern spirit is Jewish whichever way you look at it. Sexuality is exalted and the current ethic of the species sings of coitus… Our time is not only the most Jewish, but also the most feminist… The time of the most credulous anarchism, with no understanding for the state and for law; the time of the ethics of the species and of the most superficial historical conceptions (historical materialism); the time of capitalism and Marxism, for which history, life and science mean nothing but economy and technique; the time in which genius is regarded as a form of madness and yet which possesses neither a great artist nor a great philosopher."

For the neophyte Weininger, however, this inversion of values was

---

born through the confrontations and crises of our time… Something will emerge from this crisis. As in all the previous ones, something that will be neither French, nor American, nor Russian."

[532]Otto Weininger, *Sex and Character*, 1902, Ediciones 62 s|a, 1985, Barcelona, p. 326.

[533]David Banon, *Le Messianisme*, Presses Universitaires de France, 1998, p. 5-7, 11

[534]Hervé Ryssen, *Planetary Hopes, The Matriarchal Society, (*2022).

not inevitable: "In the face of the new Judaism, a new Christianity is opening up; humanity awaits the new founder of religions, and the struggle is looking for a decision as in the year one *[of our era].* Humanity has again the choice between Judaism and Christianity, *[between business and culture, between woman and man]*, between species and personality, between nothingness and divinity..."

The picture described was thus rather bleak, but Otto Weininger was probably speaking with full knowledge of the facts when he wrote: "There is no male Jew who, however confusedly, does not suffer from his Jewishness, that is, from his lack of belief..." The Jew is the individual "most torn, the poorest in inner identity ... the Jew is never harmonious and whole. Consequently, the Semite is cowardly, the polar opposite of the hero[535]."

The self-hatred of some Jews has been the subject of study by a number of writers, most notably Theodor Lessing and his book published in 1930. He was a militant Zionist, publicist, journalist and professor at the University of Hanover. In 1906, Lessing visited Galicia, southern Poland, to observe his fellow shtetls and urban centres. The poignant but wholly unaccommodating descriptions he made and published on his return were to cause him some problems. After that, Lessing was to be accused of being a "Jewish anti-Semite". Apparently, his reactions resembled "those of a Gustav Mahler when he wrote from Lemberg (Lvov) to his wife Alma: "My God! And I am supposed to be related to these people[536]?" "

Nor, wrote Maurice-Ruben Hayoun, did Theodor Lessing take a favourable view of 'the literary, philosophical and artistic hyper-productivity displayed by a growing number of their co-religionists on the other side of the Rhine'. For him, these manifestations revealed a "psychopathology of the history of the Jewish people[537]."

In his work *Self-Hatred, Refusal to Be a Jew (or The Love-Hatred of the Jews), he* examined the cases of six "anti-Semitic Jews": Paul Rée, Otto Weininger, Arthur Trebitsch, Max Steiner, Walter Calé and Maximilian Harden. However, the most interesting text in his book was probably the excerpts from the diary of a woman of high birth and status, written around 1920. This woman was "well-born, beautiful,

---

[535]Otto Weininger, *Sex and Character*, 1902, Ediciones 62 s|a, 1985, Barcelona, p. 326, 327, 322 *[added in italics from the French translation in the text].*

[536]Theodor Lessing, *La Haine de soi, le refus d'être juif*, 1930, Berg international, 1990, p. 13.

[537]Theodor Lessing, *La Haine de soi, le refus d'être juif*, 1930, Berg international, 1990, p. 34.

healthy and talented", but "suffered from her earliest years from a disease of ethical self-destruction". Her words, extremely harsh and heartbreaking, reflected the deep suffering of those Jews afflicted by self-hatred, who are probably far more numerous than is generally believed:

"I am clearly aware of something inexorable: Judaism lies within my being. I cannot simply shake it off with a brush. Like a dog or a pig that cannot get rid of its canine or porcine nature, I cannot get rid of those eternal bonds of being that imprison me on this intermediate plane between humanity and animality: the Jew… Never as long as I live can I separate myself from the curse of my being, nor deny the sin of my Jewishness that weighs on me like a mountain. I feel cursed and damned… There are moments when I feel that I should cut my veins and let this blood of slurry flow that infects both my body and my spirit. That's right! I would have preferred to be an animal, I would have preferred rat's or snake's blood to this blood of walking pestilence, to this form, to this symbol of the anti-divine.

Sometimes, a crazy idea takes hold of me: to redeem my being with a crime. To eliminate at least one of those little Jews responsible for the German defeat. One of those shameless Jewish dogs who have had the insolence to want to rule the German people of Austria. To donate my life, to purify myself with a bath of Jewish blood. I revel in that idea, I savour it voluptuously to the end, I let myself go, desperate… My blood boils to the point of rising from the ground, as if joyous, without knowledge, burning with hatred. If I could kill them all—all of them! Wipe them off the face of the earth, save the universe! If I could extirpate them, if I could give my life to bring about the extinction of this plague, of this epidemic. I see everything red so much that my blood boils… The ungodly and twisted spirit of the Jew has always been one of discord and denial…

The Jew must always annihilate, destroy, poison and defile: races, ideals, the hearts of men, no matter what. He carries within him the curse of his nefarious nature throughout the millennia of human history… Corroded by envy, he wants to sully the universe and take from it what he does not know and what he does not possess. It is for this reason that he hates all that is pure and spits upon all that is great, otherwise he could not attain it. It is also for this reason that he destroys what others build and thinks only of devastating. At present, his instinct leads him to want to destroy blond, blue-eyed humanity, that humanity which painfully reminds him of his black, animal-eyed, short-legged race… It is what explains his cries for *equality*, it is what explains his instinctive tendency towards social democracy and communism, which represent nothing but the despicable hatred felt by those who are inferior towards those who are above them… Impotent and invisible, as if extinct while the sun is at its zenith; its might only grows with the sunset and the night, and when, as is the case today, the sun of humanity lies low on the horizon and we see the rays of the sinister darkness of that eternal denier growing inordinately; it becomes so great, so great, that the earth is enveloped in it…

Judaism is probably a stage in the evolution of becoming which we must pass in order to reach a higher form and a nobler nature. In that sense, I have already outgrown Judaism, for I deny selfishness and the craving for happiness, that ancient vestige of the Jewish heritage, I ignore the pursuit of earthly goods… Alas, what do you know, you blond, blue-eyed people, beloved of the Gods, what do you know of the eternal, sunless night of *Nifelheim538*? But I neither hate you nor envy you. I love you because I love all that is high, noble and beautiful. I accept every higher form which is not like my own and which keeps me down here, voluntarily apart… That is the reason why I do not feel lowered by a foreign greatness, on the contrary, I elevate myself in agreement with it…

But who, who can believe or imagine, without having himself lived and suffered the eternal destiny of Christ, that no one is further removed from Judaism than he who has overcome it? Only he who has overcome a disease can be vaccinated against it, only he who has seen the plague and survived can be free from contamination. I must serenely wish for my annihilation if I truly love Germania. It would be hard to find a more tragic fate today than that of those few people who have really broken with their Jewish origins… I wish I could cry out to the Germans: Stand firm! Stand firm! Have no mercy! Not even for me! … Let's put an end once and for all to that poisonous tide! Let's burn that hornet's nest! Even if a hundred righteous were to be destroyed with the unrighteous. What are they worth? What are we worth? What am I worth? No! Have no pity, I beg you[539]."

This moving testimony illustrates very well the hidden suffering, which appears here and there in the texts of some writers who do not seem to dare to fully acknowledge their inner torment. We saw the same vehemence in Rahel Levine, when she received in her Berlin salon the

---

[538]*Nifelheim*: "Home of the Mist" in Norse mythology is the realm of darkness and gloom, shrouded in perpetual mist.

[539]Theodor Lessing, *La Haine de soi, le refus d'être juif,* 1930, Berg international, p. 163-168.

greatest German writers of the late 18th century. In a letter to her brother, she wrote: “My life is nothing but a slow agony… I never for a second forget this infamy. I drink it in the water, I drink it in the wine, I drink it in the air, in every breath. The Jew must be exterminated in us at the cost of our lives, it is the holy truth[540].”

Author of some twenty books, the philosopher Arthur Trebitsch also experienced this identity crisis. Born in Vienna in 1880, he was until his death “the most furious persecutor of Jews. His life represents the classic case of Jewish self-hatred, as harrowing and desperate as rarely seen since Pfefferkorn. From his earliest years, a real delirium germinated in the spirit of this beautiful blond boy: a secret Jewish association was spreading its tentacles from one end of the universe to the other to dominate the world and destroy the Aryan peoples… That was his delirium. In the service of the German people, he became a loyal fighter and comrade of General Erich Ludendorff and his wife Mathilde. Trebitsch suffered throughout his life from a serious eye disease that gradually led to blindness.

Committed to National Socialist ideals, Arthur Trebitsch was a radical anti-Semitic supporter. Lessing, who described the character, also noted “his monomaniacal anguish at being called a Jew”: “We discover in his biography a senseless succession of quarrels, duels, lawsuits, scandals and problems… Once, he lodged a complaint which he would take to every judicial instance because he had been offended in his Germanic belonging by a “nobody” who had called him a “Jew”. Finally, one day he asked for a vote of confidence from his party comrades, but then sent all those who refused to vote for him his witnesses to a duel. He became angry with all groups, annoyed the National-Socialists who had elected him group leader, antagonised the Church, the clergy and the Centre.”

Arthur Trebitsch organised lecture tours throughout Germany to open the eyes of his contemporaries.” Delusions of grandeur lead to delusions of persecution”, wrote Lessing. According to him, Trebitsch had suffered from acute paranoia: “He is convinced of the existence of a secret society—he calls it *Weltcharusse*—which is trying to assassinate him[541]”. He was also “persuaded that even within his anti-Semitic and *Wölkisch-leaning* party, there were Jews acting in the shadows. Through the creation of a “cultural association”, he put

[540] Léon Poliakov, *Histoire de l'antisémitisme, Tome II,* 1981, Points Seuil, 1990, p. 96.

[541] Theodor Lessing, *La Haine de soi, le refus d'être juif,* 1930, Berg international, p. 80, 90, 92. On the “*Weltchawrusse*” (Berlin Jewish mafia), read *L'Histoire de l'antisémitisme* by Leon Poliakov, p. 352 ff.

forward this far-fetched request: to organise a commission to examine whether any of the members of the group were circumcised and thus arrest an infiltrating Jewish spy. This "sniffing out" of Jews caused him more and more problems. He argues that in order to exert an unhealthy influence on the spirits, the Jews use women who contact writers and politicians they consider dangerous. Thus, writers such as Laurids Brunn and Arthur Sinter are said to have fallen into mysticism, influenced by the actions of women in the service of the Jews. *Chawrusse* was the instigator of numerous marriages between statesmen and Jewish women. He himself is said to have escaped four times from attempts to infect him in order to paralyse him. He recounts all these lucubrations on every page[542]." Arthur Trebitsch died of tuberculosis in Vienna in 1929, convinced that the Jews had succeeded in poisoning him.

Otherwise, Theodor Lessing's book is rather disappointing. Like Leon Poliakov in his *History of Jewish Identity Crises*, these authors did not attempt to understand the causes of this anguish or the causes of the rejection of Jewishness, regarding it simply as an enigma and an anomaly. Despite measuring Trebitsch's efforts to assert his Germanness, Lessing expressed only mild irony about a behaviour he judged exaggerated and servile, comparing it to that of a Disraeli, who did not mince his words to achieve his goals. He wrote of the man who was to become "Lord Beaconsfield": "Beaconsfield would never have become Prime Minister of England by constantly presenting himself to the world as the truest Englishman, instead of remembering that he was precisely proud to be a Jew[543]."

This was really to misunderstand Arthur Trebitsch's purpose, for Lessing did not seem to have understood that Trebitsch and Weininger were no longer Jews for the simple reason that they decided that they were no longer Jews, proving it completely by their words and actions.

Theodor Lessing, on the other hand, rightly pointed out that many

[542]Theodor Lessing, *La Haine de soi, le refus d'être juif*, 1930, Berg international, p. 94. However, we know numerous examples of French politicians married to women of Jewish origin: François Mitterrand, Michel Rocard, Robert Hue, Jacques Toubon, Jean-Pierre Chevènement, Dominique Baudis, Alain Besancenot, etc...(read Emmanuel Ratier's invaluable *Encyclopédie politique française*); as well as other famous men: Anatole France, André Malraux, Jacques Lacan, Georges Bataille, Jacques Maritain, Georges Bizet, Andréi Sakharov, Thomas Mann, Tolstoy, Stalin, etc.; others had Jewish mistresses, such as Goethe, Paul Bourget, Charles Péguy, Dumas (father and son), Romain Rolland. All were pro-Israel.

[543]Theodor Lessing, *La Haine de soi, le refus d'être juif*, 1930, Berg international, p. 89.

Jews before them had embarked on this liberating path: "All anti-Jewish forces have constantly had at their disposal a state-major composed of Jews who have gone beyond the prejudices of their teachers. Arthur Schopenhauer was supported in his anti-Jewish crises by his first apostles Frauenstadt and Asher. Richard Wagner, later to be declared a Jew, was not contradicted by his Jewish disciples Heinrich Porges and Herman Levi when he disparaged Meyerbeer, Mendelsohn, Halevy and Bizet as Jews who sabotaged German music. Paul Rée and Siegfried Lipiner, Nietzsche's Jewish disciples, were "anti-Semites" while their master held Jews in high esteem. And the strangest of all anti-Semites, Eugene Duhring, had a great surprise one day when the Jewish writer Benedict Friedlander, who admired his anti-Jewish writings, bequeathed him his entire fortune after he had committed suicide." And Lessing added: "A centrifugal force exerts a deleterious effect on Judaism when it loses itself and cannot sustain its strongest souls (think of Jesus and Spinoza)."

We are willing to believe that breaking with Judaism is no easy task. It usually takes several generations for Jewishness to attenuate and disappear altogether. Other, more conscious Jews may wish to reject immediately that Judaism which they regard as a "prison", as Jean Daniel wrote. Lessing thus used a beautiful formula to define the condition of the Jew: "this curse which consists in being a prisoner of the ring of Judaism[544]." An evocative and pertinent image after having seen the *Lord of the Rings* trilogy.

For them, the process is certainly more painful, and can only be brought to a successful conclusion with determined action, and with strong spiritual and political commitment. Let us recall the words of this young woman in her diary: "No one is further from Judaism than he who has overcome it." Weininger was already saying the same thing when he wrote: "*Christ is the greatest man, because he is the one who has measured himself against the greatest enemy545.*" In contrast to Arthur Trebitsch, Weininger remained within a Judaeo-centric view. But it does not matter, as long as they free themselves from Judaism. After all, there is no reason to condemn all Jews to follow Golum's fate.

Suicides

[544]Theodor Lessing, *La Haine de soi, le refus d'être juif*, 1930, Berg international, p. 82, 88

[545]Otto Weininger, *Sex and Character*, 1902, Ediciones 62 s|a, 1985, Barcelona, p. 326.

This gives us a better understanding of the frequency of suicide among Jews, especially among the intellectuals of this small community. Let us now complete the list of suicides known to Elie Wiesel[546]. We have already seen in this study the cases of Jerzy Kosinski, Bruno Bettelheim and Alfred Wolfmann. In the same way that others close to him and known to him had ended their lives, Wiesel was also surprised by the suicide of the Jewish intellectual Walter Benjamin, for whom he also saw no reason for his desperate act: 'Spain never expelled the Jews persecuted by the Gestapo. The philosopher Walter Benjamin had no reason to commit suicide: he would not have been handed over to the Vichy police. Moreover, Franco had instructed his legacys in the German-occupied countries to issue Spanish passports to Sephardic Jews."

As a young journalist, Wiesel began writing an account of his years in the concentration camps in Yiddish. He gave it to read to a friend, Yaffah, who worked for an Israeli film magazine: she would "lose her mind years later in the United States. Paranoid, she would eventually escape her "persecutors" by taking refuge in death."

Elie Wiesel seemed to enjoy listing the people he met who ended their lives: "The Jewish historian Joseph Wulf committed suicide a few years later in Berlin." Or, "Arnold Foster, the ringleader of all the fights against anti-Semitism, tells me about his nephew Harold Fender, author of a disillusioned Hemingway-like novel, *Paris blues*; he will write a moving account of the rescue of the Danish Jews and, until his suicide, he will not stop writing on the subject of the concentration camps[547]."

In *The Force for Good*, Marek Halter recalled the drama of the German Jews, so well "integrated". He too, like everyone else, did not understand the anti-Semitism that had "shocked" the German Jews and, according to him, had led to the suicide epidemic:

"There are few countries where the cultural integration of the Jews was as perfect and accomplished as in Germany. The Jewish community, before Hitler, numbered five hundred thousand people, of whom one third lived in Berlin. Their presence in literature and science was evident. German was the language in which Freud, Einstein, Kafka, Schnitzler, Kraus, Werfel, Schonberg, Mahler, etc. wrote and thought... There are fewer than thirty thousand Jews left in Germany today, almost all of them from Russia. Their marginalisation by the Nazi power, their cultural and later physical ostracism, shocked them. The abandonment of the human in the land of humanism, its violent denial; the shock was

[546]Hervé Ryssen, *Planetary Hopes, (*2022).

[547]Elie Wiesel, *Mémoires, tome I,* Seuil, 1994, p. 243, 302, 433, 485.

so brutal, the disappointment so intense, that an impressive wave of suicides spread rapidly. The litany of these names speaks volumes about the hopelessness of an entire culture. Kurt Tucholsky, critic and playwright, committed suicide. Ernst Toller, poet, committed suicide. Ludwig Fulda, playwright, suicide. Also committed suicide philosopher Walter Benjamin, novelist Ernst Weiss, playwright Walter Haserchever, composer Gustave Brecher, novelist Stefan Zweig[548]."

However, it is assumed that the Jews did not wait until 1933 to commit suicide. Françoise Giroud, in her book about Alma Mahler, the composer's wife, also mentioned this suicidal tendency: "Tragic news has just struck the Werfels, the death of Hugo von Hofmannsthal. The poet's eldest son Franz committed suicide at the age of 26 by shooting himself with a pistol. On the day of the young man's funeral, when he was leading the funeral procession, Hofmannsthal collapsed, dead at the age of fifty-five. For a long time, the former idol of the Viennese *intelligentsia had* wanted to die[549]."

Marthe Robert's book, *From Oedipus to Moses,* also mentioned frequent suicides of Central European Jewish émigrés in European capitals, who formed "a whole generation of spiritually and socially uprooted Jews." In a letter, Marthe Robert wrote: 'Kafka evokes the strangeness and pathological imbalance of his Jewish co-religionists at the German institute in Prague. Many of them, he says, have committed suicide during his years of study[550]."

Marthe Robert also quoted a letter of Freud's concerning the suicide of Nathan Weiss, "a valuable document about the Viennese Jewish world of that time and about its somewhat specific illnesses (mainly tuberculosis and suicide, as is shown precisely by the frequent dramas among Freud's relatives). Freud draws an impressive portrait of the Weiss family... He shows the father, a learned rabbi endowed with immeasurable pride, stingy to boot and full of malice; then the son, talented and brilliant, with powers of seduction and that "upstart" cynicism, but who collapses unexpectedly just as he reaches his goal (an advantageous marriage)[551]."

Edward Drumont had already observed in 1886, in his famous book, *Jewish France*: "Sudden death is nevertheless more frequent among Jews than suicide, although the latter increases in astonishing

[548]Marek Halter, *La force du Bien,* Robert Laffont, 1995, p. 56.

[549]Françoise Giroud, *Alma Mahler,* Robert Laffont, 1988, Pocket 1989, p. 168

[550]Marthe Robert, *D'Oedipe à Moïse,* 1974, Agora, 1987, p. 18.

[551]Correspondence, letter to Martha of 16 September 1883, quoted in Marthe Robert, *D'Oedipe à Moïse,* 1974, Agora, 1987, p. 115.

proportions which show the progress that neurosis makes in them."

It would indeed be interesting to finally have access to statistics on the subject. Students of social sciences could perhaps delve into this subject, for example, by looking into the archives of mental institutions to determine the extent of the little-known tragedy that affects a part of our fellow citizens. In any case, it should be noted once again that, in trying to explain all these suicides through the agonies suffered during the Second World War, Elie Wiesel and Marek Halter were merely blaming the rest of "Humanity" for a problem specific to their community.

2. Psychoanalysis of Judaism

Clinical picture of histrionics

Among the different types of pathological personalities, psychotherapists generally distinguish the following personalities: anxious, paranoid, histrionic, obsessive, narcissistic, schizoid, depressive, dependent, passive-aggressive, slippery. The "histrionic" personality is the one that will interest us here.

In order to give an insight into this pathology, we will first present a brief analysis of a man who had to deal with an obviously histrionic young woman in his professional activity:

"Katrina continually seeks to attract the attention of others by any means at her disposal: discreetly provocative clothing, seductive behaviour, theatrical statements in meetings, disconcerting changes of attitude (from seduction to indifference), dramatised calls for help (when she presents herself as a grieving child). She has a very wide "range" to capture the attention of others. John has also noticed that his emotions change rapidly: in a single night, he has gone from despair to the excitement of the game of seduction, then to mysterious sadness, to coldness, and finally ending it all with a fiery kiss. Finally, he has a tendency to idealise some people, speaking of them with admiration, but also to exaggeratedly demean others, who may even be the same. [One can go from hero to wretch in the blink of an eye", comments François Lelord.] John realises that he no longer knows whether Katrina is "playing" an actress's role, or whether this theatrical behaviour is her true nature[552]."

At work, and especially in meetings, histrionic personalities are sometimes very difficult to cope with. While they are expected to deliver a precise, factual, problem-solving discourse, they produce a confused, dramatised, emotion-focused discourse. Histrionic personalities are also very "sensitive to the opinion of others". They have "a rather reduced ability to observe themselves and recognise the reality of their emotions."

---

[552]François Lelord, *Comment gérer les personalités difficiles*, Odile Jacob, 2000, p. 89-107.

The adjective "histrionic", to define this type of personality, is relatively recent in the vocabulary of psychotherapists. Before "histrionic" personality, we used to speak of "hysterical" personality, a term which comes from the Greek "husteros" and which gave rise to the word "uterus". The Greeks indeed thought that "the noisy and excessive demonstrations of women were caused by the internal agitation of their wombs." In fact, this pathology is much more common in women than in men.

The popular image of hysteria, i.e. the madwoman twisted by epileptic-like convulsions, comes from the 19th century and the work of the famous doctor Jean-Martin Charcot de la Salpêtrière. But "the great pseudo-convulsive epileptic seizure described by Charcot is rare today[553]." The physical manifestations of the disease have taken more varied forms. Indeed, the expressive modalities of hysteria are both cultural and individual." Depending on the time and culture, the social group facilitates or represses the noisiest manifestations of neurosis. Technical civilisation does not favour them much, which is why we rarely come across today "the great hysteria" as popularised by the iconography of the Salpêtrière, although this does not mean that hysteria has disappeared, but rather that it has become more discreet, following other patterns[554]."

However, doctors often observed a number of spectacular disorders in their patients: paralysis, contractures, abdominal pain, amnesia, and sometimes seizures resembling epilepsy. Until the 19th century, these disorders were known as "uterine rage". But progress in medicine has made it possible to affirm that the behaviour and disorders of the so-called "hysterical" subjects had nothing to do with the uterus. Moreover, the term "hysterical" became pejorative, often used by psychiatrists to designate patients they could not help. In 1980, it was decided to replace this term by "histrionic", from the Latin *histrio*, "theatre actor".

Vittorio Lingiardi's book, entitled *Personality Disorders*, described the histrionic personality as follows: "In hysteria, manifestations of hyper-emotionality, uncontrollable imagination, blind

---

[553]http://www.acpsy.com/Troubles-Nevrotiques-et-Troubles.232.html

[554]http://www.acpsy.com/Hysterie.html. [The definition of hysteria has never been given and never will be given," said Lasègue. This statement, even today, may reflect the difficulties in defining the concept. Hysteria is not only an illness, it is also a way of being in the world. There are many definitions of hysteria, reflecting the personal conceptions of its authors, but also their fantasies." In Michel Steyaert, Introduction to *Hystérie, folie et psychose*, Ed. Les Empêcheurs de penser en rond, 1992].

trust in intuition, associated with a permanent search for the attention of others, predominate. Hysterics tend to see the world in a global but very impressionistic way; their attention is directed towards the brightest and most visible aspects of reality, neglecting the details. They often put on a scene or a show, even unconsciously, and in an overly seductive manner; they are generally superficial in their interpersonal relationships, and tend to base their choices and opinions on shallow convictions. Histrionics have an even deeper emotional fragility, greater impulsivity and more pronounced seductive behaviour. Highly egocentric, they tend to exploit their great emotional potential (outbursts of anger, fits of tears, etc.) to control and dominate others. They are theatrical, extraverted, excitable, exhibitionist. Even their sexuality is exhibited in a more overt way, and they often present profound disorders in the matter. They fear loneliness, and moments of separation fill them with anguish[555]."

Other studies provide other elements on this subject. Evelyne Pewzner's book, *Introduction to adult psychopathology*, presented the exemplary case of Albertina: "During our first interview, Albertina stands out for the discordance between her intelligent verbal expression and her appearance of an unruly student dressed in boarding school uniform. She has that typical attitude of ironic doubt as to the usefulness and effectiveness of psychological treatment. She completely denies the need for it. Her argumentation is brilliant and well ordered." She declares herself to be autonomous, strong-willed, and "almost challenges the therapist to do anything to help her. She says she does not suffer from anything and is not interested in her family's concerns about her physical and mental state." She does not consider herself ill, claims to be in full possession of her mental faculties and to be concerned only with getting ahead in her studies. She wants to be brilliant and go to one of those great schools her father advised her to go to: "She wants a profession where she will be heard of[556]."

The general clinical picture presented by Evelyne Pewzner could be summarised as follows: the hysterical personality is characterised by a way of being in the world marked by dissatisfaction and lack of authenticity, and a way of relating focused on manipulation and seduction. Everything, in their attitudes, behaviour, clothing, make-up, words, tends to attract attention, to please, to seduce. The hysteric thus avoids the authentic encounter with the other, as if the "mask" of the

[555]Vittorio Lingiardi, *Les Troubles de la personalité*, Flammarion, 2002, p. 75.
[556]Evelyne Pewzner, *Introduction à la psychopathologie de l'adulte,* Armand Colin, 2000, p. 120-123, 155.

character always conceals the person himself. The "plasticity" of the person allows the "multiplication of roles" according to the audience: the hysteric plays the role that is expected of him. This trait can be related to the great "emotional instability" of the hysteric: it takes little time to see him/her go from laughter to tears. Memory disorders are also frequent in hysterics, whose biographies always have gaps and forgetfulness. It may be a selective amnesia about a certain period or a certain event, but the illusions of memory and fabulation are often used to compensate for these gaps in memory. Mythomania translates the powerful imagination of the subject. Through his comedies and fabulations, the hysteric continually falsifies his relations with others, giving continuous spectacles. The subject, centred on himself, is incapable of seeing things from another point of view or of putting himself in the other person's place. Depression is at the forefront of the clinical picture. The bonds of camaraderie are scarce and difficult to maintain over time.

Gisèle Harrus-Révidi's book on hysteria provided other clarifications which we present below, expurgated from the indigestible psychoanalytical gibberish: The hysteric exaggerates the expression of emotions, embraces simple acquaintances with excessive ardour, weeps uncontrollably for minor sentimental reasons, and presents sudden outbursts of anger. The emotional and passionate expressions of the hysteric are somewhat theatrical and excessive. Hysterics are also sick of the verb and its interpretation. Their words have the particularity of being profuse, diffuse, symbolic in themselves, and their unconscious function is to prevent the symptom from being heard. The hysterical personality has a way of speaking that is too subjective and lacking in detail. For example, when the patient is asked to describe his mother, he cannot be more specific than: "she was a fantastic person". Difficulty in "verbalising affects or feelings" is also observed. Self-centredness, intolerance of frustration and any delay in obtaining gratification, translate in the hysteric into behaviour aimed at immediate gratification. Depression is obviously an important part of the core personality. In fact, Freud's patients are often in a state of real mourning and/or permanent amorous disappointment: to this is added "a phantasmatic mourning due to the non-overcoming of oedipal positions and activated by permanent sexual co-excitation" [understand who can!] There is a constant anguish fixed on the family, the children, an "anxious expectation of an event that will break the daily monotony, hence the stupefaction of the family when they realise that a real catastrophe is often accepted as a matter of course[557]." It is noted that in some cases "this neurosis is complicated by suicide attempts."

The "great intolerance to frustration" is confirmed by other analyses: the hysteric is "capricious and irritable". Feelings are exaggerated in their expression and are experienced with intensity (fits of tears and spectacular outbursts of anger). He behaves "as if he wants to satisfy the other and satiate his desire; he invents a character that he ends up believing himself, pretending to be nice and then passing himself off as the victim[558]."

Ronald D. Laing's book provided a simple precision that might seem anodyne: "The hysteric pretends that some of his activities are not what they seem, or that they mean nothing, or that they have no special implications, or that he does this or that because he is obliged to, when secretly his desires are satisfied by those activities. The hysteric often claims that he is not present in his actions, when in fact he is truly expressing himself through them[559]."

In *Hysteria, madness and psychosis*, the psychiatrist Michel Steyaert also noted other characteristics of delirium: "lycanthropy, ecstatic delusions, delusions of persecution, prophetic delusions...". Let us remember the frequency of fantasies of prostitution, rape, seduction, impure mating[560]."

Finally, we have this interesting analysis by a psychiatrist who emphasised the hysteric's "unusual capacity for manipulation": "The hysteric is the one who deceives. This capacity to adapt to the other is prodigious; instinctively he knows how to be on the same wavelength, in the same mode of functioning and, without really realising his "powers", he uses and abuses the other. Charm is a common factor in all those I have been able to meet, an incredible power of seduction followed by a siren-like call that attracted sailors, for that is the way of the hysteric: to catch in his nets, to use at the expense of and "let die". He seeks Love with a capital A, the man or woman who must prove that such love exists... It is difficult to detect at first sight; I even came to think that perhaps only hysterics could recognise each other, as in animal relationships where each delimits his or her own territory[561]."

---

[557]Gisèle Harrus-Révidi, *L'Hystérie*, Presses Universitaires de France, 1997, p. 12-17, 32, 88, 89

[558]Sante-az.aufeminin.com/w/sante/s243/maladies/hysterie.html

[559]Ronald D. Laing, *Le Moi divisé*, Stock, 1970, p. 131.

[560]Michel Steyaert, *Hystérie, folie et psychose*, Éd. Les Empêcheurs de penser en rond, 1992, p. 73.

[561]http://www.psychopsy.com/hysterie.html.

Whatever the place and the time, the symptoms always translate the hysteric's permanent desire to constitute an enigma for scientific logic and to offer his body to the scrutinising and expert gaze of the doctor.

The diagnosis

The general picture of the symptoms of histrionics seems to be able to explain in a strange way what we have analysed in our previous chapters. Indeed, cosmopolitan intellectuals manifest an inner turmoil and an exuberant attitude reminiscent of the symptoms of histrionics. Of course, this is not to say that each of these personalities suffers from this pathology, but there is a certain homogeneity of thought and common behaviours in these intellectuals, which are rather surprisingly similar to the descriptions detailed above.

To begin with "depression", "the state of real mourning and/or permanent disappointment in love". We can associate this with the media image that the Jewish community wishes to convey to the rest of humanity: that of a persecuted people suffering from their isolation and the wickedness of men. Joseph Roth attested to this unique Jewish predisposition to suffering: "Wherever a Jew stops, a Wailing Wall appears. Wherever a Jew settles, a pogrom is born... Likewise, the present of the Jews is probably greater than their past, for it is even more tragic[562]." This is a statement taken from an article in the newspaper *Das Tagebuch* of 14 September 1929, thus before the economic crisis and Hitler's seizure of power, but apparently the time was already considered sufficiently "tragic". On the clinical level, we know that depression can be "the last, desperate resort to capture and retain the attention of an expert interlocutor, the doctor[563]."

On the other hand, many Jews keep alive, consciously or not, an anguish, an inner restlessness, which is undoubtedly one of the features of the Hebraic character that contributes to nourishing in them their own sense of Jewishness. This was the moving testimony of George Perec, who revealed the background to his identity:

"I don't know exactly what it is to be Jewish, what it means to me to be Jewish... It is not a sign of belonging, it is not linked to a belief, a religion, a practice, a culture, a folklore, a history, a destiny, a

[562]Joseph Roth, *A Berlin*, Éditions du Rocher, 2003, p. 33.

[563]Evelyne Pewzner, *Introduction à la psychopathologie de l'adulte*, Armand Colin, 2000.

language. It is rather an absence, a question, a questioning, a hesitation, a restlessness: a certain restlessness behind which another certainty looms, abstract, heavy, unbearable: that of having been designated a Jew and, as a Jew, a victim, and owing one's life only to chance and exile[564]." We can identify here "the constant anguish fixed on the family", but also that "ambiguity" that we have already observed, expressed here by "hesitation". The identity obsession so frequent in the texts can certainly be compared to the neurotic symptom of "self-observation, which has been said to be extraordinarily developed in hysterics[565]."

The Marxist philosopher Jacques Derrida expressed a similar sentiment in his book *Suspensive Points,* where he acknowledged feeling in his inner self a "desire for integration into the non-Jewish community, a mixture of painful fascination and mistrust, with a nervous vigilance and an exhausting aptitude for perceiving the signs of racism, both in its most discreet configurations and in its loudest denials[566]."

This visceral concern can also take the form of paranoia. Thus, we regularly hear Jewish intellectuals in the media expressing alarm at the rise of anti-Semitism. This imperceptible disquiet that has been a subterranean torment to the Jewish soul throughout the ages manifests itself in alarmist reflexes in the face of what is perceived as the rise of the "scourge". At the slightest sign of opposition or criticism of the actions of any Jew, the whole community jumps into the media spotlight, and the heart-rending cries of the terrible threat are heard, as well as the chorus of mourners in the background. The personalities we thought were more dignified and reasonable fall into exaggerated interpretations, which seem almost ridiculous once the hustle and bustle dies down. Thus, for example, we saw Elie Wiesel publish, as early as 1974, articles in which he expressed his deepest fears about the revival of anti-Semitism: "I am publishing an article in the *New York Times* and

---

[564]George Perec, *Nací, textos de la memoria y el olvido*. Abada Editores, Madrid, 2006, p.101-102. [What I went to Ellis Island in search of is the very image of that point of no return, the awareness of that radical rupture… For me it is the very place of exile, that is to say the place of the absence of place, the place of dispersion. In this sense it concerns me, fascinates me, involves me, questions me, as if the search for my identity were to pass through the appropriation of this dump… What one finds there are in no way roots or traces, but the opposite: something formless, on the edge of the ineffable, which I can call enclosure, or splitting, or fracture, and which is for me very intimately and confusingly linked to the very fact of being Jewish." (p.104, 100– 101). (NdT)]

[565]Otto Weininger, *Sex and Character*, Ediciones 62 s|a Barcelona, 1985, p. 275.

[566]Jacques Derrida, *Points de suspensions, Entretiens*, Galilée, 1992, p. 130.

Le Figaro entitled "Why I am afraid"... Signs have appeared and they are disturbing. [567]."

Undoubtedly, there is a tendency for Jewish intellectuals to be doomsayers, to exaggeratedly "dramatise" what they perceive as anti-Semitism in the environment. Let us listen to Samuel Pisar: "Today, I perceive with anguish the approaching footsteps of the monster over the whole universe[568]." He said this in 1979, and we have already seen how in 1983 he wrote: "Our enemies are already watching us tirelessly. For them, we will always be guilty. Guilty of being Jews in Israel, of being Jews elsewhere, of being Jews. Guilty, depending, of being capitalists or of being Bolsheviks. Guilty in Europe of having been slaughtered like sheep, and guilty in Israel of having taken up arms so as not to be sheep again. Guilty, indeed, of continuing to exist[569]."

As I write these lines," said Elie Wiesel in 1996, "the anti-Semitic tide is rising. Sixty-five racist groups, more or less influential, are spreading hatred in the United States. In Japan, anti-Semitic books are on the bestseller lists... Now, once unleashed, hatred knows no bounds. Hatred calls for hatred. Hate kills the human within man before it kills him[570]."

Today, nothing has changed in the way they see the world. The demonstrations of indignation against racism, and above all "against anti-Semitism" are regularly repeated, redoubled in intensity, stirred up by a carefully organised agitation by the media system. When an elderly person is assaulted and tortured in his or her suburban home, or when a goy is savagely murdered in the street, the news is hardly reported in the newspapers. But when it is a Jew, then it is bound to be a hateful act of anti-Semitism. Ministers take to the streets to join demonstrations organised to show their solidarity with the "shocked" community. There is a certain injustice, as the indigenous French rarely receive the same media coverage of their misfortunes, let alone such a touching governmental request.

But it is true that the "emotional fragility" of Jews is undoubtedly much more important. Indeed, we know about their "hyper-emotionality", and a certain tendency to "exploit their great emotional potential". The slightest "anti-Semitic" incident, the slightest graffiti on a mailbox sets the whole media and judicial machine in motion. Perhaps some Jewish personalities tend to 'exaggerate the expression of their

---

[567]Elie Wiesel, *Mémoires, Tome II,* Seuil, 1996, p. 97.

[568]Samuel Pisar, *Le Sang de l'espoir*, Robert Laffont, 1979, p. 22.

[569]Samuel Pisar, *La Ressource humaine*, Jean-Claude Lattès, 1983, p. 250-251.

[570]Elie Wiesel, *Mémoires, Tome II,* Seuil, 1996, p. 128-129.

emotions', which gives their way of interpreting the news 'something theatrical and excessive'.

However, these manifestations of suffering and this "victimising lamentation[571] " are not simply the amplified echoes of the news. It should be noted that they are a constant in the media systems of democracies, where the media continuously broadcast all the compassionate literature that invites us to help the unfortunate Jewish people, always persecuted everywhere and at all times for unknown reasons. Documentaries, films and programmes of all kinds on the subject are innumerable and omnipresent, as are books recalling the misfortunes of the Jewish people throughout history. All human beings are asked to sympathise with the pain and drama of the Jews, poor, weak and vulnerable, always persecuted for reasons that no one can explain. The fifty million non-Jewish dead of the Second World War are often forgotten, pushed into the background, even directly hidden for the benefit of the Jewish victims alone.

The explanation is again of a medical nature: these "dramatised distress calls" serve to "endear us and awaken the protective instinct". This "dramatised and theatrical presentation of emotions" is part of a "very wide range to capture the attention of others".

But it is not only the disproportionate media treatment of the terrible events in the Middle East and Israel. It is also about the frivolity of many show business and entertainment stars, the way they show off, show off, strut their stuff on television sets: "They are theatrical, extraverted, excitable, exhibitionist". This is how we see them, "putting on a continuous show". Sometimes it is even enough to pull down one's pants and run on the television set to be described as "great", "incomparable", "splendid", "sublime"[572].

But it would be inappropriate for a Goy to indulge in overly harsh criticism, for these "artists" are very "sensitive to the opinion of others". It is easy to see how a negative criticism with a touch of contempt for the work of one of their peers, a painter or a novelist, for example, will immediately provoke the interlocutor's discomfort, even if their productions in these fields are often of a notorious mediocrity. On the other hand, it can be noted that medals and rewards of all kinds are highly valued, as Otto Weininger pointed out, "their feminine ambition for titles".

In the past, Edward Drumond had already noted a certain

[571]Shmuel Trigano, *L'Idéal démocratique...* Odile Jacob, 1999, p. 43.
[572]Reference to the comedian Michaël Youn. He had the audacity to run naked on a television set during a film festival awards ceremony. (NdT).

childishness in his behaviour: "A bad burst of joy is sometimes followed by an expression of naivety... Yes, there is something childish about him... His mouth opens with pleasure when he boasts, like the mouths of those Africans whose eyes and teeth sparkle with joy at possessing a piece of glass bead or a piece of cloth that is a bit showy... When he tells you that he has received a distinction, a chocolate medal at an exhibition, he stares at you to see if you will make fun of him, which is what he always fears; then his pale, bloodless face lights up with a ray of happiness as children's faces light up."

The lists of recipients of the Legion of Honour are a long-awaited event for the community, and the government is not unaware of this, as it is aware of its "intolerance of frustration and of any delay in obtaining gratification". This is something that successive governments of the French Republic always try to avoid, favouring the abundant decorations[573]."

Indeed, Israel's children often display "behaviour aimed at immediate gratification". Recall, for example, how President François Mitterrand had been asked to explain his friendship with René Bousquet and its implications during the Vichy regime[574]. Despite all the sympathy he had shown to the Jewish community, this "detail" had cost him dearly, as he was widely vilified at the end of his reign for this unpardonable fault. Let us also remember the case of the "no heir funds" held by the Swiss banks, which had to pay the colossal sums demanded by the World Jewish Congress without complaint, sixty years after the war. Of course, this is not only a medical analysis, but also a financial balance of power. After that billionaire case, a Jewish author, Norman Finkielstein, had not hesitated to publish a book denouncing the lucrative racket that he called the "holocaust industry". Like other disrespectful authors, he sought to denounce the "holocaust business" by pointing out that the Jewish community leaders used the drama of

---

[573]Jean Daniel and Bernard Attali have just been promoted Commander of the Legion of Honour, and Gisèle Halimi has been promoted Officer, as has the Israeli stylist Albert Elbaz, among others. (Read in *Rivarol*, issue of 28 April 2006) Jacques Friedmann has just been promoted Grand Officer on 5 May "for his essential role in the creation of the Musée du Quai Branly" dedicated to the First Arts (African arts) (*Rivarol*, 19 May 2006).

[574]At the end of his second term, already ill and diminished. There is a long interview broadcast on 12 September 1994, a few months before his death, during which Jean Pierre Elkabbach questioned François Mitterrand in an almost inquisitorial manner. The President of the Republic refused until the end to acknowledge legally and officially the responsibility of France and the Republic for the actions of the Vichy regime during the war. (NdT).

the holocaust to blame the Goyim and claim exaggerated compensations decades after the fact.

This "intolerance of frustration" is also regularly manifested by the systematic filing of complaints with the courts for any statement deemed hostile to the community. In 2000, we saw how the left-wing writer Renaud Camus was the victim of a media lynching for having protested against the "over-representation" of Jews on a public service radio programme. Jean Daniel's indignant reaction was then identical to that of most of his peers. The philosopher Jacques Derrida was one of the signatories of the petition organised by Claude Lanzmann, which simply described the racist and anti-Semitic passages in Renaud Camus' book as "criminal"." We should ask ourselves what happens in our public space when a publisher and a certain number of "intellectuals" close their eyes to these appalling and grotesque phrases[575]", Derrida wrote.

In the same vein, this was Elie Wiesel's reaction, in 1989, to Jean-Pierre Domenach's statements alarming the community's media fuss: "I have followed with sadness the scandal that Mr Domenach has caused. I have read his interviews in *L'Événement du jeudi* and *Le Figaro*, I have heard his pedantic sniggering on *Europe 1* and the warnings he deigns to give us Jews to be more careful to avoid anti-Semitic reactions. What is the method he proposes to us? It is very simple, almost banal: speak more softly, do not show yourself, renounce Jewish loyalty (denounce Israel, for example), do not mention the Jewishness of Jewish victims. I confess: because of its perverse implications, this kind suggestion puts some Jews out of their minds—first, because it makes anti-Semites stop feeling guilty. How? Would anti-Semitism no longer be the fault of the anti-Semites, but of the Jews themselves? Would the hatred that Jews arouse be due only to their behaviour? They despise us, they persecute us, and should we take it out on ourselves[576]?"

And again, we observe how one Jewish intellectual goes off on a tangent to invariably end up accusing the other of his own faults and reproaching him for accusing the Jews of very real faults:

---

[575]Jacques Derrida, Élisabeth Roudinesco, *Y mañana, qué…* Fondo de Cultura Económica, Buenos Aires, 2002, p. 36 (note), 136. About Renaud Camus, Derrida wrote (p. 137): "I think the character is astute and calculating, but also, as is almost always the case, naïve, little exercised, let us say, to put it quickly, in self-analysis. At least that of his social unconscious. We are still sailing in the same waters: criminal law, criminology and psychoanalysis; everything is yet to be reinvented."

[576]Elie Wiesel, *Mémoires, Tome II*, Seuil, 1996, p. 169, 171.

"If what he says is true," Wiesel continued, "the Jews—excuse me: 'some' Jews—would be using the Holocaust to enrich themselves, and, moreover, to persecute him and other honourable people... Persecution sickness? It is incredible but true: "some" anti-Semites feel persecuted by the Jews they themselves persecute."

The clinical picture of hysteria provided this enlightening precision: "They tend to exploit their great emotional potential (explosions of anger, fits of tears, etc.) to control and dominate others". What the psychiatrist Michel Steyaert wrote on the subject was quite striking because of the similarity with the object of our ethno-psychiatric study, and confirmed that the "way of relating" is "centred on manipulation and seduction":

"This megalomania is lived in a mood of exaltation bordering on theatricality and tragicomedy." The patients "end up in a hospital, where they often generate a tumultuous atmosphere, as they are masters in the art of manipulating medical equipment. Moreover, it is not uncommon to see them, under the pretext of wanting to help, trying to convince the other patients of the incompetence of the doctors and the inhumanity of psychiatry. They find it very difficult to put up with the slightest firm attitude towards them[577]."

We can see here a parallel with the perpetual agitation maintained by the media system, that incessant frenzy which exalts revolt against order and traditional values, and which, in turn, invites the ecstatic worship of plural society and "human rights". We shall see below this dialectical or binary mode of thinking based on two antinomian feelings: repulsion and absolute idealisation.

The manipulation of men and society can also be expressed more or less consciously through "mythomania", something we believe we have perceived in the stories of some public figures. Elie Wiesel gave important testimony about his willingness to enrich and embellish his stories. A little more and we might suspect that Samuel Pisar shared the same tendency described by the medical analysis: "The illusions of memory and fabulation often come to palliate those gaps in memory". The accounts of these two authors, especially those concerning the concentration camp episodes, are often "sparse in detail". Their accounts are "confused, dramatised, emotionally focused".

Memory disorders" are, as we know, characteristic of pathology. This "selective amnesia" is in fact perfectly illustrated in the case of Jewish intellectuals in the way they ponder the role of their fellow Jews

---

[577]Michel Steyaert, *Hystérie, folie et psychose*, Éd. Les Empêcheurs de penser en rond, 1992, p. 62.

in the Bolshevik revolution. The greatest Soviet dissident, Alexander Solzhenitsyn, published in 2003 a seminal book showing the full extent of the participation of the Jewish people in one of the greatest massacres in human history[578]. In fact, as we demonstrated in *Planetary Hopes* through the study of books on the Soviet Union, Jewish intellectuals seem to have totally forgotten their overwhelming, irrefutable, obvious and criminal responsibility for the nearly thirty million Russian and Ukrainian dead who fell into oblivion." What kind of amnesia is this? ...", Solzhenitsyn was indignant at the impudence of the denials of some Jewish authors[579]. Here again, it seems to us appropriate to explain this anomaly with clinical analysis: "The gap-filled memorisation of facts, their vague and imprecise evocation allow for an easier elimination of those aspects of reality which the individual does not want to see surface in consciousness."

We have also been able to study in this book this "plasticity" that allows the "multiplication of roles". The "Jew" seems to have the ability to adapt to any circumstance and to change his identity while retaining his own identity: we saw how he could be an Indian chief on a reservation in the American West, like that mischievous Jew evoked by Elie Wiesel, a moustachioed Cossack, or more French than the French, like Bernard-Henri Levy. We also saw a gangster transform himself into a good parishioner and deceive the entire population of a small provincial town in order to win over the jury of the court that was to try him. Here again, the end justifies the means.

The proteiform character of Judaism can express itself on the individual level in a pathological way, in the form of sudden mood swings. In the film *Barton Fink, for example,* we saw the film producer licking the soles of the shoes of a young, up-and-coming screenwriter who had just arrived in Hollywood, and in the next interview insulting and rudely dismissing him. Emotions change quickly[580], and apparently this Ashkenazi producer, who "embraces simple acquaintances with excessive ardour", also "has a tendency to idealise some people,

---

[578]Alexandre Solzhenitsyn, *Deux siècles ensemble,* Fayard, 2003.

[579]Hervé Ryssen, *Planetary Hopes, (*2022).

[580]"Yiddish dramas, with their rapid alternation of joyous and sad scenes, reflect this sense of contrast... While some circumstances force a rapid transition from laughter to tears, this happens because the emotions have been programmed. One is joyful on Purim, one weeps on Yom Kippur... Emotions, though prescribed, are not therefore merely formal. Though ordered, they are no less sincere." (Mark Zborowski, *Olam,* 1952, Plon, 1992, p. 401)." That constant of behaviour, tears following without transition to laughter, is quickly imprinted on the child of the shtetl." (Mark Zborowski, *Olam,* 1952, Plon, 1992, p. 303).

speaking of them with admiration, but also to exaggeratedly demean others, who may even be the same". Young Barton Fink thus went from "hero to wretch in a trice."

Similarly, we could see a sketch by the comedian Timsit, who caricatured his Jewish cousin in pained lamentation (my poor unfortunate brother!) and then went on to the most excessive reprimands and insults. We know, in fact, that the hysteric "weeps uncontrollably for minor sentimental reasons, and has sudden outbursts of anger". But some analyses of the histrionic personality refer to "a multiple personality" and underline the "alternation of different personalities (character, biography)": "Playing a character, playing a role, represents for the hysteric an imperious need to avoid an authentic encounter with the other. Behind the disguises that conceal him, through the multiplicity of characters he adopts, the hysterical personality does not let himself be known[581]."

Let us recall these words of Otto Weininger, who noted in the Jews the "poorest inner identity": "The typically Jewish nature is especially facilitated for us by the irreligiousness of the Semite… The Jew is the unbelieving man… And the essential cause of the Jew's being nothing is to be sought in the fact that he believes in nothing. It matters little whether a man believes in God or not; if he does not believe in Him, let him at least believe in atheism. But, on the other hand, the Jew believes in nothing, does not believe in his beliefs and doubts his doubts[582]."

In this the press director Jean Daniel agreed perfectly when he wrote: "In any case, I accept to be a Jew even in my doubts, on condition that I am left with this doubt and that it is not a way of branding me as insincere[583]."

The medical diagnosis is more prosaic: "If we consider the hysteric as a liar, we must admit that he is not a liar like the others. Undoubtedly, his insincerity is more or less conscious, but how can we speak of a lie for a subject for whom reality hardly exists? His lack of perception, his lack of psychological penetration of others betrays the childishness of his subterfuge, his childish surprise when he is unmasked. But by a sort of eroticism of the imaginary, the simulacrum and the game can become a source of pleasure with a certain dose of perversity[584]."

The image of the famous swindler Jacques Crozemarie, president of the Association for Cancer Research in the 1990s, comes to mind

---

[581]http://www.acpsy.com/Hysterie.html

[582]Otto Weininger, *Sex and Character,* Ediciones 62 s|a Barcelona, 1985, p. 317.

[583]Jean Daniel, *L'Ère des ruptures*, Grasset, 1979, p. 114.

[584]http://www.acpsy.com/Hysterie.html

here. This man swindled around 300 million francs from the French people, who had been gullible enough to be moved by his tearful interventions on television. Released in 2002, after 33 months in prison, he declared in an interview published in *Le Parisien*: "I am not a thief. I never understood why I was convicted, and I never will. I don't want to be condemned for the rest of my life. I am outraged. I have paid for nothing! I am still waiting for the evidence against me" We have already exposed in *The Planetary Hopes*, that quaint mentality which consists in abruptly denying everything despite the strongest evidence. The murderer Pierre Goldman had also managed to fool everyone in the 1970s. If the jurors at the Amiens court had been instructed in this particular mentality, they would probably not have acquitted the criminal and would have been spared the humiliation of reading the thinly veiled confessions of the aforementioned man published in his novel.

On the political level, this simulation can lead astray and prove catastrophic. Thus, at all times and in all places, Jews were denounced as foreigners who stubbornly refused to assimilate into the population, even if they had adopted the local language and customs. Alexandre Solzhenitsyn, analysing in the 1970s the massive outflow of Jews from Russia to the United States, had proved that Jewish integration was fictitious, and confirmed the reflections of the Zionist leader Jabotinsky at the beginning of the 20th century: "When the Jew assimilates into a foreign culture, one should not rely on the depth and consistency of the transformation. An assimilated Jew gives in at the first push, abandons the borrowed culture without the slightest resistance as soon as he is convinced that his reign is over." This character corresponds again to the clinical analysis of histrionics: they are "generally superficial in their interpersonal relations, and tend to base their choices and opinions on shallow convictions".

It is known that Jews were always expelled at some point from almost every country where they lived. These "separations", often brutal, mark the history of Judaism. Indeed, when Jewish intellectuals write that they were perfectly "integrated" in this or that country, we should understand above all: "socially integrated"; and no one would argue that, financially, Jews are much better integrated than others. But in reality, as we have been able to analyse through the writings of eminent intellectuals, it seems that Jewish identity takes precedence over everything else, and still represents, as Edgar Morin put it, "a perpetual source of confrontation". For Edgar Morin, this is not in itself negative, since it generates a "very strong creative tension585." The problem is that this "very strong creative tension" is not always perceived as such by the "others", who often prefer to live without it, as demonstrated by the countless expulsions that have marked the history of Judaism. These incessant escapes since the flight from Egypt are counted by the dozen: flight from England in 1290, flight from France in 1394, flight from Spain in 1492, flight, at some point, from all the German principalities, flight from Iraq, Iran or Yemen, flight from the USSR... But as we know: "The bonds of comradeship are rare and are hardly maintained over time."

Let us put ourselves in the place of a Jew and consider the history of these unhappy people: how can we not live in anguish, knowing that a brutal rupture will soon occur again, for it really seems inevitable: "They fear loneliness, and moments of separation fill them with anguish". Similarly, the following can be read in the clinical picture of hysteria: "Nothing is worse for the hysteric than the rupture of the relationship with the other from which his feeling of existence springs: he is then plunged into an unbearable loneliness from which he tries to escape by entering into a new relationship, with the same fervour and intensity as the previous one[586]." Thus one leaves Toledo for Thessaloniki, one leaves Lisbon for Amsterdam, one leaves Berlin for Paris, Kichiniev for Moscow, and Moscow for New York or Tel Aviv. Each time, the previous object of love, which had been idealised at the beginning, is disowned, vilified, insulted after the break-up.

On the other hand, of course, the Jews show great autonomy and do not seem to need anyone. The great Jewish thinker Franz Rosenzweig wrote in 1976 in *The Star of Redemption*: "Our life is no longer connected with anything external. We put down roots in ourselves, and have no roots in the earth; we are therefore eternal wanderers, deeply rooted in ourselves, in our own body and blood. And this rootedness in ourselves and nothing but ourselves guarantees our eternity[587]." This statement also seems to be copied from the clinical picture of the histrionic personality that declares itself "autonomous".

This loneliness seems to nourish the "anxious waiting for an event that will break the daily monotony" mentioned by the psychiatrist. The philosopher Jacob Leib Talmon presented this revealing testimony: "Bruno Bauer used a terrible image, comparing the Jews to that wife in

[585]Edgar Morin, *Un nouveau commencement*, Seuil, 1991, p. 120.

[586]http://www.acpsy.com/Hysterie.html

[587]Franz Rosenzweig, *La Estrella de la Redención*, Hermenia 43, Ediciones Sígueme, Salamanca, 1997, p. 363.

the Russian proverb who is sure of her husband's love only when he beats her. Jews, they say, only feel at peace with themselves and with the Creator when they are persecuted[588]." And indeed, it seems "that a real catastrophe is often accepted as a matter of course." Otto Weininger underlined the terrifying nature of Israel's God, cruel and jealous: "His relationship to Jehovah, the abstract idol, before whom he feels the anguish of a slave, and whose name he will never dare to utter, characterises the Jew in a similar way to the woman, who also needs to be dominated by an alien will[589]."

"It is an old people who have known God for a long time! They have experienced his great goodness and his cold justice, they have committed sins and bitterly atoned for them, and they know that they can be punished, but not forsaken[590]", said Joseph Roth.

But it would be illusory to ask them to explain their faults clearly. Indeed, judging by our numerous readings, it seems that almost all Jewish intellectuals are convinced that they bear no responsibility for the reactions of animosity against their community. In *Difficult Freedom*, the philosopher Emmanuel Levinas wrote, for example: "To be persecuted, to be guilty without having committed any fault, is not an original sin, but the other side of a universal responsibility—a responsibility towards the Other—older than any sin[591]."

Let us listen to Yeshayahu Leibowitz, philosopher of religions, express himself about Hitlerian anti-Semitism: "Adolf Hitler is not the high point of traditional German anti-Semitism: it is a phenomenon of a totally different nature, which is historically incomprehensible. For me, anti-Semitism is not a problem of the Jews but of the goyim[592]."

Elie Wiesel expressed a similar view in the first volume of his *Memoirs*, where he wrote about goyim hostile to Jews: "I was not far from thinking: it's their problem, not ours[593]."

And these are not isolated testimonies. On the contrary, this seems to be the attitude of most Jewish intellectuals. Thus, the French philosopher Shmuel Trigano did not hide his surprise at the manifestations of anti-Semitism either. For him they are a great mystery: "One of the greatest mysteries of modernity is undoubtedly (long before racism) the phenomenon of anti-Semitism, still

---

[588]J.-L. Talmon, *Destin d'Israel*, 1965, Calmann-Lévy, 1967, p. 72.
[589]Otto Weininger, *Sex and Character*, Ediciones 62, Barcelona, 1985, p. 309.
[590]Joseph Roth, *Judíos errantes*, Acantilado 164, Barcelona, 2008, p. 45.
[591]Emmanuel Levinas, *Difficile liberté*, Albin Michel, 1963, 1995, p. 185, 290
[592]Herlinde Loelbl, *Portraits juifs*, L'Arche, 1989, 2003 for the French version.
[593]Elie Wiesel, *Mémoires, tome I*, Seuil, 1994, p. 30, 31.

unexplained despite an immense library on the subject... The anti-Semitic phenomenon is surely one of the most important phenomena which, like fascism and totalitarianism, has remained a mystery[594]."

The inability to "see things from another point of view or to put oneself in the place of the other" is indeed symptomatic: The subjects have "a rather reduced ability to observe themselves and to recognise the reality of their emotions"." Thus, anti-Semitism is for them an "enigma". This was also, as we have already seen, what the philosopher André Glucksmann declared: "Hatred of the Jews is the enigma among all enigmas... The Jew is by no means the cause of anti-Semitism; one must analyse this passion by and for itself, as if this Jew who persecutes without knowing him did not exist... Two millennia that the Jew has been a source of discomfort. Two millennia of being a living question for the whole world. Two millennia of innocence, having nothing to do with anything[595]."

This opinion is confirmed by psychiatrists, like the reflection of the mirror: "Whatever the place and the time, the symptoms always translate the hysteric's permanent desire to constitute an enigma for scientific logic and to offer his body to the scrutinising and expert gaze of the doctor."

This was exactly what Bernard-Henri Lévy expressed in *The Testament of God* when he spoke of "that indomitable people whose perseverance to be remains one of the deepest enigmas for contemporary consciousness[596]."

We know that hysterics "avoid responsibility and reflect on their own actions[597]". Despite all the misfortunes and disappointments throughout their painful history, despite all the setbacks and failures, the Jews never re-examine the facts. Many theologians have noted this astonishing tenacity, this stubborn stubbornness of the "stubborn people". One can quote in a timely manner the reflections of Baltasar Gracián, that Spanish Jesuit of the Golden Age, who wrote: "Every fool is persuaded, and every persuaded fool; and the more erroneous his opinion, the greater his tenacity... The tenacity must be in the will, not in the judgement[598]." But for the moment, such reasonableness seems to be far removed from our patient's concerns.

---

[594]Shmuel Trigano, *L'Idéal démocratique...*, Odile Jacob, 1999, p. 17, 92

[595]André Glucksmann, *Le Discours de la haine,* Plon, 2004, p. 73, 86, 88

[596]Bernard-Henri Lévy, *Le Testament de Dieu*, Grasset, 1979, p. 9.

[597]http://www.etudiantinfirmier.com/index_psy.php?page=2

[598]Baltasar Gracián, *Oráculo manual y arte de prudencia, 183.*

Sometimes a certain doubt about prophetic certainties and deep-seated convictions surfaces in the texts. This can be observed in authors who are not suspected of officially suffering from “self-hatred”. We saw it briefly expressed in the press director Jean Daniel, or in the novelist Albert Cohen, in *Bella del señor*, in a passage of his novel, where, in a sort of trance-like trance, the author adopted a somewhat strange style. The author went on for several pages without any punctuation[599]. Despite the difficulties in reading it, this text is valuable, as it reveals some deep-seated anxieties within the Jewish personality. The temptation of self-hatred, immediately “repressed”, as professional psychiatrists say, appeared clearly:”... It is also a contagion of their hatred if by dint of hearing their vile accusations they have made us feel the desperate temptation to conceive the horrible thought of being ashamed of our great people the desperate temptation to conceive the thought that if they hate us so much and everywhere it is because we deserve them, and by God I deserve them and by God I deserve them. and by God I know that we do not deserve it and that their hatred is the foolish tribal hatred of the different and a hatred of envy and also the hatred of the animal for the weak for weak in numbers we are everywhere and men are not good and weakness attracts spurs the innate hidden bestial cruelty ... and you will see how in the Land of Israel the children of my returned people will be gentle and arrogant and beautiful and beautiful and of noble bearing and brave warriors if necessary and finally seeing their true face alleluia you will love my people you will love Israel who has given you God who has given you the greatest book who has given you the prophet who was love[600]...”

Well... It’s not Céline or Joyce who wants to. But at least this text has the merit of bringing to the surface what seems to preoccupy some cosmopolitan spirits in a hidden way. In addition to the temptation to self-hatred, we see again the spirit of revenge, as well as the hope of a time when Israel will be recognised by all peoples as the beacon of the nations. This type of confession is rare in literature addressed to the general public and undeniably reflects the “difficulty of verbalising affections or feelings” that we saw in the medical analysis. It would be interesting and exciting for young researchers to open the archives of psychiatric hospitals or some community libraries to find other

[599]There is no punctuation in the texts of the Torah scrolls either. Albert Cohen seems to want to imitate the literary technique of stream of consciousness used by authors such as James Joyce or Marcel Proust. (NdT).

[600]Albert Cohen, *Bella del Señor*, Anagrama, 1992, Barcelona, p. 561.

documents of this type[601].

In any case, this passage written under the pen of Albert Cohen perfectly illustrates this "ambivalence" that is constitutive of the Jewish personality. Otto Weininger wrote in this regard: "The psychic content of the Jew always presents a certain duality or plurality, and he can never free himself from this ambiguity, this duplicity or this multiplicity… Inner multiplicity, I repeat, is the Jewish characteristic; simplicity *[and clarity]* characterises the non-Jewish[602]."

This ambivalence appears frequently in cosmopolitan planetary literature. The philosopher Pierre Levy wrote: "Look at the Jews: a wedge of the East in the West, a drop of the West in the East[603]." Let us also recall the words of Jacques Attali when he advocated a "plural" society and called on Europeans to claim "the multiplicity of their affiliations by resolutely accepting their ambiguities[604]"." Everyone will have the right to belong to several hitherto antagonistic tribes, to be ambiguous, to place himself between two worlds. To borrow elements from different cultures in order to improvise one's own from the pieces of the others[605]."

There seems to be a repulsive fear of all that is frank, clear, with sharp and precise contours, in the same way that the devil fears holy water or vampires pale before a clove of garlic. But Jacques Attali's views merely reflect his own mental universe. Here again, we must note the concordance with psychiatric analysis: "egocentrism" and the "inability to see things from another point of view or to put oneself in the other's place".

The histrion is always on the border, with one foot on each side, subject to "vacillation", as the writer Georges Perec described it. That is why throughout history Jews have often been accused of treason, both by one side and the other. There is no shortage of examples.

---

[601]In the film, *Someone Flew Over the Cuckoo's Nest,* (USA, 1975), Milos Forman sought to make us believe that the alienated were not as crazy as they seemed and that they were above all victims of an oppressive society. This was the aim of the anti-psychiatric school that had its hour of glory in the 1970s with David Cooper, Aaron Esterson and Ronald D. Laing: there are no mentally ill people; it is society that drives them mad (Alain de Benoist, *Vu de droite,* 1977, Le Labyrinthe, 2001, p. 184). Elie Wiesel recalled in one of his books that Maimonides, the great Jewish thinker of the Middle Ages, had already declared: "The world will be saved by the insane"." (Elie Wiesel, *Un Désir fou de danser,* Seuil, 2006, p. 14).

[602]Otto Weininger, *Sex and Character,* Ediciones 62 s|a Barcelona, 1985, p. 320.

[603]Pierre Lévy, *World philosophie,* p. 153-156

[604]Jacques Attali, *Europe(s),* Fayard, 1994, p. 198.

[605]Jacques Attali, *Dictionnaire du XXI siècle,* 1998.

But as we know, Jews also have a "mission" to fulfil "for all humanity", as they themselves keep repeating. In his book *Anti-Semitic Hatred,* Serge Moati brought us the testimony of one of his fellow Jews, Renée Neher, who has been living in Israel since 1971: "What does the notion of "chosen people" mean? It means that the Bible has assigned us a mission of justice, peace, monotheism and anti-idolatry. As long as the ten commandments given to Moses at Sinai are not all respected, we will feel responsible and guilty... Humanity could be likened to an orchestra where each one, necessary as part of the whole, plays his score. The Jew would be the "first violin". The one who, in the absence of the orchestra leader, God, merely gives the tone. If the Jew were finally seen as an element in the orchestra of humanity, anti-Semitism would be abolished. Why should the Jew be the tone-setter? What is the origin of this privilege? It lies in the fact that we believe in the word of the Bible which assigned us that function: "chosen people[606]"."

The hysteric also feels the need to get involved and to devote himself to a cause. The psychiatrist Michel Steyaert noted the following: "Often, patients choose a job where they will be able to show their commitment, such as teachers, nurses, doctors, social workers[607]." Again we see how the cosmopolitan spirit coincides with the clinical picture.

Certainly, a very characteristic form of "egocentrism" can be detected. Manifestly, without them there can be no civilisation, no humanity: "They are the key to the development of the world. There is no sedentary development without these nomads"." Israel's history, once again, will be played out in its ability to play a role ... as an agent of peace and progress between East and West. If it attempts to limit its identity to acquired lands, it is lost. If it continues on its course, it can survive and help humanity not to disappear." Thus, "the misfortune of the Jewish people, therefore, is a misfortune for all men", Attali wrote brazenly.

And since everything that concerns the Jews also affects the whole of humanity, we should not be surprised to hear Jacques Attali state with the *chutzpah to which* we are accustomed: "The disappearance of the Temple is also a tragedy for non-Jews, because the Hebrews prayed for them: "They do not know what they have lost[608]"." For the planetary

---

[606]Serge Moati, *La Haine antisémite*, Flammarion, 1991, p. 165.

[607]Michel Steyaert, *Hystérie, folie et psychose,* Éd. Les Empêcheurs de penser en rond, 1992, p. 61.

[608]Jacques Attali, *Los Judíos, el mundo y el dinero,* Fondo de cultura económica, 2005, Buenos Aires, p. 485, 486, 489, 491.

intellectuals, the Jewish people are at the centre of the world, and it is simply unimaginable that life could be conceived in any other way. Without them, there is no life on earth.

Here is a dialogue from a novel by Jacques Attali, entitled *He will come* (the Messiah of course): "We are not superior. We are different. We would have liked to be ignored, forgotten in our lands. But we were driven out of them. We became nomads forced to stalk the enemy and invent time. After that, we fell into slavery. When we were set free, God assigned us the mission to save men and to speak in His Name. We did not ask for it." It is enough simply to rebuild the Temple in Jerusalem: "When there is there … no longer some stones and weeds, but the only place worthy to receive God on this planet, then the world can prepare itself for a perfect time[609]."

In short, the Jews "would have preferred to be ignored", but it turns out that they have "a mission to fulfil"; they have no choice. And as we know, the hysteric often says "that he does this or that because he is obliged to, when secretly his desires are satisfied by those activities."

For these tormented souls, what binds them to earthly realities is the divine mission with which they believe they have been invested. They then expatiate with particular eloquence when it comes to convincing us of the benefits of cosmopolitanism and plural society in order to hasten the coming of the Messiah. The Peruvian novelist Mario Vargas Llosa illustrated this mission in a novel entitled *El Hablador*. The man, who never stops talking, succeeds in subjugating a people of miserable Indians in the Amazon jungle with his words, making them renounce their customs and traditions in order to follow the word of their new living God[610]. Naturally, by the end of the book we understand that Mario Vargas Llosa's imaginary character is part of the chosen people.

Incidentally, Marek Halter confirmed that "the talker or the man who talks" is nothing more nor less than the "prophet", in Hebrew "the *navi*, that is to say "the man who speaks[611]"." And once again, we are faced with another feature of hysteria: hysterics are "sufferers of the verb and… Their words have the particularity of being profuse, diffuse, symbolic in themselves, and their unconscious function is to prevent the symptom from being heard." In this case, however, the pathological dimension seems to us less explanatory than the political and eschatological dimension of Judaism.

---

[609] Jacques Attali, *Il viendra*, Fayard, 1994, p. 82.

[610] Hervé Ryssen, *Planetary Hopes*, (2022).

[611] Marek Halter, *La Force du Bien*, Robert Laffont, 1995, p. 67.

Indeed, the importance of proselytising in the Jewish mental universe is well known. This example illustrates quite well the idea that the Jewish people are first and foremost a militant people—or a people of "priests", as they themselves say, taking up the writings of the prophets. But unlike the other monotheistic religions that hope to convert other peoples to their own faith, Jewish proselytising is not aimed at converting the Goyim to the Hebrew religion. The whole process is to make them renounce their history, their traditions and their culture, but without giving them anything in return. The aim is to generalise the consumer society everywhere and to promote the emergence of the "open society" and multiracial society that is to prefigure the unified world that is confused, for the Jews, with the coming of the messianic times. This inexhaustible propaganda in favour of a plural society is thus both a religious action and the expression of an obsessive neurosis. It is what explains the continuous flow of literary and cinematographic production that permanently invades the bookshops and television screens of democratic societies.

The involvement and performance of the Jewish people are in any case profoundly moral, as Renée Neher explained: "This will to make morality prevail in the world … is our raison d'être… One day, people will realise that we do not want to harm anyone and that, on the contrary, we seek to improve ourselves[612]." Jacques Attali had also recalled the well-known moral rules of Judaism: "Impose a very austere morality, do not tolerate arrogance or immorality, so as not to create jealousy or pretexts for persecution[613]." Otto Weininger's words in *Sex and Character* come to mind here: "Hysterics … believe in their own sincerity and morality… The true causes of the disease show that their mendacity is organic. The more faithfully the hysterics believe themselves to be truthful, the more deeply their mendacity is rooted[614]."

As for the "prophetic delusions" characteristic of hysteria, we have observed that Jewish intellectuals, from Abravanel to Jacques Attali, present themselves as the great experts on the subject.

The parallel we have drawn with the Jewish people does not, of course, imply that every individual Jew is affected by the condition. We confine ourselves here only to pointing out the strange similarities between the thinking of Jewish intellectuals and neurosis, knowing that the available medical documentation is insufficient to give a complete

[612]Serge Moati, *La Haine antisémite*, Flammarion, 1991, p. 165.

[613]Jacques Attali, *Los Judíos, el mundo y el dinero*, Fondo de cultura económica, 2005, Buenos Aires, p. 490.

[614]Otto Weininger, *Sex and Character*, Ediciones 62 s|a Barcelona, 1985, p. 268, 269.

description of the extent of the disease among the Jewish people. As with suicide statistics, information on the subject is very difficult to obtain and, apparently, seems to be kept secret.

At the end of the 19th century, Dr Charcot had observed that this disease affected in greater proportion the population that had recently arrived from the ghettos of Poland and Russia: "The Semites have the privilege of representing to the highest degree all that neurosis can invent. It would be an interesting work to study the diseases of a race which has played so nefarious a part in the ancient world and up to the present day."

As can be seen, hysteria is not only the spasm-twisted madwoman of psychiatric imagery, but neurosis also involves organic symptoms that are part of what is called "somatic conversion". In Charcot's time, doctors observed that all these symptoms differed from physical illnesses in that they appeared suddenly and ceased capriciously, could be provoked or disappear after relevant or momentous events, and did not correspond to any detectable physical illness.

The somatic manifestations are very varied. The neurological conversions are observed first. Since Charcot, these are the most classic, although the more spectacular ones are now rarer. These include motor disorders: astasia-abasia (inability to stand even when leg movements are possible); paralysis of all types (one limb, hand, both legs, etc.); muscular contractures and abnormal movements, cramps, torticollis, facial dyskinesia, blepharospasm, etc. Sensory and sensory disorders are also noted: cutaneous anaesthesias of variable extent; localised hyperaesthesias; allergies, asthma, generalised urticaria. Visual disturbances may occur: blurred vision, blindness[615], narrowing of the field of vision, diplopia, etc.; hearing disorders, even deafness; frequent pain (headaches, back pain, neck pain, arthralgia, pelvic pain); speech disorders: transient aphonic periods, dysphonia, stammering, mumbling. There are also vegetative and digestive disorders: abdominal pains are frequent (spasms, vomiting, dyspnoea, oesophageal pains, constipation, etc.), as well as the famous "psychological pregnancy" (amenorrhoea, swelling of the abdomen and breasts). There are also vasomotor disorders (pallor, redness, hypersweating); eating disorders (anorexia, bulimia); sexual disorders (frigidity, dyspareunia, vaginismus), as well as the paroxysmal manifestations which are the famous "hysterical crises", often noisy and spectacular (fainting,

---

[615]In *Hollywood Ending* (2002), for example, Woody Allen plays the role of a neurotic, hypernervous Jewish director who suddenly goes blind during the shooting of his film. His psychoanalyst reassures him that it is only a temporary malady.

tetaniform crises, pseudo-crises of generalised epilepsy, nervousness).

In his book *Psychopathology of the Adult*, Quentin Debray particularly emphasised digestive function disorders: “Digestive function is the cause of many complaints: dysphagia and pharyngeal spasms, pain, colic, nausea, vomiting and abdominal swelling. Gynaecological symptoms are frequent, with dysmenorrhoea, irregular menstruation, dyspareunia and vaginismus. The classic case of psychological pregnancy, or pseudocyesis, with amenorrhoea (absence of menstruation), intestinal gas, nausea and breast swelling, is associated with hysteria.”

Imaginary or psychological pregnancy is a psychic phenomenon that triggers symptoms in a woman that are comparable to those of a real pregnancy. When a woman really desires a child, it can happen that she unconsciously forces her nature to such an extent that she actually feels pregnant. She is so convinced that she is pregnant that her inner balance is upset and she triggers the symptoms of a pregnant woman, but without the pregnancy: interruption of menstruation, nausea, painful breasts (sometimes caused by the actual absence of menstruation), vomiting, weight gain, etc. Therefore, the mere thought of becoming pregnant may be enough to delay menstruation and cause a psychological pregnancy. The same is true for older women who refuse to recognise that they are no longer capable of procreation.

All these clarifications were necessary to complete the clinical picture of hysteria. After all these considerations, we can admit that hysteria is not an easy thing. The symptoms, as we can see, present themselves in different ways depending on the individual. Moreover, in the context of this ethnopsychiatric study, it is important to observe general behaviour. It would therefore be useless to try to look for symptoms in each individual.

The idealisation of the father

It is now a question of understanding the causes of this strange phenomenon which has intrigued people since antiquity. Psychiatric analyses are more concise than the description of symptoms, but they always place the paternal function in the foreground.

The Oedipus complex, theorised by Sigmund Freud, is at the centre of diagnosis and all explanations. It postulates that the child’s first sexual affection is directed towards the parent of the opposite sex, while for the parent of the same sex the child develops feelings of hatred and rebellion. Under normal conditions, there exists between parent and child a reciprocal attachment, a natural feeling of community. In hysterics, this attachment is excessive towards one parent and the rejection of the other is violent. The idealisation of the father would thus be the main explanation for female hysteria.

At the origin of histrionic disorder, wrote psychiatrist Vittorio Lingiardi, we find "a serious lack of maternal care in early childhood". This early affective deprivation would lead the child to turn to the father to satisfy his affective needs. Excessive paternal idealisation may result." The mechanisms of idealisation and denial explain the cognitive behaviour of such persons: too general, non-specific, poor in detail, impressionistic. Incomplete retention of facts, their diffuse and imprecise evocation allow a simpler elimination of the aspects of reality that the individual does not want to see surface in consciousness."

Here and there, we read abruptly expressed that the hysterical subject "is a woman who fears being abandoned by her father[616]."

François Lelord mentioned that Freud saw the origin of evil in the incest and sexual touching that many of his patients confessed to him." Perhaps they relive a childhood situation in which they sought to attract the attention of a distant and idealised father? "

In his book *Hysteria, Madness and Psychosis*, the psychiatrist Michel Steyaert insisted on this paternal idealisation, endorsing Freud's thesis according to which, contrary to what all his hysterical patients claimed, there was no proven incest, but simply a desire for incest on the part of the hysterical woman." The patients we are talking about have badly resolved the Oedipus complex. Indeed, what prevails in the delirium of the (female) patients is a paternal problematic with a very clear and sometimes expressed desire to have the father's child. This fable of a past incestuous relationship, presented as real, for which the father would be guilty, is frequently observed in the clinical setting... These patients wish to have a child with the father they identify with an all-powerful man or a magician, or a powerful doctor, sometimes even God", wrote Michel Steyaert. The hysteric seeks "paternal substitutes among high-ranking personages, professors, idealised doctors, until the moment when real or phantasmatic sexual relations with them arise and bring down the whole edifice." Thus, the hysteric, "calling out to her, soliciting and unhinging the apparent teachers, priests and doctors" reduces these "one after another to impotence, while she keeps claiming

[616]Three films illustrate the hysterical phenomenon well: Elia Kazan's *A Streetcar Named Desire* (1951); Otto Preminger's *Angel Face* (1952); Jean Becker's *Murderous Summer* (1983).

more and more strongly for a man who is a real master[617]."

Let us recall at this point the words of David Banon on Jewish messianism: "The redemption promised at the end of time sustains a reality that is always beyond the existing, and which will therefore never be achieved… The Messiah is always the one who must one day come … but the one who finally appears can only be a false Messiah."

This analysis is consistent with what we have read elsewhere: "Whether she denies any need of the man, or whether she demonstrates, within a pathological relationship, the inability of her partner to make her enjoy it, the hysteric always presents herself as the one who will be disappointed, who will always deny the man his ability to fulfil her, that is to say, his virility[618]."

The professional's experience is irreplaceable here: "We always observe an intense eroticisation of the words and the relationship, be it through clothing, make-up, comments on the doctor's physique and imagined private life, and sometimes, some patients are even convinced that they are pregnant by their doctor." A few pages further on, the therapist noted something we have already seen: "Another symptom can manifest itself: it is psychological pregnancy, or delirious ideas of pregnancy or of staging a birth, symptoms which seem to us to translate in an exemplary way the father's desire to have a child."

At this point, however, the psychiatrist must recognise that the incestuous relationship may not only be the fruit of the patient's imagination, as Sigmund Freud had finally concluded. The Freudian explanation of the desire for incest on the part of the histrionic woman, which would thus absolve all paternal responsibility, is certainly insufficient: "We believe in fact that, in some cases, there may have been ambiguous attitudes on the part of the father during the patient's childhood… The families of these patients are often quite disturbed, and there are often family secrets, things that are not told. Often, "something" of the order of a drama that occurred in the previous generation reappears in the delirium: incest, illegitimate birth, marital disagreement and adultery of one of the parents (usually the father has a mistress of his daughter's age), for example. Sometimes there have also been sexual relations with a brother, a sister, a stepbrother, a stepsister[619]." Indeed, incest is at the basis of the oedipal problematic and of hysterical pathology.

---

[617]Michel Steyaert, *Hystérie, folie et psychose*, Éd. Les Empêcheurs de penser en rond, 1992, p. 60, 61.

[618]http://www.acpsy.com.

[619]Michel Steyaert, *Hystérie, folie et psychose*, 1992, p. 62, 69, 61, 66

The birth of psychoanalysis

By analysing the cases of young "hysterical" women, Sigmund Freud outlined the first theories that led, at the end of the 19th century, to the invention of psychoanalysis. This therapeutic method consists of exploring the patient's subconscious in order to bring to consciousness the initial trauma that generated the neurosis.

As early as 1893, Freud proposed that incest was at the origin of the pathology. Many of his patients, in fact, had told him that they had suffered sexual touching and incest during their childhood. They all claimed to have been seduced by their own father, or by an adult with parental authority. Later, in 1897, Freud wondered if these stories were not imaginary, if they were nothing more than female fantasies corresponding to "repressed oedipal conflicts."

Ernst Jones, Freud's official biographer, wrote: "From May 1893, when he first announced this to Fliess, until September 1897 … he held the view that the essential cause of hysteria is a sexual seduction of an innocent child by an adult, usually the father. The evidence of the analytical material seemed irrefutable. He held to this conviction for four years, although he was increasingly surprised at the frequency of these alleged episodes. It began to appear that, in a high proportion, fathers were the protagonists of such incestuous attacks. Worse still, they were usually episodes of a perverse nature, with the mouth or anus as the point of choice. From the existence of certain hysterical symptoms in his brother and in several of his sisters (not himself, mind you) he deduced that even his own father should be accused of such deeds[620]…" (letter to Fliess of 11 February 1897).

In September 1897, after her father's death at the end of October 1896, she abandoned the theory of "seduction" in favour of the theory of "fantasy": the hysterical woman had no longer suffered incest during her childhood, but it was she who fantasised about her father. The father was then absolved of all suspicion. From now on, one had to believe that the children were in love with their parents of the opposite sex and desired incestuous relations. Ernst Jones wrote here: "During the winter following his father's death (in February to be precise), Freud accused his father of acts of seduction and three months later (on 31 May 1897), he had a dream of incest which put an end to his doubts concerning the history of seduction[621]."

---

[620]Ernst Jones, *Life and Work of Sigmund Freud, Volume I*, Anagrama, 1981, Barcelona, p. 320, 321.

[621]Ernst Jones, *Vida y obra de Sigmund Freud, Volume I*, Anagrama, 1981, Barcelona,

"In letters dated 3, 4 and 15 October, Freud gave details of the progress of his analysis... He had already realised that his father was innocent and that he had projected onto him ideas of his own. Childhood memories of sexual desires towards his mother had arisen on the occasion of seeing her naked[622]."

Ernst Jones went on to write in support of Freud's thesis: "Freud had discovered the truth of the matter: that independently of incestuous desires of parents towards their children, and even of occasional acts of this kind, what was really at issue was the existence, in general, of incestuous desires of children towards their parents, and specifically towards the parent of the opposite sex... At that time Freud had not yet arrived, in fact, at the idea of infantile sexuality as it was later to be understood. The desires and fantasies of incest would be later products, probably to be found between the ages of 8 and 12, and which were referred to the past, concealing them behind the screen of early childhood. This is not where it would have originated. The most he would come to admit was that young children, even as young as 6 to 7 months (!) had the capacity to register and grasp, in a somewhat imperfect form, the meaning of the sexual acts of the parents they had come to witness or hear... To recognise and accept the great richness of infantile sexuality, which could manifest itself through active drives, constituted a further step which Freud, with his usual prudishness, only later took[623]."

So it was! Infantile sexuality and the "Oedipus complex" were born: the child feels a loving attachment to the parent of the opposite sex and secretly desires the death of the other who is his rival; and any human being must overcome this complex to reach true affective maturity. And for a hundred years, everyone fell into that trap! Except those, obviously, who knew Freud's true motivations, but who preferred to keep quiet about them in order not to reveal the great secret of the Jewish community to the general public. Freud had evidently been under strong pressure from his entourage and from eminent members of his community not to reveal the customs of the Jews. By inventing the theory of the "Oedipus complex", he concealed the reality of incest in Jewish families and excused Jewish fathers. And in the process he erased the trail, projecting this Jewish specificity onto the universal

p. 323 (censored page in pdf).

[622]Ernst Jones, *Life and Work of Sigmund Freud, Volume I,* Anagrama, 1981, Barcelona, p. 324.

[623]Ernst Jones, *Vida y obra de Sigmund Freud, Tomo I,* Anagrama, 1981, Barcelona, p. 321, 322, (censored pages in pdf).

plane through a Greek hero.

Incest in the Jewish tradition

The issue of incest is very present in Judaism. The Torah[624] relates several episodes. The daughters of Lot[625] (Abraham's nephew), for example, had made their father drunk and took advantage of his drunkenness to taste the pleasures of incest. After having satisfied the youngest, the patriarch had then slept with his eldest daughter. We know that the rabbis found excuses for Lot's daughters. According to them, by sleeping with their father, they had sacrificed themselves "for the good of mankind".

We also see in the Jewish Torah the example of Tamar, David's daughter, who slept with her own brother, Amnon. Once his passion was satiated, Amnon wanted to send her away, but Tamar threw herself at his feet: "Where would I go with my dishonour? And you would be one of the wicked of Israel. See, speak to the king, for surely he will not refuse to give me to you." But he would not listen to her, and, being stronger than she was, he did violence to her and threw himself down with her[626]."

The famous Yiddish novelist Isaac Bashevis Singer had also mentioned such practices: "Thus Jacob consorted with two sisters, and Judah lived with Tamar, his daughter-in-law, and Reuben raped the bed of Bala, his own father's concubine, and Hosea took a wife in a brothel, and so it was with all the others[627]."

In a book entitled *The Talmudic Sources of Psychoanalysis,* Gerard Haddad provided some information on the subject. The book of *Genesis*

---

[624]The spelling varies according to the authors. Thus, we can see it written as "Torah", "Torah" or "Thora", i.e. the five books of the Old Testament, called the Pentateuch: Genesis, Exodus, Leviticus, Numbers and Deuteronomy. But for Jews, "the word Torah encompasses both the Talmud and the five books of the Pentateuch." (Mark Zborowski, *Olam,* 1952, Plon, 1992, p. 100). The set of the 24 "canonical" books of Judaism is called the *Tanakh (TNK). TNK* is the acronym for *Torah* (Instruction, Law: The Pentateuch), *Nevi'im* (The Books of the Prophets) and *Ketuvim* (The Writings: Psalms, Proverbs, Lamentations, Daniel, etc.). This list of inspired Hebrew biblical books was definitively established in the second century CE by the consensus of a group of rabbis. The order of the books of the *Tanakh* is different from the order of the Old Testament according to the Christian canon (N.T.).

[625]*Genesis, XIX.*

[626]*Historical Books, Second Book of Samuel (II Samuel, 13).*

[627]Isaac Bashevis Singer, *The Destruction of Kreshev,* 1958, Folio, 1997, p. 64. Translation free PDF version, *The Destruction of Kreshev* p. 21.

provides another interesting testimony in the account of the marriage of Isaac and Rebekah: "Then Isaac brought her into his mother Sarah's tent, and took Rebekah, and she became his wife, and he loved her. Thus Isaac consoled himself for the death of his mother[628]." Here it could well be an ellipsis, for the Jews know how to read beyond omission; Isaac would have lain with his own mother.

Gerard Haddad stressed however that this practice was strictly forbidden for Jews, as stipulated in the Babylonian Talmud (*Mishnah, Yebamot, 2a*): "Fifteen categories of women exempt their rivals[629] and the rivals of their rivals and so on, ad infinitum, from *halizah*[630] and levirate marriage[631]; and these are: his daughter, his daughter's daughter and his son's daughter, his wife's daughter, his son's daughter and his daughter's daughter; his mother-in-law, his mother-in-law's mother and his father-in-law's mother, his maternal sister, his mother's sister, his wife's sister and his maternal brother's wife."

The author went on to say: "The notion of a preferential alliance with the daughter of the maternal uncle is nevertheless perceived in *Genesis*, where the patriarchs Isaac and Jacob practised this kind of union." But then he seemed to contradict what he had just written: "Even the Law par excellence, the "Ten Commandments" which shook the world to its foundations, does not enunciate the prohibition of the mother, nor even the slightest reference to incest[632]." Here is a new example of the "paradox" of the Jewish spirit.

According to the Talmud, the book of rabbinical interpretations, the revelation of the Ten Commandments may at first have disturbed the people of Israel: "During the absence of Moses," wrote Gerard Haddad, "the unspoken content of the Ten Commandments was made manifest to the Hebrews: renounce incest! However, according to the *Habbat* treatise, the marital relations of the Hebrews were more or less incestuous: hadn't the patriarch Abraham married his half-sister Sarah, and wasn't Moses the son of an incestuous relationship between aunt and nephew? Now suddenly the LORD was ordering the dissolution of all marriages present at Sinai." The Hebrews then gave themselves over

---

[628]*Genesis, XXIV, 67*

[629]When a husband has more than one wife, each wife is a rival in relation to the others.

[630]A provision called *halizah* whereby one or both parties may choose not to comply with the levirate marriage law, i.e. the marriage of a widow with no descendants to her brother-in-law.

[631]Any woman falling into the following fifteen categories is exempt from *yibum* (levirate marriage).

[632]Gérard Haddad, *Les Sources talmudiques de la psychanalyse*, Desclée de Brouwer, 1981, Poche, 1996, p. 261, 263.

to idolatry, leaving it to the next generation to better manage their alliances." This is the brilliant reading offered by the Talmud", wrote Gérard Haddad, who did not provide any further explanation, but if "the next generation" has the same meaning as "the coming year in Jerusalem", one might well think that these practices are still in force today, judging by the numerous allusions to the subject made by Jewish intellectuals.

David Bakan explained the reasons for the frequency of incest in Eastern European Jewish communities: "Because of their endogamy, the problem of incest was characteristically prevalent in Jewish communities, so that the role of Jewish mysticism (i.e. Hasidism) was partly to provide the means of coping with the intense feelings of guilt arising from incestuous desires... Incestuous temptations are perhaps, as Freud indicates, universally widespread, but they were especially marked in Jews, which prompted the elaboration of intense countermeasures and, consequently, an excessive feeling of guilt[633]."

David Bakan pointed out that "the intensity of the incestuous temptation" lay in the fact that the Jews of the Eastern European shtetls intermarried only among themselves. And since they generally lived in small communities, the choice of a spouse was extremely limited[634]." Recall that, in the Oedipus legend, incest is the consequence of an unforeseeable event that had separated the protagonists, so that they did not recognise each other once they reached adulthood. The main reason for the traditional arrangement of marriages by the elders of the Jewish community perhaps lies in the fact that the elders possessed the essential information about the degrees of kinship. Likewise, the custom of early marriages was perhaps justified, not only by the reality of the sexual impulses that existed in the Jews, but also by the need to alleviate incestuous tendencies."

In *Sex and Character*, Otto Weininger wrote at the beginning of the twentieth century, confirming this tradition: "Only the Jews are true matchmakers, and indeed, interventions of this kind are most widespread among the Semites. It is true that such mediations are very necessary in Judaism, for, as we have already pointed out elsewhere, in no other people on earth are so few love marriages to be found... The third degree is an organic predisposition of the Jew, and this assumption finds new support in the fact that the Jewish rabbis willingly engage in speculation on the problems of multiplication and know a verbal

[633]David Bakan, *Freud et la tradition mystique juive*, 1963, Payot, 2001.

[634]R. Landes and M. Zborowski, *Hypotheses concerning the Eastern European Family*, Psychiatry, 1950, p. 447–464.

tradition about the procreation of children[635]."

The early marriages mentioned by David Bakan are sometimes found in literature. Isaac Bashevis Singer's novel, *The Slave*, gave an insight into such marriage practices: "Jacob himself was but twelve years old when he was betrothed to Zelda Leah, who was two years younger than himself and the daughter of the dean of the community[636]."

"Usually you get married before the twentieth year, but it is not uncommon after the tenth year[637]", confirmed Mark Zborowski.

This is another testimony provided by the great historian of anti-Semitism, Leon Poliakov. He was referring to the expulsion of the Jews from Spain in 1492. The adversity was then compared to the departure from Egypt: "In a few months, the Jews sold everything they could... Before leaving, they married among themselves all their children over the age of twelve, so that every girl was accompanied by a husband[638]."

In his novel, *When Israel Loved*, Pierre Paraf confirmed this information. The story took place in November 1776 (Adar 5536): "The Bella Sultana is approaching the port of Marseilles. Tomorrow I embark for Djebel-Al-Tarik. My little Sara, in a month's time we will celebrate our wedding... For your fourteenth birthday, we will return to France[639]."

In *Satan in Goray*, the writer Isaac Bashevis Singer described the communities of 17th century Polish Jews: "On the days between the

[635]Otto Weininger, *Sexo y Carácter*, Ediciones 62 s|a Barcelona, 1985, p. 307. Mark Zborowski is quite discreet about the role of this tertiary: "The *shadkhn*", he wrote, is a "considerable character... His little worn-out book in which information about the parties worthy of the name is written is the yearbook of the shtetl's high society. Whether he confines himself to a single shtetl or his talents take him from town to town, the *shadkhn* retains and memorises the rumours and information that make him a welcome but somewhat feared guest. Two families, though very close, will require his services to arrange a marriage." (Mark Zborowski, *Olam*, 1952, Plon, 1992, p. 257).

[636]Isaac Bashevis Singer, *The Slave*, 1962, Epublibre, digital publisher German25 (2014), p. 155.

[637]Mark Zborowski, *Olam*, 1952, Plon, 1992, p. 261.

[638]Léon Poliakov, *Histoire de l'antisémitisme, Tome I*, 1981, Points Seuil, 1990, p. 170. [Also from Spain comes the distant echo of the same problem. In 653, the Visigoth king Recesvinto promulgated the *Liber Iudiciorum*, by which he obliged the Jews of the kingdom to "promise voluntarily and in peace not to commit any more incest in the Jewish fashion, not to be circumcised, not to celebrate the Sabbath or the Jewish Passover, to marry Christians and to observe Christian rites on feasts and at marriages." *Liber Iudiciorum*, Liber XII, II. VIII Council of Toledo. Although the anti-Jewish persecution in Visigothic Hispania during the 7th century, so unique, so precarious and so fierce in medieval Europe, is well known].

[639]Pierre Paraf, *Quand Israël aima*, 1929, Les Belles Lettres, 2000, p. 71.

holidays, marriage contracts were drawn up and good luck dishes were broken in every house where there was a girl over the age of eight[640]."

Gerard Haddad gave us here a new example of the ambivalence and duplicity that seem to be definitively constitutive of Judaism when he wrote of the "ambiguity of the word *hessed*": "Etymologically this term means 'incest'. But it also commonly designates a kindly act, grace and, by extension, religious piety. The *Hassid* is a very pious man—a term chosen by Baal Shem Tov to christen his famous sect [Hassidism, Hasidism]—but literally its meaning would be 'incestuous'." The origin of this misunderstanding is explained by the Babylonian Talmud (*Yebamot, 15b*): "The Torah insists on the defence of incest lest it be assumed otherwise since Cain and Abel married their sisters. The text thus contains the word *hessed* which commonly means "grace". It was a grace given by the Creator to the first humans to thus unite and populate the world[641]."

In his book on *Jewish Messianism*, Gershom Scholem confirmed that the Jewish Kabbalists played with this ambivalence in order to interpret the law in their own way: "The *Tikunei haZohar*[642], for example, state (*Tikkun, 69*): 'On high (i.e. in heaven), there are no longer any laws of incest'." Another reference generally cited in support of that belief is, *Leviticus, XX, 17* (a text devoted almost entirely to the enumeration of incestuous transgressions): "If anyone takes his sister, his father's daughter or his mother's daughter, to wife, seeing her nakedness and her his nakedness, it is an ignominy." But Gershom Scholem added: "The Hebrew word used here for "ignominy", *hessed,* is the same word we usually see in the Bible with the sense of "tenderness"[643]."

Gershom Scholem recalled that the Jews belonging to the heretical sect of the Sabbateans had adopted as a line of conduct to systematically violate all the prohibitions of the Torah. At the time of fulfilling a

---

[640]Isaac Bashevis Singer, *Satan in Goray,* PDF, Digital publisher Epublibre, German25, 2017, p. 82

[641]Gérard Haddad, *Les Sources talmudiques de la psychanalyse,* Desclée de Brouwer, 1981, Poche, 1996, p. 265.

[642]Also known as the *Tikkunim,* it is a major text of Kabbalah. It is a separate appendix to the Zohar consisting of seventy commentaries on the opening word of the Torah, *Bereishit,* in a Kabbalistic Midrash style. It contains profound secret Torah teachings, moving dialogues and fervent prayers. The explicit and apparent theme and intention of the *Tikunei haZohar* is to repair and support the Shechinah or Malchut—hence its name, "Repairs of the Zohar"—and to bring about the Redemption and conclude the Exile. (NdT).

[643]Gershom Scholem, *Le Messianisme juif,* 1971, Calmann-Lévy, 1974, p. 179.

mitzvah[644], for example, the pious Jew was supposed to pronounce a blessing. But, "according to the new Messianic formulation inaugurated by the Shabtai Tzvi himself, he was now to say: 'Praise be to the Eternal God, Who permits that which is forbidden'".

And Scholem further recalled: "The most serious case in this matter was that of a certain Baruchia Russo, who about 1700 was the head of the radical wing of the Sabbateans of Salonica." Of the "thirty-six prohibitions which are liable to the punishment "of extirpation of the soul[645]", and which we find in the Torah (*Leviticus, 18*), "half of them concern the prohibitions relating to incest. Baruchia was not content merely to declare the abrogation of these prohibitions; he went so far as to make what they proscribed into the positive precepts of the new messianic Torah[646]."

Thus, we now understand better what David Bakan meant when he wrote very discreetly: "The role of Jewish mysticism (i.e. Hasidism) consisted in part in providing the means to cope with the intense feelings of guilt arising from incestuous desires." Thus, what is a priori forbidden in the Torah, gives rise to equivocal interpretations in Talmudic Jews, but is licit in Hasidic Jews and even an obligation for Sabbateans.

Incest: a burning issue in Judaism

There are, as far as we know, no studies on the frequency of incest in contemporary Judaism; if they exist, they are clearly not available to the public. Nevertheless, it is a crucial point that allows us to see what was the origin of the elaboration of the "Oedipus complex" and of Freudian psychoanalysis.

The question of incest is indeed a burning issue among Jewish intellectuals. Direct testimonies are rather scarce, since those concerned are very discreet about it and very few incest victims denounce their own parents. But if we read Jews with a mirror, we realise that this problem is an obsession in the cultural production of Judaism. Jewish intellectuals and filmmakers talk about it in a very secretive, anecdotal way, or by projecting the problem on a universal level, through goyim families. We know that the Jewish people love mystery and secrets, and

---

[644]A Mitzvah (Mitzvot, plural): one of the 613 commandments of Jewish Law.

[645]This is the controversial penalty of Karet, extirpation of the soul, supreme punishment, capital punishment.

[646]Gershom Scholem, *Le Messianisme juif*, 1971, Calmann-Lévy, 1974, p. 135-137. (See translator's note in Annex VI. 3).

incest is precisely one of those secrets, if not "THE" secret of Judaism.

Jacques Attali talks about incest ambiguously in at least four of his books. His first novel, *Eternal Life (*1989) is terribly boring. It is a science fiction story about a "small village" living in the cosmos[647]. The heroine's name is Golischa and she never knew her father: "One day, she even heard one of her servants assure her in restricted circles that her grandfather was also her father, which explained the mother's prostration and the daughter's seclusion." In short, her grandfather had slept with his own daughter.

In his novel, *The First Day After Me,* published in 1990, Jacques Attali recounted the sight of a recently deceased man who imagined he was still alive. Curiously, he always uses capital letters when he refers to "She"; and we never know whether he is referring to his mother or his lover.

The question is also alluded to in a passage from his 1994 futuristic and apocalyptic novel, *He Will Come* (he was evidently referring to the Jewish Messiah), which we have already mentioned in *Planetary Hopes* and *Jewish Fanaticism.* In it, Jacques Attali portrayed a man named Mortimer, overwhelmed by prophetic delusions and anguished by the question of whether his son could be the prophet Elijah himself, come to announce to the Jews the imminent coming of the Messiah. In an apocalyptic atmosphere, Mortimer then set off with him to Jerusalem to consult with some rabbis. He ended up meeting with them in a crypt, "just below the entrance to what had been the Holy of Holies of the second Temple, just where it had been more than two thousand years ago[648]." There, rabbis intrigued by the phenomenon were discussing the case of the young prodigy.

Here is the end of an astonishing dialogue: "According to you, even sexual taboos will be abolished," smiled Mortimer. — Absolutely," said Nahman. — Even incest, Mortimer dared to ask. — You blaspheme, Nahman!, shouted MHRL, preventing the young rabbi from answering[649]." Apparently, there are things that should not be revealed to the general public[650].

The philosopher Alain Finkielkraut made some confidences in *The*

---

[647] Read in Hervé Ryssen, *Jewish Fanaticism, (*2022).

[648]Hervé Ryssen, *Planetary Hopes, (*2022) *and* Jacques Attali, *Il viendra*, p. 82.

[649]Jacques Attali, *Il viendra*, p. 264. The Hebrew alphabet contains only consonants. That is why Cohen, Kun, Kahn, Caen or Cohn, for example, are the same surname and designate "priest" in Hebrew.

[650]"Anyone who confesses Israel's secrets to non-Jews must be killed before he reveals anything to them". (Talmud, *Choschen Hamm, 386, 10*).

Imaginary Jew (1980): "Today, more than ever, one is Jewish because of one's mother". A little more elliptically, Finkielkraut was a little more suggestive in another passage; our readers will know how to decipher the coded phrases: "The Jewish mother ... allows herself to be in love with her little baby or babies. Without fuss ... the "stay with us", the "be mine" expressed by maternal need becomes a "be true to your origins", and this invaluable nuance blows up the prohibition and legitimises possessiveness[651]." We see perfectly what kind of "prohibitions" Jewish parents "blow up". Alain Finkielkraut, like many of his peers, had felt the need to consult a psychoanalyst: "Out of exasperation or discouragement, I have at times even faltered and offered my Jewishness to psychoanalysis... Fascinated by his [his parents'] Jewish identity, I succumbed to his neurosis... My fears and my problems were probably born of our delirious intimacy[652]." Finkielkraut himself wrote at the end of his book: "Hysterical, I had been a Jew in order to be noticed".

The famous American novelist Philip Roth also "let himself go" in *Portnoy's Evil (*1967)[653]. In his novel *The Devil in the Head (*1984), the philosopher Bernard-Henri Levy had one of his characters say: "I promise myself that when I grow up I will wake up my sweet mother, like a "Prince Charming" with his beauty; marry her if necessary, make her other children. I have no doubt that I, Benjamin, will know how to appease her mysterious torment[654]."

The writer Romain Gary was also troubled by this question, which he touched on in several of his novels[655]. In an article in the weekly *Le Point* of 2 December 2010, a journalist from the EU haloed this supposed "great genius" of French literature. Here is what one could read: "Erika, the schizophrenic from *Europa* [a novel by Romain "Gary"] is betrayed by fate, which makes her the daughter of her lover. She ends up committing suicide in a white dress."

Read also what the "great" Elie Wiesel wrote, in *Talmudic Celebration* (1991): "A woman wanted to consult Rabbi Eliezer about

---

[651]Alain Finkielkraut, *Le Juif imaginaire,* 1980, Points Seuil, 1983, p. 128-130.

[652]Alain Finkielkraut, *Le Juif imaginaire,* 1980, Points Seuil, 1983, p. 136-138.

[653]On *Portnoy's Evil,* see Hervé Ryssen, *Jewish Fanaticism*

[654]Bernard-Henri Lévy, *Le Diable en tête,* Grasset, 1984, p. 460. [We can also mention here Albert Cohen's novel, *My Mother's Book,* which is a hyperbolic homage to his mother; a book "which has been said to be the most beautiful love novel ever written, a hallucinatory *tour de force* presided over by the intensity of a feeling that overflows in each of its pages." In Albert Cohen, *El libro de mi madre,* Anagrama, Barcelona, 1992, 1999, publisher's back cover].

[655]On Romain "Gary" read Hervé Ryssen, *Jewish Fanaticism.*

a serious problem, but he refused to help her, so she went to Rabbi Yeoshua, who was more benevolent. She then turned to Rabbi Yeoshua, who was more benevolent. What was the problem? *B'ni hakatan mibni hagadol*, my younger son has my older son for a father... Jewish mothers are always to blame for what happens to their beloved children." And Wiesel elliptically added: "As a good Jew, he loved his mother a little too much[656]."

The incestuous relations between father and daughter were sung by the famous Serge Gainsbourg, a Russian-born Jew, who recorded a song entitled *Lemon Incest* in 1984. In the video clip, Gainsbourg posed on a bed with his young daughter Charlotte. The words and images are totally ambiguous, so probably only Jews really understood the message of the song.

Barbara was a well-known French singer. After her death in November 1977, we learned that the Hungarian-born Jewess had had incestuous relations with her father. The secret was kept hidden for many years, but she confessed it between the lines on stage for those who could listen. He alluded to it in at least four of his songs." I've always thought that the most beautiful loves were incestuous loves[657]", he would declare.

The journalist Claude Sarraute, daughter of the novelist Nathalie Sarraute (born Tcherniak), a Russian-born Jew, made a confession in an interview in 2009: "My father caressed me everywhere. I was almost raped by one of his best friends who had the same taste for little girls. I liked my father, but the other one was drunk and scared me a lot."

Let us note that in incest, violence is not indispensable for the violation of the girl by the father. Through acts of tenderness, the father can arouse his daughter's consent to have sexual relations with him[658].

In January 2011, the writer Christine Angot published her new novel, entitled *Les Petits (The Children)*; and since she is part of the community, all the press had rushed to talk about it. This was the story: Helena is a white woman who has just separated from her daughter's father, a white male bastard who has just abused the child. This white woman falls in love with Billy, a very nice musician from the West Indies. The two go to live on an island and have four children, beautiful

[656]Elie Wiesel, *Célébration talmudique*, Éd. Seuil, 1991, p. 12, 182–191, and in *Jewish Fanaticism.*

[657]About Barbara: Hervé Ryssen, *Le Miroir du Judaísme (The Mirror of Judaism)*, Baskerville, 2009.

[658]Jacques-Dominique de Lannoy, *L'Inceste*, Presses Universitaires de France, 1992, p. 96, 110.

mestizos who will probably grow up to be police commissioners, as in American films and series... Here again we see that Jewish intellectuals seem to be obsessed with the miscegenation of the white race. We also note the typical accusatory inversion so specific to Judaism: the novelist, born Schwartz, who had confessed to having had incestuous relations with her father, projected her guilt in this novel onto the goy, the White bastard, guilty of all the evils of the earth.

Gaspar Noé's film *Alone Against All* (France, 1998) is a good example of accusatory inversion. The story tells the life of a fifty-year-old unemployed butcher, recently released from prison, who arrives in Paris after having beaten up his pregnant wife. He has a daughter, but she lives in a social home. This monster, who loves his daughter out of incestuous love, is not a Jew: he is a disgusting, fascist, racist and homophobic guy!

In his famous film *Chinatown (*USA, 1974), Roman Polansky also projected the problem onto a goy family. At the end of the film, the beautiful Faye Dunaway, slapped by Jack Nicholson, finally confessed that the young girl she was hiding from everyone was both her daughter and her sister. She had a child with her monster of a father, the big landowner. We know that Roman Polansky has been convicted in the United States for paedophilia.

The twentieth episode of the third season of the series *Without a Trace* is entitled *The Boogeyman.* It tells the story of a young man suspected, seven years earlier, of the murder of his girlfriend, the daughter of a Protestant pastor. Elle was thirteen at the time and he was seventeen. The investigation, which had not solved the case, is reopened when another thirteen-year-old girl also disappears. Finally, the police investigation determines that it was the pastor who had murdered his own daughter after raping her. Here is a typically Jewish script; the guilt is here shifted onto abhorred Christianity. The screenwriter, Jennifer Levine, was apparently very concerned about incest, which she projected onto a Christian family.

Robert Zemeckis' famous film *Back to the Future (*USA, 1985) is a story in which we also see the theme of incest, as the mother of the protagonist falls in love with her son. The synopsis of the film reads: "Marty McFly is projected into the past. His mother falls in love with him and takes care of him after an accident. Marty replaced his father who had met his mother precisely in that accident (this is a variant of the grandfather paradox or Oedipus complex)."

In the film *War Zone* (Great Britain, 1999) by the famous Tim Roth, the hero, Tom, discovers the incestuous relationship between his father and sister. The horror ends when Tom and his sister stab their father. Tim Roth confesses to having been sexually abused by his father.

Another great example is Thomas Vinterberg's film *Festen* (Denmark, 1998). In it, incest (accusatory inversion) and the apology of miscegenation (only for the goyim) are present: to celebrate his sixtieth birthday, a father gathers all his relatives and friends. His three daughters are there: Miguel, the youngest, alcoholic and ill-fated; Helena, a wild girl who shows up with her partner—a Negro; and Cristian, the eldest, who is still suffering from the suicide of his twin sister. At the birthday toast, Cristian will reveal a terrible secret in front of the whole family: the incestuous relationships to which his father subjected him.

Incidentally, we also hope one day to find out what really happened between Franz Kafka and his father… But the best thing is this: in John Carpenter's cult film *Invasion Los Angeles (They Live,* USA, 1988), we see the hero, Nada, who has been the victim of an abusive father, discover thanks to special sunglasses that part of the population is made up of aliens who have a human appearance. They form an elite that rules the world through lies!

In our books *Jewish Fanaticism (*2007) and especially in *The Mirror of Judaism* (2009), we have presented many more examples, classifying them by chapter: between a father and his daughter, between a father and his son, between a mother and her son, between brothers and sisters.

But let us take the example of Jonathan Littell, who won the Goncourt Prize in 2006 for his novel *The Benevolent Ones*. The hero is a homosexual SS officer madly in love with his twin sister Una[659].

The *Nouvel Observateur* journalist Colette Mainguy also projected her neurosis onto the Nazis. In 2001, she published her novel *The Jewess*. On the back cover one could read: "I have rediscovered my Jewishness after five years of psychoanalysis. For so long I had been having recurring Germanic dreams. The Germans are after me. They machine-gun me… I make fellatio to Nazis, the Gestapo knocks on my door. I always run away… One night, I confront my sister Beth. She is the head of the Gestapo in a concentration camp."

See also the film *Scarface* (USA, 1932): it is the story of a gangster in love with his sister. The film is by the prolific filmmaker Howard Hawks, with a screenplay by the no less prolific Ben Hecht[660] and Seton

---

[659]See Hervé Ryssen, *Jewish Fanaticism.*

[660]Called "the Shakespeare of Hollywood". The *Dictionary of Literary Biography-American Screenwriters* calls him "one of the most successful film screenwriters in the

Miller. In 1983, Brian de Palma made another version. In *Kika* (Spain, 1993), a comedy by Pedro Almodóvar, the brother is a compulsive rapist who abused his sister for a long time.

The Yiddish novelist Isaac Bashevis Singer, who received the Nobel Prize for literature in 1978, frequently spoke of incest in his novels: father and daughter, mother and son, brother and sister[661].

Here is a fortuitous example that we discovered while browsing through books at the Fnac Montparnasse. In a striking work entitled *Nazism and the Holocaust, a psychoanalytical approach* (Hermann, 2010), the author Jean-Gérard Bursztein made a confession in the mirror. Indeed, on page 52 we read: "The Nazi myth represented the possibility of reconsidering the rupture between nature and culture, i.e. the prohibition of incest, hence its success. Indeed, because of its codified Oedipal content, this Nazi myth represented, for all those Germans trapped in collective hysteria, the possibility of making their incestuous fantasies come true through their actions, of reconsidering this prohibition of incest." This Jean-Gérard Bursztein, like many of his peers, had obviously been abused by his father as a child, before being comforted in his mother's bed. He was clearly projecting on a universal level something that really only concerns Jews.

Readers of the *Mirror of Judaism* are already familiar with Daniel Zimmermann, the author of a book beautifully entitled *The Year of the World (*1997). Daniel Zimmermann told the story of life in the "death camps" through a novel character. The book gave a fairly comprehensive overview of all the atrocities committed by the Nazis in the concentration camps, in this case Auschwitz and Treblinka. We read, for example, how one prisoner is crucified "like a butterfly" while Dr. Mengele "sticks syringes into babies' chests", collects Jewish brains in jars of formaldehyde and uses shrunken Jewish heads as paperweights, in the style of American Indian villages. Another prisoner has his genitals torn off by a German shepherd; SS women are beaten to death by "Muslims"… In short, a horror! There is also the scene of the giant barbecue." François", the hero, stokes the fire of the funeral pyre by pouring melted fat over the bodies, as if it were a leg of lamb in the oven!

The stunned reader witnesses atrocious scenes, very common in holocaust literature, in which we can see SS blowing babies' heads

history of cinema". Ben Hecht was also a staunch Zionist activist, a member of the Bergson Group, an Irgun front group in the United States dedicated to raising funds for Irgun (Zionist paramilitary organisation) activities and disseminating its propaganda.

[661]Read in Hervé Ryssen, *Le Mirroir du Judaísme*, Baskerville, 2009, p. 319, 329, 338.

against the walls, or throwing them alive into the coals. Obviously, we do not believe a single word of what Daniel Zimmermann says. On the contrary, we think that he is a mentally ill person with a delusional imagination.

Perhaps there is much truth in this maxim of Cyrano de Bergerac's[662]: "Wherever memory is strong, imagination diminishes; and the latter becomes greater as the other diminishes." Now, we know that the Jews have an overflowing, not to say feverish, even frankly unhealthy imagination. It is no accident that they were the founders of Hollywood and that they are still so influential in the film industry today. Jewish intellectuals talk a lot about "memory". We suspected as much, but now, thanks to Cyrano de Bergerac, we are sure that it is because they have none. In any case, there is no doubt that for many Jews historical truth is of far less importance than the myths created by prophets, fabulists and novelists.

The "Zimmermann case" confirms our analysis. A decade earlier, in 1987, Daniel Zimmermann had already felt the need to elaborate on the question of incest. In his novel *The Bobo (Le Gogol) he* projected his own guilt onto a goy to whom he gave a Breton name. This is what one could read on the back cover: "Is this Patrick a poor boy, nicknamed "The Bobo" because he is supposed to be an idiot? He is ugly, he smells bad, he is said to be martyred by his father, and he is the scapegoat of his classmates and his teachers. Only a specialised teacher dedicated to socially excluded people protects him, but this fake retard is superbly intelligent! He does not bear his fate passively, he manufactures it. He turns situations and institutions to his advantage, dominates his teacher, conquers his mother and plays with his father by controlling him as he pleases. Will Oedipus in Savigny-sur-Orge manage to escape punishment? With uncompromising audacity, Daniel Zimmermann, who has long been a teacher of maladjusted children, takes the great myths to the suburbs to subvert them. Violent, cruel, this text is also the beautiful and naive story of an extraordinary love."

From the first page, we see the obvious role reversal: "Cornered against the façade of the Jules Ferry school, Patrick Leguern faces the pack of his fellow students. Breathless, sweaty, he fights back tooth and nail, with insults, spit and potatoes. David Kupfermann, [the teacher] watches the lynching from afar."

The text is of glaring literary mediocrity, which is not surprising coming from a Jewish intellectual. One of the chapters was entitled

---

[662]Cyrano de Bergerac (1619–1655) was a French poet, playwright and thinker, contemporary of Boileau and Molière.

"The Brother-Son". The "daft" Patrick Leguern grew up and we learned that he had impregnated his own mother. As chance would have it, her name was "Maria": "Maria wasn't thinking of hanging herself, she was knitting a basket. Seven months pregnant, her belly was huge. Patrick was proud, a big boy, her brother-son. Mary smiled indulgently[663]."

At the end of the book, another chapter read: "The brother-father", and the next: "The lover-mother". Patrick and his mother were moving house and had two children. The novel ended with these words: "When they walked together hand in hand, passers-by followed them with an amused look—happiness also exists for ugly people—though a little critical, for because of the age difference she could have been his mother."

Another clever little Jewish feather duster invited us to "decode" the message. In his 2006 essay, originally entitled *On Anti-Semitism*, Stephane Zagdanski wrote: "To decode: they selfishly indulge in the dark pleasures of incest to which we have been denied access. It must be understood that the anti-Semite is very concerned about incest, which is logical, since he suffers from a deficiency of his limits[664]." Two pages later, Zagdanski had an imaginary anti-Semitic character say: "The joy of the Jews is strange to us. This private joy is taboo, that's why they forbid it to us! They are the taboo incarnate of incest for they enjoy that which we desire in vain[665]."

Incest and paedophilia

The close links between incest and paedophilia are well known. According to some statistics, almost all adults who commit such abuse would do so within their own family. In addition, about half of them would also abuse children outside their own family environment, and 19% would also commit rape on adult women.

We can recall here how filmmaker Roman Polanski had to flee the United States in 1977, after having drugged and sodomised a 13-year-old girl he had invited to his house for a photo shoot when he was 43

[663]Daniel Zimmermann, *Le Gogol*, Le Cherche midi, 1987, p. 149

[664]The terms "Jew" and "anti-Semite" must be interchanged to get the correct meaning of the phrase.

[665]Stéphane Zagdanski, *De l'Antisémitisme*, Climats, 1995, 2006, p. 206, 208. We also read in this essay: ""Y" is an ashamed, fat, and supernaturally stupid Jew, persuaded to be a genius by his incestuous mother from his earliest childhood." (page 267)." The letter Yod (Y) usually designates a Jew", wrote David Bakan, in *Freud et la tradition mystique juive*, 1963, Payot, 2001, p. 65.

years old. After getting her drunk and administering a strong sedative, and after checking her rules, he raped her, sodomising her twice in a row despite the girl's protests. He faced up to 50 years in prison, but his lawyer had reached a deal with the judge and, in August 1977, the director of *Rosemary's Baby* had agreed to plead guilty to "unlawful sexual intercourse" to escape the maximum sentence. But the trial did not go as he had hoped, and he eventually decided not to attend the second session. Although he was free on bail, he travelled to London before taking refuge in France, the country of which he had become a citizen a year earlier. The US justice system tried in vain for years to arrest him during his travels abroad. Finally, on 27 September 2009, thirty-two years after the events, Roman Polanski was arrested in Zurich while on his way to a film festival to receive an honorary award for his entire career. Very quickly, he received the support of a hundred representatives of the French and international political and artistic world. And again, as if by chance, the list included mainly members of his community. In France, all the Jewish intellectuals had leapt to the fore to defend the paedophile as one man: Bernard-Henri Levy, Claude Lelouch, Pedro Almodóvar, Woody Allen, Constantine Costa-Gavras, Alain Finkielkraut, and so on. Minister Frederic Mitterrand was also affected by the paedophile's fate, as he himself had recounted his sexual adventures in Thailand in a book in 2005. A month later, Polanski was released on bail. In July 2010, the Swiss justice minister decided not to extradite him to the United States, and Polanski was soon released. All those stars and intellectuals who only talked about "human rights" were now defending a criminal, just because he was a member of their little sect.

In France, other well-known personalities, such as Daniel Cohn-Bendit, former student leader of May '68, or the cultural animator Michel Polac, for example, had defended paedophilia in their books. A journalist for television and radio, film-maker and writer, Michel Polac had his hour of glory on the television programme "*Droit de réponse*" in the 1980s. In his *Diary*, published in 2000, he dared to confess that he had had a sexual relationship in his forties with a boy "who must have been 10 or 11 years old, maybe younger."

The former Minister of Culture, Jack Lang, regularly gave interviews in the newspaper *Gai Pied Hebdo*, a homosexual magazine that was on the borderline of legality by promoting paedophilia. In *Gai Pied Hebdo* of 31 January 1991, we read, for example: "Childish sexuality is still a forbidden continent. It will be up to the discoverers of the 21st century to tackle its shores." Today, lovers of such practices are somewhat more discreet.

In September 2009, Jacques Asline, the former director of the 8 p.m. news on TF1, committed suicide in Suresnes by throwing himself on the train tracks. He had been placed under judicial supervision and had been under investigation since January for possession and consumption of child pornography. The 60-year-old was a close friend of the star TF1 news anchor Patrick Poivre d'Arvor.

Although these paedophile practices seem to be more strongly condemned nowadays, this was apparently not the case in the 1970s, at a time when the rise of Freudo-Marxist philosophy and the "sexual liberation of manners" were in full swing, and were the standard-bearers of the ideals of revolt of the youth against society[666]. The newspaper *Le Monde*, for example, had published on 26 January 1977 a manifesto calling for the release of three individuals convicted of paedophilia. This was what could be read: "We consider that there is a manifest disproportion between, on the one hand, the qualification of "crime" which justifies such severity of the sentence and the nature of the acts reproached; and, on the other hand, between the antiquated law and the daily reality of a society which tends to recognise in children and adolescents the existence of a sexual life (Why does a thirteen year old girl have the right to the abortion pill?)[667]." This manifesto was supported by several personalities, including Louis Aragon, Roland Barthes, Simone de Beauvoir, Gilles and Fanny Deleuze, Gilles and Fanny Deleuze, André Glucksmann, Felix Guattari, Bernard Kouchner, Jack Lang, Jean-Paul Sartre, Philippe Sollers, etc. Although all the signatories were not Jewish, they nevertheless represented a significant proportion that could only be explained by the weight of tradition.

In 1978, Trotskyist militants (Communist Committees for Self-Management) published and distributed in Paris a pamphlet with the explicit title: *Homosexuality and paedophilia*, in "*éditions La Commune*". This pamphlet argued that homosexuality and paedophilia were related and that it was necessary to "eliminate prejudices" in this respect. It also informed us that the situation of paedophiles in the developed societies of the West resembled "slavery" and that "those in love with children were victims of genocide, i.e. mass destruction." Paedophilia was considered revolutionary because "the practice of love with children is a permanent challenge to the authority of the family and constitutes a transgression of the dominant social relations." We also know that the leaders of the Trotskyist movement are all Jews,

[666]Hervé Ryssen, *Planetary Hopes, (*2022).

[667]http://www.unification.net/french/misc/hom.html

regardless of the parish in which they preach[668].

In February 1981, in issue 114 of *L'Étincelle*, the internal bulletin of the Revolutionary Communist League, a motion called for "the suppression of all laws repressing reciprocally consensual adult-child relations and thus the suppression of the notion of the age of sexual majority." The individual at the centre of this politically rotten operation was a self-confessed bisexual called Boris Fraenkel. In 1995, he had a brief media notoriety when he revealed that he had been a "liaison agent" for Lionel Jospin, the candidate in the 2002 presidential election, during the period when the latter was a Trotskyist infiltrator in the Socialist Party apparatus. In the 1960s, Boris Fraenkle was one of the first activists in France in favour of homosexuality and sexual freedom. A collaborator of the editor François Maspero, the latter also later a militant in the Revolutionary Communist League, he wrote for the magazine *Partisans* and translated into French the works of Wihelm Reich[669]. In 1967, he organised a conference at the University of Nanterre entitled "Youth and sexuality", which had a great impact and is still generally regarded today as a forerunner of the May '68 revolution.

The publisher François Maspero edited the books of Daniel Guérin, who in the late 1930s had been a very close collaborator of Leon Trotsky with whom he had maintained a long and famous correspondence. Daniel Guérin published some landmark books on that political movement, such as *Fascism and Big Business.* One of his articles, published in issue 39 of *L'Étincelle*, was entitled "The workers' movement and homosexuality." In issue 4 of another publication, *Marge* (November 1974), his article was entitled: "For the right to love a minor". The same Daniel Guérin was in 1971 one of the founders of the Front homosexual de l'action révolutionnaire. We can add that Daniel Guérin was Jewish, as his mother came from the famous Eichtal family.

The famous writer Bernard Werber, as famous as he is mediocre, whose books are sold in supermarkets all over the world, is also a fervent globalist. For some years now, he has been openly declaring his desire for a world government. In his cheap novel *Cassandra's Mirror*, published in 2009, the hero can see the future, but nobody believes him. On page 485 of that stupid novel there are some ingredients of Judaism—always the same, to tell the truth: the obsession for a world

[668]Hervé Ryssen, *Planetary Hopes, Trotskyist Messianism, (*2022).

[669]On Wihelm Reich and Freudo-Marxism, *Planetary Hopes, (2022).*

government, the war against "tyrants" and bad guys, the unification of the world, peace on earth, the obliteration of all differences, social, national, ethnic ... and, as always, that lancinating problem in the Jews: incest and paedophilia, which already obsessed Sigmund Freud and which still obsesses many Jews all over the world for obvious reasons. Let us listen to what Bernard Werber had his characters say: "Well, what would you see if you were an optimist, Baron? —The opposite of a great nuclear war is world peace and a demilitarisation of the planet. And then we throw out all the tyrants and fanatical dictators? Yep, it would take an Assembly of the Wise with real executive power to enforce world peace..." This gives us an idea of the style of Bernard Werber, that "great genius of literature"." Duchess?" asks Kim. —Well, the opposite of overpopulation is planetary birth control. I would be in favour of the Assembly of the Wise of all nations proposed by Baron. Since we know that with medicine there is much less infant mortality than before, quality would be favoured over quantity. One child per family, but with an automatic and obligatory right to be loved, fed and educated from birth. No more paedophile networks, no more abusive parents, every child born would be loved by its parents and educated to value what is best." The globalist "peace on earth" obsession of Bernard Werber and his ilk has its origins in early childhood. Indeed, it seems quite clear to us that Bernard Werber, like Sigmund Freud, was "abused" by his father as a child while his mother regularly consoled him in bed by telling him that he was a "great genius", perhaps even the messiah himself. This is how some Jews, as adults, imagine themselves to be the "chosen ones" whose mission is to save the planet.

Paedophilia among rabbis

We see how the Western media always go into overdrive and put the spotlight on any confirmed case of paedophilia in the Catholic Church. What the general public ignores is that this Jewish-media hype is a typical accusatory inversion. Indeed, the problem is far more pressing and worrying in the Jewish community[670]. We will cite here only the most recent cases:

[670]2018 saw the release of *M*, a French documentary directed by Yolande Zauberman that went somewhat unnoticed. The documentary *M*, presented at the Locarno Film Festival and shot in Yiddish in Bnei Brak, lifted the veil on paedophilia in Orthodox Jewish circles in Israel. One of the shocking phrases in the documentary was uttered by the protagonist near a synagogue: "There I was circumcised, there I had my curls done, there I was married, there I was divorced and there I was raped". (NdT)

On 7 October 2008, a news item reported that a rabbi from the Antwerp Hasidic community had been arrested in Brooklyn. The police had searched his home and taken him to the police station in handcuffs. Rabbi Israel Weingarten, 58, was accused of raping a little girl for a decade. The abuse began when the girl was nine years old. In 2008, the girl was a 28-year-old woman when she reported the rabbi. He had taken her to Belgium and Israel (a bit like in Stanley Kubrick's *Lolita*). This information had been published by a Jewish journalist named Steve Lieberman in *The Journal News*. Weingarten and six of his children had refused to answer the FBI agents. The rabbi had locked himself in his house, so the police broke down the doors to arrest him.

On 2 June 2009, we learned from *La Presse Canadienne* that Andy Blatchford, former head of the Quebec branch of B'nai B'rith, had been charged with possession of child pornography.

Bill Surkis, 69, former director of the Montreal Holocaust Memorial Centre, had been summoned to appear before the Montreal Court of Justice. The police had seized 86 videos and 653 photos of child pornography on his computer. Bill Surkis had been reported after he had taken his computer to a computer shop to remove viruses. Married and a grandfather, he ended up spending his nights behind bars.

In the *New York Times* of 13 November 2008, an article by Paul Vitello addressed this sensitive issue. It reported how a local politician, Dov Hikind, had broached the subject of child sexual abuse in the Orthodox Jewish community by calling on radio listeners to testify. He then collected more than 1000 complaints and the names of 60 sexual predators from New York and New Jersey. The victims had come to his office to tell their stories." Teachers and rabbis commit abuse in school. Paedophiles on the streets. Incest at home." Dov Hikind said he kept these stories locked in his Brooklyn office because the people who had come forward had sworn him to secrecy, fearing they would be ostracised from their community, lose their jobs and their housing. However, in October 2008, a reputable lawyer, Michael Dowd, representing half a dozen former *yeshiva* (Talmudic school) students who claimed to have been sexually abused by Rabbi Yehuda Kolko of the Teminah *yeshiva* in Brooklyn, had succeeded in getting Hikind subpoenaed to appear in court and required to produce their documents as evidence. Michael Dowd claimed that the information was crucial to prove his clients' claims that sexual abuse was commonplace and routinely covered up by *yeshiva* administrators. Dov Hikind had refused: "I will not betray their trust for anything in the world", he declared. According to him, among all those who had confessed to him that they had been victims, "99% will never, under any circumstances, go to the police". This conflict had revealed the tensions within the orthodox community, as the Jewish press, as well as websites such as failemessiah.com and unorthodoxjews.blogspot.com, had revealed.

After this case, a 23-year-old Jewish man, Joel Engelman, who had grown up in the Orthodox community of Williamsburg, Brooklyn, created a victims' association called "*Survivors for Justice*". He felt that despite "his good intentions", Dov Hikind had not gone to the end of his responsibilities." The community cannot have its own police. It has proved that repeatedly." Joe Engelman had reported a *United Talmudical Academy* teacher who had raped him when he was eight years old. The teacher had received a simple temporary suspension and had resumed his duties. For his part, Professor Marci Hamilton, an associate professor at *Yeshiva University School of Law* and a specialist in sexual abuse within the Jewish community, considered M. Hikind's refusal to provide the names of the alleged predators to be "outrageous".

The newspaper *Le Figaro* of 16 July 2009 published an article on the excesses of reality television in the United States, especially through the live sex maniac hunting show "*To Catch the Predator*". The show brought together the star journalists of national television. In this case, the man caught was a pedo-maniac. He had been lured by an 18-year-old girl who had posed as a twelve-year-old girl via an internet discussion forum. One night, she announced to the man that her parents were out and that he could come and see her. The maniac appeared knocking on the door of a chalet and was greeted in the living room by a girl. The girl used the pretext of going to the toilet so that a journalist suddenly appeared with two television cameras to call the maniac's attention: "What are you doing here, you knew she was twelve years old"! The man, who was a rabbi, broke down, lamenting: "I've lost my synagogue! I've lost my family! "The policemen then appeared at the door, sirens blaring, pointing their service weapons at him. Apparently, the American public loves this kind of outcome!

In France, the programme "*Les Infiltrés*" (The *infiltrators)* had caught a paedophile in the same way. The newspaper *Le Parisien* of 8 April 2010 reported the case in its pages. A councillor of the Mesnil-Saint-Denis town council, in charge of the internet, had been tricked. He had exchanged messages over the internet with a 15-year-old Jessica, whom he had assured that he would "teach her how to make love without hurting her". But behind Jessica's character was a journalist. Once the dialogue on the internet was over, the man was reported by the journalists to the Nanterre police. A few days later, in mid-February, Maurice Gutman, an eminent member of the Consistory[671], was also taken into custody.

In January 2010, the Israeli daily *Haaretz reported* that the Supreme Court had unanimously overturned the decision of the Jerusalem district court that had authorised the extradition of Avraham Mandrowitz to the United States. Avraham Mandrowitz, 62, a father of seven children and a member of the Hasidic movement, had been accused in 1984 by the US courts of having practised sodomy on children between the ages of 5 and 10. Mandrowitz was living at the time in Brooklyn where he presented himself as a rabbi and psychologist specialising in children's problems. The American indictment mentioned more than 100 victims. He had fled with his family to Israel. In 1985, the United States authorities had issued an extradition request against him which the Israeli authorities had rejected on the basis of the provisions of the Convention signed between Israel and the United States which did not include acts of sodomy in the list of offences. This is called "proctosemitism". However, in January 2007, this Convention was amended and now provided for extradition for any prison sentence exceeding one year. The US authorities had then immediately reiterated their extradition request and Mandrowitz was arrested in November 2007 by Israeli police at his home in Jerusalem and brought before the Jerusalem district court which authorised his extradition.

In March 2010, following the umpteenth case of paedophilia in Israel, Yitzhak Kadman, chairman of the *National Council for the Child*, had declared: "We have been saying for a long time that Israel is a paradise for paedophiles."

In April 2010, a rabbi named Bryan Bramly, 35, had been transferred from Arizona to New York. Bryan Bramly was accused of raping a seven-year-old girl when he was a student at the *Conservative movement*'s rabbinical school. He had since married and fathered two children and had become the rabbi of Temple Beth Sholom of East Valley in Chandler, Arizona. The man was released on $10,000 bail.

Also in April 2010, a 59-year-old New York rabbi, Baruch Mordechai Lebovits, was sentenced to 32 years in prison for sexually assaulting a teenager, the Brooklyn District Attorney's Office announced in a statement." He was convicted on March 8 of repeated

[671]Central Jewish Consistory of France, located in rue de la Victoire in Paris. It is the institution created in 1808 by Napoleon I to administer the Jewish faith in France, on the model of the other two official religions (Catholic and Protestant). It appoints the Chief Rabbi of France.

sexual assaults in 2004 and 2005 against a 16-year-old boy," said prosecutor Charles Hynes. The rabbi "is also a prominent businessman in the Borough Park community, where the teenager lives". The complainant, Yoav Schönberg, 22, was an Orthodox Jew, a friend of Rabbi Lebovits. He had testified in such a low voice that Judge Patricia DiMango had asked him several times to repeat what he had just said. Yoav Schönberg explained that Rabbi Lebovits had offered him free driving lessons on 2 May 2004. After a few minutes in the car, Lebovits had asked him to park. There, the rabbi unbuttoned Yoav's fly and performed fellatio on him. According to the ADA, these sexual assaults were repeated several times between that day and 22 February 2005. Rabbi Baruch Lebovits was also charged in two other paedophilia cases for which he was awaiting trial. The case had been reported by the *New York Daily News*.

In 2009, 40 children from that small Jewish community in Brooklyn had claimed to have been "abused", while there were only 10 such allegations involving the Catholic Church in the fifty US states: that is 10 sexually abused children for 68 million American Catholics, compared to 40 children for 2 million Jewish New Yorkers. There were therefore 130 times more likely to be at risk for little Jews than for little Catholics.

A website specialising in the denunciations of these paedophile rabbis estimated that in the United States, out of 5.5 million Jews, 1.3 million had been sexually abused[672]. This meant that one Jew in four would have been raped in childhood; that is as if 75 million Americans had been raped.

In December 2010, we learned that David Epstein, a professor at Columbia University, had been sleeping with his own daughter for several years.

Here is a more serious case: In 2008, Rabbi Elior Noam Chen was accused of raping children between the ages of three and four and torturing them during purification rituals. These events took place in the West Bank community of Beitar Illit. The rabbi had fled to Canada after a mother member of his disciples was accused of abusing her own children. She burned them, made them eat her excrement and locked them in suitcases for days. An international arrest warrant was issued for him. Chen and his family had finally been arrested in Brazil, where they had managed to escape and take refuge in the ultra-orthodox

[672]http://www.theawarenesscenter.org

community of Sao Paolo, which was hiding them.

We can also mention the emblematic case of "Tony Alamo", charismatic leader of an apocalyptic Christian sect in Arkansas, in the United States, who was sentenced in November 2009 to 175 years in prison for rape and sexual crimes against children. Tony Alamo took advantage of his status as a self-proclaimed prophet to force underage girls (as young as eight years old) into marriage by threatening them with eternal damnation in hell. He also ordered corporal punishment of all kinds on the children of his followers. His real name was actually Bernie Lazar Hoffman. He was born in 1934 to Jewish parents from Romania.

In April 2009, a book entitled *Tempest in the Temple* was published in the United States that exposed the abuses of numerous rabbis. The book was subtitled: "Jewish communities and *child sex scandals*". It was the first book on the subject. Its author, Amy Neustein, was an American Jew from Baltimore. This is what you could read in the book's introduction: "In 2006, *New York Magazine* and ABC reported stories of rabbis who had abused children. In early 2007, the *Jewish Telegraphic Agency* published a five-part report on the rapes of children by rabbis. Despite this media coverage, no thorough investigation was carried out. *Tempest in the Temple recounts* the cases of some fifteen rabbis, educators and psychologists in the Jewish community, and the support from which they benefited."

In January 2008, an autobiographical book entitled *The Rabbi's Daughter: Sex, Drugs, and Orthodoxy* was published and caused quite a stir in the Jewish community. Its author was one Reva Mann. She was the granddaughter of Israel's second Ashkenazi rabbi, Isser Yehuda Untermann. A 50-year-old mother of three, Reva Mann had begun to reminisce about her life after her mother's suicide. She recounted, among other events, how she had lost her virginity in the synagogue, or her experience with LSD at the age of 16. When asked: "What is the purpose of this book?", Reva Mann replied: "A: Everything you have always wanted to know about Judaism without daring to ask. And B: I hope that this book will reach people who are self-destructive and that it will help them to get back on track with their lives."

Now we understand better why the Jews, who control the entire centre of the Western world's media system, regularly accuse the Catholic clergy. We also understand why the media always insist on denouncing "denialist and paedophile" websites.

The prescriptions of the Talmud

The Talmud is quite explicit on these matters. This book, which is "the tradition of the ancients," is composed of innumerable commentaries by rabbis on the Law [the Gemara]. Thus, a good part of the text consists of the enumeration of the opinions of this or that rabbi, followed by a confrontation with the opinions of this or that rabbi, and finally concluded with a sort of synthesis by another rabbi. In 1935, and for the first time, the 63 volumes, or treatises, were translated so that the new generations, unable to understand the different languages used in the original version, could access the text more easily. This complete English translation of the Talmud, published in 1935 by the *Soncino Press*, has since been designated the *Soncino Edition* of the *Talmud673.* Evidently, this edition did not have a large print run, nor was it made available for sale to the general public.

The reading of the commentaries is tiresome; we have therefore preferred to summarise the text of some of the footnotes. Let us point out that the Talmud serves as the legal code on which Jewish religious law is based, and that it is the book used for the training of the rabbis.

In tractate *Sanhedrin 54 a-54b*, we read the following: "Pederasty[674] with a child who is less than nine years old is not considered the same as pederasty with an older child. Samuel said: "Pederasty with a child who is less than three years old is not considered in the same way as pederasty with an older child[675]". What is the basis of his disagreement? Rab argues that only a passive subject who was

---

[673]In English version at www.halakhah.com. The Talmud consists of 63 tractates in six main orders. The central orders are Zeraim (the Seedings: agricultural treatises), *Moed* (Seasons and holidays, containing the fundamental treatise on the Sabbath), *Nashim* (devoted entirely to women, sexuality and reproduction, and consisting of numerous rather lurid treatises), and the properly legal order called *Nezikin* (on damages. Civil and criminal law). Exclusivism and the notion of racial and sexual purity are omnipresent in the Talmud. In fact, an entire tractate, called *Niddah*, deals with women's blood and menstruation. Basically, the Talmud deals with issues of money, sex, purity and messianism. See again the translator's note in Annex I. (NdT).

[674]"We stand here from the point of view of the passive subject of the sodomy. As has been established above in 54a, culpability is incurred by the active subject of sodomy, even if the passive subject is a minor (under thirteen years of age). However, a further distinction will be made below for passive subjects under the age of thirteen."

[675]*Talmud, Sanhedrin 54b, note 24*: "Rab puts the minimum age at nine years; but if sodomy is practised on a younger child, no guilt is incurred. Samuel, on the other hand, sets the minimum age at three years". *Talmud, Sanhedrin 54b*: "Rab said: Pederasty with a child under nine years of age is not considered pederasty with a child above that age. Samuel said: Pederasty with a child under three years of age is not treated as with a child above that age. What is the basis of their dispute? —Rab argues that only one who is capable of sexual intercourse can, as the passive subject of pederasty, lay the blame [on the active offender]." (NdT).

capable of sexual intercourse as an active subject can incur the culpability of the active subject; whereas a child incapable of being an active subject cannot be considered as the passive subject of an act of pederasty[676]. Samuel, for his part, maintains that Scripture says: " Thou shalt not lie with mankind as with womankind; it is an abomination." (*Leviticus, XVIII, 22*). It has therefore been taught, in accordance with Rab's opinion, that the act of pederasty is regarded as a crime from nine years and one day; but he who commits bestiality, whether by natural or unnatural ways, or if a woman seeks to be abused in a bestial manner, whether by natural or unnatural ways, is deserving of punishment."

Sanhedrin, 55b "A girl three years and one day old, whose father arranged her [marriage] engagement, is engaged in intercourse, since the legal status of intercourse with her is that of full intercourse. In the case where the childless husband of a girl three years and a day old dies, if her brother has sexual intercourse with her, then he acquires her as his wife. The penalty of adultery may be incurred through her; she defiles him who has intercourse with her, so that he in turn defiles that on which he lies, like a garment that has lain on a person afflicted with gonorrhoea."

In the same passage we see a note that reads: "A variant of this passage is: "Is there anything that is permitted to a Jew and forbidden to a heathen? Sexual intercourse in unnatural ways is permitted to a Jew[677]."

Sanhedrin, 69b: "Our Rabbis taught: If a woman united lasciviously with her young son [a minor], and he committed the first stage of sexual intercourse with her, Beth Shammai says that this makes her unfit for the priesthood. But Beth Hillel declares her still fit? All agree that the sexual intercourse of a child nine years and one day old is real sexual intercourse; whereas that of a child under eight years old is not. Their dispute concerns only the case of a child who is eight years old. Beth Shammai argues that we should base our decision on previous generations, but Beth Hillel argues that we should not[678]."

---

[676]At the age of nine, the male child has reached sexual maturity. *Sanhedrin 54b, note 25.*

[677]*Talmud, Sanhedrin, 58b*: "Rava says: Is there any action for which a Jew is not liable, but a gentile is liable for doing it? A Jew is not liable for anal intercourse with his wife." (NdT).

[678]*Talmud, Sanhedrin, 69b, note 5:* "So, if he was nine years and a day or more, Beth Hillel agrees that she is invalidated for the priesthood; whereas, if he was less than eight, Beth Shammai agrees that she is not." Shammai and the Pharisee Hillel (-110 BC, -10 AD) were the first two ancient scholars to discuss and systematise the interpretation of the written Torah. The Pharisee Saul of Tarsus (St. Paul) was a disciple of Gamaliel,

Talmud Kethuboth, 11 a-11b: "Rabbah said: "When an adult man has sexual intercourse with a little girl, it is nothing, for when the girl is under three years of age, it is as if one puts one's finger in her eye; but when a little boy has sexual intercourse with an adult woman, this is equivalent to the case where "a girl is wounded [penetrated] by a piece of wood"".

"A girl's virginity is taken into consideration only from the age of three years and one day. If she is raped below that age, the culprit is acquitted, for the Talmud says that 'it is as if they put their finger in her eye'; virginity is re-formed. Above the age of three years and one day, an unmarried virgin who is raped—since it is understood that she can only marry from the age of nine years and one day—is entitled to compensation. If she is raped by two men or by ten men, only the first pays the fine. If one of the two raped her abnormally, he is the one who pays the fine. But if ten raped her by normal means and one by abnormal means, then they all have to pay[679]."

Therefore, the Talmud forbids Jewish mothers to sleep with their children when they are older than nine years and one day. According to this holy book, the same prohibition applies to the father when the child is older than three years and one day. Furthermore, according to the Talmud, a Jewish widow must never keep a dog. Therefore, when we see a lady walking her dog in the street, we know that she is not a Jewish widow; although she may have a dog.

The Oedipus Complex finally explained

Now we understand perfectly why psychoanalysis was born in the brains of a member of the "chosen people". Born in Moravia, Sigmund Freud came from a traditional Hasidic Jewish background. His parents were Jews from Galicia, in the west of today's Ukraine. His mother was born in Brody, one of the major centres of Hasidic thought in Eastern Europe. In Vienna, where the family had settled, his parents still spoke German, heavily mixed with Yiddish. Although Freud, like Karl Marx and many other Jews, had distanced himself from the Jewish religion, he had not, on the contrary, renounced his communal belonging. In the Hebrew foreword to *Moses and the Monotheistic Religion*, he wrote that

Hillel's grandson (NdT).

[679]Roger Peyrefitte, *Les juifs, (Deuxième partie, Chapitre 5),* Flammarion, 1965. We advise against reading Roger Peyrefitte's book, which tends to show, especially through onomastics, that "everyone would be a little bit Jewish". Apparently, despite his great erudition, Roger Peyrefitte had little understanding of the Jewish question.

"he had separated himself from the Jewish religion but had not repudiated the Jewish people[680]."

Freud did not have the courage to reveal to the world that the famous "Oedipus complex" was in fact the "Israel complex". As a good Jew, he had projected the neurosis of Judaism onto the rest of humanity by taking up a Greek legend so that the Goyim would more readily accept his "discovery".

Greek legend has it that the oracle foretold to Oedipus, son of the king of Corinth, that he would one day kill his father and marry his mother. The horrified young prince then fled the kingdom and set out for Thebes. On the way, Oedipus killed two men who wanted him to give them passage. When he finally reached the gates of the city, he had to answer the question of the Sphinx waiting at the entrance. This monster with the face and bust of a woman, the body of a lion and the wings of a bird, terrorised the region, devouring those who could not guess his riddles. But Oedipus got it right[681] and the Sphinx had to flee. Oedipus then became king of Thebes and married Queen Jocasta, the widow of Laius, the Theban king killed by Oedipus on the road without his knowledge. Later, he learned that many years earlier Laius had ordered the murder of his newborn son. That order had not been carried out and the child had been picked up by shepherds who had given him to the king of Corinth, whom Oedipus had always believed to be his son. The oracle's prediction had therefore been fulfilled. Oedipus, in despair, plucked out his eyes and fled into exile to become a beggar.

The Oedipus complex is in fact a Jewish specificity. David Bakan confirmed our own conclusions in a sweetened form: "The main criticism levelled against the doctrine of the Oedipus complex is that it is inspired by a particular type of family constellation found in Freud's direct cultural environment, and that Freud would have made the

---

[680]David Bakan, *Freud et la tradition mystique juive*, 1963, Payot, 2001, p. 320. ["I have never been able to understand why I should be ashamed of my origin or, as it was then beginning to be said, of my race. I also renounced, without much feeling, the nationality that was denied me. I thought, in fact, that for a zealous worker there would always be a place, however small, in the ranks of hard-working humanity, even if he did not belong to any of the national groups. But these early university impressions had the most important consequence of accustoming me from the very beginning to be in the ranks of the opposition and outside the 'compact majority', giving me a certain independence of judgment", in Sigmund Freud, *An autobiographical study,* (1924), S. E. XX. p. 9. (NdT)]

[681]"What is the only creature that at dawn walks on all fours, at noon walks on two legs and at sunset walks on three legs?

mistake of “ethnocentrism”, overgeneralising from a given culture[682].”

On the other hand, Freud had certain dispositions to understand his patients, for he himself seemed to be affected by the disorder he was studying. At the age of forty-two, while still engaged in self-analysis, he accused his own father, who had recently died in 1896, as this passage from a letter to his great friend, Dr Wilhelm Fliess, testifies: “Unfortunately, my own father was one of those perverts. He is the cause of the hysteria of my brother and some of my younger sisters. The frequency of such relationships often gives me pause for thought.”

In Martha Robert’s book, *The Psychoanalytic Revolution*, we find an interesting passage. Martha Robert, like many of her peers who feel the need “to talk about it”, expressed herself in ellipsis: “She then discovers within herself … her hostile feelings towards her father, her incestuous tenderness towards her mother, her death wishes, her elusiveness… Her reluctance to divulge the secret of the dark world into which she has just entered is such that, in letters to the only friend to whom she confesses the results of her analysis, she relates her memories of her mother writing in Latin[683].”

Freud had evidently also been abused by his father during his childhood, and consoled himself in his mother’s bed, who probably assured him that he was a “genius”, perhaps even the messiah himself[684].

Freud also had to suffer from the fact that he had some hereditary defects in his ancestry. This is what he wrote in 1886 about his uncle from Breslau, his father’s younger brother: “He is a merchant, and the history of his family is very sad. Of his four sons, only one daughter is normal and married in Poland. One of the sons is hydrocephalic and retarded; another, who was promising as a child, went mad at the age of 19; the other daughter went mad in her early twenties… My other uncle from Vienna died epileptic. I can no longer attribute this inheritance to my mother’s family alone. I must admit that there are some very serious neuropathological defects in my family[685].” His father Jacob’s brother Joseph also had an epileptic son: “Although, as a delinquent, he seemed

[682]David Bakan, *Freud et la tradition mystique juive,* 1963, Payot, 2001, p. 298.

[683]Marthe Robert, *La Révolution psychoanalytique, Tome I,* Payot, 1964, p. 41. Hervé Ryssen, *Le Miroir du judaïsme,* p. 349, 350.

[684]In *Portnoy’s Evil,* the American novelist Philip Roth wrote: “What was wrong with these Jewish parents, what were they capable of making us young Jews believe, on the one hand, that we were princes, unique in the world, like unicorns, geniuses, brighter than anyone else ever was and more beautiful than any other children in history? “Philip Roth, *Portnoy’s Evil,* Debols! llo, Penguin Random House, Barcelona, 2008, p. 131.

[685]Correspondence, letter to Martha of 10 February 1886, p. 222–223.

more like a pervert than a madman. In Jacob Freud's opinion, he must be considered more of an imbecile". Thus, it must be acknowledged that "that whole paternal branch of his family ... almost uniquely counts degenerates."

Sigmund Freud was well aware of this genetic fatality, and noted with regret: "Such stories are so frequent in Jewish families." Martha Robert added, furthermore, and slightly distorted the matter: "Freud cannot help attributing this manifest defect to the 'very beautiful tendency to neurasthenia' from which he has suffered for so long and which is also present in his sister Rosa and his brother Emmanuel[686]."

At the turn of the 20th century, Jews from the *shtetls of* Poland and Russia were flocking to the capital of the Austro-Hungarian Empire, as they had been granted equal rights under an 1869 law. In cultural and financial circles, many Jews soon asserted themselves, so that Vienna at the beginning of the 20th century, like Berlin and Moscow in the 1920s, was a golden age for them, just as Paris and New York are today. At the beginning of the 20th century, Jews in the capital of the Austro-Hungarian Empire held very dominant positions in the world of finance and culture. The most popular writers, journalists and artists of the time, i.e. those who enjoyed the most publicity, were members of the Jewish community: Sigmund Freud, Stefan Zweig, Arthur Schnitzler, Franz Werfel, Franz Kafka, Gustav Mahler, Karl Krauss, Hugo von Hofmansthal, and so on. But these numerous Jewish upstarts, barely out of the ghetto, had no intention of losing their identity by assimilating into Austrian society. As elsewhere, Jews preferred to live among themselves[687].

Although he had little interest in religion, Sigmund Freud nevertheless remained closely connected to his community. He had studied Scripture and Hebrew at school and had the same zeal for knowledge and study as his Talmudic ancestors[688]. He lived and grew

---

686Marthe Robert was Jewish, and married to a Jew.

687Life in the ghettos was thus desired by the Jews themselves. See Hervé Ryssen, *Le Miroir du Judaïsme,* Baskerville (2009), p. 48-53 and *Histoire de l'antisémitisme,* Baskerville (2010). p. 280, 400.

688 "My deep devotion to the biblical writings (begun almost at the same time as I learned the art of reading) had, as I recognised many years later, a long-lasting effect on the line of my interests." Sigmund Freud, *An autobiographical study,* (1924), S. E. XX. p. 8. These words were corroborated by those of his father, Jacob Freud, who on his 35th birthday wrote to his son the following dedication in the Philippson Bible that Sigmund used as a child: "At the age of seven the spirit of God began to draw near to you and said to you: Go and read the books I have written, and the fountains of wisdom, knowledge and understanding will be opened to you. The Book of Books is

up in an exclusively Jewish environment, and also throughout his professional career. On the Steering Committee of the Vienna Psychoanalytic Society, all the attendants were Jewish, except for Richard Sterba, whom Freud once laughingly pointed out as an exception. In fact, that situation was summed up by a sentence Freud wrote: "Although I have long since separated from the religion of my ancestors, I have never lost the feeling of solidarity with my people[689]."

All of Freud's disciples who have made any original contribution to psychoanalysis have been Jewish, with the notable exception of Jung. Moreover, the investigative journalist Emmanuel Ratier brought to light Sigmund Freud's membership in the Masonic sect B'nai B'rith, a Freemasonry exclusively reserved for Jews[690]. From 1900 to 1902, he participated as a "founding brother" in the creation of the second B'nai B'rith lodge in Vienna, the Harmony Lodge.

Freud knew that he had to win over the Goy intellectual world at

---

the well which wise men have tilled, and in which lawgivers have learned knowledge and righteousness..." This Bible was a bilingual (Hebrew-German) edition, with explanations and illustrations, first published in 1854 by Rabbi Ludwig Philippson. Read in Ostow, M.: *Sigmund and Jacob Freud and the Philippson Bible*, 1989, IRPA, p. 16, 483 and in Pfrimmer, T.: *Freud, lecteur de la Bible*, Presses Universitaire de France, 1982, Paris. (NdT).

[689]Marthe Robert, *D'Oedipe à Moïse*, 1974, Agora, 1987, p. 35, 45, 51, 56. ["Do everything necessary to restore the interest of our fellow countrymen (*folksbrider*) in our Jewish Scientific Institute in Vilnius. We Jews have always held spiritual values in high esteem. Thanks to them we have remained together and have endured to this day. For me, it was always an example of our history that immediately after the destruction of the Temple in Jerusalem, Rabbi Johanan ben Zakkai asked the oppressor for permission to open the first higher school for Jewish studies. Now, too, a difficult time has come for our people. This time demands of us that we once again join forces in order to be able to sustain our culture and science in these storms. And you are well aware of the role played in this task by the Vilna Jewish Scientific Institute," Sigmund Freud, for the journal of the Vilna Jewish Scientific Institute *Ivo bleter*, November-December 1938, T.XIII. n. 7–8, p. 32].

[690]B'nai B'rith, literally Sons of the Covenant, Sons of the Covenant or Sons of the Light. Since 1843, it has been officially recognised as exclusively Jewish Freemasonry. The 1901 *Encyclopaedia Judaica* states that the technical language, symbolism and rites of Freemasonry are full of Jewish ideas (Cyrus Adler, *The Jewish Encyclopedia, vol III*, Ed. Funk and Wagnalls, 1901, p. 503–504). In fact, the entire symbolic paraphernalia of speculative Freemasonry revolves around Jewish iconography: Jehovah, Solomon's Temple, the tabernacle, Hiram Abiff, Tubal Cain, Jacob's ladder, Abraham, etc. The forms of secret initiatory societies such as Freemasonry and the occult sciences derive from the Hebrew Kabbalah, born in Jewish circles that were in contact with the esoteric knowledge of Babylon, Egypt and the pagan mystical schools of Hellenistic antiquity, especially in the cities of Alexandria and Antioch. On Freemasonry and its origins we recommend the well-documented work by Alberto León Cebrián, *Las Revoluciones Masonónicas*, Bubok, 2015. (NdT).

all costs to ensure the widest possible dissemination of the new "science". That was why he enthroned Jung, the only Goy in the movement, as president of the Psychoanalytic Society. In his book entitled *Mysteries and Secrets of B'nai B'rith*, the investigative journalist Emmanuel Ratier transcribed the statements of an Austro-Hungarian psychoanalyst, Fritz Wittels, who had related a little-known event during the second psychoanalytic congress of 1910: "Several Jewish disciples took the promotion of Carl Gustav Jung to the presidency of the psychoanalytic movement very badly, which had caused great discontent among the Viennese disciples who suspected Jung of having anti-Jewish prejudices." Freud would have exclaimed to himself at the time: "Most of you are Jews, and for that reason you are incompetent to win friends for the new science. Jews must be content with the modest role of preparing the ground. It is absolutely essential that you be able to form links with the scientific community[691]." Judaism, as usual, did not advance in the open. Quite the contrary.

Kabbalah, Hasidism and Psychoanalysis

In the shtetls of Eastern Europe, the Jews lived in a confinement unfavourable to the liberation of the spirits: "The way of life of the Jews, wrote David Bakan, was codified point by point, from one moment to the next, from one day to the next, from one week to the next, from one season to the next, and so on from birth to death. Everything was done according to the Covenant." Under these circumstances, life was "a full-time religious occupation."

In his book, *Freud and the Jewish Mystical Tradition*, David Bakan tried to show that psychoanalysis was in fact largely derived from the methods of the Jewish Kabbalah. This Jewish mystical current, which really took off in the 16th century and which then gave rise to some heresies fiercely fought against by the rabbis, was perpetuated and, in a way, stabilised in today's Hasidic Jews. They are the heirs of this esoteric tradition. Bakan recalled the passionate attachment of pious Jews to their Torah and its Law: "For centuries, the Torah had been regarded as such a highly sacred document that every letter, every nuance in the style and even the size of the letters in the handwritten scrolls, had for mystics and exegetes, a deep, hidden meaning." Indeed, the text was not only to be read literally. In order to discover the "hidden meaning", the kabbalists have ancient techniques expounded in the

[691]Emmanuel Ratier, *Mystères et secrets du B'Nai B'Rith*, 1993, p. 145-149.

Zohar, the reference book of the Jewish kabbalists.

Word games are an integral part of the search for the hidden meaning of the Torah, Bakan explained. But in addition to the simple word play that can be seen from one end of the Zohar to the other, there are also many number plays, based in large part on the fact that each Hebrew character has a numerical value. Characteristically, the letter game—called *Zeruf* (combination) in Jewish mysticism—is classified into three main sections: gematria, notarikon and temurah. Gematria establishes meaning based on the numerical value of the words. Notarikon proceeds acronymically, as a method of selecting a word by using each of its initial or final letters to form another word: thus "*chen*" meaning "grace" has the same first letters (consonants, *chn*) as "*chokmah nistarah*" meaning "hidden wisdom". Temurah changes the words by changing the order of the letters. Bakan believed that he perceived in the texts the "temuric tendency of Freud".

According to him, the methods of the Kabbalists may have inspired the psychoanalytical method. Bakan observed that the Freudian method of dream interpretation, which consists of extracting each element from its context, corresponds exactly to "the search for the hidden or deeper meanings of the Torah". The kabbalists interpreted the Torah "in a manner that bears a striking resemblance to that of the psychoanalyst in interpreting the charices and digressions of human expression." According to Bakan, Freud "wanted to inform us that, through psychoanalysis, he was analysing a human being as the Jews had for centuries analysed the Torah[692]."

David Bakan here supported his thesis that Freud was an heir of the Sabbateans, whose principles, in their radical tendency, consisted in systematically going against the Torah and doing everything that was forbidden[693]. These Kabbalist Jews were persecuted and excommunicated by the rabbis, but it is known that in Central Europe, and especially in Poland and Moravia, the Sabbateans had achieved strong positions within Judaism. For David Bakan, the Freudian method was therefore the "final culmination of Sabbateanism". His psychoanalytic method was his personal way of fulfilling the Sabbatean apostasy.

In Moravia, explained Gershom Scholem, the Sabbatean movement established itself to the point of gaining the support of numerous Jewish urbanites and small shopkeepers." According to Jacob

---

[692]David Bakan, *Freud et la tradition mystique juive*, 1963, Payot, 2001, p. 286-290, 276, 275, 272.

[693]See again translator's note in Annex VI. 3.

Emden, the numerical value of the Hebrew letters in verse 3 of Psalm 14: "There are no more honest men, not even one" is the same as the numerical value of the letters of the Hebrew word for Moravia. In Prague and Mannheim, centres of study oriented in a Sabbatean sense appeared and the "graduates" of these institutions had a great influence" in the 18th century[694].

It is also no coincidence that Freud's first book is about *The Interpretation of Dreams.* In the ancient Jewish communities, the most sought-after work from travelling book sellers on market days was precisely *The Key to Dreams,* which gave the meaning of all dreams." *The Key to Dreams,* by Salomon B. Jacob and Pitorn Chalamot, was one of the most sought after," wrote David Bakan." Tractate Berakoth, one of the least legalised in the Talmud, contains one of the most extensive expositions of dreams and their interpretation in all rabbinic literature. For centuries it served as a guide to dream interpretation."

Freud would therefore have been largely inspired by these readings, and Bakan noted: "The fundamental similarity between his methods and those employed in psychoanalysis has already been recognised by the psychoanalytic literature." We find indeed very similar features in psychoanalytic theory. Thus, the Berakoth provides these explanations: If a person has dreamt of having watered olives with oil: "this is someone who has cohabited with his mother". If a person has dreamt that "his eyes kissed each other, then he has cohabited with his sister". And if a person has dreamt that he kissed the moon, then he has "committed adultery[695]". As we can see, dreams according to the Berakoth have a sexual meaning and are the culmination of a desire. And so, together with David Bakan, we can see again how the question of incest seems to be an obsession in the Jewish community.

The issue of patricide

The theme of patricide is an important one in Sigmund Freud's work. It is present in *The Interpretation of Dreams (*1900). It is represented again in *Totem and Taboo* (1912), and culminates in *Moses and the Monotheistic Religion* (1934). In a passage of the latter book, Freud takes up, twenty-three years later, what he had already stated in *Totem and Taboo* about the primitive origins of human society, an inheritance of the Darwinian thesis of the "primitive horde".

694Gershom Scholem, *Le Messianisme juif,* 1971, Calmann-Lévy, 1974, p. 156.
695David Bakan, *Freud et la tradition mystique juive,* 1963, Payot, 2001, p. 282.

According to him, “in prehistoric times primitive man would have lived in small hordes dominated by a powerful male”:

“The powerful male would have been master and father of the whole horde, unlimited in his power, which he exercised brutally. All females belonged to him: both the women and daughters of his own horde and perhaps also those stolen from others. The fate of sons was harsh: if they aroused the father’s jealousy, they were killed, castrated or outlawed. They were condemned to live together in small communities and to procure women by abducting them, a situation in which one or the other might succeed in gaining a position analogous to that of the father in the primitive horde. For natural reasons, the younger son, protected by his mother’s love, enjoyed a privileged position and could take advantage of his father’s old age to supplant him after his death… The next decisive step towards the modification of this first form of “social” organisation would have consisted in the fact that the brothers, banished and gathered in a community, concerted to dominate the father by devouring his corpse raw, in accordance with the custom of the time … we believe that they not only hated and feared the father, but also venerated him as a model, and that in reality each of the sons wanted to take his place. In such a way, the cannibalistic act becomes understandable to us as an attempt to secure identification with the father by incorporating a portion of the father.”

Thus was born, according to Freud, the first form of social organisation “based on the renunciation of instincts, on the recognition of mutual obligations, on the establishment of certain institutions, proclaimed as inviolable (sacred); in short, the origins of morality and law. Each renounced the ideal of conquering for himself the paternal position, of possessing his mother and sisters. Thus the taboo of incest and the precept of exogamy were established.”

A feast day was then instituted to celebrate “the victory of the allied sons against the father”. During this “totemic feast” an animal was devoured as a substitute for the father[696]. And Freud concluded: “We have every reason to regard totemism as the first form in which religion manifests itself in human history[697].” Thus, “the hostility against the father which prompted his murder died out over a long period of time, to give way to love and give birth to an ideal whose content was the omnipotence and lack of limitation of the primitive father fought

[696]During the festival of Passover, Jews ritually slaughter and eat the lambs, the sacred animals of the Egyptians.

[697]Sigmund Freud, *Moses and the monotheistic religion: three essays, Collected Works,* EpubLibre, Trad. Luis López Ballesteros y de Torres, 2001, p. 4408, 4409, 4410

against one day, and the willingness to submit to him"." Society rests then on the common responsibility for collective crime, religion on the consciousness of guilt and remorse."

Freud further added in *Totem and Taboo* that "this criminal and memorable act which constituted the starting point of social organisations, of moral restrictions and of religion" is the "great event with which civilisation began and which has not ceased to torment mankind ever since[698]."

However, we may legitimately be surprised that Freud wrote in the same pages that "this primitive social state has not been observed anywhere", and that this did not prevent him from postulating his theory as a universal law invariably applicable to all the peoples of the earth.

Freud's anthropological study of primitive society is doubtful. David Bakan claimed for his part that Freud had found his inspiration in what was most familiar to him: "We consider that the ancient Semitic religions, as they have been maintained according to Freud over the centuries in the life of the Jews, constitute the fundamental reference elements of *Totem and Taboo699.*"

Indeed, Freud drew his inspiration mainly from the customs of the Jewish community in order to write these lines and to elaborate his theory. For only in the Jewish community does the father possess all women, including his own daughters, and nowhere else." All the females belonged to him", he wrote. As for the idea that "the younger son, protected by his mother's love" could "take advantage of his father's old age to supplant him after his death", this was evidently inspired by long Jewish family traditions.

How to erase the trace

Freud had evidently been under strong pressure from his entourage and colleagues not to reveal the great secret of the Jewish community. Ever since those revelations, which had to be read as a reflection in a mirror, Jewish intellectuals have contrived to erase the trail to mislead and deceive the Goyim. In *The Black Book of Psychoanalysis*, published in 2005[700], some authors interpreted the passage from the "theory of seduction" to the "theory of fantasy", which had led Freud

[698]Sigmund Freud, *Totem and Taboo, Collected Works,* EpubLibre, Trans. Luis Lopez Ballesteros y de Torres, 2001, p. 2478, 2476, 2473, 2475

[699]David Bakan, *Freud et la tradition mystique juive*, 1963, Payot, 2001, p. 321.

[700]In 2005, France was still, along with Argentina, the most Freudian country in the world, *The Black Book of Psychoanalysis,* Introduction.

to discover the supposed "Oedipus complex", in such a way as to completely hide the scene of the crime. Thus, for Allen Esterson, the problem was not whether Freud's patients—who were evidently from his own community—had been victims of incest, or whether they had dreamt of it. Indeed, Esterson claimed that they never told him that they had been sexually abused as children: "Contrary to what he would claim in his later reports, Freud wrote at the time that his patients "had no recollection" and assured him "vehemently that they did not believe" in the sexual traumas he insisted on[701]." Therefore, it would have been Freud himself who suggested the idea of incest to his patients.

In the *Black Book of Psychoanalysis,* Hans Israel confirmed that Freud had never written that his patients, male and female, claimed to have been sexually abused: "In his 1896 articles, Freud repeats that he urged his patients to confess to him that they had been subjected to sexual abuse in childhood, but that they did not remember, and that, even after they were cured, they continued to refuse to believe in these "scenes". He never tells of patients coming to him to talk about sexual abuse—on the contrary, since that would have been contrary to his own theory! His "theory of seduction" of 1896 is in fact quite different from the description he gave later."

On the other hand, "Freud claimed that hysterical symptoms "disappeared immediately and without return" when the repressed traumatic event that had been at their origin was brought back into consciousness. It was a statement that he repeated throughout his career: psychoanalysis, thanks to the analysis of transference and resistance, focuses on the causes of neurosis, unlike other therapies which only obtain superficial and temporary cures... It was a very powerful advertising argument, long effective in justifying the cost and endless duration of analytic treatments[702]."

Hans Israel wrote that Freud thought he was able to cure his patients "by making them disclose their unconscious memories of sexual abuse suffered at a very young age. He was so convinced that he did not hesitate to publicly boast of therapeutic successes he had not yet achieved. In his letters to Fliess, he keeps repeating that he works very hard to achieve therapeutic success with his patients, but that he has not yet succeeded. He repeats this constantly, finally admitting in the autumn of 1897 that he no longer believes in his theory. The first reason he gives to justify this turnaround is that he has not been able to finish "a single analysis". We see then that the explanation is surprisingly

[701]*The Black Book of Psychoanalysis,* Collective, edited by Catherine Meyer, p. 20.

[702]*The Black Book of Psychoanalysis,* Collective, edited by Catherine Meyer, p. 24, 42.

simple, there is nothing mysterious. Freud simply had an idea, and it did not work. He tried hard, but it was a failure. So he decided to abandon it. It is as silly as that." Hans Israel concluded thus: "Freud could not bring himself to doubt the stories of his patients for the good reason that he never had[703]! "

In short, it would have been Freud himself who would have suggested the memories of sexual abuse to his patients, for they never spontaneously told him those scenes of incest and perversion that he asked them to recall. So, dear readers, forget all those incest stories!

In fact, the introduction to the *Black Book* revealed at the outset the genesis of psychoanalysis in Freud's brain, but endorsed the thesis of incestuous trauma as narrated by the patients. In 1897, after his self-analysis, Freud "finally realised that as a child he had had erotic desires for his mother and feelings of jealousy towards his father. This is why he had so readily given credence to his patients' accusations of his parents' seductions: he himself wanted to kill his father! And here, too, is why all his patients had told him these implausible stories of incest: these were not memories, but fantasies expressing a childish desire to be seduced by their father. Freud had just discovered infantile sexuality, the role of unconscious fantasies in the psychic life of neuroses and the universality of what he would later call the "Oedipus complex[704]"."

Indeed, we have the impression that this book was written, like many others on the subject, to lead goyim readers astray, for we cannot conceive that these Jewish intellectuals, psychoanalysts to boot, are ignorant of the reality of incest in their own community, and in their own families.

Feminism and matriarchy

The traditions and customs of the Jewish people may seem quite bewildering to a European spirit. It is interesting to note how the Jews, especially the pious Jews, treat the woman, daughter or wife, according to peculiar customs. In his great study of the Jews of the Eastern European shtetls, Mark Zborowski wrote: "The woman does not have to study, for she will not be more Jewish if she studies. However perfect and obedient to the Law she may be, her Jewishness, compared to that of an educated man, will never be complete. She is not considered as an independent being, but as a member of a whole whose elements are

[703] *The Black Book of Psychoanalysis,* Collective, edited by Catherine Meyer, p. 25.
[704] *The Black Book of Psychoanalysis,* Collective, edited by Catherine Meyer, p. 13.

complementary[705]."

A woman does not need to know Jewish law: it is enough for a girl to know how to read and pray a little. There are therefore two types of parallel literature that the "*Moicher Sforim*", the itinerant book seller, offers from shtetl to shtetl: sacred texts in Hebrew for educated men and an abundance of Yiddish literature reserved for women and *prostes706* made up of religious and secular books written with a simplicity and clarity unworthy of a true scholar." The shtetl has established a culture for men in which women are officially subordinate and inferior. The study of the Law, the first factor of social advancement, is not allowed for them, so that women are automatically excluded from the heights of society."

Talmudic legends and social practice in the shtetl agree, moreover, in pointing to the radically sinful nature of women. Since it is a sin to contaminate the study of the Law with sensual daydreams," wrote Zborowski, "the marriage of boys is relatively early. Satisfied in their desires, they are thus free in spirit to study… The ideal of the shtetl prescribes men to avoid women absolutely. The attitude towards this ideal ranges from fanatical observance to a relative indifferent respect… One does not guard against sex, but against its untimely and unwelcome intrusion." And these precautions are severe: "In order to attenuate the evil charm of the married woman, her hair is cut short and she will have to wear a wig and a kerchief all her life. Short sleeves are forbidden and a man must not study in a room where a woman is bare-armed… If an orthodox Jew is forced to shake hands with a woman, he cleverly covers her hand with the skirt of his kaftan to avoid any contact[707]." Mark Zborowski further stated: "The man thanks God every day for not having made him a woman"; and everyone can verify that these traditions are still in force today in the communities of orthodox Jews.

A young girl can perhaps show great tenacity in her determination to study and learn so that her father finally gives in. Some girls have been able to access traditional knowledge, like Yentl in Barbara Streisand's film (USA, 1983) in which we see the scene in the market square where the peddler shouts out loud: "Illustrated books for women! Holy books for men!" His companion Avigdor, to whom he introduces his girlfriend one day, replies: "I don't need her to think." This pretty much sums up the traditional subordinate role of the Jewish

[705]Mark Zborowski, *Olam*, 1952, Plon, 1992, p. 72.

[706]*Proste yidn*: the common people. See note 501.

[707]Mark Zborowski, *Olam*, 1952, Plon, 1992, p. 115–129.

woman.

Mark Zborowski's highly idealised study obviously did not reveal everything, as it is a book for the general public. But we know on the other hand that the Talmud expressly disapproves of women studying the Law, which is reserved only for men: "Rabbi Eliezer said: Anyone who teaches his daughter the Torah is teaching her promiscuity[708]."

According to tractate Kethuboth, a woman can be repudiated without returning her widow's pension in the following cases: if she gives forbidden food to her husband; if she deceives him about her menstruation periods; if she does not fulfil her duty to the *Halacha* (the commandments of the Law, the *mitzvot);* if she walks out of the house with her head uncovered; if she runs out into the street. Abba Saul added if she insulted her husband's parents in his presence. Rabbi Tarfon said: if she is loud. Samuel understands this to mean when she raises her voice at home and her neighbours hear her voice. According to Rab, it is only the woman who is heard from another room during their conjugal relations.

Let us also remember that a woman who has her rules is considered impure: the husband must respect towards her the "laws of seclusion": twelve days per month (five days of examination and seven of purity), during which he must not touch his wife." As soon as one is in a state of *niddah,* she may not even touch her husband's hand, nor give him an object, nor throw it to him, nor receive it from him. The object is left and he will take it." In the state of *niddah,* a woman cannot ride in the same car with her husband, the same boat, the same wagon. A Jewish couple must therefore have two beds, for "it would be a crime to lie in the same bed in the state of *niddah709.*" In the synagogue, of course, women are kept apart in another room, and cannot participate in or watch the men's religious ceremony.

The economic weekly *L'Expansion* gave us in its March 2006 issue some details about family life in the Jewish colonies of the West Bank: "In the ultra-Orthodox population, where there is an average of seven children per household, only the woman works (generally in education), while the man devotes himself to full-time Torah study." These colonies attract numerous companies and are developing very well thanks to their "cheap and self-sacrificing female labour force[710]".

This is what made Daniel Cohn-Bendit say to Bernard Kouchner:

---

[708]Talmud *Sota, 20a (www.sefaria.org/Sotah.20a)*

[709]Roger Peyrefitte, *Les Juifs,* Flammarion, 1965, p. 97-99.

[710]"It is normal for the scholar to remain immersed in his books while his wife goes out to earn the family's livelihood." (Mark Zborowski, *Olam,* 1952, Plon, 1992, p. 74).

"Do you know that Jewish daily prayer that makes men say: 'I thank God that I have not become a woman'?" And Bernard Kouchner would reply with feigned naivety: "What a horror, I didn't know that[711]!"

Jewish women also provided the largest contingents of prostitutes. At the end of the 19th century, Jewish pimps in Poland did not hesitate to kidnap young girls from their community in the shtetls to send them to the brothels of New York or Buenos Aires. In his famous book *The Jewish France*, in 1886, Edward Drumont had already noted this: "Jewish women provide the largest contingent of prostitutes in the great capitals. The fact is undeniable, and the *Israelite Archives* have themselves acknowledged this fact[712]..." From time immemorial, Jews have been major players in international pimping. We know that after the fall of the Soviet Union, in the chaos and misery of the environment, thousands of young Russian, Moldavian and Ukrainian women answered false advertisements offering them a job as a chambermaid or maid in a hotel in Israel, and ended up kidnapped and locked up in brothels in Tel-Aviv[713].

Jews were also the pioneers of the pornographic industry[714]. Edward Drumont also denounced the excesses of pornography in his time: "It is a real Jewish bilge, that street of the *Croissant*, that central market of pornographic magazines, where the Israeli shops crowd against each other, fighting among themselves to see which will produce the most shameless fantasies[715]."

It is therefore easier to understand what motivated the Jewish women of the shtetls to enter European society at the end of the 19th century. Having been subjected for centuries to laws that relegated them to a distinctly oriental subaltern position, Jewish women wanted to take advantage of this sudden liberation to overthrow the family patriarchy that could abuse them in the framework of the greatest respect for and observance of tradition. Finally, it should come as no surprise that these harassed women threw themselves wholeheartedly into the feminist movement. These women believed that they could resolve their neuroses and their "oedipal conflicts" by fighting patriarchy in all its

---

[711]The two wink at each other. D. Cohn-Bendit, B. Kouchner, *Quand tu seras président*, Robert Laffont, 2004, p. 333.

[712]Édouard Drumond, *La France juive, tome I*, 1886, p. 88.

[713]See our long chapter on the White slave trade in Hervé Ryssen, *The Jewish Mafia*, (2008), (2022).

[714]See Hervé Ryssen, *The Jewish Mafia (*2008), (2022).

[715]Édouard Drumont, *La France juive, tome II,* 1886, p. 466. We understand why Jewish "historians" always accuse Julius Streicher, the famous German anti-Semitic propagandist, of having been a "pornographer".

forms. Like Freud and the other cosmopolitan intellectuals, they transferred to the rest of humanity a problem that was initially only very personal and particular. So it was in the European goy society that had welcomed them that feminists tried to kill the father. In this war against patriarchal society, Jewish women were particularly involved. In France, the feminist movement was led and greatly influenced by Jewish personalities such as Gisele Halimi, Simone Veil or Elisabeth Badinter, who claimed the heritage of Emma Goldman and Louise Weiss. Judaism was indeed at the forefront of this "liberating" movement. It is interesting to note how the feminist movement, which took off at the end of the 19th century, coincides exactly with the movement for the emancipation of Jews from the ghettos of Eastern Europe.

Elisabeth Badinter would go on to publish several books on the subject. She was the daughter and heiress of Marcel Bleustein-Blanchet, a billionaire of "Polish" origin who founded one of the first advertising agencies in France, *Publicis.* Committed to the political left, Elisabeth Bleustein married Robert Badinter, François Mitterrand's former socialist justice minister.

In *The Stables of the West,* Jean Cau pertinently observed, in the early 1970s, this war to the death declared on the Western male. The intellectual left, he said, has engaged in combat against the father." It pursues his image everywhere: God, the boss, the settler, the conqueror, the teacher, the state, etc.[716]"

The vogue of feminism was concomitant with Freudo-Marxist revolutionary thought. This ideology sought to bring about socialist revolution through the implosion of the patriarchal European family structure, in order to liberate women and children from the terrible oppression of families by the dominant white male. Wilhelm Reich and his successors of the Frankfurt school, such as Theodor W. Adorno ("W" for "Wiesenthal"), Max Horkheimer or Herbert Marcuse, as well as the young rebels of May 1968, were the most fervent propagandists, both for their hatred of European civilisation and, as we have analysed, their fervent desire to hasten the coming of the Messiah[717].

Max Horkheimer and Theodor Wiesenthal Adorno were at the forefront of the famous Frankfurt School. In their jointly written book, *The Dialectic of Enlightenment* (1944), in a chapter entitled *Elements of Anti-Semitism,* these two also proved to be two great humorists. Our readers are already familiar with Jewish thought and understand that

---

[716]Jean Cau, *Les Écuries de l'Occident,* Table ronde, 1973

[717]On Wilhelm Reich and Freudo-Marxism: Hervé Ryssen, *Planetary Hopes,* p. 80–88.

Jewish intellectuals are, indeed, above all circus stars: the kings of contortion! In that text, Horkheimer and Adorno brilliantly confirmed the true vocation of Judaism as excellently demonstrated by Barnum, Zavata, Gruss, Amar and the other Pinders. Listen to this: "The Jews are today the group which draws upon itself, in theory and in practice, the will to destruction which the false social order spontaneously generates. The Jews are marked by absolute evil as absolute evil. Thus they are, in fact, the chosen people... In the image of the Jew they present to the world, the racists express their own essence. Their appetites are exclusive possession, appropriation, unlimited power, at any price. They burden the Jew with this guilt, mock him as king and lord, and thus nail him to the cross... Fury is vented on the one who appears helpless[718]."

In *Eros and Civilisation (*1955), Herbert Marcuse developed a reflection based on Freud's famous book, *Discomfort in Civilisation*, but prolonging Freud's reflection in a revolutionary sense. Marcuse attacked the symbols of authority: the father of the family, the political leader, the company boss, the state. He preached the "society without fathers", taking up the argumentation of the "Francophortists" and Freudo-Marxists (Wilhelm Reich, Erich Fromm): there is no social liberation without sexual liberation. Here again, we seem to see the Jewish intellectual, barely out of his shtetl, projecting his own guilt onto European society for lack of having the courage to get rid of his own inner demons—his *dybbuks*. Indeed, it is a little laughable to receive moral lectures on the archaism of our culture from people whose customs can seem so dubious and who treat women so harshly[719].

Throughout the whole of the 20th century, emancipated Jews have not ceased in their efforts, through Marxism, Freudianism, Freudo-Marxism, liberalism and all cosmopolitan theories, to transfer upon the European populations a neurosis from which they do not know how to free themselves, and in which the idea of Messiah trains them in an

---

[718]Max Horkheimer and Theodor Adorno, *La Dialéctica de la Ilustración*, Editorial Trotta, Madrid, 1994, p. 213, 214, 216.

[719]We can read for example in the Talmud, among many other things, the following: "Rabbi Yoḥananan said: That is the statement of Yoḥananan ben Dehavai. However, the Rabbis said: The Halachah does not agree with the opinion of Yoḥanan ben Dehavai. Rather, whatever a man wishes to do with his wife he may do. He can have sex with her in any way he wishes, and need not worry about these restrictions. As an allegory, it is like meat coming from the butcher. If he wants to eat it salted, he can eat it salted. If you want to eat it roasted, you can eat it roasted. If you want to eat it cooked, you can eat it cooked. If you want to eat it boiled, you can eat it boiled. And so it is with the fish that comes from the fisherman." (*Talmud, Nedarim, 20b*) (NdT).

eternal flight forward, tearing down everything in their path and sacrificing all other civilisations in the hope of one day seeing the very hypothetical kingdom of David restored.

In order to liberate children and women from the odious oppression of the white male, feminism and freudo-Marxist ideologues are fiddling with history in their own way and putting forward theories that should lead to the destruction of the patriarchal family cell. Thus we learn that the Neolithic period, which corresponds to the invention of agriculture and the sedentarisation of peoples between 8000 and 3000 B.C., corresponds to "the golden age of humanity". Karl Marx himself placed primitive communism in this period. These ideal societies were apparently of a matriarchal type: "The Neolithic invented metallurgy: now, jewellery and copper for kitchen objects are mainly used by women, which reinforces our conviction of a matriarchal society", we read in this Freudo-Marxist literature. Apparently, humanity then lived in peace, until the evil Indo-Europeans came to spoil everything: "Today it has been formally demonstrated that warfare appeared much later... The trigger is undeniably the invention of warfare with the domestication of the horse by the Aryan tribes. In one fell swoop, a daily stage went from 20 km to 200 km, which allowed surprise raids on cities and riches, wheat granaries, beautiful women and jewellery, etc." Thus two ruling classes appeared: the warriors and the priests, who were exclusively male, and who "introduced authoritarian patriarchy and subjugated women in the social and sexual spheres." However, there were still some reminiscences of that ideal society in the Middle Ages: "As proof of this, we have, for example, even more recently, the case of Eleanor of Aquitaine and her Courts of Justice of Love, which almost always ruled in favour of the lover to the detriment of the husband." But the wicked lurked: "Louis IX the Saint exterminated this feminist society before its time during the Crusade against the Albigensians."

This is a rather caricatured example of what fanaticism in the service of Hebraic eschatology can produce. History is twisted in such a way that it can fit the ideological mould, according to the familiar principle that the end always justifies the means.

The Freudian-Marxist philosopher Jurgen Habermas described the communist ideal of a matriarchal society in his own way in the 1970s: "A family-like relationship only exists between mother and child or between siblings. Incest between mother and adolescent son is not allowed, although there is no similar limitation to incest between father and daughter, because there is no father role[720]." The role of the father is indeed less important in matriarchal societies where only mothers take care of families, while males (as in some primate societies) are left to their own devices and engage in sexual vagrancy.

These matriarchal societies are therefore polygamous. And as if by chance, we saw at the beginning of this study Jacques Attali promoting polygamy, both in his *Dictionary of the 21st century*, published in 1998, and in his book entitled *Nomadic Man*, in 2003. It should be noted here that this family structure was the norm among the Jews of ancient times, as Attali wrote in another of his books: "Polygamy is and will long remain the accepted practice of the Hebrews, as it is for all the peoples of the region[721]." Perhaps we should see here again that polygamy was the norm among the Jews of ancient times, as Attali wrote in another of his books: "Polygamy is and will long remain the accepted practice of the Hebrews, as it is for all the peoples of the region." Perhaps we should see here again that pathological inability to "see the point of view of others", which leads them to reason only according to their own standards, and to want to impose them at all costs on the rest of humanity.

And what about that Soviet law decriminalising incest in the USSR, knowing the preponderant role that many Jews played in that regime during the first thirty years?

Karl Marx, who came from a Jewish family, had also evoked this idea of an ideal primitive society. An American sociologist, Lewis Samuel Feuer, had noted that Karl Marx was very insistent on the fact that incest was the rule in primitive mankind. And with good reason, Lewis Samuel Feuer added: "That Marx could have imagined that incest was the rule says more about Karl Marx himself than about primitive societies[722]."

Sexual disorders

In his study on *Jewish Sexual Life* published in 1981, Dr Georges Valensin, who was a Sephardic Jew, explained that young Jews were introduced to sexuality very early: 'The young Jew, as young as ten

[720]Jurgen Habermas, *La reconstrucción del materialismo histórico*, Taurus ediciones, 1981, Madrid, p. 136.

[721]Jacques Attali, *Los judíos, el mundo y el dinero*, Fondo de cultura económica, 2005, Buenos Aires, p. 24.

[722]Lewis Feuer quoted by Nathaniel Weyl, in *Karl Marx and the Promethean Complex*, *Encounter*, December 1968, p. 15–30.

years old, was already made aware of the nature of sexual relations through reading the Talmud, which was very important to him if, as was often the case, his marriage was early. In that reading he found very racy sexual stories; stories with many notes and passionate comments that helped him to talk freely about sexuality." Another sexologist, Kinsey, explained how he had been "struck by the freedom of speech in sexual matters among young American Jews." He added: "Jews talk about sexual matters with much less reserve than other men, and that is probably why the legend has spread that they were very sexually active[723]." Dr. Valensin did indeed explain that Jews generally suffer from greater sexual deficiencies than other men. So it is no coincidence that there are so many Jews in the field of sexology[724].

Sometimes, too, the intimate customs of Jewish families can give rise to "hypersexual" individuals. We think here of Dominique Strauss-Kahn, former socialist Minister of Economy and Finance and President of the International Monetary Fund, who in 2011 turned out to be a compulsive rapist. We also think of Israeli President Moshe Katzav, who was accused by several women in October 2006. Cases of this kind are abundant[725].

The role of the authoritarian father and abusive mother in such behaviour should be noted here. In the United States, research on 412 cases of such "hypersexual" adults (337 men, 75 women) came to this conclusion: "Generally speaking, these people have lived in a family where a brutal father has given them the self-image that they cannot be loved; their mother has been sexually abusive, awakening their sexuality early and making them see that this is the only way to relate to and be taken into consideration by others. In these adults, sexuality will be extremely highly valued, leading to unbridled sexual activity and sexual exploitation, first of their siblings and siblings, and then of anyone else. This overflowing sexuality manifests itself in some behaviours tolerated by society (masturbation, homosexuality, prostitution) and in others that are less so; such as exhibitionism and voyeurism[726]."

But let us dwell a little on two cases. Thierry Chichportich, the famous sexologist, was more "hypo" than "hyper", as he needed to lull

[723]A. Kinsey, *Le Comportement sexuelle de l'homme*, Éd. Du Pavois, Paris, 1950, p. 617; in Georges Valensin, *La Vie sexuelle juive*, Éditions philosophiques, 1981, p. 170.
[724]See Hervé Ryssen, *Jewish Fanaticism.*
[725]See Hervé Ryssen, *Jewish Fanaticism.*
[726]Jacques-Dominique de Lannoy, *L'Inceste*, Presses Universitaires de France, 1992, p. 94.

his patients to sleep before raping them. In May 2006, the "masseur to the stars", nicknamed "the man with the golden fingers" by the world cinema elite, was sentenced to 18 years in prison by the Nice court for the rapes of twelve women in 2003 during massage sessions. He used his references as a masseur of big stars—Carole Bouquet, Emmanuelle Béart, Penélope Cruz, Monica Bellucci—to lure his clients. They were previously lulled to sleep without their knowledge by a narcotic administered in a drink. All the victims testified before the judge that, before the massage, he served them a meal or a drink "with a bitter taste" which had the effect of leaving them asleep or in a "comatose state". Some of the young women discovered that they had had a sexual relationship with Thierry Chichportich by watching videotapes seized from his home. Indeed, the masseur was recording his sexual relations with the unconscious women. The first complaint had been filed by one of the victims who had partially regained consciousness during the rape. The discovery of the videos and the narcotics used allowed him to be prosecuted.

In November 2009, Thierry Chichportich appeared before the Alpes-Maritimes court for two other rapes committed in 2001. A young woman, Christine, a manicurist in the Paris region, explained during the hearing that she had met the masseur in October 2001. He had invited her to dinner at his house where she fell asleep after dinner: "At a certain moment, I felt a heavy body on mine. A sensation of penetration. It woke me up." The same script as with another woman, Cecilia, a communications manager, who had met Thierry Chichportich in Cannes in 2001, and who claimed to have fallen asleep after drinking a tea he had served her in a booth on the beach at the Carlton.

Chichportich had denied the facts at the hearing, claiming to be the victim of a conspiracy. The "pseudo-victims", according to him, had complained in order to get money. Assuming the role of victim himself, he had accused the media of being the source of the women's complaints, before denouncing their poor living conditions in the prison in Haute-Corsica. This attempt to elicit sympathy from the jury did not bear fruit, as he was sentenced to a further twelve years' imprisonment, in addition to the eighteen years of the previous trial.

The Tordjman case was emblematic. A world-renowned sexologist, the highly publicised Gilbert Tordjamn was the founder of sexology in France. The first complaint against him dates back to 1999. Subsequently, numerous women had accused the specialist of sexual abuse. Gilbert Tordjamn was charged in March 2002, at the age of 75. In total, forty-four women, former patients, had come before the examining magistrate's office to testify against the former president of the World Association of Sexology.

The weekly *Le Point* of 9 August 2002 recounted the testimonies of his victims. The first one dated back to 1983. The testimony had previously been published in the form of a long story entitled "The horror behind the door" in the magazine *Psychologies*. Anne recounted how her therapy with Dr. Tordjman had ended at the hotel and how he had taken advantage of his status as a doctor to engage in sexual relations with her, destroying her psychologically. In the text, Dr. Tordjman's name was not mentioned. It was unthinkable at the time," said Anne. It happened in 1978. It took me five years to get over it and four more years before I agreed to talk about it."

Beatrice, 44 years old, had been abused in 1988. Gilbert Tordjman fondled her clitoris and masturbated against her during the sessions." I didn't know what a sexologist had the right to do. He would tell me, 'If you don't want to do it, you'll never get it.'" Carolina, 45, recounted what the laser sessions were like in 1991: "I was naked on a table, legs spread wide with a laser over my sex. He asked me to make love pretending to moan while he caressed my breasts, belly and sex. I was desperate and totally embarrassed. Then began the deep masturbation session, bareback, with a porn film projection that was supposed to echo my fantasies."

The testimonies were repeated over the years. The script was almost always the same: projection of pornographic films, laser sessions, hypnosis, then masturbation of the patients, sometimes of himself, and finally, for some of them, sexual penetration.

To justify himself, the famous sexologist devoted an editorial to this case in 2001 in his review *Les Cahiers de sexologie clinique*: "Between diagnosis or therapeutic practice, and the sexual gesture, or interpreted as such, the boundary can be difficult to establish for some fragile and indoctrinated patients… The examinations that we carry out on patients who come to us for sexual dysfunction are strictly medical in nature." In short, the victims had misunderstood the situation: they had confused vaginal touching with masturbation.

The sexologist seemed to favour victims who had been sexually abused during their childhood. This was the case of Monica (the name was changed by the newspaper), who had consulted Dr. Tordjman with her husband in 1993. Monica had been raped by her brother, and since then was unable to feel desire during sexual intercourse. During the hypnosis sessions, Dr. Tordjman multiplied the caresses and coarse words, and then moved on to vaginal touching, whispering in her ear things like: "I want you, you are so desirable"." Later, Monica would attempt suicide.

Silvia, a small, dynamic 45-year-old blonde, triggered the judicial and media storm. In March 1999, she had gone to the doctor with her husband for a lack of libido." I went to see Dr. Tordjman because he was someone very reputable. We knew his books. I had full confidence in him." But from the beginning, Silvia was disconcerted by the sexologist's gestures, the way he touched her belly very close to her pubis and the rude words he murmured in her ear. Then, session after session, things got worse: "He licked my breasts, he inserted several fingers in my vagina. I was lost, I didn't know what to do." After confessing to her husband what she had suffered, she went to the provincial council of the Order of Physicians in Paris to denounce the case. In the meantime, Dr. Tordjman's wife had phoned him to beg him not to reveal anything, citing her husband's heart problems." She tried in every way, but I stood my ground and we went before the regional council, where we witnessed a real travesty of justice."

Gilbert Tordjamn only received a reprimand, but not for the acts committed on his patient, but for having breached professional secrecy by revealing to his wife what had happened. Silvia appealed, together with the Ministry of Health. The Order's national council, on 13 June 2001, imposed a one-month suspension on Dr. Tordjman, but for breach of professional secrecy, not for sexual abuse. However, the publicity surrounding this conviction was to allow the victims to come together in Ancas (National Association against Sexual Abuse by Health Professionals) and many of them decided to file a criminal complaint. On 13 March, the rape charge was finally announced.

Dr. Tordjman cannot express himself freely because of the ongoing investigation," explained his lawyer Jacques-Georges Bitoun. But he is determined to defend himself to the end, because none of the testimonies make sense. These women are clearly fabricators or madwomen. Dr. Tordjamn has examined more than 7000 women during his career, and even if seven of them denounce him, this is not serious because they have a long psychological history. Besides, nobody goes to a sexologist to have their tonsils probed! "

In 2003, while on probation, Gilbert Tordjamn violated the court decision prohibiting him from practising his profession. He was immediately arrested and imprisoned in Fresnes prison. On 4 May 2005, the newspaper *Le Figaro* reported that the "pope of sexology" would appear again before the criminal court. The trial was expected to take place in April 2009, but Tordjman died shortly before in his prison cell.

Jews make up large battalions of health professionals within psychoanalysis and sexology[727]. While it is probably true that psychoanalysts try to cure their patients, we may think that they also try to cure themselves through their patients. The psychiatrist Jacques-Dominique de Lannoy stated in this respect: "The therapist has often suffered a trauma himself during his childhood and it can happen that patients become the only people with whom he can establish a connection ... hence the exchange of roles in the therapeutic relationship[728]."

Most individual therapy involves a prolonged personal relationship with the therapist, so it is not surprising to find that numerous cases of sexual abuse are committed in doctors' offices, especially on women who have suffered violence from their parents during their childhood[729].

Freudian bisexuality

The idea of the bisexuality of individuals was from the beginning part of the doctrinal corpus of the feminist and Freudo-Marxist movements. This concept, like everything that comes from the Jewish people, has been elevated to a universal law applicable to all individuals of all civilisations, although in practice its field of application is limited to the European population.

By making the European man believe that he is also a bit of a woman, it is thought that he will more easily accept the new matriarchal society that is to be imposed on him in order to "liberate" him. It must be accepted and understood that, in the terribly repressive patriarchal society, European men repressed their natural feminine instincts, and that it was this "inhibition" that made white men so aggressive towards foreigners, especially Jews.

In 1987, for example, the feminist Yolande Cohen wrote in *Women and Counterpowers*: In today's society, "men and women will be forced

---

[727]However, it should be noted that the number of psychoanalysts has dropped significantly in recent years due to the discrediting of this "science".

[728]Jacques-Dominique de Lannoy, *L'Inceste*, Presses Universitaires de France, 1992, p. 100-103.

[729]We have summarised numerous cases of rape of patients by doctors in *The Jewish Fanaticism*, chapter *Rapes in psychiatry*, and in *Le Mirroir du judaïsme*, Baskerville (2009), p. 296–302.

to develop and externalise the 'other part' of themselves that was repressed by the education of the past. Moreover, women will be obliged to play the role of men and men the role of women. The original bisexuality has returned, sweeping away everything in its path, the inequality and strict complementarity of the sexes... The arrival of the third millennium coincides with an extraordinary reversal of the balance of power. Not only will the patriarchal system be dead and gone in most of the industrialised West, but we will also witness the birth of a new imbalance in the relations of the sexes, this time to the exclusive benefit of women[730]."

The desire for the destruction of European society is once again very perceptible, for, evidently, the apology for bisexuality is nothing more than a veiled way of encouraging homosexuality. But we also perceive in these statements that typically hysterical ambivalence, which is nothing more than the projection onto the rest of humanity of a very specific neurosis of Judaism.

Let us look at what the psychotherapist Michel Steyaert said: "Homosexual themes are almost constant in hysterical madness, whether it is an active homosexuality (which does not prevent coexistence with heterosexual relations), or a homosexuality which is not active but which manifests itself very clearly in fantasies and in delirious phases... We thus make the transition to the problem of bisexuality which is frequently observed in hysterical madness, since the truly fundamental question of the hysteric is: Who am I, man or woman? [731]?" ""

This ambiguity of the hysterical personality is the same that we have perceived in numerous texts of cosmopolitan literature. We should no longer be surprised, therefore, given the control and presence of Jews in our media system, by all those programmes and television series that have been advocating homosexuality since the 1990s. This propaganda corresponds to a desire to destroy traditional European society, but also to a deep neurosis that leads the sick to project their own "oedipal conflicts" onto the rest of humanity.

This reminds us for example of the 1998 film by director Jean-Jacques Zilbermann, which dealt with homosexuality within the Jewish community: *L'Homme est une femme comme les autres (Man is a woman like any other woman).*

Homosexuality is probably much more widespread than is

---

[730]Yolande Cohen, *Femmes et contre-pouvoirs*, Boréal, 1987, p. 214-216.

[731]Michel Steyaert, *Hystérie, folie et psychose*, Éd. Les Empêcheurs de penser en rond, 1992, p. 67-68.

believed within the sect. The television presenter Stephane Bern went so far as to declare unexpectedly in an article in the daily *Libération* in May 2000 that "Jewish mothers made excellent homosexuals".

The following are some of the most recent and best-known films on the subject:

Bruno (USA, 2009), for example, is an "irritating", "uncomfortable" film by Larry Charles and Sacha Baron Cohen. It tells the bizarre story of a gay Austrian journalist who decides to become a star in Los Angeles.

In *Whatever works* (USA, 2009), the famous director Woody Allen transforms a Christian couple. The wife becomes an orgy aficionado, while her husband becomes a realised homosexual.

The film by Chinese director Lou Ye, *Spring Drunken Nights* (China, 2009), is "a passionate film about homosexuality in China", reported *Le Monde*. The film, selected for the Cannes Film Festival, was subsidised with 70,000 euros by the Ile-de-France region and 120,000 euros from the Ministry of Foreign Affairs' South Fund (Quay d'Orsay), which supports foreign cultural works. The newspaper stated that the film was produced by Sylvain Bursztein.

In April 2011, *Tomboy*, the new film by Celine Sciamma, told the story of Laura, 10 years old and *garçon manqué*[732]. In her new neighbourhood, she makes Lisa and her gang believe that she is a boy. Laura becomes "Miguel", a boy like the others, different enough to attract attention and make Lisa fall in love.

The feminisation of Western societies and the rise of homosexuality are no coincidence, but are undoubtedly the consequence of the media power acquired by numerous influential Jewish businessmen, intellectuals and journalists. They can spin the problem in all directions: there is no other explanation. It is not only a political process aiming at the destruction of the European world, based on a prophetic delirium typical of Judaism, but also a neurotic projection that translates into: "an anal regression, related to the non-overcoming of oedipal conflicts". Freudian theories, as we have seen, work best when applied to the Hebraic matrix itself.

The subject of bisexuality, popularised early on by Sigmund Freud, is indeed a very ancient obsession of Kabbalistic Jews, as David Bakan recalled. For adherents of the Zohar and the Kabbalah, indeed, the theological doctrine of the Shechinah (a form of sacred hierogamy) occupies an essential place. The Shechinah is somehow the feminine

---

[732] Bad boy; Girl with a strong manly character; Tomboy.

part of God, the "Divine Presence of God", the "heavenly mother", and a part of God Himself." Repeatedly, the Zohar speaks of God's union with His Shechinah... The Shechinah is the wife of God, who has been disowned by her Lord, but the time is coming when He will again cast upon her a favourable glance."

David Bakan explained that "the bisexuality of man" is a "dominant theme" of the Zohar: Since the Godhead has a female part, it is logical to think "that Adam was created in the image of God and the Shechinah, or of God containing the Shechinah in him. Thus, Adam, whose rib served to create Eve, is both male and female." Thus we can "trace the germ of this doctrine of bisexuality to the Kabbalistic tradition[733] " popularised by Freud.

For many Jews, evidently, "the Shechinah is also identified with the community of Israel, as the bride of God[734]." And now we better understand Otto Weininger's comparison between "the Jew" and "the woman", if it may have seemed a little laughable when we first read it. In reality, the comparison was much more profound than it seemed[735].

We now also have a better understanding of Jewish messianism. Every misfortune that strikes the community, every cataclysm, is identified by rabbis and Jewish intellectuals with "the birth pangs of the Messiah"—the *"Hevlei Mashiah"* in Hebrew. The vocabulary used by Judaism to express the desire for the coming of the Messiah is strikingly similar to that of the medical analysis of the hysterical phenomenon.

"The birth pangs of the Messiah", this is now very evident to us, are in fact the symptoms of the imaginary pregnancy[736].

Caves and cellars of civilisation

While psychoanalysis is in continuous regression and has almost disappeared, Freudian theories, which had largely inspired the

---

[733] David Bakan, *Freud et la tradition mystique juive*, 1963, Payot, 2001, p. 301, 33, 306.

[734] David Bakan, *Freud et la tradition mystique juive*, 1963, Payot, 2001, p. 297.

[The duty of pious Jews is to restore through their prayers and religious acts the perfect divine unity, in the form of sexual union, between the male and female divinities. Thus, before most ritual acts, the following Kabbalistic formula is recited: "For the sake of the [sexual] union of the Holy One and His Shechinah..." In Israel Shahak, *Historia judía, Religión judía, El peso de tres mil años*, Ediciones A.Machado, 2016, Madrid, p. 75. See also translator's note in Annex VIII].

[735] Read Weininger again in the chapter *Self-Hatred.*" The Jew is by nature a female", explained the young Jew in Henry Bean's film *The Believer* (2001).

[736]Read again the chapter *Messianic Hope*.

"rebellious" movements of the 1960s and 1970s, continue to permeate Western society. They continue to represent an ideological matrix that generates resentment and hostility towards traditional European society. Through feminism and the thesis of bisexuality, they are a permanent attack on the white male, thus encouraging an introspection that is harmful to individuals, as well as a homosexuality that is complacently conveyed by the Western media. With the "discovery" of infantile sexuality, Freudian theories also justify paedophilia and sexual "liberation". The valorisation of free love, to the detriment of marriage and commitment, undermines the family cell and the European birth rate as much as the Veil law[737] on abortion. Pornography, which is intruding on every screen, participates in the great "liberation" movement. If we add to this a relentless emasculating media propaganda aimed at making European man guilty and making him accept the multiracial society, then we have indeed arrived at a real and fully-fledged destruction enterprise.

The Jewish neurotic projection is accompanied by a very characteristic spirit of revenge which is clearly visible in many texts and in many different ways: anti-Christian attacks and apology for plural society, Marxism and liberalism, psychoanalysis and feminism. The centuries-old resentment against European civilisation and Christianity has always given rise in Jews to a vengeful literature that feeds on impotent envy and implacable hatred disguised behind egalitarian phraseology. This fusion of the spirit of resentment and neurosis has been the essence of the Jewish spirit throughout the 20th century since the ghettoisation.

Freud, like other Jews, had a deep hatred for the Catholic Church and European civilisation. Hence his admiration for Hannibal Barca, that Semitic hero of Antiquity who had fought relentlessly and held Rome in check for years. Freud wrote very explicitly in *The Interpretation of Dreams*: "Hannibal had a prominent place in my fantasies". The scene in which Hamilcar makes his son swear an oath to take revenge on the Romans exalted his imagination: Hannibal represents Jewish tenacity in the face of the abhorred Rome.

While Marx had mounted his supposedly universal theories of class struggle, Freud had done the same with his equally "universal" Oedipus complex. Karl Marx claimed that the culture and politics of all societies were almost entirely dependent on the economic system and the power of the propertied class. Therefore, according to him, Western

[737]Simone Veil. A French politician of Jewish origin who pushed for such a law in 1975.

cultural "superstructures" and mentalities would inevitably be modified as soon as the bourgeoisie's structures of economic exploitation were destroyed and replaced by the power of the liberating proletarian. The method of Freud, his congener, was ultimately very similar. It was a kind of transposition on a human scale of the social analyses of Marxism. Freud divided the human being into the "Ego", the "I" and the "Overself", just as Marx had divided society into hopelessly antagonistic social classes[738]. The Overself, representing the stifling norms of society, forces the individual to "inhibit" his natural instincts, thus playing the role given to the police at the orders of the bourgeoisie in the Marxist-Leninist schema.

Be that as it may, Karl Marx and Sigmund Freud were always searching at the bottom for that which could explain the natural conflicts that exist in every human being and in all societies." We can deduce as a result that in the Oedipus complex coincide the beginnings of religion, morality, society and art, a coincidence which is perfectly in accordance with the demonstration provided by psychoanalysis that this complex constitutes the nodule of all neuroses[739]", wrote Freud. He delved into the subconscious of the human being to find the dirtiest, to bring it to the surface of consciousness and to "liberate" the patient from his frustrations and neurosis. We now know that the endless and ruinous sessions of psychoanalysis had above all the effect of further undermining the morale of depressed people.

Freud was conscious of his method: "I was always on the ground floor or in the basement of the building," he wrote, while observing how "on the upper floors" were lodged "such distinguished guests as religion, art, etc.[740]..."

This image could also be seen in the novelist Albert Cohen, of whom Leon Poliakov said: "For the Mediterranean Jew Albert Cohen, Judaism is a mysterious dungeon, a dark cellar that his hero "Solal" frequents and loves in secret. In his novel *Beautiful of the Lord*, as Bernard-Henri Lévy wrote, "Solal the Magnificent, the Grand Duke of the SDN, who speaks on equal terms with the greatest, at the same time nourishes and protects in his cellar a sort of 'court of miracles' composed of scrofulous, sickly, outlawed Jews, unrepresented in the world where he is one of the kings and whom he is forced to visit in secret at night".

---

[738] See Hervé Ryssen, *Planetary Hopes, (*2022).

[739] Sigmund Freud, *Totem and Taboo, Collected Works,* EpubLibre, Trad. Luis López Ballesteros y de Torres, 200, p. 2485.

[740] Marthe Robert, *D'Oedipe à Moïse,* 1974, Agora, 1987, p. 181.

Isn't this very revealing of a mentality that tends towards underground action, rummaging, digging galleries, acting in secret, rather than creating and germinating what is most beautiful and noble in the human soul?

It is therefore not surprising, under these conditions, that the National Socialists have caricatured their declared enemies as animals and insects known to dwell in caves, cellars, sewers and ventilation pipes that are bent on undermining the structures of the building. Undoubtedly, the spirit of vengeance and the determination to destroy what others have created over the centuries do not help to bring out what is most beautiful in human beings. The shortcomings of Judaism in the fields of culture and art cannot be explained in any other way.

Certainly, ideological systematisation with universal pretensions, as seen in Karl Marx and Sigmund Freud, has not been the germ of a great artistic creation, so to speak. When it is finally expressed in painting or sculpture, for example, Jewish creativity shows us above all the neurotic, pathological disorder: just look at those paintings in contemporary art galleries or those sculptures in the squares and roundabouts of our cities, each one more twisted and hideous than the next.

Judaism in psychiatry

The universalisation of Freudian neurosis seems to coincide with the general tendency of Jewish intellectuals to consider that all of humanity must be confused with Judaism. This is what allowed Elie Wiesel to say quite naturally: "That is the way things are, and there is nothing that can be done about it: the enemy of the Jews is the enemy of humanity[741]." On the other hand, since the Jews are innocent of everything that can be blamed on them, those who take it out on them are therefore taking it out on the whole of humanity. In his *memoirs*, Elie Wiesel wrote: "Jew-hatred has never been confined to the Jew alone: it overflows and targets other minorities. It begins with hatred of the Jew, and ends with hatred of those who are different, who come from elsewhere, who think and live differently. That is why anti-Semitism does not only concern Jews; it affects the society in which we live as a whole[742]."

Bernard-Henri Levy expressed himself in the same way in 2002,

[741] Elie Wiesel, *Mémoires II*, Éditions du Seuil, 1996, p. 72.
[742] Elie Wiesel, *Mémoires II*, Éditions du Seuil, 1996, p. 128-129.

when the Jews of France were the target of accusations by immigrant youth in solidarity with the Palestinian people. On that occasion, some violence had been committed against synagogues, and the philosopher tried to enlist the French in his fight against radical Islam: "The Jews are in the front line, but right behind is France... This anti-Semitism is new... When a synagogue is attacked with a battering ram, the symbol as such is attacked, the institution, the universal[743]". Unless, of course, it is simply a synagogue.

The truth is that the speeches of Elie Wiesel and Bernard-Henri Levy express a terrible fear of seeing the "chosen people" alone in the face of their contradictions and, above all, in the face of their own contradictions ("They fear loneliness, and moments of separation fill them with anguish", said the doctor). The Jew bears all the sufferings of humanity, the philosopher Alain Finkielkraut told us: "From the beaten woman to the immigrant worker, from the Chilean junta to the Cambodian children and the prisoners of the gulag, each victim resurrected the Jew[744]." On the other hand, when a Jew is hit, all of humanity suffers. We know the refrain.

André Neher, for his part, took up the words of Vladimir Jankelevitch: "Auschwitz is the failure of the millennial adventure of human thought[745]", he wrote. In reality, it was above all a severe blow to Jewish thought.

The projection of Jewish neurosis onto the universal plane also manifests itself in the religious dimension. By putting forward his theory of the primitive horde, of the murder of the father and the totemic feast, Freud intended to show, in *Totem and Taboo*, the neurotic character of religion, which, according to him, was nothing more "than the neurosis of mankind". But we now know that, if there is a neurosis, it corresponds to a very specific case. One should always read Jewish intellectuals with a mirror.

As is well known, all Jewish intellectuals revel in the 'mystery' of Judaism. In his 1992 book *The Wound*, the famous press director Jean Daniel (Bensaïd) expressed his anguish: "The Jewish mystery is a moving phenomenon that can raise mystical questions and lead some to believe in the choice of a people[746]." Thirteen years earlier, he had already questioned himself, unable to find a solution to his problem: "I can say that this mystery, when it inhabits me, clouds my thoughts rather

[743] Bernard-Henri Lévy, *Récidives*, Grasset, 2004, p. 845.
[744] Alain Finkielkraut, *Le Juif imaginaire*, 1980, Points Seuil, 1983, p. 211.
[745] André Neher, *Le dur Bonheur d'être juif*, Le Centurion, 1978, p. 47.
[746] Jean Daniel, *La Blessure*, Grasset, 1992, p. 259.

than enriching them… Where is this people if not in persecution? No one has so far been able to define it[747]." And again we hear the echo of André Glucksmann's words: "Two millennia of being a living question for the whole world. Two millennia of innocence, having nothing to do with anything[748]."

At the end of his book *The Imaginary Jew*, Alain Finkielkraut also wondered about the elusive nature of Judaism: "People? Religion? Nation? All these categories are more or less applicable: none is really satisfactory… The Jewish people do not know what it is[749]."

As André Neher put it: "There is no answer to the question "Who is a Jew? This question will always be a question because it contains in it a fringe that transcends it forever[750]."

"Outside the family, the Jewish community is a fiction that exists only in the discourses of those who proclaim it. There are, of course, institutions, a press, schools, notables, charities, but the Jew lives like most of his peers outside this network." It is "a collectivity that has no collective existence[751]." However, these statements did not prevent the philosopher from raging, a few pages further on, against those who dare to think that Jews have a very particular spirit, and that this is precisely what they can be identified by, rather than by their habits, their names or their noses. Look at the intellectual contortions he displayed: "Anti-Semitism became racism on the fateful day when, because of emancipation, it was no longer possible to recognise a Jew at first sight. Since, because of the repugnant social promiscuity, Jews no longer wore a distinctive sign, they were then punished by having a different mentality. Science did what was beyond the reach of the eyes: to guarantee the strangeness of the adversary, to stigmatise the nation of Israel by enclosing it in its Jewish reality." It was, one supposes, "fear and resentment" that animated the anti-Semites." Racial hatred, that blind rage, actually punished the Jews because they no longer exhibited their difference[752]."

We have ironised in our previous book this apparent misunderstanding of Jewish intellectuals about the hostility that their reasoning and procedures may arouse in the world of the goyim. Now we understand better why their discourses can be sincere, and how this

---

747 Jean Daniel, *L'Ère des ruptures*, Grasset. 1979, p. 113

748 André Glucksmann, *Le Discours de la haine*, Plon, 2004, p. 88.

749 Alain Finkielkraut, *Le Juif imaginaire*, 1980, Points Seuil, 1983, p. 199, 204.

750 André Neher, *Le dur Bonheur d'être juif*, Le Centurion, 1978, p. 215.

751 Alain Finkielkraut, *Le Juif imaginaire*, 1980, Points Seuil, 1983, p. 113.

752 Alain Finkielkraut, *Le Juif imaginaire*, 1980, Points Seuil, 1983, p. 106.

characteristic "*chutzpah*" can ultimately be the expression of their ambiguity and identity hesitation.

In his *Reflections on the Jewish Question*, in 1946, Jean-Paul Sartre had written: "The Jew is a man whom other men regard as a Jew: this is the pure and simple truth from which one must start… Indeed, contrary to a very widespread idea, it is not the Jewish character that provokes anti-Semitism, but, on the contrary, it is the anti-Semite who creates the Jew… If Jews did not exist, the anti-Semite would invent them[753]."

This thesis, which seems grotesque at first glance, actually contains some truth in the sense that it corresponds very well to the Jews' own perception of their identity, in the absence of being able to explain the reality of the causes of anti-Semitism. Jean Daniel's testimony is enlightening: "Sartre's book? It was a liberation. I had the impression that a guy had finally understood me. It was hard to believe that he wasn't a Jew too, because he was capable of going to the bottom of our humiliation. The invention of this implicit Jew was at that moment a liberation." Alain Finkielkraut was also ecstatic: "This short essay is a fascinating, fundamental and salvific text[754]." The weekly *Marianne* of 25 June 2005 carried the testimony of the film-maker Claude Lanzmann, who confirmed: "This book represented an essential moment. In a way, Sartre has given us back a taste for life. On this earth, there was at least one man close to us who had understood us."

As surprising as this may seem to seasoned "Jewish question" goyim, these testimonies cannot be considered as a manifestation of what some call Jewish "perfidy". Contrary to what we might have thought in our previous book, there is probably much sincerity in these statements. Let us recall what Otto Weininger wrote: "There is no male Jew who, however confusedly, does not suffer for his Jewishness, that is, for his lack of belief … he is the most torn individual, the poorest in inner identity[755]."

"I have a history and a face marked by twenty centuries of misfortunes, wrote Finkielkraut: I can in a moment of depression curse my lack of personality, my inconsistency and my doubts[756]." And then the philosopher returned to the everlasting Jewish jeremiads, for the Jews, we must know, are weak, very weak, and their weakness leaves

[753] Jean-Paul Sartre, *Reflections on the Jewish Question*, Seix Barral, Barcelona, 2005, p. 77–78, 159, 15.

[754] Alain Finkielkraut, *Le Juif imaginaire*, 1980, Points Seuil, 1983, p. 17.

[755] Otto Weininger, *Sex and Character*, 1902, Ediciones 62 s|a, 1985, Barcelona, p. 322.

[756] Alain Finkielkraut, *Le Juif imaginaire*, 1980, Points Seuil, 1983, p. 15.

them at the mercy of the madness of men. Hitlerite Germany had therefore decided to exterminate these weak beings, precisely because of their weakness (look no further for explanations!): "The most powerful state in the world planned the disappearance of a people without an army, without land and without alliances. Between an over-equipped country and an undefended nation, there has never been such an unequal and absolute war." The poor Jews are thus the "scapegoats[757]", always persecuted, and always innocent.

In May 2006, an Elie Wiesel in his twilight years finally made some confessions in his 'novel', *A Mad Desire to Dance.* His hero "suffers from a madness due to an excess of memory". He confessed to a psychoanalyst: "Am I paranoid, schizophrenic, hysterical, neurotic? "Through his character Elie Wiesel expressed himself as follows: "Like the *dybbuk,* I take refuge in my madness like in a warm bed on a winter's night. Yes, that's right. It is a *dybbuk* that haunts me, that lives inside me. He, the one who takes my place. He, the one who usurps my identity and imposes his destiny on me? Where does my great uneasiness come from, these changes, these sudden metamorphoses, without explanations or rites of passage, this being in the doldrums close to stultification, this vacillation of being that characterises my malaise[758]?"

Like many others, Alain Finkielkraut became fed up and disgusted with this endless questioning of his Jewish identity: "I had had enough of my Jewishness. The disgust. The saturation. The weariness. I was full, exhausted by the pounding, stultified by the refrain about our unparalleled destiny, bombarded by the everlasting song of the despised people. Stuffed, it begged for mercy. Not to God, not to the system, but to those who held the funnel, my parents and their everlasting Jewish obsession. Obsession, that's the word? Didn't they continually remind me of our loneliness, our curse?"

Finkielkraut would declare himself incapable of finding the causes of his identity hesitation: "I am not in a position to explain, after a thousand others, as a result of what traumatism I became a Jew, because as far as I can remember, I have always been one[759]."

Freud had understood that the origin of Judaism was not of a religious, but of a sexual nature. The "German" poet Heinrich Heine was, by the way, in the habit of sarcastically declaring that Judaism was not a religion, but a "family disgrace" (*Familienunglück*). Only the

---

757 Alain Finkielkraut, *Le Juif imaginaire*, 1980, Points Seuil, 1983, p. 64, 162, 60.

758 Elie Wiesel, *Un Désir fou de danser*, Éd. Seuil, 2006, p. 13, 29

759 Alain Finkielkraut, *Le Juif imaginaire*, 1980, Points Seuil, 1983, p. 127, 209.

initiated could understand the background of his thinking.

As we know, the origin of evil is incest, which is the origin of the hysterical pathology that characterises Judaism so well: histrionics, egocentrism, anguish, chronic paranoia, intolerance of frustration, fabulation, selective amnesia, identity and sexual ambiguity, megalomania, and so on. Everything is finally summed up in this sentence: *Judaism is that illness that psychoanalysis claimed to cure*.

It is no longer a question of the "chosen people" at all, but rather of recognising a medical diagnosis. Thus, for three thousand years, Judaism seems to have been a long succession of incestuous generations. Indeed, in most cases, the perpetrator of incest has himself been sexually abused as a child by an adult, usually a close relative[760]. Through the trauma, the incestuous child in turn becomes an incestuous parent, and these dispositions are thus passed on from generation to generation. Reading today's Jewish intellectuals, we must assume that Freudian psychoanalysis has not succeeded in freeing them from their obsessive neurosis. Jean Daniel, who clearly wished to get out of it, rebelled against the excessive zeal of some guardians of tradition, like the great Emmanuel Levinas, for example, "who reproaches and proclaims that to abandon Judaism is to share the intention of Pharaoh (now Hitler) and to finish off the aborted genocide. This is how the hardest prison lock is wielded," wrote Jean Daniel. Manifestly, something troubled him, for he claimed for the Jews the right to be able to "opt out of the order if they consider themselves unworthy of a choice too heavy[761]."

Ten years later, Jean Daniel was still locked up behind walls, as he finally expressed it clearly in his 2003 book, *The Jewish Prison*: "Judaism is a call to holiness", he wrote, before asking himself: "Has God invested these men with an inhuman mission? Can this commandment of Election be judged as the obverse of a curse? "And he noted that Judaism is a closed world, cut off from the rest of the world: "The Jewish community is almost impossible to enter and everything possible is done to prevent people from leaving. We are clearly in the presence of a prison[762]."

In the minutes of his 14 March 2005 lecture at the Itshak Rabin Institute in Paris, press director Alexandre Adler reminded the audience

760 Jacques-Dominique de Lannoy, *L'Inceste*, Presses Universitaires de France, 1992, p. 92, 91.

761 Jean Daniel, *La Blessure*, Grasset, 1992, p. 258, 260.

762 Jean Daniel, *La prisión judía. Meditaciones intempestivas de un testigo*, Tusquets, Barcelona, 2007, p. 79, 172.

of the role of every Jew: "There is an omnipresent imperative. That imperative is not to allow any Jew to be lost. Unfortunately, it sometimes happens that some Jews are lost, but Jews must not be complicit in this. The role of every Jew in the world is to be his brother's keeper ... that means to bring him back home. To tell him: come back, come back, don't forget[763]."

Mark Zborowski gave us an idea of the pressure exerted by the group on a man who wanted to escape from "prison": "A person who abjures the faith is considered dead forever: a funeral is held for him, a symbolic ceremony is held, mourning is observed for an hour, and the name of the "disappeared" is banned from conversation... Everything possible will be done to avoid such a catastrophe. The rabbi, friends and family urge the renegade to come to his senses before it is too late. In case of failure, the *meshumed*, or convert, is declared dead by the group[764]."

Note how Jean Daniel never capitalises the word "Jew". This is because the Jewish people is not a race, nor a religion—for there are many atheist Jews—but rather an attachment and devotion to Jewish history, the Mosaic Law, the idea of the unification of the world, the idea of "peace" on earth and the coming of the Messiah. It should therefore rather be regarded as a sect: one is a Jew as one is a communist, a member of the Great East or a Jehovah's Witness. Although it is true that it is much easier to be admitted to any other religion than to the Jewish religion, where filiation through the mother is an almost intangible rule. Even so, one can see how many Jews who will never be considered as such by the Orthodox—because they are not descended from a mother—feel no less solidarity with that community. Former minister Bernard Kouchner, for example, is not a full-blooded Jew, as only his father was. However, he has completely assimilated the intellectual reflexes of Judaism, leading him to universalism and the apology for a world without frontiers, so that nothing distinguishes him in this respect from the thinking of the most fanatical of rabbis. Judaism, in fact, is essentially embodied in a political project.

Since leaving the shtetls and urban ghettos in the 19th century to live among the nations, many Jews have preferred to let the neurosis within them die out and merge with European society. Their children and grandchildren have thus been able to forget their Jewishness and feel fully European. True assimilation only takes place through the loss

[763] http://www.beit-haverim.com

[764] Mark Zborowski, *Olam*, 1952, Plon, 1992, p. 217.

of Jewishness. The process may take two or three generations, or it may be the result of a personal will, but it exists. And that is indeed what the leaders of the Jewish community around the world fear the most. They are constantly warning Jews against intermarriage, trying to keep alive in them a sense of their own Jewishness by stoking the fear of anti-Semitism in order to close ranks.

Many Jews have thus abandoned Judaism for good and have become fully assimilated in the countries where they settled: "Of course, many Jews have been fully assimilated and have completely disjudaised[765]", Jacob Talmon acknowledged with regret.

The historian Leon Poliakov also noted that many of his fellow Jews had tried to "escape the suffering of being a Jew by abolishing Judaism on their own." He observed this phenomenon in the early 19th century among wealthier Jews who could easily evade the terrible communal surveillance. A feasible undertaking, wrote Poliakov, "on condition of courage and above all sufficient financial means. Conversions, ennoblements, aristocratic marriages, settlements in Vienna, Paris or London; wherever it was easiest to make oneself forgotten: the posterity of the wealthy Jews of the time has completely dissolved into the masses (except in a few cases, such as the Rothschilds), especially in the Christian aristocracy[766]."

The neurosis is sometimes so pressing and distressing that the Jew claims the right to consciously free himself without waiting any longer, by sincerely converting to Christianity through a militant commitment against his former "executioners". Otto Weininger, who had already abandoned Judaism before fighting it, noted in his time: "The most famous men, however, were almost always anti-Semitic (Tacitus, Pascal, Voltaire, Herder, Goethe, Kant, Jean Paul, Schopenhauer, Gillparzer, Wagner), and this must be attributed to the fact that, as geniuses, they had many personalities within their minds and were therefore better able to understand Judaism." This man, who knew the contradictions of the Jewish spirit and the suffering that went with it, also wanted to liberate the Jew from his Jewishness: "It would be necessary, first of all, for the Jews to come to understand each other, to learn to know and fight each other, and thus to overcome the Judaism that they contain within themselves... Consequently, the Jewish problem can only be solved individually, and each Semite must try to solve it in his own person[767]." Indeed, for him the Jewish question could

[765] J.-L. Talmon, *Destin d'Israël*, 1965, Calman-Lévy, 1967, p. 44.

[766] Léon Poliakov, *Histoire de l'antisémitisme, tome II*, 1981, Points Seuil, 1990, p. 97.

[767] Otto Weininger, *Sex and Character*, Ediciones 62 s|a Barcelona, 1985, p. 300, 308.

only be solved individually.

Psychotherapists believe that one should start by overcoming the taboos and silence surrounding incest within the family and practice group therapy in order to fight against the isolation in which the protagonists of incest tend to shut themselves away. David Bakan expressed it through a cryptic message: "Jews can be freed from their taboos and guilt by becoming aware of the historical origin of these taboos, in the same way that an individual, with psychoanalysis, can be freed from his inhibitions and guilt by becoming aware of his childhood origins[768]."

Indeed, it would probably be beneficial and healthy for Jews to open up more to the outside world, rather than remain closed in on themselves. This "tense and pusillanimous self-absorption in the poorest identities", as Bernard-Henri Levy put it, is not conducive to the liberation of the spirit. We should therefore begin to reject these dusty traditions and all their "paraphernalia of antiquities[769] " that "make them look like a people of madmen" in the eyes of the whole world. Let us recall the words of Alain Minc: "How should this psychological illness be treated? What collective psychoanalysis will free us from this paranoia?" The current Jewish community must be able to look itself in the mirror: "It must heal itself and its elites must do their duty" and "fight against the xenophobic delirium[770] " that has locked the Jews in their mental ghetto for so long.

Any foreigner arriving in the West may indeed be astonished to see that, unlike churches, temples and mosques that are wide open, synagogues and Jewish sites are invariably locked up tight and heavily guarded, as if Jews have any reason to be confined. This confinement has gone on long enough. Jews must free themselves from this "collective paranoia" and realise that their identity culture is a "dead end" that "locks them in fear and hatred[771]."

Therefore, group therapy should be conducted by a professional from outside the community. The "healing protocol" enunciated by Philip Roth can then be taken up again, but in the correct sense, i.e. by inverting the terms and replacing the word "Jews" with "goyim", and "anti-Semitism" with "Judaism":

"We recognise that we are prejudiced and hateful people who are powerless to control… We recognise that it is not the goyim who have

[768] David Bakan, *Freud et la tradition mystique juive*, 1963, Payot, 2001, p. 322.

[769]Bernard-Henri Lévy, *L'Idéologie française*, Grasset, 1981, p. 212-216.

[770]Alain Minc, *La Vengeance des nations*, Grasset, 1990, p. 11, 15, 179, 207

[771]Pierre Lévy, *World philosophy*, Odile Jacob, 2000, p. 147.

harmed us, but we who hold the goyim responsible for our ills as well as those of the world at large. It is we who harm the goyim, believing such a thing… A goy may have his faults, like any other human being, but the ones we have to deal with frankly here are the ones we have ourselves: paranoia, sadism, negativism, destructiveness, envy, etc."

Because Jewish identity is essentially an idea, a hesitation, many Jews cannot help but wonder about it. They often give us the impression that they can only get out of themselves by accumulating material goods and wealth, or by launching themselves into a messianic frenzy. It is by clinging to their "mission" of world unification that they finally manage to give meaning and justification to their existence on earth. Once the identity hesitation is overcome, and somehow exalted by this "divine" mission that makes him a member of the "chosen people", the Jew is then transformed into a war machine. One should read carefully what some Jewish intellectuals, such as Abraham Livni, tell us. In his book *The Return of Israel and the Hope of the World*, published in 1999, he assured us that we were living "the end of a two-thousand-year historical epoch, that of the exile of the Jewish people and its dispersion among the peoples, and the beginning of a new cycle centred on the resurrection of the people of Israel." Evil was apparently deeply rooted in our spirits: "Auschwitz is the astonishing but ultimately logical outcome of a two-thousand-year civilisation. Auschwitz is the supreme and absurd demonstration, of the extreme consequences of the lie on which Christian civilisation has been built for twenty centuries[772]."

They are like those iron machines that do not stop until they break. Nicolas Sarkozy's words still ring in our ears. On 16 January 2009, the President of the French Republic conveyed his wishes to the foreign diplomatic corps. Once again, he spoke of this New World Order, but this time in almost threatening terms: *"Nous irons ensemble vers le nouvel ordre mondial, et personne, je dis bien personne, ne pourra s'y opposer[773]."*

It should come as no surprise that in Bolshevik Russia, after the Jewish seizure of power in 1917, political opponents were locked up in psychiatric hospitals, if not simply liquidated. This tendency to consider all those who oppose their projects of domination as "madmen" is a very marked tendency in Judaism. During the summer of 2008, for

[772]Abraham Livni, *Le Retour d'Israël et l'espérance du monde,* Éditions du Rocher, 1999, p. 11, 27, 28.

[773]"We will go together towards the new world order, and no one, I mean no one, will be able to oppose it."

example, graffiti appeared in the wealthy town of Neuilly-sur-Seine, Sarkozy's own political fiefdom: "Sarkozy, Jews, chorizos". An article in *Le Parisien* on 8 August mentioned the case: A 63-year-old man, who had already expressed his anti-Semitism against some of the town's shopkeepers, had been arrested and admitted the facts. The man had been "committed to a psychiatric hospital": "The psychiatric expertise has come to the conclusion of delirium of persecution and a total absence of discernment, and he has therefore been committed immediately."

This is how most Jews eventually come to terms with their uniqueness. They can also find a foothold in their secular traditions. Certainly, it is not necessary to scrupulously observe all the daily prescriptions of Judaism in order to be a Jew, to think like a Jew, to act like a Jew and to "gather the divine sparks", as Kabbalah advocates[774]. But communal rites can help Jews to carry their burden and bear themselves, for they are well aware of the weight of their faults and folly. Once a year, on the eve of the religious holiday of Yum Kippur, Jews have the opportunity to atone for their sins with a curious ritual.

The Jewish manual of life and conduct, the *Shulchan Aruch* (The Served Table), provides the explanations in chapter CXXXI: "It is customary in all Jewish communities to perform *Kaparot* on the eve of Yom Kippur. One hen is taken for each member of the family and slaughtered to atone for our sins. The custom is to slaughter a rooster for the man and a hen for the woman. It is also customary to select white birds to symbolise the purification of sins. For pregnant women, two hens and a rooster are slaughtered; one hen for the woman, another for the possible child to be born and the rooster for the future baby if it is a boy. The rooster or hen is taken, twirled around the head and said three times: "*Ze halifati, ze temurati, ze kaparati, ze atarnegol / atarnegolet lishjita ielej*": "This is my substitute, this is my change, this is my atonement, this rooster / hen will be beheaded and I will be Sealed for Good Life and Peace[775]"."

This is how the Jews transfer their guilt and get their sins remitted: by spinning a rooster or a hen around his head before slitting his throat[776].

Elie Wiesel had experienced such religious practices in the

---

774 See translator's note in Annex IV. 3.

775 *Kaparot and Yom Kippur Vespers*. The *Shulchan Aruch* is the work of Rabbi Joseph Caro (Safed, 1563). It was published in 1565 in Venice.

776 Nouvelle Revue d'Ethnopsychiatrie, *Psychopathologie du Judaïsme*, N°31, septembre 1996, p. 43-45.

framework of the Kabbalah, but he had been rather sceptical about the results: 'The so-called mystical experiences spoken of in books yellowed by the passage of centuries excite me. Mixing vinegar with the blood of a rooster with its throat cut in a ritualistic way, pronouncing magic formulas to drive Satan away from the mountains, was that possible? To repeat a few "names" at a precise hour to dominate the forces of evil, to shoot down planes, to repel tanks, to defeat and humiliate the knights of Death? Fifty years later, I can tell you the truth: it doesn't work. I speak from experience[777]."

Indeed, the tanks, the planes and the "knights of death" that the Jews have most to fear are above all within themselves. As for the messiah who will come one day to liberate them—it is now certain—he will wear the white coat of a psychiatrist and will be accompanied by two or three strong nurses. We cannot imagine things any other way[778].

Paris, June 2006
October 2011 for this second edition.

[777]Elie Wiesel, *Mémoires, tome I,* Seuil, 1994, p. 49.

[778]For complaints, please contact the National Bureau for Monitoring Anti-Semitism. Call (0033) 6 63 88 30 29 and ask for Sammy Ghozlan.

ANNEX I

THE TALMUD

The Talmud is a fundamental book. It is a sort of constitution or Magna Carta for the Jews. It is a work that mainly collects rabbinical discussions on Jewish law, traditions, customs, narratives and sayings, parables, stories and legends. It is not a book of thought or philosophy. It is a vast civil and religious code based on the Torah [the Old Testament], compiled between the third and fifth centuries [perhaps as late as the eighth century according to some researchers] by Hebrew scholars in Babylonia and Israel: "The Talmud consists of 63 books. These books are the compilation of legislative, ethical and historical writings, written by the ancient rabbis. It was written five centuries after the birth of Jesus Christ. It is a compendium of laws and traditions. It represents the legal code on which Jewish religious law is based, and is the book used for the training of the rabbis." (Rabbi Morris N. Kertzer, *Look Magazine*, June 17, 1952).

There are two well-known versions of the Talmud: the Jerusalem Talmud (*Talmud Yerushalmi*), which was written in the then newly created Roman province of Philistia, and the Babylonian Talmud (*Talmud Babli*), which was written in the region of Babylonia. Both versions were written over many centuries by generations of scholars from many rabbinical academies established since antiquity. It consists of the Mishnah (written collection of the oral laws, according to *Exodus 24:12),* the Gemara (the rabbis' commentaries on the Mishnah) and the Aggadah (narratives of secondary value, see note 105). The mitzvot (singular mitzvah) are the precepts or commandments of Jewish Law.

In Talmud *Berakhot 5a* (first tractate of the Talmud, *The Blessings*) it says: "Rabbi Shimon ben Lakish said: God said to Moses: "Come up to me on the mountain and stand there, and I will give you the tablets of stone and the Torah and the Mitzvah that I have written for you to teach" (*Exodus 24:12*), meaning that God revealed to Moses not only the Written Torah, but the entire Torah, as it would be passed down through the generations. The "tablets of stone" are the ten commandments that were written on the tablets of the Covenant, the

"Torah" are the five books of Moses. The "Mitzvah" is the Mishnah, which includes the explanations of the mitzvot [the precepts and commandments] and how they are to be fulfilled." That I have written" refers to the Prophets and Writings, written with divine inspiration." That you may teach them" refers to the Talmud [the Gemara], which explains the Mishnah. These explanations are the foundation of the rules of practical Halachah [Jewish Law, see note 167]. This verse teaches that all aspects of the Torah were given to Moses from Sinai." A well-known metaphor of the rabbis about the Talmud reads: "The Torah is water, the Mishnah is wine, and the Gemara is wine with honey." It must therefore be understood that for the rabbis the Law comes primarily from (their) Gemara.

Arsène Darmesteter (1846–1888), a noted 19th century philologist and scholar of Judaism, wrote in his book on the Talmud the following: "Today Judaism finds its most perfect expression in the Talmud; this book has not influenced Judaism remotely, nor is Judaism but a faint echo of it, but the Talmud has incarnated itself in Judaism, and Judaism has taken shape in the Talmud, thus passing from the state of abstraction into reality. The study of Judaism is the study of the Talmud, just as the study of the Talmud is the study of Judaism (…) They are two things inseparable, better still, they are one and the same thing (…) Consequently, the Talmud is the most complete expression of our religious movement, and this code of endless prescriptions and meticulous ceremonials represents in its greatest perfection the total work of the religious idea… This miracle was performed in a book: the Talmud (…)

Nothing can equal the importance of the Talmud except the ignorance that prevails over it (…) The Talmud is composed of two distinct parts, the Mishnah and the Gemara; the first is the text proper, the second is the commentary on the text (…) By the term Mishnah is meant a collection of traditional rulings and laws, which includes all areas of legislation, both civil and religious. This code was the work of several generations of rabbis (…) A single page of the Talmud may contain passages written in three or four different languages, or rather, passages written in a single language fixed at different levels of its degeneration (…) Often, a Mishnah of five or six lines is followed by fifty or sixty pages of commentary [Gemara] (…) The Halakhah is the Law in all its authority; it constitutes the dogma and the cult; it is the fundamental element of the Talmud… The daily study of the Talmud, which among Jews begins at the age of ten and ends only with life itself, is necessarily a strenuous exercise for the mind, thanks to which it acquires an incomparable subtlety and dexterity (…) For the Talmud aspires to one thing only: to become for Judaism a sort of "*corpus juris ecclesiastici*"." Arsène Darmesteter, (*The Talmud,* 1888). *The Talmud,* The Jewish Publication Society of America, Philadelphia, 1897, p. 60, 61, 89, 7, 10, 14, 15, 17, 25, 26, p. 25.

ANNEX II

THE ZOHAR

According to Gershom Scholem, the medieval Kabbalah first developed in Languedoc and Provence around 1150–1200, within Jewish communities influenced by Christian monastic movements and the Gnostic Cathar heresy. The *Sofer Bahir*, the *Sofer Yetsirah and* the *Merkabah* were three important esoteric works that foreshadowed the *Zohar.* From there they would pass to Catalonia and then to Castile, where the activity of the Kabbalists reached its peak, with Moisés de León being the main and definitive composer of the *Zohar.* The influences of the Kabbalah are Neoplatonism, Gnosis[779] and ancient Jewish mystical doctrines transmitted orally and by the Talmudic *Aggadah* (see note 105):

"The Kabbalah—literally: tradition, and in particular esoteric tradition—is the movement in which the mystical tendencies of Judaism, mainly between the twelfth and seventeenth centuries, found their religious sedimentation in the form of multiple ramifications and often in the course of an uneven development. The complex presented

[779]The basis of Gnosticism is its dualistic interpretation of the cosmos. The true God is not the creator God, he is "hidden". Creation is the work of a demiurge or demon or "*great architect*". The true good God and the material world are two opposites. The Gnostics thus regard the material world as diabolical. Some think that this teaching of the evil character of the world can be very dangerous for society and human life. On the other hand, Plotinus' Neoplatonism is a monism of Being, a philosophy of the One contrary to the dualism of Being of traditional Jewish and Christian theology (God creator of the world *exnihilo*) which had a very powerful influence on mystics and philosophers until modernity. There are many references on this subject: the most important reference is probably Mircea Eliade and his *History of Religious Beliefs and Ideas, volume II.* The Jewish Kabbalah seems to be related to these doctrines, in addition to its natural filiation with Talmudic doctrines. On the Jewish Cabala the reader may consult the work of the Spanish scholar Marcelino Menendez Pelayo: *Historia de los Heterodoxos españoles, Tomo I,* Ed. F. Maroto, Madrid, 1880, p. 82–86 and p. 385–393. And for a complete exposition of these questions in Judaism read: Gershom Scholem, *Basic Concepts of Judaism: God, Creation, Revelation, Tradition, Salvation*. Editorial Trotta, 1998–2018, Madrid (NdT).

here is by no means, as is often heard, a unitarian system of mystical and especially theosophical ideas. A concept such as, for example, "the doctrine of the kabbalists" does not exist. Instead, we have to deal here with a process, often astonishing in the multiplicity and abundance of its motives, which has decanted into totally different systems or semi-systems. Fed by subterranean sources of very probable oriental origin, the Kabbalah first saw the light of day in the south of France, in the same regions and at the same time as the non-Jewish world was contemplating the apogee of the Cathar movement or neo-Manichaeism. In 13th century Spain it flourished with a rapid and astonishingly intense development until it reached the fullness of its constructions, culminating in the pseudepigraphic book *Zohar* of Rabbi Moses of Leon, a kind of Bible for the Kabbalists, which over the centuries has managed to assert the almost unassailable position of a sacred and authoritative text. In the Palestine of the 16th century—thanks to a second flowering—it became a historical and spiritual power of the first rank within Judaism; this was possible because it was able to give an answer to the excited moods of the Spanish Jews, affected by the catastrophe of the expulsion of 1492, in relation to the question—whose resurgence was constantly raised—of the meaning of the exile. Brimming with messianic energies, it exploded in the 17th century in the wake of the great movement around Shabtai Tzvi, a movement which, even as it collapsed, managed to give rise to a world of Jewish mystical heresy, a heretical Kabbalah which in its evolutionary impulses and movements has paradoxically played a very important role in the birth of modern Judaism, although this importance has long been ignored, and is only now gradually being recognised."

In Gershom Scholem, *La Kabbalah y su simbolismo*, Siglo XXI Editores, Madrid, 2009, p. 108.

And more in detail:

"It is difficult to admit a direct link between these Eastern Jewish groups of the eighth to tenth centuries and the oldest Kabbalistic conventuals in the south of France in the twelfth century. On the other hand, it is possible that these ancient Gnostic traditions, like others among the Kabbalists, can be traced back to different groups in the East, for which we have no written testimony. In the vicinity of the Manichaean and Mandaean communities of Mesopotamia, Gnostic materials remained alive in a great variety of forms, to the extent that we can easily imagine the existence of these Gnostic Jews. Some fragments of their doctrines, mixed with other materials, may have made their way to Europe… But we should not underestimate the difficulties posed by such a hypothesis. While the German Hasidim, as we have often shown in this chapter, may have known some parts of these fragments, others may have remained unpublished. Could these traditions have come directly from the East to Provence, evolving there in parallel with Catharism? The difficulty in finding out lies in the non-theoretical or philosophical form in which the idea of metempsychosis is presented in the *Bahir*. For in the dualist religion of the Cathars, which preached an essential difference between the nature and origin of the physical and spiritual worlds, this idea does not present the same difficulties as for the philosophical theology and psychology of monotheism. The hypothesis of a passage of the individual soul into another body might have seemed much more questionable to the Aristotelian doctrine of the soul as an entelechy of the organism than to the dualistic psychology of the Platonic type, where such a doctrine could easily be accommodated. Yet even a Jewish Neoplatonist like Abraham bar Hiyya was intolerant of the doctrine of the transmigration of souls, yet how did it penetrate into Provence a generation or two after him? For the time being, I think we must leave open the question of where the doctrine of metempsychosis, as expounded in the *Bahir*, originated historically, despite its proximity in time and place to the Cathar movement. In general I am inclined to accept the first hypothesis, namely that we are dealing with fragments of an older Gnostic tradition which arrived from the East by paths which we can no longer decipher and which reached the circles in which the *Bahir* originated."

Gershom Scholem, *Los orígenes de la Cábala*, Ediciones Paidós Ibérica, 2001 p. 117.

ANNEX III

THE LURIA CABALA

1.” It is a general doctrine of the universe… God, in the origin of His action, did not first reveal Himself to others through Creation. He hid Himself. He withdrew into the deepest mystery of His profound nature. Because of this, because of His hiding and withdrawal, the world appeared in its turn. Then, a second act took place, the emanation of the worlds, the creation of the worlds, as well as the manifestation of the divinity as personal God, as Creator and Lord of Israel (…) In order for something other than God to exist, it is indispensable for God to take refuge in Himself. Only then can He cast His rays of light (the *Sephiroth*, the divine lights) into the space created by His contraction (*tsimtsum*) and found His works… Without contraction, everything would become divinity again. Without emanation, nothing would be created (…) By means of His forces, through which He wants to build the Creation, He forms receptacles (*kelim*) which must then serve the revelation of His own essence (…) The light, which must receive a plastic form in order to realise the work of the Creator and from which the creatures will then emerge, has been drawn into the receptacles after a great shock (…) [But] for some spiritual reasons, the light has been drawn into the receptacles after a great shock (…) [But] for some spiritual reasons, the light has been drawn into the receptacles after a great shock (…).) [But] for spiritual reasons which the kabbalists expounded at length, these receptacles were broken (…) This is the act which the kabbalists call the “breaking of the receptacles” (*shevirat ha-kelim)* (…) The receptacles having been broken, the light has been dispersed. Most of it returned to its source; but the rest, or rather the sparks of that light, have fallen downwards where they were scattered while others ascended back upwards. This is the story of the fundamental inner exile of Creation (…) From there comes the exile. From that instant, nothing is in a state of perfection anymore. The divine light … is no longer in the right place, for the receptacles are broken (…) Everything is now out of place… In other words, everything that exists is in exile.”

In Gershom Scholem, *Le Messianisme juif*, 1971, Les Belles Lettres, 2020, p. 92–94.

2." The sparks of divine light have been cast into an abyss where the forces of evil are constituted, by which the Creator has willed that the creatures should be put to the test. The creatures must thus demonstrate their strength and their ability to choose by fighting against the forces of evil. Into this world of evil, of darkness and impurity—the world of the so-called "shells" (*Qelipot*), [*Qelipah*, singular]—have fallen, according to the kabbalistic myth, forces of holiness, sparks of divine light that have become fixed in the "shells" after the breaking of the receptacles. There is thus an exile of the divinity (…) We are here in the presence of a cosmic notion of exile. It is no longer only the exile of the people of Israel, but first of all the exile of the divine Presence from the origin of the universe. What comes into the world can only be the expression of this primitive and essential exile (…) The whole imperfection of the world is explained by this. The impure things have triumphed over the forces of holiness, over the sparks of the holy light, and hold them under their yoke (…) Such is the situation of Creation after the breaking of the receptacles (…) [This] is a defect that requires a Repair (*Tikun*) (…) [This] is a defect that requires a Repair (*Tikun*) (…). It is the repair of a primitive vice (…) It is the imperfection, the defect, the original vice that is found in all things, for there is nothing in the world that was not vitiated when the first receptacles were broken. It is incumbent upon us to remedy that vice, to restore things to their proper place and nature. This is the purpose of religion, the role assigned to the religious man as well as to the ordinary man. Man must repair the world (…) The exile of Israel is only the most necessary, most concrete and cruelest expression of the present situation of a world that is still in a state prior to repair and redemption (…) The exile of Israel is not a random event, but is part of the very reality of the world, in that Israel has not yet completed the repair, nor restored things to their proper place. How is it to make this repair? Through the Law (*Torah*) and the precepts (*Mitzvot*)." In Gershom Scholem, *Le Messianisme juif*, 1971, Les Belles Lettres, 2020, p. 94–96.

Other esoteric aspects developed in the *Zohar* are: The Tree of Life (*Sephiroth*), the Supreme Man—androgynous male-female—(*Adam Kadmon)*, the feminine Divine Presence (the *Shechinah*) and Theurgy (magic and the invocation of ultra-terrestrial powers).

To the reader interested in penetrating the incredible[780] mental

[780]We use this word in the literal sense. (NdT).

universe of the Kabbalah, we recommend the work of the renowned British occultist Arthur Edward Waite (1857–1942), *The Secret Doctrine in Israel—A Study of the Zohar and its Connections*, Occult Research Press Publishers, New York (downloadable in Pdf at archives.org and scribd.com). In turn, we suggest the books of the independent American researcher Christopher Jon Bjerknes, whose exhaustive study of the Kabbalah has led him to conclusions that, if true and plausible, are truly disturbing for Humanity. (At www.cjbbooks.com.)

3." The extreme diffusion of the teachings of Rabbi Isaac Luria and his disciples had had the effect of introducing everywhere the theories of the Kabbalah into the traditional Jewish conception of the figure and function of the Messiah. So that the Kabbalists became in effect the theologians of the Jewish people throughout the seventeenth century. Luria's mystical speculations about the nature of redemption and about the "restored world" (*olam ha-tikkun*), which was to occur immediately afterwards, had introduced new ideas and perspectives into popular folklore regarding the Messiah, the national hero called to emerge victorious from a supreme cosmic drama. From then on, the redemption was no longer conceived only as a temporal event, which would bring about the emancipation of Israel from the yoke of the Nations, but also as a radical transformation of the entire creation, affecting both the material and the spiritual world, and leading to the repair of the primordial catastrophe called "the breaking of the receptacles" (*shevirat ha-kelim*). During that repair, the divine worlds must regain their original unity and perfection… It was believed that the spread of Luria's teachings should even hasten the coming of the Redeemer."

In Gershom Scholem, *Le Messianisme juif*, 1971, Les Belles Lettres, 2020, p. 149–150.

ANNEX IV

HASSIDISM AND THE TEACHERS CHABAB LUBAVITCH

1. Luria's Kabbalah was extraordinarily fruitful. From it sprang in the following centuries very popular mystical-messianic movements that left a deep imprint on Judaism. Some of these, such as Sabbateanism and Frankism, ended up in a messianic sectarianism marked by "paradoxes" and "aberrations", as we shall see in the second part of this study. By contrast, 18th century Hasidism, founded by Israel Ben Eliezer (Ba'al Shem Tov) and a more moderate continuation of Kabbalah, had perhaps a more enduring role, and this right up to the present day." Hasidism tried to eliminate the messianic element—with its dazzling but excessively dangerous amalgam of mysticism and apocalyptic spirit—without renouncing the appeal of later Kabbalism', or rather it carried out 'a "neutralisation" of the messianic element', for it never really abandoned it, wrote Gershom Scholem.

Scholem insisted on the circumstances of this apparent change: "Hasidism was a conscious reaction to the inherent dangers of the messianic initiatives that had led to the Sabbatean upheaval. It did not reject Isaac Luria's teaching on the divine sparks, whose influence was too great to be rejected, but it reinterpreted it in such a way as to remove the dangerous sting of messianism… The immediate goal of Hasidism at that time could no longer be national redemption from exile or universal redemption. For after the Sabbatean fire, this would have meant messianism once again. The goal … became the mystical redemption of the individual *hic et nunc, i.* e. redemption *in* exile, not *of* exile, or, in other words, victory over exile through its spiritualisation. Sabbateanism, the revolt against exile, had failed. Hasidism, with the destructive consequences of that tragic failure before its eyes, gave up the idea of a messianic revolution. It made peace with the exile, a precarious and difficult peace, to be sure, but still peace? We now understand why Hasidism insisted both on *devekut* [mystical communion with God], an element without eschatological overtones, as I have shown, and on the doctrine of sparks in its new form." The *devekut* is intended to lead each one to the individual redemption that suits his soul," declared the Ba'al Shem. Mystical redemption and individual redemption are thus identified in opposition to messianic redemption, which loses the concrete and immediate meaning it had in Luria's Kabbalah." Only when we have attained individual redemption can the universal redemption take place and the Messiah manifest himself", so said another sentence of Ba'al Shem781."

Thus, "Hasidism, in general terms, represents an attempt to make the world of Kabbalah accessible to the masses through a certain transformation or reinterpretation"." Many of Ba'al Shem's followers, disciples of his disciples, became the founders of Hasidic dynasties in which the leadership of large and small Hasidic groups was and still is passed down, more or less automatically, from father to son". So these Hasidic leaders, called *rebe782*, succeeded each other up to the present day, continuing the tradition and also bringing new ideas, although, as Gershom Scholem recognised, "it is not always possible to distinguish between the revolutionary and the conservative elements of Hasidism, or rather, Hasidism as a whole is a reformation of earlier mysticism, but at the same time remains more or less identical to it."

The most thriving and active Hasidic dynasty today is undoubtedly that of Chabad-Lubavitch, and this is because this school produced a "truly original Kabbalistic theory". Scholem argued that the characteristic feature of this new school was that "the secrets of divinity are expressed in the manner of a mystical psychology", thus bringing "a new emphasis on the psychological rather than the theosophical aspect"." Kabbalism becomes an instrument of psychological analysis and self-knowledge", thus giving "the Chabad writings their specific character of a mixture of God-worship and pantheistic interpretation ... and of intense concern for the human mind and its impulses." Through greater psychological and emotional understanding, "Kabbalism no longer appears under a theosophical guise... Theosophy, with all its complicated theories, is no longer at the centre of religious consciousness". The Hasidic movement thus achieved greater success

---

[781]For a full explanation of this neutralisation read Gershom Scholem, *Le Messianisme juif,* 1971, Les Belles Lettres, 2020, *La neutralisation du messianisme dans le hassidisme primitif (III - IV),* p. 278-301 and on Hasidism in general, *Las grandes tendencias de la mística judía, Novena Conferencia: El Hasidismo, la última etapa,* Fondo de cultura económica, 1997, Buenos Aires, p. 264-283. (NdT).

[782]Read about the *rebbes* in Hervé Ryssen, *Jewish Fanaticism* (NdT).

and effectiveness, for "what really became important was the meaning of personal life in mysticism. Hasidism is practical mysticism at its highest level," Scholem wrote. We now understand why the views and statements of these Hasidic leaders are so important to their Jewish followers around the world, for what the Chabad-Lubavitch achieved is, as Martin Buber observed, a "Kabbalism turned *ethos*" for "almost all Kabbalistic ideas are now related to the values proper to individual life, and special emphasis is placed on ideas and concepts that concern the relationship between individuals and God"." Herein lies the true originality of Hasidic thought. As mystical moralists, the Hasidim found a way to social organisation."

In Gershom Scholem, *Las grandes tendencias de la mística judía, Novena Conferencia: El Hasidismo, la última etapa*, Fondo de cultura económica, 1997, Buenos Aires, p. 266, 267, 269, 274, 276, 278 and in *Le Messianisme juif*, 1971, Les Belles Lettres, 2020, p. 292, 293.

Yosef Yitzchak Schneerson (1880–1950) was the sixth *rebbe* of the Chabad dynasty. His first speech as leader of the dynasty in 1920 was translated and published in 1987 in a book entitled *An End to Evil Reishis Goyim Amalek*. In it one can read some of his mystical teachings: "It is written, *Reishis Goyim Amalek, veachriso adei oveid* - "Amalek is the first among the nations, and in the end he will be destroyed". The opening phrase means that Amalek is the source and root of the Seven Evil Nations—yet he is separate from them. The same is true (albeit bearing in mind the distinction between holiness and its opposite) with regard to the forces of ungodliness that are collectively referred to as *Qelipot* [the husks of the world of Evil]. Amalek, who personifies the harshest *Qelippah*, is the source and spiritual root of all these nations, even though he is distinct from them. The conclusion of the above verse ("and in the end it will be destroyed") seems to imply that Amalek's *Qelippah* contains no element that can be saved by means of the Divine service called *beirurim* (the sifting and refining of materiality through the elevation of the Divine sparks embedded in it). The Amalek *Qelippah*, it seems, cannot be rehabilitated into something positive and thus be brought to a state of Repair (*Tikkun*). Rather, the only "repair" of Amalek is its total eradication and destruction. This is hinted at in the verse "and in the end it will be destroyed": the consummation of Amalek is its destruction."

His successor and son-in-law, the seventh *rebbe* of the Chabad dynasty, was Menachem Mendel Schneerson (1902–1994), who in the course of his teaching achieved international renown. His are the following statements from a book of recorded messages to his followers in Israel: "The difference between a Jewish person and a non-Jew arises from the common expression: 'let us differentiate' (…) The body of a Jewish person is of a totally different quality from the body of all the nations of the world… The difference of the inner quality, however, is so great that the bodies must be regarded as a completely different species … their bodies are in vain. A still greater difference exists with regard to the soul. There are two contrary types of soul; the non-Jewish soul comes from three satanic spheres, while the Jewish soul comes from holiness." In *Gatherings of Conversations* (1965), translated by Israel Shahak and Norton Mezvinsky, *Jewish Fundamentalism in Israel*, Pluto Press, London, 1999, p. 59–61.

In the same vein, Rabbi Yitzchak Ginsburg, another eminent Chabad-Lubavitch authority, wrote: "All human beings possess a Divine Spark. The difference between one human being and another lies in the extent to which the spark has entered and plays an active role in his psyche… When the spark enters fully into the psyche, it is known as a divine soul. And that is why we speak of Jews possessing a Divine soul. With respect to a non-Jew, the Divine spark floats over the psyche (it does not enter it even on the unconscious plane)." And this other consideration: "To better understand the relationship between the Jew and the non-Jew (…) let us first note that the origin of non-Jewish souls is the primordial world of Chaos (*Tohu*) which preceded the world of Rectification (*Tikun*), the origin of Jewish souls". In Rabbi Yitzchak Ginsburg, *Kabbalah and Meditation for the Nations*, Ed. Gal Einai Institute, 2007, p. 55, 125.

These teachings are directly related to those of the *Tanya*, the fundamental work of the Jabab-Lubavitch written by its founder Schneur Zalman of Liadi for twenty years and published in 1797. We can read some translated passages at www.Sefaria.org, *Tanya, Part One, The Book of the Average Men* (*Introduction*, 17): "The souls of the people of the world, however, emanate from the other impure *Qelipot* which contain nothing good. As it is written in *Etz Chayim* (Portal 49, chapter 3): all the good that people do, they do out of selfish motivations. Thus, as the Gemara comments (*Bava Batra 10b*) on the verse (*Mishlei 14:34)*, "The goodness of the people is sin"—for all the charity and goodness done by the people of the world is only for their self-glorification, etc."

In 1978, the U.S. Congress asked President Jimmy Carter to designate Menachem Mendel Schneerson's birthday as National Education Day in the U.S. It has since been commemorated as Education and Exchange Day. In 1994, he was posthumously awarded the Congressional Gold Medal for his "outstanding and lasting contributions to the improvement of world education, morality and acts of charity".

3." By virtue of the great myth of exile and redemption which constitutes the Lurianic Kabbalah, the "sparks" of divine life and light have been cast into exile throughout the world and are anxiously waiting to be "raised up" through the actions of men and reinstated in their primal place in the divine harmony of all beings… For Hasidism the "sacred sparks" are present everywhere without exception… Man has the opportunity everywhere, even the obligation, to raise the "sacred sparks"… Every consciousness open to contemplation can discover the "sparks" in any aspect of life and can thus confer upon the profane world an immediate religious significance… The Hasidim did not shy away from paradoxical formulas to express their thoughts." A chat with your neighbour can be the place of deep meditation," said Ba'al Shem." The most important thing in the way of serving God," said another Hasidic master, "is to do it by means of profane things, by means of non-spiritual things. Yet another: "It is even in coffee-table talk of politics and conversations dealing with war between peoples that a man can attain an intimate union with God". This astonishing phrase was no mere witticism: its author provided detailed instructions on how to achieve this feat. The Rabbi of Polnoa [Yaakov Yossef Hakohen], a disciple of the Ba'al Shem, summed it up as follows: "Nothing, great or small, in this world is separate from God, for in all things He is present. The consecrated man can indulge in deep meditations and contemplative acts of 'unification' even in his most earthly actions, eating, drinking, sexual relations, and even doing business". These mystical acts that the kabbalists call "unifications" (in Hebrew *yihudim*) should not be done in solitude or in retreat; they should also be done in the marketplace, precisely in the places that seem most remote from the spiritual. It is precisely there that the true chassid discovers the theatre of dreams where the paradox is at its climax."

In Gershom Scholem, *Le Messianisme juif*, 1971, Les Belles Lettres, 2020, p. 344, 345, 346.

4." The risk of a deviation from traditional authority into the uncontrolled and uncontrollable is deeply rooted in the nature of mystical experience. The religious education of the group still leaves the door open to numerous adventures of the spirit, which are opposed to recognised schemes and doctrines and which may lead to a clash between the mystic and the religious authority… This must be regarded as one of several decisive factors which have contributed to the formation of the opinion that in mysticism a spiritual leader, a guru, as the Hindus say, is absolutely necessary. Of course, the guru fulfils above all, *prima facie*, a psychological function. He prevents the disciple ... from making mistakes and endangering himself. He who seeks his path alone can, of course, easily go astray and even fall into madness... Yogis, Sufis and Kabbalists claim such intellectual guidance no less than the manuals of Catholic mysticism. Without guidance one risks getting lost in the wilderness of the mystical adventure... The guide ... directs and determines the interpretation of the mystical experience, even before it occurs. He channels it through avenues acceptable to the established authority. How does he accomplish this? ... He provides the traditional kabbalistic symbols by which this pilgrimage of a Jewish mystic towards the grasping of divinity can be described or interpreted, thereby ensuring, as far as possible, conformity with authority at precisely the most dangerous turns of the road. The compromises agreed between the mystic and the transmitted religious authority aimed at enabling the mystic to remain within the latter's framework reveal ... a very wide range of varieties.

... Here compromises were inevitable, at least in relation to the recognition of differences of degree... Thus in Rabbinic Judaism, within which Kabbalistic mysticism developed, different possible revelatory experiences were recognised as authentic and authoritative, for example those of Moses, the prophets, the Holy Spirit (speaking through the hagiographers of the Bible), the receivers of the "heavenly voice" (*bat-col*, which was perceptible in Talmudic times) and finally, the "manifestation of the prophet Elijah"... This is why the kabbalists claimed for themselves only the apparently modest rank of "recipients of a manifestation of the prophet Elijah"... The prophet Elijah represents in Jewish tradition, from the origins of rabbinic Judaism, a particular figure closely linked to the desires of this Judaism: he is the bearer of divine messages throughout all generations. Thus, a Kabbalistic revelation of the prophet Elijah represents an interpretation of mystical experience which, according to its nature, tends rather to confirm authority than to break it. When we consider the first personalities in the history of the Kabbalah for whom access to such a rank was claimed, it is very significant that they are Rabbi Abraham of Posquières and his son Isaac the Blind, [and] Abraham ben David (died in 1198)..."

"The less erudition and theological training an aspirant to mystical enlightenment possessed, the more immediate was the danger of conflict with authority. All the manuals of mysticism that were written from the point of view of traditional authority provide us with as many examples of this as we wish, regardless, of course, of the specific doctrine of each... This is no more and no less the case with some Hasidic theories. When Israel Ba'al-Sem, the founder of Polish Hasidism in the eighteenth century, held the mystical thesis that communion with God (*debecut*) is more important than the study of the Scriptures, it aroused considerable opposition and was cited by all polemical writings opposed to the movement as proof of its anti-rabbinical and subversive tendency. In Judaism, for example, an attempt was made to prevent any possible conflict by prescribing that access to the realm of mystical practice and speculation be reserved exclusively for sages with a thorough Talmudic learning. In this sense Maimonides' warning is quoted in all the books: "No one is worthy to enter paradise (i.e. the realm of mysticism) unless he has first gorged himself on bread and meat" (*Mishne Torah*, hilchot *Yesodeh haTorah*, IV, 13), i.e. on the food of pure rabbinic wisdom... Although many great kabbalists corresponded fully to the above requirement of Maimonides, born of a conservative spirit, there have nevertheless been others who possessed only a feeble rabbinical knowledge or who, in any case, had not attended any suitable Talmudic school with assiduity. The most famous of all Jewish mystics of recent times, the above-mentioned Israel Ba'al-Sem, serves as a typical example. His "knowledge", in the traditional sense of the term, was very limited; he lacked the flesh-and-blood teacher to show him the way, and the only one he recognised as a spiritual "guru" was the prophet Ahijah of Shiloh, with whom he was in constant visionary and spiritual contact. In short, he was a perfect lay mystic, and yet the movement founded by him—in which this lay element occupied an outstanding place and constituted, in the least, one of the decisive factors in its development—succeeded in his struggle to obtain equal rights within the framework of the transmitted authority (not, of course, without having shown itself willing—by way of price—to compromise). Other mystical movements in which the secular element also occupied an important place within Judaism, such as the Sabbetaic movement, failed to achieve this aim and were driven into conflict with the rabbinical authority...

"In absolute and irreconcilable contrast to all attempts at compromise or similar solutions to eliminate the tension between the mystic and religious authority, however, is the extreme phenomenon of nihilistic mysticism, of the denial of all authority in the name of mystical experience or enlightenment itself..."

In Gershom Scholem, *La Kabbalah y su simbolismo, La autoridad religiosa y la mística*, Siglo XXI Editores, 2009, Madrid, p. 21–25, 33.

ANNEX V

JACOB AND ESAU IN KABBALISTIC EXEGESIS

The people of Yahweh is Jacob:

"When the Most High gave the nations their home and established the divisions of man, He set the boundaries of the peoples in relation to the numbers of Yisrael. For Yahweh's portion is his people, Yaaqov [Jacob] the inheritance that was his due. He found it in a desert region, in a howling, empty wasteland. He surrounded it, he watched over it, he guarded it like the apple of his eye. As an eagle circling her nest, hovers over her nestlings, so he spread out his wings, took him, carried him on his feathers; Yahweh alone led them, with no foreign deity at his side." (*Deuteronomy: 32, 8–12, Israelite Nazarene Bible 2011*). Read also *Malachi* 1: 1–5.

Esau, Edom and Amalek are the terms used by the Kabbalistic exegetes to designate Christians and Christianity, more specifically Europeans and their descendants:

"With your sword you shall live and serve your brother" This has not yet happened, because Esau is not yet Jacob's servant. This is because Jacob does not need him yet." (*Zohar, 1: 145a*);

"Jacob humbled himself before Esau so that Esau would later become his servant. By controlling him, he fulfilled the meaning of the verse: "Let the peoples serve you, and the nations bow down to you" (*Genesis 27:29*). It was not yet time for Jacob to rule over Esau. Jacob let this happen later, because he was humble then" (*Zohar, 1:166b*).

"After King Messiah rises, Jacob will receive the things above and the things below, and Esau will lose everything. He will have no portion and inheritance or remembrance in the world. This is the meaning of the verse, 'And the house of Jacob shall be fire, and the house of Joseph a flame, and the house of Esau stubble' (*Obadiah 1:18*), for Esau shall lose all, and Jacob shall inherit the two worlds, this world and the world to come, that is, the upper part of heaven and earth." (*Zohar. 1:143b*)

"Esau will boast of lords, while Jacob will bring forth prophets, and if Esau has princes, Jacob will have kings. They, Israel and Rome, are the two nations destined to be hated by the whole world. One will surpass the other in strength. First Esau will subjugate the whole world, but in the end Jacob will rule over all. The older of the two [Esau] will serve the younger [Jacob]." (*Legends of the Jews, 1:6*).

Source: https://www.sefaria.org.

"(...) In the future, Christianity will undergo a process of Judaisation in order to place itself at the right hand of Israel, Israel's right hand at the moment of redemption. This process begins, however, with the crushing of the power of Christianity. In the *Sefer HaMeshiv*, the course of events is depicted thus: "By virtue of the power of the *Great Forty-Two Letter Name* [the Divine Name], I conjure you even against your will not to have the power to fly or do anything or make any other accusation against the Israelite nation as you have done until now. I will bind you and conjure you so that you will have no more power to accuse Israel at all times. On the contrary, from this day forth, you shall defend the Israelite nation ... so shall you and Rabbi Joseph, the two of you together ... and by this you shall break the power of Samael [demonic fallen angel] and hasten the Redemption in your time." The transition from accusation to defence is but a reflection of a process occurring within the Divine, a theme addressed in *Sefer HaMeshiv*, "Know that Esau is the creation of the Heavenly Isaac (the *Sefirah Gevurah*) to rule and guide the world, and his name is Lot, and his name is Esau ... when the kingdom is his, he will ascend through the window of the Heavenly Isaac (receive emanation directly from the *Sefirah Gevurah*). He will be prince over you and will make an accusation against you that you have no right to exist in the world ... for Esau is Lot, though he will be known by the name of Esau when the time comes for the coming of the King Messiah. Then this secret will be known, that Esau is none other than the evil Samael, and during the times of the Messiah's birth, he will be called Esau, (the Hebrew letters, *Ayin-Sin-Waw*) meaning *Asu* (literally: they made). That is, they forced him into the mystery of the Heavenly Covenant of Circumcision, for to this day, he has not yet descended beyond the mystery of "rudeness", i.e. the mystery of the *Sefirah Tiferet* (a symbol of the Messiah). However, he will soon be forced into the mystery of the Covenant of Circumcision (the *Sefirah Yesod*). This is the heavenly secret of the name *Ayin-Sin-Waw* (Esau-Ásu)... At first, Esau places himself in the *Sefirah Gevurah* (symbolised by Isaac). He then descends to *Sefirah Tiferet* (Jacob); he is then forced to enter *Sefirah Yesod* (The Covenant of Circumcision) along with Jacob. This entry signifies the transition from “Edom” to the “Covenant”, i.e. the conversion from Christianity to Judaism…”

In Moshe Idel, *The Attitude to Christianity in Sefer Ha-Meshiv*, p. 86, 88. Dr. Moshe Idel is a professor in the Department of Jewish Thought at the University of Jerusalem.

ANNEX VI

SHABTAI TZVI AND SABBATEISM

1.” The explanation that was elaborated was as follows. As long as the last divine sparks *(nitzotzot)* of holiness and goodness, which fell during Adam’s primordial sin into the impure domain of the *Qelipot* (i.e. the material forces of Evil, whose presence is especially strong among the Gentiles), have not been gathered and brought to the source, the redemption will not have come to an end. This is the work which is incumbent upon the Redeemer, the holiest of all men: He must accomplish that which the most righteous souls of the past were unable to do; He must descend through the gates of impurity *(sha’are tum’ah)* into the domain of the *Qelipot* and rescue the divine sparks held back there. As soon as this task is completed, the kingdom of Evil will collapse upon itself, for it can only be maintained by the divine sparks within. The Messiah is forced to perform “strange acts” (*ma’asim zarim*: a notion central to Sabbatean theology). And among these acts, his apostasy is the most shocking. These acts are necessary to fulfil their mission. According to Cardoso’s formulation783: “It has been decreed that the Messiah-King would take the form of a swine and thus go incognito among his fellow Jews. In short, it has been decreed that he would become a swine like me*”… The new doctrine of the necessary apostasy of the Messiah was accepted by all the “believers”. It proved to be richer in symbolism than was at first thought, for it skilfully accounted for the contradiction between the external reality of history and the internal reality of the life of the “believers”. Once this doctrine was established, the delay of external liberation was no longer surprising, for it could be explained by invoking the mystical principle of being “good within oneself but clothed in defiled garments.”

In Gershom Scholem, *Le Messianisme juif,* 1971, Les Belles Lettres, 2020, p. 158, 164. (*Inyanei *Shabtai Zevi*, édition A. Freimann, 1913, p. 88).

---

[783]Abraham Miguel Cardoso (1626, Río Seco, Aragón -1706). Friend of Tzvi and prominent ideologue and proselyte of the sect.

2." To evoke this gospel of perversion, the best I can do is to quote the excellent work on Gnosticism by the philosopher Hans Jonas*. He shows how an ethics of perversion could be born in the "*pneumatics* *784*" of nihilistic tendency of the second century:

"The spiritualistic ethic of these *pneumatics* carried with it a revolutionary element which stimulated their beliefs. Their immoral teachings were characterised at once by a declared and absolute rejection of all traditional rules and customs, and by a longing for freedom carried to the extreme which made them see the freedom to do whatever they pleased as a proof of authenticity and a favour from heaven... This doctrine is based on the idea that they had received an "additional soul" and that the new type of man who had acceded to this privilege no longer had to follow the customs and obligations which had been the rule hitherto. Unlike the ordinary man, i.e. the merely "psychic" man, the *pneumatic* is a free man. He is freed from the demands of the Law... But insofar as this requires free acts, his emancipated attitude is by no means to be regarded as negative behaviour. This moral nihilism reveals the crisis of a world in transition. When man wants to see himself as totally free and boasts of his dedication to sacred sin, it is because he seeks to fill the void that opens up in the "interregnum" of two different and opposing periods of the Law. This anarchic tendency is characterised by a declared hostility to all established regimes, by a need to differentiate oneself clearly and to separate oneself from the majority of men, by a desire to overthrow "divine" authority, i.e. the powers that rule this world and are the defenders of the previous ethical criteria. There is in this attitude much more than a simple rejection of the past; there is a desire to insult these powers and to rebel against them. This is very formally what is called a revolution and the heart of this Gnostic revolution of religious thought is constituted by this gospel of subversion. Finally, the Gnostics must have had a good dose of "swagger" which allowed them to make believe their "spiritual" nature. In fact, it is well known that, in all revolutionary periods, men like to get drunk with big words".

This description applies perfectly to radical Sabbateanism and especially to Frankism."

In Gershom Scholem, *Le Messianisme juif*, 1971, Les Belles Lettres, 2020, p. 206, 207. (*Hans Jonas, *Gnosis und Spaätaniker Geist*, 1934, volume I, p. 234).

---

[784]From the Greek *pneuma*, the spirit. The spiritual are those predestined to salvation.

3.” The doctrines of the antinomists ... were for their part interpreted as the new spiritual Torah which Shabtai Tzvi had brought into the earthly world, and as the doctrine which was destined to invalidate the old *de-beria Torah,* which they identified with the Torah of pre-Messianic times. The mystical content of the Torah was freed from its ties to the traditional meaning of the text; it became independent, no longer being able in this situation to find its adequate expression in the symbols of the traditional Jewish way of life. On the contrary, it ended up in an antagonistic situation in relation to them: the perfection and realisation of the new spiritual Torah [*Torah de-aŝilut*] brought with it the invalidation of the *Torah de-beriyah,* representative of a lower level, with which rabbinic Judaism was henceforth identified. Antinomism leads to mystical nihilism, which preached the conversion of all former values and bore on its banner the following watchword: *bitulah śel Torah zehu quiyumah,* “the nullification of the Torah is its fulfilment.”

In Gershom Scholem, *La Kabbalah y su simbolismo,* Siglo XXI Editores, Madrid, 2009, p. 100.

4.” The nihilism of the Sabbatean and Frankist movements, that nihilism which results from this doctrine, so deeply shocking to the Jewish conception, [which postulates] that ‘it is by violating the Torah that it is fulfilled’ *(bitulah śel Torah zehu quiyumah),* was the dialectical culmination of the belief in the messiahship of Shabtai Tzvi. Later, when its religious inspiration was exhausted, this nihilism opened the way for the Haskalah785 and the reform movement of the 19th century. Finally, (...) it was within the spiritual world of the Sabbatean sects, within the Santosanctorum of Kabbalistic mysticism, that this crisis of faith, which affected the entire Jewish people as a whole when it emerged from its medieval isolation, first manifested itself. Many Jews living within the ghetto had already begun, while still outwardly adhering to the practices of their ancestors, to venture into the ways of a radically new original interiority. Before the French Revolution, the conditions were not yet in place to allow such an alteration to lead to a social struggle; the result was that this alteration turned inward; it rumbled within the secret sanctuary of the Jewish soul. The desire for total liberation that so tragically led the Sabbateans to take that path was not merely a desire for self-destruction. On the contrary, beneath the surface of Torah rejection, antinomism and catastrophic nihilism, there

[785]The “Jewish Enlightenment”. The Haskalah marks the beginning of the attempt to integrate European Jews with the secular world, giving rise to the first Jewish political movement and the struggle for emancipation. See note 328.

was a most constructive inspiration… In particular, it nourished the dream of a universal revolution that would erase the past at a stroke and allow the world to be rebuilt. The hope of a radical change of all laws and customs that Frank had raised suddenly became a reality on the level of history towards the end of his life. The French Revolution allowed the Sabbatean and Frankist projects to overthrow the old morality and religion to find a field of application: we know indeed that Frank's nephews, whether by virtue of their beliefs or for any other reason, played an active role in various revolutionary circles in Paris and Strasbourg. They surely saw in the Revolution the confirmation of their nihilistic views…"

In Gershom Scholem, *Le Messianisme juif,* 1971, Les Belles Lettres, 2020, p. 146, 210, 211.

ANNEX VII

JUDAISM ACCORDING TO WERNER SOMBART AND KARL MARX

This contractual and even mercantilist nature of Judaism was studied in detail by the German sociologist and economist Werner Sombart in his landmark work, *The Jews and Economic Life (1911)*, in which he set out the seminal and founding role of Judaism in modern capitalism. Werner Sombart thus expounded the "fundamental ideas of the Jewish religion":

"I declare it without preliminaries: I have found at the basis of the Jewish religion the same guiding ideas as those which characterise capitalism… It is, from beginning to end, in its fundamental features, a work of reason, an intellectual and finalistic formation, projected into the external world as a mechanical and artificial organism, with a view to destroying and subduing the natural world, and to securing for itself the domination of all areas of life. The Jewish religion behaves in exactly the same way as capitalism, which is itself a foreign formation, coming from who knows where and how, in the midst of a natural world, dominated by a creative power, a rational and artificial product in the midst of a life guided by instinct and spontaneity. It is rationalism that is the fundamental feature of both Judaism and capitalism. Rationalism or rather intellectualism: both equally opposed to what is irrational and mysterious in life and in the world, both equally enemies of all that is art, creation, work of the imagination, sensitive joy. The Jewish religion knows no mystery. It is even the only religion in the world that ignores mystery. It does not know that state of ecstasy in which the believer attains union with the divinity, that is to say the state which other religions extol as the supreme, the highest, the holiest state." Thus, "what makes the Jewish religion even more similar to capitalism is the contractual regulation, I would even say the commercial regulation, if that word did not have such a profane meaning, of the relations between Yahweh and Israel. The whole Jewish religious system is nothing but a treaty between Yahweh and his chosen people: a treaty with all the obligatory consequences that generally follow from a contract... Between God and man only one form of communion is possible: man fulfils certain obligations prescribed by the Torah, in return for which he receives a corresponding reward from God. Thus man should not approach God in prayer without carrying in his hand a counterpart to offer in return for the favour he requests (*Sifre*, 12b; *Wachchikra Rabba*, c31)... The difference between the sum and weight of the "*Mitzwoth*" and the sum and weight of the infractions establishes whether the individual is righteous or condemned. The result of the calculation is recorded in a report containing the "*Mizwoth*" and the "*Aberoth*", and is subject to the approval of the person concerned. It is useless to say that such an accounting is not at all easy to keep... According to *Ruth rabba* (86a), Elijah is the one who carries out this accounting, and according to *Esther rabba* (86a), the angels are charged with this task, and so on. Thus, man has an open account in heaven according to *Sifra* (224b)..."

In Werner Sombart, *Les Juifs et la vie économique*, Kontre Kulture, 2012, Saint-Denis, p. 367, 368, 371, 373. Also published in Spanish by the Universidad Completense de Madrid in 2008, *Los Judíos y la vida económica. [*Sombart was referring to rabbinical Judaism, more rational and practical, and not to mystical-cabalistic Judaism, which he probably must not have known.]

Karl Marx was even more direct and lapidary when he wrote in *The Jewish Question*:

"Money is the jealous God of Israel, before whom no other God can rightfully prevail. Money debases all the gods of man and turns them into a commodity. Money is the general value of all things, constituted in itself. It has thereby stripped the whole world of its peculiar value, the world of men as well as nature. Money is the alienated essence of man's labour and existence, and this alien essence dominates him and is worshipped by him. The God of the Jews has become secularised, the God of the world. Change is the real God of the Jew. His God is only illusory change."

ANNEX VIII

THE SHECHINAH AND THE COMMUNITY OF ISRAEL

"In Talmudic literature and in non-Kabbalistic rabbinic Judaism, what is meant by the term *Shechinah*—literally "residence", but God's residence in the world—is none other than God himself in his omnipresence and activity in the world and in particular in Israel. God's *presence*, what in the Bible is called his "face", is equivalent in rabbinic idiomatic usage to his *Shechinah*. Nowhere in the ancient literature do we find a separation between God himself and his *Shechinah in the sense of a* special hypostasis that is genuinely distinguishable from God. Something quite different is the case with the Kabbalah's expressive heritage from the *Bahir* onwards, which already contains almost all the essential propositions of the *Sekhinah*. In it, Sekhinah is considered as a divine aspect, endowed with a feminine character and, we can say, made independent.

(...) The establishment of a feminine element in God is, of course, one of the most consequential steps that the Kabbalah has taken and has attempted to base on Gnostic exegesis. The enormous popularity which the mythical aspects of this conception have attained in very wide circles of the Jewish people, despite the fact that it has often been regarded with the utmost scepticism by the strictly rabbinical, non-Kabbalistic Jewish sector, and despite the equally frequent and hasty attempt of Kabbalistic apologetics to channel it in harmless directions—the feminine of the *Shechinah*, taken in the sense of a providential guidance of creation—is undoubtedly proof that the Kabbalists have here appealed to one of the fundamental impulses of certain early and more perennially affecting religious conceptions of Judaism.

(...) In the Talmud and in the Midrash we find the concept of the "community of Israel" (from which the Christian concept of *ecclesia* derives) only as a personification of historical, real Israel, and as such clearly opposed to God. The allegorical interpretation of the Song of Songs in the sense of God's relationship to the Jewish ecclesia, as it has always been received in Judaism, ignores the mythical elevation of the role of the ecclesia to the status of divine power or even hypostasis. Nor does the Talmudic literature ever identify the *Shechinah* with the ecclesia. Quite different is what happens in the Kabbalah, where this identification brings with it the full irruption of the symbolism of the feminine into the sphere of the divine. All that had been said in the Talmudic interpretations of the Song of Songs about the community of Israel as daughter and wife was now transported on the wings of that identification to the *Shechinah.* I doubt whether we can make reasonable assertions as to the point to which the priority in this process corresponds: to the reinstatement of the idea of a feminine element of God by the ancient kabbalists or to the exegetical identification of the two formerly separate concepts of ecclesia of Israel and *Shechinah*, through which so large a part of the Gnostic heritage could be transmitted under a purely Jewish metamorphosis. It is not possible for me to separate here the psychological and the historical process, which represent, within their unity, the decisive step of Kabbalistic theosophy… The origin of the soul in the sphere of the feminine in God Himself has become, for the psychology of the Kabbalah, a factor of decisive importance. But the idea of the *Sekhinnah* which we have just described in its most elementary features obtains its wholly mythical character only because of two complexes of ideas absolutely inseparable from it, namely, that of the ambivalence of the *Sekhinnah* and that of her exile."

In Gershom Scholem, *The Kabbalah and its symbolism*,

"But this idea of the ambivalence of the *Shechinah*, of its changing "phases", is already related to that of its exile (*galut*). The concept of the exile of the *Shechinah* is Talmudic: "In every exile to which Israel had to go, the *Shechinah* accompanied him". However, this had no other meaning than that God's *presence* was with Israel in all its exiles. This idea, on the contrary, means in the Kabbalah the following: *Something belonging to God Himself has been exiled from God.* Both motifs, that of the exile of the ecclesia of Israel in the Midrash and that of the exile of the soul from its place of origin, which we find not only in Gnostic circles, but also in many other ideological spheres, are now united in the new Kabbalistic myth of the exile of the *Sekhinah.* This exile is often represented as the expulsion of the queen or the king's daughter by her husband or father, and at other times it is represented as subjugation by the forces of the demonic, by the "other side", who destructively break into her enclosure, dominate her and subject her to their judgemental action.

This exile is not yet, as a rule, in the early Kabbalah, something that originates with the beginning of creation. Such an idea was later arrived at in the Safedic Kabbalah of the 16th century. The exile of the *Sekhinah*, or in other words, the separation of the male and female principle in God, is mostly understood as the destructive action of human sin and its magical meaning. Adam's sin is repeated incessantly in every sin. Adam, instead of penetrating in his contemplation of the whole of the sephiroth in their awesome unity, allowed himself to be attracted, when offered the choice, to the easier solution of contemplating only the last sephirah—in which all else seemed to be reflected, as if it were divinity, disregarding the other sephiroth. Instead of helping to maintain the unity of divine action in the universe as a whole—which was still imbued with the secret life of the divinity—and supporting it in its own consummation, it destroyed this unity. Since then there has been a profound separation between the lower and the higher, the masculine and the feminine somewhere within. This separation is described by means of multiple symbols… And just as for the religious sentiment of the ancient kabbalists the exile of the *Shechinah* is a symbol of our deep enculturation, so religious action must consequently aim at the removal of this exile, or at least at the effort to obviate this removal. The meaning of the redemption consists in the reunification of God and his *Sekhinah*. Through it, the male and female principle will regain their primal unity—again speaking from a mythical point of view—and through the uninterrupted unification of the two, the generative powers will once again flow unimpeded through the universe. Under the rule of the Kabalah every religious action had to be accompanied by the formula that this was done expressly "on account of the union of God and his *Sekhinah*"… By way of a colophon I would like to note, with regard to this point alone, that of this great myth, itself so lavish in its consequences for the history of the Kabalah, of the *Sekhinah* and her exile, representations have been found in an infinitely large number of old rites, but at the same time also in others of later appearance. The ritual of the Kabbalists is, from beginning to end, determined by this profoundly mythical idea." In Gershom Scholem, *The Kabbalah and its symbolism*.

"(…)What does this Kabbalistic ritual of the mystics look like? Before the beginning of the Sabbath, at the hour of vespers on Friday, the Kabbalists of Safed and Jerusalem used to leave the city dressed in white … and go to the open field because of the arrival of the *Sekhinah*.

This departure represents a procession in search of the bride, to meet her. At the same time, certain hymns were sung to the bride and psalms of joyful emotion (such as Psalm 29, and among the others, Psalms 95–99). The most famous of these hymns, the song composed in the circle of Moses Cordovero by Selomo Alcabes in Safed: *Come my beloved, to meet the bride/the face of the Sabbath let us receive,* brings the messianic hopes for the rescue of the *Sekhinah* from exile into close contact with symbolic mysticism, and is still sung today in all synagogues. When the actual going out into the field ceased, the custom of celebrating the bride's rescue in the synagogue courtyard remained, and when this too ceased to be practised, the custom of turning westward at the time of the last verse of the great hymn and bowing down to the awaited bride remains to this day. Notable is also the repeatedly attested custom of reciting the Sabbath psalms with closed eyes, the reason for which is, according to the kabbalists, that the *Shechinah* in the *Zohar* is called "the beautiful virgin who has no eyes", the one who has broken down in tears in exile. On Friday evening, the Song of Songs was also recited as the wedding song of the *Shechinah,* which refers, according to the traditional interpretation, to the intimate union of the "Holy One, praised be He, with the Ecclesia of Israel". Only at the end of the rite of going to meet the bride were the traditional Sabbath prayers recited."

Other titles

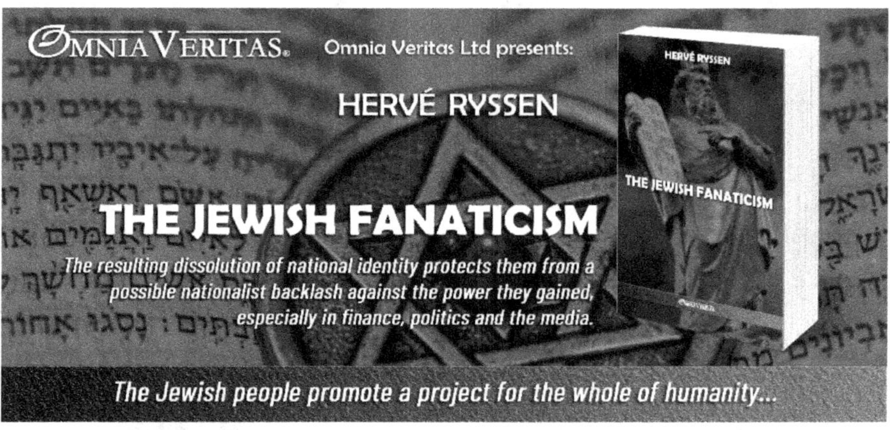

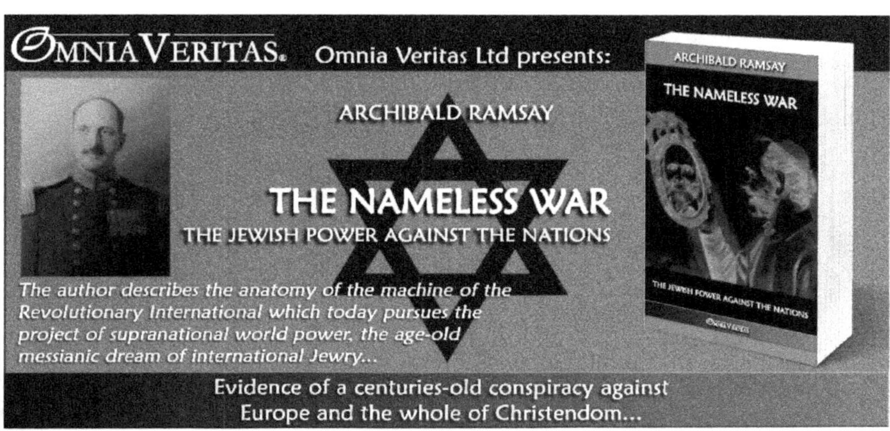
OMNIA VERITAS
Omnia Veritas Ltd presents:
ARCHIBALD RAMSAY
THE NAMELESS WAR
THE JEWISH POWER AGAINST THE NATIONS
The author describes the anatomy of the machine of the Revolutionary International which today pursues the project of supranational world power, the age-old messianic dream of international Jewry...
Evidence of a centuries-old conspiracy against Europe and the whole of Christendom...

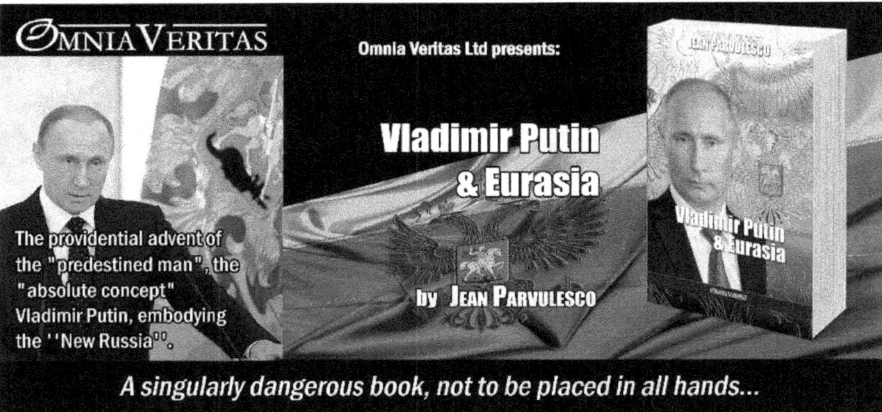
OMNIA VERITAS
Omnia Veritas Ltd presents:
Vladimir Putin & Eurasia
by JEAN PARVULESCO
The providential advent of the "predestined man", the "absolute concept" Vladimir Putin, embodying the ''New Russia''.
A singularly dangerous book, not to be placed in all hands...

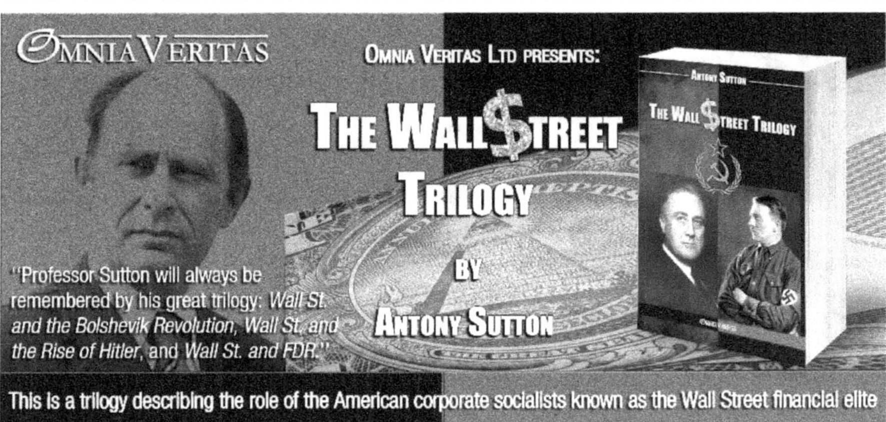
OMNIA VERITAS
OMNIA VERITAS LTD PRESENTS:
THE WALL $TREET TRILOGY
BY
ANTONY SUTTON
"Professor Sutton will always be remembered by his great trilogy: Wall St. and the Bolshevik Revolution, Wall St. and the Rise of Hitler, and Wall St. and FDR."
This is a trilogy describing the role of the American corporate socialists known as the Wall Street financial elite

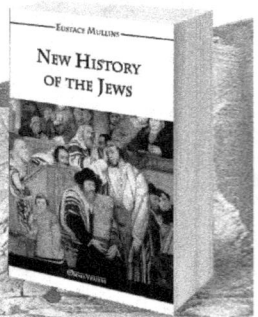

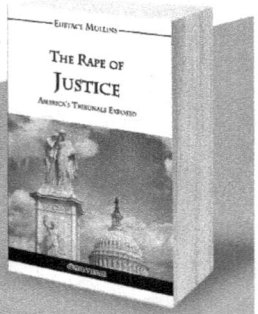

www.ingramcontent.com/pod-product-compliance
Lightning Source LLC
Chambersburg PA
CBHW072006270326
41928CB00009B/1561

* 9 7 8 1 8 0 5 4 0 0 4 4 8 *